Profiles of BLACK SUCCESS

Profiles of BLACK SUCCESS

Thirteen Creative Geniuses Who Changed the World

GENE N. LANDRUM, Ph.D.

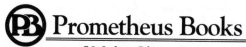 Prometheus Books

59 John Glenn Drive
Amherst, New York 14228-2197

Published 1997 by Prometheus Books

01 00 99 98 97   5 4 3 2 1

Library of Congress Cataloging-in-Publication Data

Landrum, Gene N.
    Profiles of Black success : thirteen creative geniuses who changed the world / Gene N. Landrum.
        p.   cm.
    Includes bibliographical references (p.   ) and index.
    ISBN 1–57392–119–X (cloth)
    1. Afro-Americans—Biography. 2. Celebrities—United States—Biography.
I. Title.
E185.96.L255   1997
920'.009296073—dc21   96–39376
                                                                                                              CIP

Printed in the United States of America on acid-free paper

To

my loving son, Glen,

a role model for living and loving in a diverse world

Contents

List of Figures

9

Acknowledgments

Many people were supportive in the creation of this book. I want to personally thank Ruth Sawyer, librarian at International College in Naples, Florida, who contributed greatly to the research effort. She provided computer search assistance and located many interlibrary loan books as did Elizabeth Nagangast of the Naples Public Library. I would like to thank Kevin Luckett, an African-American member of the Naples Mensa organization, who provided valuable input. Kevin gave me insight into his approach to business biases and his mature approach to resolving them. He told me, "I am far too busy searching for knowledge and success to worry over other people's hangups and prejudices," with the added admonition that one should never "allow others to interfere with their life or to be knocked off course by small inconveniences." What insight! His personal experiences are what I have found to be the foundation of the success patterns in these thirteen subjects. All adamantly refused to be deterred by bigotry and discrimination and often used it as a motivating force for even greater achievement.

Others who contributed to this research effort were International College students Lourdes Barrera and Carol Little; two astute African-American women I met on a plane, Margaret Taylor and Michelle Willingham; as well as many others who offered insight into the genesis of greatness in minorities. Fred Nerone, the business chair at International College of Naples, was very helpful in providing historical texts and out-of-date biographical materials on my subjects. In addition he offered intellectual insights on the motivating forces of mankind in general. As always, my wife, Diedra, proved to be my greatest critic and psychosocial editor. She also functioned as the expert on personality and behavior modalities due to her work as a professional counselor, her educational background in psychology, and her master's work on the Myers-Briggs Type Indicator Test.

Preface

Profiles of Black Success is about thirteen special individuals who changed the world for the better. They were not helped by others. They did it themselves. Their professional achievements have placed them head and shoulders above their peers and often above anyone of any race. The subjects selected personify excellence and the crème-de-la-crème in six professional fields and thirteen vocations. In addition to the thirteen contemporary subjects, three historical subjects were selected to further validate the similarities and differences between these subjects and the norm. These three are Martin Luther King, Jr., Frederick Douglass, and George Washington Carver, ranked numbers one, two, and twenty-seven, respectively, by Columbus Salley in his 1993 work, *The Black One Hundred: A Ranking of the Most Influential African-Americans Past and Present*. Most of the sixteen subjects have been acknowledged by one or more sources as one of the greatest blacks who ever lived.

The selection process included researching hundreds of preeminent twentieth-century black people who achieved eminence in various disciplines. The original intent was to include more subjects, but space and time did not permit this luxury even though many more subjects certainly qualified for inclusion. Superstars like Duke Ellington, the most prolific jazz composer ever, should have been included. Likewise, Toni Morrison, James Baldwin, Barbara Jordan, Muhammad Ali, and Arthur Ashe, among others, should be in this book, but space and other limiting criteria forced me to eliminate these great individuals.

In selecting the final thirteen, I purposely eliminated many of the great civil rights reformers who have made significant contributions to black equality. I decided to include just one such subject, and after careful consideration I chose Nelson Mandela. He brings a global perspective to the work in addition to the enormous contributions he has made to black equality throughout the world. His winning the Nobel Peace Prize in 1993 and his election as president of South Africa in 1994 further validates choosing him, since he has gone from the lowest

13

to the highest possible position of any potential subject. Consequently, leaders such as W. E. B. Du Bois, Marcus Garvey, Malcolm X, and Jesse Jackson were considered but not used.

Definition of a Creative Genius

Who qualifies as a creative genius? I think any person who changes the world in some dramatic way. *Webster's Dictionary* defines a genius as a person who "influences another for the good or bad" or has "an extraordinary intellectual power especially as manifested in creative activity" or has "a marked capacity or aptitude." *Webster's* defines creativity as "bringing something new into existence." I have elected to use the following definition of creative genius fashioned from the above definitions: "Creative genius is any person who has a dramatic influence on society or brings something new into existence which effectively changes the world in some way."

Based on this definition, these thirteen subjects qualify as creative geniuses even though their intelligence quotient scores may not qualify them on the quantitative scale. I prefer to use a *qualitative* measure of achievement, and not a quantitative one, since the world is qualitative, not quantitative, and analog, not digital, as some researchers would have us believe. For some reason the world has become enamored with numbers, where the terms *genius* and *gifted* require a minimum SAT score of 1400 or an IQ score of 140 to qualify. On the contrary, a genius is someone who has changed the world for the better whether some test says he or she did or did not.

This book is about people who "achieved," not people who scored highly on tests. It aims to demonstrate that great achievement has little to do with answers on a test, but more to do with performance on the stage of life. Henri Poincaré scored at the imbecile level on Alfred Binet's IQ test at a time when Poincaré was universally acknowledged as the world's foremost mathematician. Skid Row is littered with people touting IQs of 150. In many cases a high test score becomes a person's greatest handicap.

Normal People with Abnormal Drives

This book is about normal people who have achieved far beyond the norm due to an insatiable internal drive. It is about you and me, and anyone else who demands excellence in life despite few inherited advantages. It is about a tenth-grade dropout with a net worth in excess of $300 million who earned a Ph.D. in his forties (Bill Cosby). It is about the son of a slave who ascended to the pinnacle of success as a scholar and athlete to become the world's greatest Shakespearean actor (Paul Robeson). It is about the son of a Jamaican immigrant who escaped the degradation of Fort Apache in the Bronx to become head of the Joint Chiefs of

Staff and a front-running presidential candidate in 1995 (Colin Powell). It is about a basketball player who wasn't good enough to make his high school team as a sophomore but who used the rejection to mold himself into the greatest basketball player who ever lived (Michael Jordan). It is about a kid who was called a "flake" by both friends and family, but persevered to create the greatest entertainment dynasty in American history, and along the way found time to change the world of music forever (Berry Gordy). And it is about a woman raised in the Deep South who never had the opportunity to go to college but through tenacity has been called America's first female and first black poet laureate (Maya Angelou).

These are all normal people with "abnormal" drives who achieved unbelievable success by living out their dream of reality. It is about simple people who used their vision, energy, passion, and tenacity to reach the top, people who dared to be different and thereby became rich and famous. It is not about race, since "race is a myth" according to anthropologist Dr. Jefferson Fish, who makes a valid argument that "race is a social classification, not a biological one" and is not a "biological variability" but a "cultural classification" based on the color of one's skin. It is about people with dark skin who helped change the world for the better by starting with little and making it into a lot. Their stories are inspirational road maps for those desirous of realizing their greatest fantasies, because without fantasy and imagination there can be no great successes, only mediocrity.

The Selection Process

To be chosen for inclusion in this book a subject had to be:

Self-made. These subjects had to have created their own niche in the world or innovated a product or concept that would not have existed if it had not been for their influence. They could not marry into or inherit their success.

Cream of the crop. All subjects must have risen to the very top of their professions. They must have been acknowledged by some reputable critic as "the best" that ever lived in their given area of expertise.

International in scope. The individuals must have had a national and international influence, not just a regional influence.

Dominant for ten years. Once the superstar reached the pinnacle of success he or she must have had the staying power to remain at the very top for at least ten years.

Contemporary. They must have operated in the twentieth century and preferably within the past forty years. The only marginal subject in this respect is Paul Robeson, who is arguably one of the greatest black talents ever in any profession. The enormity of Robeson's multifaceted powers, his erudition and sheer bravado, are truly amazing. Robeson made his greatest contributions to art during the mid-twentieth century and would have been more active later had it not been for his political activism, for which he was denied the right to work after 1950. All other subjects are not only contemporary, most are still living and professionally active. The exceptions are Thurgood Marshall and the recently deceased Reginald Lewis.

The Subjects

Figure 1 lists the subjects and describes their major contribution to society, their particular creative ingenuity, and their unique success that qualifies them as one of the thirteen blacks who best met the above criteria as a creative genius. They were selected from a rich source of references, including Michael Hart's *The 100 Ranking of the Most Influential Persons in History* (1978), Columbus Salley's *The Black One Hundred: A Ranking of the Most Influential African-Americans Past and Present* (1993), Jackie Carney Smith's *Black Firsts: Two Thousand Years of Extraordinary Achievement* (1994), Sande Smith's *Who's Who in African-American History* (1994), Herb Boyd and Robert Allen's *Brotherman: The Odyssey of Black Men in America* (1995), Arnold Ludwig's *The Price of Greatness* (1995), and the annual rankings of eminent blacks by *Black Enterprise* and *Ebony*.

It became obvious in the research that greatness is "learned" and available to virtually everyone willing to pay the price. As Daniel Goleman wrote in *Emotional Intelligence* (1995), "Even the most deeply implanted habits of the heart learned in childhood can be reshaped. Emotional learning is lifelong." The Harvard psychologist further validates this premise by declaring, "No human quality is beyond change!" James Cone gives further confirmation with this quote from *Martin & Malcolm & America* (1991), "Martin and Malcolm . . . were not messiahs. Both were *ordinary* human beings." I can say without equivocation these thirteen were also normal people with an abnormal drive who were driven to fulfill their internal dreams of reality.

This book aims to show that "nurture" not "nature" is the secret for becoming a creative genius. Richard Herrnstein and Charles Murray's *The Bell Curve* proclaimed that a "cognitive elite" was a critical factor in great success. This book aims to refute that claim by showing how these thirteen, who did not qualify as part of a "cognitive elite," became rich and famous anyway and changed the world in the process. They were not from money, from social privilege, educated at Harvard (except for Lewis), or exceptionally brilliant, but became eminent through other factors to be explored.

Being born with a Mensa-level IQ, rich, with a social pedigree or an Ivy League education is nice but not necessary for great achievement. Such a background is based on the luck of the genetic draw but has little to do with molding a person into a superstar. These fifteen creative geniuses made their own luck. Many were transformed with a "success imprint" that became a part of their persona. Some were changed by traumatic imprints that conditioned them for greatness or armed them with the key success traits that ultimately made them great: charisma, competitiveness, confidence, energy/work ethic, independence, passion, perfectionism, temerity, tenacity, and vision. These ten key success traits will be discussed at length in chapter 5.

FIGURE 1
BLACK CREATIVE GENIUSES

Maya Angelou. Writings altered society's views on race
Creative Genius: Renaissance woman as entertainer, poet, playwright, author, scholar, educator
Success: Wrote 12 books, tenured professor at Wake Forest College

Shirley Chisholm. First black U.S. congresswoman, proving "You don't have to sell out"
Creative Genius: Founder of Brooklyn's Unity Democratic Club to defeat 17th District political machine
Successes: N.Y. State congresswoman and U.S. congresswoman from New York City

Bill Cosby. Altered American TV sitcoms, changing image of black stereotypes
Creative Genius: Created family sitcom comedy for blacks and whites alike—"The Cosby Show"
*Successes:*Worth $315 million through dominant role as Mr. TV during 1970s and 1980s

Berry Gordy. Molded Motown into America's most successful black enterprise
Creative Genius: Transformed black gospel music into Motown Sound = "Mainline Pop"
Successes: Turned $800 family loan into entertainment fortune of $367 million

Michael Jackson. Arguably the greatest entertainer in history; certainly during 1970s & 1980s
Creative Genius: Moonwalk and innovative dance routines made him into a media icon
Successes: Every Grammy; largest-selling album in history, *Thriller*; $500 million net worth

John Johnson. Publishing & entrepreneurial guru of black entertainment in magazines
Creative Genius: Ebony and *Jet,* most successful black magazines; created largest black cosmetics firm
Successes: Ebony #1 for fifty years; America's most successful black businessman worth $250 million

Michael Jordan. Arguably the greatest basketball player (athlete?) who ever lived
Creative Genius: Innovated "reverse slam dunk" and idyllic image into highest "Q" rating in TV
Successes: All-world, with two Olympic gold medals and $100 million net worth—an icon

Reginald Lewis. Preeminent corporate LBO business tycoon and wealthiest black ever
Creative Genius: Used wits to succeed: Harvard without application; turned $1 million investment in *McCall's* into $90 million
Successes: CEO of largest black enterprise in world: TLC Beatrice, a $950 million acquisition

Nelson Mandela. Africa's political wunderkind, who destroyed apartheid & found freedom
Creative Genius: Perseverance in the face of enormous odds to become charismatic leader of Africa
Successes: Spent life destroying apartheid and became first black president of South Africa

Thurgood Marshall. Pioneer who changed the social and political thinking of power elite
Creative Genius: Social/political astuteness using judicial system for NAACP and black freedom
Successes: First U.S. Supreme Court justice

Colin Powell. Mediocre student who used work to become first black top military leader
Creative Genius: Delicate balancing of force and diplomacy to maintain organizational balance & power
Successes: First black chairman of the U.S. Joints Chiefs of Staff; highest personal image rating for any black

Paul Robeson. Renaissance man and first black role model, was bigger than life
Creative Genius: Multitalented Princeton All-American, lawyer, Broadway star, scholar/athlete
Successes: Preeminent Shakespearean actor fluent in twenty languages including Chinese and Russian

Oprah Winfrey. America's TV talk show "Everywoman" transcends race, creed, religion
Creative Genius: Intuitive feel for audience and guests make her "Everywoman" to everyone
Successes: Highest-paid entertainer ($75 million per year) owns every talk-show award/rating; worth $350 million

Paradoxes of Power and Genius

Most of these individuals were shocked by their monumental success. John Johnson, who founded *Ebony* and *Jet,* said, "The reason I succeeded was that I didn't know that it was impossible to succeed . . . ignorance was a blessing. Since I didn't know it was impossible . . . I did it." Both Michael Jordan and Oprah Winfrey were similarly shocked by their awesome success. Winfrey has described her success as "amazing." Both of these superstars admit to driving themselves to the limit in search of success. None of the subjects were born of eminent parents or with some genetic talent. Most became great the old-fashioned way: through hard work, tenacity, and an indomitable will to succeed. Even so, many paradoxes pervaded their lives. Their stories give credence that anyone, from any background, can capture the golden ring, but few are willing to pay the enormous price such success exacts.

This book will attempt to explain the paradoxes and demonstrate what forces were at work in overcoming the enormous odds of these subjects becoming great creative geniuses. The book's aim is to uncover the similarities and differences that exist between these powerful creative geniuses and the average person, whether black or white. Chapter 19 has been included to delineate those areas where eminent blacks and nonblacks differ. One chapter is dedicated to each subject with a complete analysis of their personal and professional lives, innovative contribution, and key traits that allowed them to get to the top. These subject chapters aim to delve into the inner selves of these subjects to find out what made them tick.

No book on black creative genius would be complete without touching on the historical factors of the black renaissance. Therefore, chapter 1 will discuss those blacks on whose shoulders these subjects stood in order to become great. Chapter 2 explores the nature vs. nurture argument with a discussion of the *Bell Curve*'s thesis that "cognitive elite" individuals will rule the world. I conclude that nurture is far more critical to success than nature. Chapter 3 discusses the early backgrounds and the psychological armaments (imprints) that endowed these individuals with their key success traits. The ten success traits are discussed in detail in chapter 4. The traumas, crises, and other dysfunctional factors that transformed these thirteen otherwise normal children into creative genius adults will be covered in chapter 5. Chapters 6 through 18 are dedicated to the psychobiographical sketches of each subject.

Subjects Considered but Not Selected

Selecting the greatest individual from various professions is difficult at best and impossible at worst. How could one not select Joe Louis, Jackie Robinson, Muhammad Ali, Wilma Rudolph, Arthur Ashe, or Jackie Joyner-Kersee in sports? For starters, I elected to limit athletic subjects to just one individual which, though

---

FIGURE 2
PARADOXES OF BLACK POWER AND SUCCESS

- How could a woman without a college education became a college professor, well-known poet, and a best-selling author?

- How did a tenth-grade dropout create a music empire that changed the face of American music and earn $350 million in the process?

- How did a shy school teacher, with no political experience, defy New York City's political machine to become America's first black female congresswoman?

- What motivated a timid, abused, and uneducated boy from Gary, Indiana, to become America's "King of Pop" and then marry the daughter of the "King of Rock"?

- Why was a South Bronx teenager who flunked out of solid geometry able to rise above West Point graduates to become the chairman of the Joint Chiefs of Staff?

- How did a kid who grew up in a city with no radio or newspaper create the most powerful and influential black publishing empire in history?

- What motivated the son of a Pullman car waiter to become America's first black Supreme Court justice?

- How did a boy with small parents (the taller five foot seven inches) but big ideas transform himself into a six-foot-six-inch giant and become the greatest basketball player in history?

- What were the tools used by a mediocre student from the streets of Baltimore to get into Harvard and then become America's wealthiest black?

- How was a boy from an inner-city ghetto able to revolutionize American television situation comedies and go on to earn a Ph.D. even though he was a high school dropout?

- How could a boy without shoes or pants until high school, who didn't discover indoor plumbing until college, become president of a nation of forty million people?

- What drove an illegitimate Mississippi girl who was molested as a child to rise above it all to become America's highest-paid entertainer?

- How was the son of a slave able to perform *Othello* in twenty-seven different languages and become America's preeminent Shakespearean actor?

---

difficult, forced the selection of Michael Jordan, who is arguably the greatest athlete who ever lived.

Even more difficult choices existed in the field of entertainment. Where is the great Louis Armstrong, Sammy Davis, Jr., Quincy Jones, Ella Fitzgerald, Billie Holiday, or Duke Ellington? And in politics how could I not select Barbara Jordan, Jesse Jackson, Adam Clayton Powell, or the first Nobel Peace Prize winner, Ralph

Bunche? Alex Haley should have been in the book as well as Alice Walker and Toni Morrison, but these people were omitted, not because they were not great, or did not fit the profile, but because I elected to limit the number of subjects in order to cover many professions and to keep the study to a manageable limit. The objective was to select the quintessential power broker and creative genius in each of thirteen professional fields and this seriously restricted the use of many renowned personalities. The individuals reviewed at length but not selected include:

Ralph Abernathy	Ella Fitzgerald	Joe Louis
Muhammad Ali	Marcus Garvey	Malcolm X (Little)
Wally (Famous) Amos	Alex Haley	Toni Morrison
Marian Anderson	Billie Holiday	Mary McLeod Bethune
Louis Armstrong	Benjamin Hooks	Adam Clayton Powell
Arthur Ashe	Charles Houston	Jesse Owens
James Baldwin	Jesse Jackson	Jackie Robinson
Ralph Bunche	Barbara Jordan	Wilma Rudolph
George Washington Carver	James Jones	Clarence Thomas
Sammy Davis, Jr.	Quincy Jones	Alice Walker
Charles Drew	Jackie Joyner-Kersee	Madam C. J. Walker
W. E. B. Du Bois	Martin Luther King, Jr.	Andrew Young

This book details how these subjects achieved success and concludes that ten key traits were the factors which made them great. A summary of these traits are listed in figure 3. Each trait is shown with the individuals who best personify that given trait. Many of the subjects had all traits but, as in all things, were stronger in one than another.

I am convinced "greatness is greatness" and color or ethnicity has nothing to do with the process. This book is about black success and genius but it should not have had to be written. Our society is homogenizing rapidly, and diversity in these eminent subjects was a critical factor in their uniqueness and success. Examples are abundant, but the three most prominent were Thurgood Marshall, Colin Powell, and Paul Robeson. Marshall was known as the "Mulatto Lawyer" due to his mixed racial heritage. Powell was of African, English, Irish, Scottish, and Arawak Indian descent. Robeson was of African, Indian, and English ancestry. The very diversity of these three wunderkinds contributed to their uniqueness and imbued them with an inner resolve to become individuals, not stereotypes of a given race. As our society intermarries, it will gravitate toward a variegated mix of white, black, and brown, and the twenty-first century will close on a society that is colorless. Classifying a person by color will have gone the way of the horse and buggy. When this occurs, the words *black, yellow,* and *brown* will be relegated to the trashcan of bigoted history.

FIGURE 3
DOMINANT TRAITS OF BLACK CREATIVE GENIUSES

Charisma
Magnetic attraction and inspirational leadership qualities
Most Exemplary: Oprah Winfrey, Nelson Mandela, Paul Robeson

Competitiveness
Awesome need to win regardless of casualties
Michael Jordan, Paul Robeson, Reginald Lewis

Confidence
High self-esteem with optimistic view of life
Thurgood Marshall, Reginald Lewis, Bill Cosby

Energy
Workaholic Type A characteristics with hypomanic tendencies
Colin Powell, Shirley Chisholm, John Johnson

Independence
Renegades who ignore the experts and tradition
Paul Robeson, Nelson Mandela, Shirley Chisholm

Passion
Psychic drive and hyperenergy incarnate
Berry Gordy, Michael Jordan, Michael Jackson

Perfection
Control freaks who must excel and are intolerant of mediocrity
Bill Cosby, Berry Gordy, Reginald Lewis

Temerity
Risk-takers who live on the edge and are comfortable with ambiguity
John Johnson, Maya Angelou, Berry Gordy

Tenacity
Perseverance and persistence despite all adversity
Nelson Mandela, Maya Angelou, Thurgood Marshall

Vision
Right-brain intuitive-thinkers with macro and long-term view of life
Michael Jackson, Oprah Winfrey, Maya Angelou

1

Historical Mentors of Black Success

History is made by minorities—or, more precisely, history is made by intellectual movements, which are created by minorities.

Ayn Rand, *Philosophy: Who Needs It*

Every man must decide whether he will walk in the light of creative altruism or the darkness of destructive selfishness.

Martin Luther King, Jr.

A Disneyland of the Mind!

We control our destiny or it controls us. That is the gospel of the superstars in this book. These visionaries could easily have given up the fight in the face of overt discrimination and prejudice which they constantly faced on their long and arduous treks to the top. They consistently chose the more difficult road, which always leads to a more gratifying win. Most were able to turn discrimination into opportunity rather than allowing it to bend their lives to its negativity and nihilistic ends. They ignored prejudice and bigotry as if it did not exist and in fact, it did not in their minds. Focus, long-term vision, and optimism pervaded their thoughts and became the essence of their personae. These visionaries refused to allow innate feelings of insecurity to gain a foothold or impact their lives. They actually used the imminent danger, which often surrounded them, as a catalyst for achievement and ultimate greatness, both personally and professionally.

These supersuccessful men and women were fortunate to have had others pave the way in their struggle to break through the black ceiling of subjugation. These visionaries allowed neither imaginary nor real roadblocks to deter them. Sir Isaac Newton was very perceptive in understanding that his success was realized by "standing on the shoulders of great men." This axiom was never more true than in the history of blacks who made it. They owe much of their success to those who broke down the barriers, who gave them a voice, the liberators who opened doors to the most fundamental opportunities. In order to be heard above the din of suppression these thirteen stood on the shoulders of Frederick Douglass, Harriet Tubman, Booker T. Washington, Mary McLeod Bethune, George Washington Carver, W. E. B. Du Bois, Charles Houston, Marcus Garvey, and other blacks of note. These people cleared the paths for Martin Luther King, Jr., Jackie Robinson, Adam Clayton Powell, James Baldwin, Jesse Jackson, Malcolm X, and Barbara Jordan, who have carried the torch passed to them by the aforementioned pioneering blacks. Other greats who proved inspirational were Wilma Rudolph, Jesse Owens, Arthur Ashe, and Joe Louis in sports; Louis Armstrong, Duke Ellington, W. C. Handy, Bessie Smith, and Josephine Baker in entertainment; and Langston Hughes, Alex Haley, and Toni Morrison in the arts.

In his *Black One Hundred* Columbus Salley ranks the most influential African Americans in history. Salley selected the Rev. Dr. Martin Luther King, Jr., Frederick Douglass, and Booker T. Washington as the three who contributed most to black success. I have elected to use the first two and George Washington Carver as historical examples of great blacks in order to further validate the findings on these thirteen contemporary subjects. King was ranked first, Douglass second, and Carver twenty-seventh in Salley's work. I believe George Washington Carver deserves more accolades for his enormous contributions to black achievement in the areas of science and education.

Frederick Douglass (1817–1895)

Frederick Douglass has all the traits exhibited by these thirteen subjects. His mother died when he was seven and he overcame the oppression of slavery to become a self-made, driven, and tenacious visionary who allowed no person to keep him from achieving his goals. When his mistress, Mrs. Auld, began teaching him to read at age eight, her husband became irate, saying, "If you teach that nigger to read, there will be no keeping him. It would forever unfit him for being a slave." These words became a "revelation" for young Douglass, who suddenly "understood the white man's power to enslave the black" and keep him ignorant. From that moment on Douglass knew the way. He wrote, "I understood the pathway from slavery to freedom." He escaped slavery to become the first great black statesman in history and the first great role model for many of the superstars in this book.

Douglass was born a Maryland slave, escaped as a teen to Massachusetts, and a few years later fled to England in fear of being caught. Douglass's tenure in Europe groomed him with the traits necessary to fight the establishment on its own ground—effective communication with the written and spoken word. This would be a fight he would take on for the rest of his long life. When Douglass returned to the United States he began a serious battle for freedom as editor for the *North*

Star abolitionist paper in Rochester, New York, and later as lecturer, advisor to Abraham Lincoln, writer, and ultimately ambassador to Haiti. Douglass was a giant of a man physically, emotionally, and mentally. He possessed prodigious energies, which he used to break new ground and to ensure that others like him understood that freedom was inextricably tied to literacy.

This innovator never allowed fear to interfere with his freedom or success. He became an eloquent speaker and lecturer on the individual rights of all men and produced prodigious amounts of written material to educate those of his race who could read. He was a man who was never deterred from his lifelong objective for black freedom and, true to his preachings, learned to speak French while in his seventies. One contemporary said of him, "Were ever so many miracles crowded into a single life?" Douglass is symbolic of one who was self-taught and internally driven and, like those in this work, self-made. He assumed his rightful place as a great person and has gone down in history as an inspiration to anyone dealt a poor hand but driven to play it to the hilt. His legacy is the one adhered to by these thirteen, which was close to Douglass's own words: "What we colored people want is character. And this nobody can give us. It is something we must earn for ourselves. . . . Our destiny is largely in our own hands. If we find, we shall have to seek. If we succeed in the race for life it must be by our own energies, and our exertions."

Frederick Douglass had the classic macrovision that is so critical to anyone desirous of changing society or innovating. He had traits similar to those of the contemporary visionaries in this book. Like these superachievers, Douglass made success his personal duty and defied anyone to stop him from achieving it. He was an immense intellect and personality who proved to be a huge historical influence on twentieth-century blacks. Of Douglass's death the *Washington Post* said, "He died in an epoch which he did more than any other to create."

George Washington Carver (1864–1943)

Carver made enormous contributions to agricultural innovation. He was often called the "Columbus of the Soil" for his work in the South converting cotton fields to more nutritional and productive crops such as peanuts and other edibles. Carver is arguably the greatest black scientist who ever lived. His great achievements, personally and professionally, can all be attributed to his driven need for self-actualization.

Born a slave, this obsessive overachiever spent forty years grooming himself as a scientist and educator. Carver worked his way through Iowa State University as a janitor and laundry hand and then worked feverishly in developing such world-renowned products as salad oil; an oil remedy for infantile paralysis; dyes of nineteen different shades from peanuts; stains and face powder from clays; flour and shoe blacking from sweet potatoes; paving blocks from cotton; dyes from dandelions, tomato vines, and trees. This self-made man held bachelor's, master's, and doctorate degrees as an agricultural chemist and became a fellow in the Royal Society of Arts of London. All of this from a man who taught himself to read with a Bible and left home at age ten to find his way in the world.

Carver's tenacity caught the eye of Booker T. Washington, who enticed this driven visionary to Tuskegee Institute, where he created more than three hundred derivative products from the peanut and one hundred eighteen products from the sweet potato. Carver was a man of unquestioned integrity who never sought money. When asked about not patenting his many creations, he responded, "God gave them to me. How can I sell them to someone else?"

George Washington Carver pursued perfection in whatever he did just as the thirteen wunderkinds in this book. That is their style and what made them successful. It is also what made Carver the consummate role model for blacks of any generation. Carver is the perfect example of learning to be great through personal dedication to a goal and never allowing anything or anyone to interfere with that quest. He was so determined to get an education that nothing could deter him. If not for Carver, the black farmers in the Deep South would have had it much tougher than they did. Carver opened many doors and paved the way for others to follow in his footsteps.

Martin Luther King, Jr. (1929–1968)

"From my Christian background I gained my ideals," said Martin Luther King, Jr., and "from Gandhi my operational technique." He emulated Gandhi in using non-violent revolution to institute social change, which earned him the Nobel Peace Prize in 1964 at age thirty-five. Those key personality traits found to be critical to great success in this book were all present in the visionary and driven Dr. King. He is the embodiment of the ten behavioral characteristics used by these subjects to break through the illusory black ceiling of achievement. He was tenacious, energetic, driven, competitive, and self-confident and married these traits with charismatic vision, temerity, and a risk-taking propensity that he used to pursue his great "dream" of freedom for all people.

King admonished his people to "feel responsibility" to discover their mission in life and became a role model by adopting his own dream as his obsessive mission. These thirteen had great empathy for King. Maya Angelou became his northern director in Harlem in the late fifties and John Johnson gave King enormous editorial space to tell his story to the people. Most also empathized with his great vision, in which he challenged them as "children of darkness." King was convinced that pacifism was the road to freedom and equality and was the foundation for all great achievement. King knew intuitively, as these thirteen also discovered, "Crisis is often the mother of creativity." He said, "Courage faces fear and thereby masters it" and "Courageous men never lose the zest for living even though their situation is zestless" while "cowardly men, overwhelmed by uncertainties of life, lost the will to live."

Martin Luther King, Jr., lived and died for his internalized dream of freedom for all people. His life and sacrifice is the essence of all great success in the world. King, like seven of these subjects, was the first son of a self-employed minister. He was influenced by the philosophical tenets of Frederick Douglass, Booker T. Washington, and W. E. B. Du Bois. As a boy King read voraciously and by age six had experienced a number of psychological imprints that were to alter his life. His two best friends were white boys whose father refused to allow them to play with young Michael (his name until age six) because of his color. This was a crushing experience for a young boy and devastated him for reasons he could not fathom. He would later write, "I was greatly shocked and from that moment on I was determined to hate every white person."

King's father appealed to his son's religious belief, saying that "love" is the true passion for transformation. He convinced his son to use love instead of hate to convert people's thinking. It was during this impressionable period when King's father changed both of their names to Martin Luther after the father of the Protestant Reformation. Martin Luther King, Jr., would live his life fulfilling his internal self-image as the revolutionist Martin Luther. He took on a mythological mask, as Joseph Campbell would have predicted, and emulated the great religious reformer for the rest of his life. Martin Luther's philosophy of truth and equality became his own, and an iconoclastic renegade was born of injustice and rejection. King used his own personal crisis to institute positive change. He was prepared to destroy myths and dedicate his life to a new way that would prove providential for his people.

King grew up to become a driven pacifist renegade. Conformity and security were absent from his armory and King never backed down from any fight even though he insisted on fighting with words and deeds rather than fists and guns. King's greatest contributions occurred during America's most turbulent era, during which he became a casualty of his own cause. With his martyrdom came many of the changes he so cherished. King's name became the rallying call of the masses, which helped enact many of his most cherished teachings. Just like the others in this book, Martin Luther King, Jr., went through a positive metamorphosis that not only changed his life but helped make him great in the process. He adopted the Hegelian philosophy of "Growth through struggle" and, true to his aphorism, proved that "freedom is not free" by sacrificing himself in the struggle, which turned out not to be in vain. King is the only black American to have a national holiday commemorating his life and achievements.

Professional Mentors

Five general areas of achievement are represented by the thirteen black creative geniuses in this book. Each of these areas was explored and conquered by notable past black heroes and heroines. The individual who best personified supreme achievement in *entrepreneurship and business* (covered in this book by Gordy, Johnson, and Lewis) was Madam C. J. Walker; in *entertainment* (Cosby, Jackson, and Winfrey), Sammy Davis, Jr.; in the *humanities* (Angelou, Robeson), Mary McLeod

Bethune; in *politics and government* (Chisholm, Mandela, and Marshall), W. E. B. Du Bois; and in *sports* (Michael Jordan), Joe Louis and Jesse Owens.

The above historical role models and mentors were critical to the achievement of these thirteen. Douglass, Tubman, Du Bois, and Bethune were role models for fighting white supremacy and the black right to success, equality, and freedom. Shirley Chisholm was inspired early in life by Mary McLeod Bethune and Harriet Tubman and then proceeded to follow their lead in making her own mark in the United States Congress. These older women clearly demonstrated to Chisholm that adversity was only a temporary roadblock on the road to the top. Sammy Davis, Jr., proved to be the same inspiration for Bill Cosby as was W. E. B. Du Bois for Paul Robeson. Whether through fantasy or cognitive reality these contemporary high achievers were inspired by their historical counterparts. Berry Gordy said that Joe Louis "was the first person that made me know what the word *hero* meant" and "started a fire deep inside me; a burning desire to be special, to win, to be somebody." Gordy felt he would never have achieved any semblance of greatness had it not been for Louis leading the way.

Louis Armstrong, Sammy Davis, Jr., Duke Ellington, and Billie Holiday similarly opened many doors for Paul Robeson, Bill Cosby, Maya Angelou, and Michael Jackson. Jesse Owens, Joe Louis, Jackie Robinson, and Muhammad Ali made it far easier for Michael Jordan to become an athletic icon, just as Madam C. J. Walker demonstrated that black entrepreneurs could aspire to great wealth and success which proved inspirational for John Johnson and Berry Gordy. George Washington Carver gave credence to blacks who attain high levels of intellectual achievement and became a role model for Reginald Lewis, Colin Powell, and Nelson Mandela. Maya Angelou has been Oprah Winfrey's inspirational guru and both were inspired by the achievements of Diana Ross and Billie Holiday.

C. J. Walker—Entrepreneurial and Business Role Model

America's first black female millionaire was the quintessential entrepreneur as well as the inspiration for John Johnson and Berry Gordy. She personifies the classic Horatio Alger rags-to-riches story. A daughter of slaves, Walker was orphaned at age seven, married at fourteen, and widowed at twenty. Perseverance characterized everything she accomplished in life. She created a product called the "Wonderful Hair Grower" in 1905. When her husband thought her marketing ideas were invalid, she left him and did it her way. One of her ways was to create an original sales organization featuring door-to-door black sales agents. Her organization was similar to the latter-day innovations of Mary Kay Cosmetics and other multilevel marketers who pay commissions to everyone who helps create the sales organization.

Madame Walker's innovative ideas took off like a rocket and by 1919 she employed 25,000 black women selling her unique hair products to black women. Walker was a woman who not only taught herself to read and write but "knew" where she wanted to go and refused to be deterred by anyone, including her husband.

Crisis defined Walker's frenetic life. Her product creations were developed from her own needs. Her hair began falling out around the turn of the century and one night she awoke from a dream with a "Eureka" solution to her hair loss. That solution became the product that would make her rich and famous. It was her "success imprint" (see chapter 4) that turned out to be her formula for success. She recalled, "One night I had a dream, and in that dream a big black man appeared to me and told me what to mix up for my hair. Some of the remedy was grown in Africa, but I sent for it, mixed it, put it on my scalp and in a few weeks my hair was coming in faster than it had ever fallen out. . . . I made up my mind I would begin to sell it." Walker told the *New York Times* in 1916, "If I have accomplished anything in life, it is because I have been willing to work hard." Her work was not in vain, as she became a hero mentor to John Johnson, Berry Gordy, and Reginald Lewis, all of whom followed her lead in creating unique entrepreneurial ventures. Hard work and vision made Walker a success and these men followed in her footsteps in every way including becoming very wealthy.

Sammy Davis, Jr.—Entertainment Mentor

Bill Cosby revered Sammy Davis, Jr., to such a degree that he went out of his way to produce a number of television specials with him just before his death. Cosby emulated Davis in many ways and told a reporter after his death, "Nobody I know could do everything he could do." Davis was "Mr. Show Business" to his peers. When Eddie Cantor saw Davis perform in Hollywood he was so impressed he called him "the greatest talent I have ever seen." Davis had decided to show off his multifaceted skills to enhance his career. He not only sang, danced, and did impersonations, he also started with the piano and played every instrument in the band. The man never had a music lesson and became a self-taught master through sheer drive and determination.

Davis was a driven man and succeeded in spite of many obstacles: poverty, no family life, one eye, drug and alcohol addiction, small stature, and relative physical unattractiveness. Inside, Davis was beautiful because he believed in himself and his friends and associates. And his beliefs led him to the top of the entertainment world. Davis could impersonate virtually anyone, male or female. He was an accomplished comedian who disdained derogatory jokes and foul language. He made movies, cut records, played the nightclub circuit, did television specials, and made television sitcoms. Nothing was beyond the scope of his enormous talents. He was a diminutive man with few redeeming qualities like money or education, but he had the soul of an angel and the will of a rock. He sometimes joked that he was a "one-eyed black Jew married to a blonde Scandinavian [Mai Britt]."

Few men worked as hard as Davis to overcome racial prejudice and his tenacity gave hope to those for whom he became a role model, like Harry Belafonte and Bill Cosby. Davis's biggest hits are the finest illustrations of his hip but sincere persona. "Candy Man," "What Kind of Fool Am I," and "Mr. Bojangles," brought down the house and won him fame and fortune, but it was his tenacity and charisma that endeared Davis to his peers. Here was a child star who learned to live with the fact that he could play major resorts in the Catskills, Miami Beach, and even Manhattan, but was unable to stay in the hotels or eat in the dining rooms of those very establishments. He survived this ridicule and rejection and fashioned himself into the most universally respected entertainer, actor, and human being in Hollywood. Sammy Davis, Jr., is the personification of entertainment, and the entertainers in this book—Cosby, Winfrey, and Jackson—should be deeply indebted to this Hollywood legend.

Mary McLeod Bethune—Humanity's Role Model

Mary McLeod Bethune was undoubtedly the most influential and famous black female in American education and politics during the first half of the twentieth century. She took it upon herself to solve the problems of her race. She founded what is now known as the Bethune-Cookman College for girls in Daytona Beach, Florida. Bethune was later appointed Franklin D. Roosevelt's Director of Negro Affairs—she was the first black woman to hold a federal office and became a key advisor in Roosevelt's "black Cabinet." John Johnson wrote in his autobiography that Bethune was "one of the most unforgettable characters I've known. . . . She was not what the world considers beautiful, but she had so much soul force and authority that when she walked into a room all eyes pulled to her, as if to a magnet." When Johnson was close to failing with *Ebony* during the late forties, this great woman was a huge influence on his survival, telling him, "Hang on. . . . Keep faith, keep trying." Johnson followed her sage advice and is now the master of his destiny.

Shirley Chisholm was enormously influenced by Bethune, as were many other contemporary blacks who followed her advice or modeled their lives after this inspirational woman. Chisholm was a teenager when she first saw Bethune's picture in the newspaper alongside President Roosevelt and his wife, Eleanor. She was emotionally moved by the thought of a poor uneducated black woman who had begun life as a slave but was able to overcome that beginning to appear in public with the president of the United States. If Bethune could do it then Shirley Chisholm should be able to—and Chisholm did so, being photographed with numerous United States presidents and running for president herself in 1972.

W. E. B. Du Bois—Agitator/Prophet and a Founder of the NAACP

Du Bois was the most respected and effective spokesperson for black people during the first half of the twentieth century. He was one of the founders of the Niagara Movement, which in 1909 became the National Association for the Advancement of Colored People. Du Bois led the way for educated blacks as an erudite philosopher of human rights based on his own intellectual credibility. Du Bois attended Fisk University but is better known as the first black to earn a Ph.D. in the social sciences from Harvard University. As the editor of the NAACP *Crisis* paper he gained wide notoriety during the early part of the twentieth century. He was a man of enormous presence who defied authority and demanded equality, just as those in this book achieved power by taking it. As friend and mentor, he influenced Paul Robeson who became a political nonconformist. Du Bois was also a hero and mentor of Nelson Mandela. Mandela made it a point to meet his hero in Ghana before Du Bois's death.

Du Bois's enormous influence took place through his writings in the *Crisis* in addition to his many scholarly books, including his two classics, *Black Reconstruction* and *The World and Africa*. Du Bois cofounded the Pan-African Congress in 1919 "for the future emancipation of the Africans in their own country" and then saw fit to cochair with Paul Robeson the Council of African Affairs. His influence lasted half a century, until he passed the gauntlet to Martin Luther King, Jr., on his death in Ghana in 1963.

In addition to Robeson and Mandela, Thurgood Marshall and Colin Powell also were inspired by this man. Although many of the other subjects in this book were not politically driven, most were highly influenced and motivated to higher achievement because of him. John Johnson and Maya Angelou were especially influenced by Du Bois, who correctly predicted, "The color line poses the twentieth century's greatest challenge." Angelou read him extensively prior to writing her poem for President Clinton's inauguration. Du Bois wrote the philosophical tenet of this book saying, "Herein lies the tragedy of age: not that men are poor—all men know something of poverty; not that men are wicked—who is good? Not that men are ignorant—what is the truth? Nay, but that men know so little of men."

Joe Louis—Athletic Role Model Extraordinaire

The man known around the world as the Brown Bomber was the childhood idol of many of the subjects in this book, including Berry Gordy, Colin Powell, Maya Angelou, and John Johnson. Many of the males saw in Louis the redemption of their manhood and the great black hope that would capture for them equality and freedom. When the Brown Bomber defeated Max Schmeling—Hitler's model for the master race—blacks everywhere saw hope for themselves. Louis reigned as heavyweight champion of the world longer than anyone in history—eleven years—and became a fantasy hero for many blacks, who saw his success as a potential vehicle of achievement and acceptance. Louis is arguably the greatest fighter in history. He achieved success despite a childhood bathed in tragedy. His father died when he was four and he was forced to survive in a Detroit ghetto until he found freedom in the ring.

Louis's influence was pervasive in both the white and black communities and his success even played a part in the lives of black women who saw his adoration by white society as redemption for themselves. Maya Angelou was in Sparks, Arkansas, and heard the famous radio broadcast of Louis's historic fight and wrote about the commotion it caused in the black community of Sparks. She said the celebration and jubilation was enormous, as it was one of the few things Southern blacks had to cheer for. Joe Louis and Jesse Owens were the first blacks in America to make world headlines and bring pride and camaraderie to their race. Blacks in the thirties could hardly identify with track and field, but they all related to fighting and Joe was their God.

Racial pride was an unknown feeling before Joe Louis. He set the standard for others to follow and became a role model for all those attempting to find personal liberation. To Berry Gordy, age eight at the time of Joe's great victory, Louis was the "greatest hero in the universe" who lit a "fire inside me." Berry said Louis's success created in him "a burning desire to be special, to win, to be somebody." He said Louis made him "know what the word *hero* meant." Even Nelson Mandela, in far-off South Africa, was inspired and took up boxing as a hobby to keep in shape but also to emulate the power of the Brown Bomber.

Summary—Catalysts for Equality

The thirteen subjects of this book not only became rich and famous in their own right, they were catalysts for change among their people. Berry Gordy legitimatized gospel music and made it mainstream. He took rhythm and blues from Harlem and Watts and made it acceptable on Madison Avenue and Rodeo Drive. He took black music and made it synonymous with American culture and music, thereby changing the musical habits of a nation. If Elvis was King then Berry was Prime Minister for his pervasive influence on contemporary music.

In a similar manner, Maya Angelou absorbed her Southern heritage—infiltrated with hatred and fear—and communicated it to a desensitized world. She used her unique autobiographical writing style to depict the gross inequities and hatred of a nation. Using Southern colloquialisms, Angelou subtly and poignantly portrayed racism and bigotry at its worst and made white readers reevaluate their unconscious view of people of color.

Colin Powell became a catalyst for equality by taking a whole different approach to the resolution of racial unrest in the military, especially during the turbulent 1950s and 1960s. Powell resorted to diplomacy and individual pride (esprit de corps) to meld a diverse group of people into one body with a common goal and spirit. His work earned him the patronage of his military peers and bosses and was instrumental in his fast-paced advancement in the military. In October 1995 *USA Today* blared, "More blacks back Clinton than Powell." Powell actually was ahead of Clinton at the time due to his enormous appeal to whites who had a Republican bent but were disenchanted with their party's platform. Powell was seen as an Uncle Tom to many of the more militant blacks and therefore favored Clinton for the 1996 presidential election. However, Powell can become an important catalyst for black success, as he is the first great black hope, according to most media, for putting a person of color in the White House.

Bill Cosby became a catalyst through a succinct and subtle use of humor and black situation comedies to affect a change in network programming. He was the first black featured in a television series—"I Spy" (1965)—and was highly influential in the depiction of blacks in what before him were known as "white" situation comedy roles. Nostalgic humor was his forte and he used it to reach the masses and squelch prejudice and ignorance. He used a vivid imagination to turn the negativity of the projects into a mega-million-dollar empire and used his windfall to further black education through philanthropy.

Michael Jackson was another who relied on mental imagery and emotional shock in his entertainment venue to affect change. It is pertinent that the "outlandish" and "weird" is often required to perceive the obvious with more candor. Jackson has become an icon to the industry. He is considered the master of creative dance and sets the standard for others to shoot for, even though he has repeatedly resorted to the occult and bizarre to achieve his objectives. No matter, Jackson has become the standard bearer for creative music and dance and the acceptance of blacks as innovators in those fields.

Ebony and *Jet* magazines are the standard-bearers for black entertainment in magazines and this occurred due to the vision of John Johnson, who chose to emulate *Life* and *Look* magazines during the forties. He chose to create a vehicle for beautiful black people to be seen not as stereotypes but as normal and successful. This was not available anywhere in America prior to Johnson.

"Air Jordan" became such a black icon due to his phenomenal talents on the basketball floor that he was able to become the first great hero to both black and white teenagers. His Airness very adroitly molded a "spartan" image with abnormal athletic skills to become a role model for millions of teenagers of all races, creeds, and nationalities. Millions of white teenagers wanted to be more like Mike than their own fathers, which tore down more barricades to equality than all of Washington's rhetoric, King's marches, or affirmative action programs and committees.

Reginald Lewis took on the white establishment on its own turf. Once successful, he became an enormous role model for blacks everywhere. There are no greater standards for acceptance by any race or creed than Harvard, Wall Street, and $400 million in the bank. Lewis very adroitly conquered each on his own terms. First he graduated from Harvard without ever filling out an application, through sheer bravado. Then he set up shop as a lawyer on Wall Street and through that vehicle became the world's master at leveraged buyouts, earning $400 million in less than ten years. These successes turned the heads of the most cynical of skeptics and made millions of nonbelievers understand that color had nothing to do with talent or success.

Others like Shirley Chisholm and Thurgood Marshall used the political arena and legislation to make their mark on equality. Nelson Mandela used passive resistance to affect change and made enormous personal sacrifices to himself and his family in order to free millions from the tyranny of apartheid. He had to hit the bottom to get to the top and was willing to do so in a life of sacrifice. Paul Robeson took a similar path and was forced to leave the United States to make his statement and search for equality and freedom. Robeson sought freedom in Soviet Russia, which turned out to be counterproductive to his objectives. But this driven man was willing to pay any price to avoid the denigration of Jim Crow America. He defied Congress and the State Department but ultimately overcame their defamation to become his own man. Oprah Winfrey joked about being a token black in her first job as a television anchor but used that opportunity to become a role model for America. Her integrity, empathy, and communications skills have made her into an icon for freedom and equality.

2

Nature vs. Nurture—
Metamorphoses:
A Concomitant of Success

I have cousins who can neither read nor write. I have had a chance. They have
not. That is the only difference.

Paul Robeson, *Here I Stand* (1958)

I maintain that nurture, rather than nature, is the primary molder of personality.

Nelson Mandela, *Long Walk to Freedom* (1994)

Born or Bred—Hit Men or Supermen?

Successful blacks, like nonblacks, *learn* to be great. They are not born that way.
Nurture, not nature, imprint them with the drives, obsessions, and needs that lead
them to the top of their professions. Imagination and dreams build strong self-esteem.
Charisma is the backbone of their persona. Drive keeps them alive. Optimism
obliterates pessimism. Energy replaces lethargy. Passion overcomes indecision.
Superiority usurps inferiority. Tenacity ends incapacity and attitudes
displace platitudes. Dreams drive them and set them apart from peers. Virtuosity
and excellence define them and these traits were all acquired on the highway that
led them to success. This is the most important message of their lives and should
be acknowledged by history. There success was not the result of some mysterious
genes or family heritage but the result of hard work and diligent imagery, all of
which emanated from their psyches and ultimately played out on the streets of life.

Dreams Build Imaginative Self-Esteem

Many of these subjects were molded by a kind of metamorphosis that altered their behaviors during their formative years. Most experienced a "success imprint" during their impressionable years or some other key point in their lives that armed them against the insecurities of failure and instilled a positive attitude and awesome self-esteem. Bill Cosby was inspired by Mark Twain and borrowed his down-home humor from the master, which he then used for his onstage comic routines. Cosby's psychological plagiarism not only contributed to his enormous success in show business but enabled him to forget the horror of being raised in the "Jungle" section of North Philadelphia. He found success accidentally from a childhood story about Tom Sawyer and rode that imagery to greatness.

Berry Gordy rode a different horse to the top. He was inspired by Joe Louis's victory over Max Schmeling—Hitler's master-race model. Michael Jordan's "success imprint" came from the last-second shot that won his team and coach their first NCAA basketball championship at the University of North Carolina. Thurgood Marshall went through his "success" transformation when he was snubbed by the University of Maryland Law School and then, after graduating from Howard University *cum laude,* filed the lawsuit that ended the Maryland school's segregationist policy. Paul Robeson was recast by refusing to be denied a position on the Rutgers football team as an eighteen-year-old freshman. His teammates broke his nose and shoulder in an attempt to get Robeson to quit the team but the tenacious Robeson refused to be defeated and became a unanimous All-American and Phi Beta Kappa student.

Success—A Self-Fulfilling Prophecy

Successful visionaries seem to experience a positive "success imprint" that propels them to greatness. Those people who experience "failure imprints" are those who appear in the headlines only for criminal behavior or other nefarious deeds. Both positive and negative experiences become indelibly imprinted in young people. Some use these to get to the top; others find themselves on the bottom and never quite know why. The reason is that we all live out our internal self-images and these self-images become the fuel that drives us through life. Be very careful who you choose as a role model or mentor. It will certainly determine your status as an adult. Losers are those people who experience a "failure imprint," while winners are those who experience a "success imprint." The only difference between the winners and losers is that winners externalize their failures and internalize their successes while losers do just the opposite.

Two young black phenomena in the mid-nineties add credence to the "bred, not born" hypothesis. Both Venus Williams and Tiger Woods are California youths who came out of the inner city of Los Angeles to become the greatest young tennis and golf players in the United States. The fathers of these two otherwise normal children groomed them for greatness and each became superstars in their given field of sports. Their fathers were rewarded for their dedicated training when their inner-city children became exceptional world-class athletes. By age eighteen Tiger Woods became the youngest ever United States Amateur Golf Champion and by nineteen played number one for Stanford and won his second consecutive title. Venus Williams is being touted as the next Chris Evert and will undoubtedly reach the top ten in tennis before age twenty. Both of these phenomena owe their success not to any genetic gifts but to dedicated parents and to their own work ethic, passion to win, and tenacity.

Success and Failure Imprints—Learned Behaviors

These subjects learned power and success during their impressionable youths or through some metamorphosis, crisis, or other experience that molded them with the key traits for success. Daniel Goleman writes in his 1995 *Emotional Intelligence,* "Emotional learning is lifelong. . . . The emotional lessons of childhood can have a profound impact on temperament, either amplifying or muting an innate disposition." Jerome Kagan, eminent Harvard psychologist, has studied childhood development and believes all infants are born with a proclivity for being timid, bold, upbeat, or melancholy. But he found that those predispositions can be altered starting with their life in the crib. In a study of childhood development he says, "Emotionally competent . . . children spontaneously outgrew their timidity." Goleman observes, "We are not necessarily limited to a specific emotional menu by our inherited traits. . . . Our genes alone do not determine behavior; our environment, especially what we experience and learn as we grow, shapes how a temperamental predisposition expresses itself as life unfolds." These scientific observations can be noted in the lives of these subjects. They all questioned their ability at times and experienced failures but always rebounded into a success mentality.

Harvard pediatrician T. Berry Brazelton found that infants in a crib learn "success" and "failure" by interacting with their environment. In a study of placing blocks together in their cribs, Brazelton found they were imprinted with a "greatness" or a "hangdog" image of themselves depending on their success or failure in the block experiment. He said those who failed would look as if "I'm no good. See. I've failed." These children had what I refer to as a "failure imprint," which results in a losing persona that continues into adulthood unless changed. Brazelton observed that the children who put the blocks together successfully experienced "success imprints." They would beam with a bright-eyed look of omnipotence that communicated, "Tell me how great I am."

Success Imprint and Trauma

Many of the subjects in this book went through a spontaneous transformation as a result of some trauma: Winfrey's abuse and pregnancy led her to become a model high school student, as did Michael Jordan's cut from his high school team and Berry Gordy's record shop bankruptcy. Others, like Maya Angelou, were traumatized numerous times. Angelou was first traumatized by rape at age seven, then a stabbing and survival on the streets of Los Angeles at age fifteen, and having a child at sixteen. Johnson flirted with bankruptcy at *Ebony* for a number of years and Lewis failed repeatedly before his LBO successes. And of course the consummate trauma was that of Nelson Mandela, who spent twenty-seven years in prison to realize his dreams. These crises taught these subjects resilience and courage, and instilled the drive to master destiny.

Internalized Expectations

Parental expectations were a factor for many of these superstars. Martin Luther King, Jr., changed his internal image of himself after his father changed his name from Michael to Martin Luther at age five, a time when he was just learning about prejudice. The unrealistic expectations of Paul Robeson's father—100 percent in everything—motivated him to unrealistic success in school, in sports, and on the stage. A few were given names to live up to, like Berry Gordy III, who was expected to carry the mantle of the family's name. And Colin Powell was saddled with the name of a World War II hero—that of Colin Kelly—whom he was expected to emulate. Others, like Reginald Lewis and Michael Jordan, were driven to fulfill an internal drive for perfection. John Johnson, Bill Cosby, Berry Gordy, Oprah Winfrey, Nelson Mandela, and Colin Powell were driven to never, ever return to the poverty whence they came.

Hero Worship Alters Internal Imagery

To some success imprints emerge out of hero worship. Shirley Chisholm modeled her life after Mary McLeod Bethune, Susan B. Anthony, and Harriet Tubman, while adopting the philosophy of Marcus Garvey. Bill Cosby modeled his act and comedy after Mark Twain while Michael Jackson was inspired to emulate his childhood hero Peter Pan. Others found their inspirational heroes in books. John Johnson became obsessed with the life of Frederick Douglass and the positive winning attitude of Dale Carnegie. Winfrey became enamored of the Horatio Alger rags-to-riches heroes, which were an incentive for her to escape the degradation of a ghetto life. All of these individuals had some special hero even if their parents were role models for a successful life.

Heuristic (Trial-and-Error) and Empirical Learning

Nelson Mandela was convinced that his success was due to early nurturing and experiential learning and had little to do with any genetically inherited skills. He talks at length in his autobiography about arbitration skills learned at the foot of the Great Chief Jongintaba, an apprenticeship he served after his father's death. At age nine, he says, "I watched and learned from the tribal meetings—profoundly influenced by observing regent and his court." Mandela concluded that his "long walk to freedom" was a result of all those things he had learned and experienced in life and was not due to any genetic gifts: "I maintain that nurture, rather than nature, is the primary molder of personality. . . . I was not born with a hunger to be free. I was born free. . . . It was the desire for freedom . . . that transformed a frightened young man into a bold one, that drove a law-abiding attorney to become a criminal, that turned a family-loving husband into a man without a home, that forced a life-loving man to live life like a monk."

Even a physically gifted individual such as Michael Jordan, whose success most people would attribute to his inherited physical attributes, was self-made. His father, James Jordan, told Al Thomy of the *Sporting News* in 1984, that his son "was not a born basketball player, Michael set goals and worked hard to achieve them. His leaping ability didn't just happen. He worked at it." An even more implausible thought is Jordan's obsessive desire to be tall when he was a small boy. He would spend hours hanging from monkey bars in an attempt to stretch his body to become taller. He stretched, pulled, and dreamed of becoming tall. And guess what? He grew to a lanky six foot, six inches—a full foot taller than any other person in his immediate family, including his father and two brothers who are five foot, seven inches in comparison. And we think we are limited by our genetic origins.

Further evidence that nurture, not nature, transformed these thirteen slightly above average people into eminent superstars comes from James Cone, the biographer of Martin Luther King, Jr., and Malcolm X. Cone writes that "Martin and Malcolm . . . were not messiahs. Both were 'ordinary' human beings who gave their lives for the freedom of their people. They show us what ordinary people can accomplish through intelligence and sincere commitment." Recent research by Daniel Goleman on "emotional intelligence" says that "emotions, not IQ" are more responsible for great success than any inborn intelligence. In other words, it appears a person's ability to effectively and emotionally interact with the world and its conflicts is far more important than any other factor.

John Johnson contends that the trial-and-error aspects of his life had more to do with his success than anything. He writes, "Moving to Chicago changed my life." The environmental influences presented by a life in Chicago as opposed to Arkansas allowed him the chance to excel and gave him the opportunity to succeed in life. Johnson felt so emotionally indebted for the opportunity he became a driven man in order to show his mother that he was grateful for the chance to succeed. He immediately was transformed into a model student and overachiever.

The Bell Curve—Good Data, Bad Conclusions

The Bell Curve was written by two brilliant Harvard researchers who, like most writers, wrote to validate their own success and psychohistory. Richard Herrnstein and Charles Murray wrote *The Bell Curve* to authenticate the pedigree required to become a Mensa intellectual, rise to the presidency of Harvard, the New York Stock Exchange, Citibank, General Motors, or head the Federal Reserve banking system. The above are all positions reserved for the "cognitive elite" that the authors tout as the source to all great success and productivity in America. The authors used "cognitive elite" interchangeably with "intelligence" and gave innumerable examples of how these individuals will be pedigreed with an Ivy League education and carriage-trade social graces as a prerequisite for achievement in the twenty-first century.

Despite what *The Bell Curve* says about the "cognitive elite" ruling the world in the new millennium, the great and powerful such as these thirteen are definitely not governed by such genetic constraints. These subjects were not the by-products of prestigious social environments, did not attend Ivy League schools (with one exception: Reginald Lewis), were not products of country clubs or the upper classes, and did not have abnormally high IQ or SAT scores except in respect to their own race. They were quite in line with the findings for superstars of other races, none of whom qualified for Herrnstein and Murray's cognitive elite. In fact, most of these thirteen were very average and often considered mediocre students during their early years. Colin Powell admitted to Larry King in a September 1995 interview, "I was a very, very, average student. If it were not for the ROTC I would have had difficulty getting through college." All were very normal people with abnormal drives who achieved abnormal success due to their drive, not their genes. Confirmation of this comes from Dinesh D'Souza in his controversial 1995 book *The End of Racism,* in which he says, "Psychologists are virtually unanimous in declaring IQ to be a product both of genes and the environment, each interacting with the other." He, like most scientists, believes that 60 percent of intelligence is a function of heredity with the 40 percent balance acquired through environmental influences.

Fallacious Reliance on Exterior Factors

Most parents and academia erroneously believe that supersuccess is a function of four factors: wealth, extensive education, family heritage, and genius-level intelligence. This misconception is one of the sad commentaries on our society. It causes many people to give up their dreams prematurely, especially if they were losers in the genetic draw or were born in the inner city and unable to attain the necessary SAT scores required to get into college. Those not fortunate enough to have been the recipient of a trust fund, Mensa-size IQ, Ivy League education, or Rockefeller name have few expectations placed on them by family or society. Due to this terrible misconception they have been relegated to a life of mediocrity. I guarantee that none of these are necessary for great success, although they are nice accoutrements for a résumé and for acceptance at the country club. But none are important factors in achieving great success, which can be seen in the lives of these thirteen.

The Bell Curve contributes to the above fallacy when it suggests that "Intelligence is fundamentally related to productivity." The book drives the nail in deeper by declaring that, "Success and failure in the American economy are increasingly a matter of the genes that people inherit." The authors conclude their research findings with this terse statement: "The twenty-first century will open on a world in which cognitive ability is the divisive dividing force in determining where an individual will end up in the social scale." On the contrary, supersuccess is a function of a person's will, drive, and other nongenetic variables that will be covered later. It has virtually nothing to do with the above four factors.

The Bell Curve's concluding hypothesis predicts that America will become a "custodial state" headed by an "overclass" of "cognitive elites" managing a massive "underclass" of "cognitive deficients." They predict a "custodial state" that is a "more lavish Indian reservation for some substantial minority of the nation's population" and is necessary to control the problems of the twenty-first century. They suggest that minorities will represent the vast majority of the underclasses that must be managed for their own good. This sounds like another master race hypothesis. Their solution is to "implement an expanded welfare state for the underclass" since they "cannot be trusted to use cash wisely." Specific solutions propounded on page 523 of the book were:

- Child care in the inner city will become primarily the responsibility of the state

- The homeless will vanish

- Strict policing and custodial responses to crime will become more acceptable and widespread

- The underclass will grow

- Social budgets and measures for social control will become still more centralized

- Racism will reemerge in a new and more virulent form

I don't think so! Daniel Goleman in *Emotional Intelligence* confirms my thesis, saying when people of "high IQ flounder and those of modest IQ do surprisingly well . . . the difference quite often lies in the abilities called here *emotional intelligence,* which include self-control, zeal, and persistence, and the ability to motivate oneself." The entrepreneurial and creative individuals in this society (and in this book) are not a by-product of any cognitive elite and usually disdain the useless conformity demanded by institutional control. They are right-brain-driven visionaries who pursue their dreams qualitatively, not quantitatively. The creative visionary is the exact opposite of the personality type that adorns bureaucratic institutions. They are rebellious and take inordinate risks since living on the edge of any product or service is where great creativity is found. It is not found in the members of the overclasses with three-piece suits managing all aspects of the creative process. Creative geniuses are found tinkering in garage workshops, producing new magazines on their home computers, writing poems that are different, and recording music that defies traditional standards. Creative destruction of the existing way is the fuel of greatness, not the established modeling techniques so revered by the cognitive elite in institutional bureaucracies.

The Bell Curve's Hypothesis

The Bell Curve suggests that genetics is the critical ingredient for great success in any profession. The book's authors are convinced that being born right is the only way to become a great creative genius. Their statistical data is impressive, as the authors have gone to great lengths to show the effect of intelligence on various demographic profiles. They use various indices to show that blacks have IQs scores averaging one standard deviation below American Caucasians with Latinos ranging in the middle of blacks and whites and Asians ten points higher than whites. The authors' main point is that: "Whites for three decades have tested one standard deviation above blacks." So what! Even if it is true *it has absolutely nothing to do with becoming successful or in gaining professional achievement.* Additionally, it is impossible to use a group to evaluate any individual's potential, since the one given in life is that we are all uniquely different.

The Bell Curve did show that when black IQs were held constant (when they were the same as whites) blacks actually had a higher propensity to graduate from college (68 percent graduated compared to only 50 percent of whites). Why did this happen? Because motivation and drive are the key variables in all great success, as detailed in chapter 5. It is self-evident that those who try harder regardless of race, religion, or national origin will perform better. Once in college, blacks try harder, which is far more important than any inherent ability. It is not the hand dealt but how one plays the hand that contributes to all wins in life.

Herrnstein and Murray have arrived at their conclusions because of their environmental influence, which is my premise throughout this book. They are by-products of the institutional megacenters that revere the pedigrees that perfectly fit into their *Bell Curve* psychometric models. Propounding their own pedigree is a well-calculated game guaranteed to keep them and their kind on top as "overclasses" with control of the cognitively deficient "underclasses." It will take dynamic people with dynamic personalities to become the movers and shakers in the next millennium. It is the overachieving personalities, like those in this book, who will become the great, independent power brokers in the twenty-first century. Ted Turner has said, "I couldn't even get a job at Turner Broadcasting. I don't fit their profile." Such visionaries become successful innovators, not any cognitive elite who will always fear deviation from the norm or "what the book says" or dare destroy tradition in order to create the new. It will be left to the Liz Claibornes, armed with a tenth-grade education, to change how we dress. It will be the Berry Gordys who will change our music, the Maya Angelous who will alter our literary approach, and the John Johnsons who will change our reading habits. These dynamic people are the rebels who would never have been invited to Harvard and if they were would not have gone. (Thurgood Marshall was asked to accept a Harvard Fellowship but declined in order to join the fight for educational equality.) The fringe, not the overclasses, become eminent successes.

Creative Geniuses Always Come from the Fringe

None of these thirteen subjects was reared in an upper-class or "overclass" family environment. None were nurtured in a country club setting, although Paul Robeson and Reginald Lewis both worked as waiters in country clubs while attending school. Bill Cosby and Colin Powell were both raised in crime-ridden ghetto environments so infamous they were given names by the media: "The Jungle" and "Fort Apache." Both John Johnson and Maya Angelou spent their youths in rural Arkansas, where they suffered the indignities of flagrant discrimination and prejudice. Shirley Chisholm, Berry Gordy, and Oprah Winfrey were raised in inner-city environments. Money, education, name, and IQ are nice accoutrements but are of little use in achieving great professional success in life. Being different is far more important to great success than fitting some statistical mold created by those who want everyone to conform to their perception of reality. These thirteen emerged out of the fringe and became successful despite their background, not because of it.

No Socioeconomic Advantages

In his 1995 *The End of Racism,* Dinesh D'Souza writes, "It is a reasonable hypothesis that IQ differences can be explained by culture and environments." This theory was based on blacks excelling or failing and had little or nothing to do with their race or cultural background. It was based on their developmental experiences with role models and nurturing. In his *Emotional Intelligence* Daniel Goleman suggests that people's success is more due to "self-awareness, empathy, persistence, and social deftness." These are quite similar to those factors I found to be important in the success of these thirteen visionaries.

Nothing in the family heritage of these subjects gave any indication that family ancestry had any bearing on their later success. Maya Angelou's brother was a monumental failure and spent much of his life in San Quentin. Angelou had the same limited advantages as her brother Bailey but was able to rise above them due to her drive, tenacity, and confidence. Berry Gordy had seven brothers and sisters who were talented but most of whom ended up working for him in some middle-management slot. All were more educated than Berry but he had the critical ingredients they lacked: awesome drive, great temerity, tenacity, and a competitive perfectionism that would not accept anything but the very best from himself or his people. Gordy transformed his internal self-image into the psychic energy necessary to grab the gold ring. In other words, he became the person that his internal script had recorded on his psyche. He lived out his internal self-image, which is what I believe happens in all creative geniuses.

None of the brothers or sisters of these subjects achieved anything close to their success. Paul Robeson had five brothers and sisters, one of whom became a medical doctor, but none came close to approaching his creative genius. Thurgood Marshall had an older brother but he was a failure in life and died a broken man, destroyed by prejudice and discrimination, which became Marshall's motivating catalyst. No examples of supersuccess were found in the family histories of these thirteen visionaries.

IQ and Formal Education Not a Factor

Asians have perennially scored higher on IQ tests than Americans of any race, with median IQs of 110. Researcher James Flynn argues that "the real explanation for the success of Asian-Americans is that they are overachievers." Plomin and Bergeman in 1991 demonstrated that a twenty-point swing in IQ was possible due to environmental influences. This experiment confirms that nurture is a very critical factor in any great achievement or success. It also demonstrates that the environment in which you are born is not nearly as important as the one in which you are raised. These subjects were fortunate to have had the right mix of experiential influences that worked.

Henri Poincaré was universally acknowledged as the world's greatest mathematician during the early part of the twentieth century. At the time of his acclaim, his friend Alfred Binet asked him to take the Stanford-Binet intelligence test. Poincaré scored at the imbecile level on the test—not once but twice. Picasso is another example of a universally acclaimed genius who couldn't get through grade school. Dean Keith Simonton, in his 1994 book, *Greatness,* comments, "Mensa gatherings seem to amass the biggest collection of misfits and underachievers on this planet." Frank Barron, who spent his life assessing creative genius at Berkeley's famed Institute for Personality Assessment, found that, "For certain intrinsically creative activities a specific IQ is necessary to engage in the activity at all, but beyond that minimum, which is often surprisingly low, creativity has little correlation with scores on IQ tests." Even one of the cognitive elite, Harvard President Derek Bok, wrote in 1985, "Test scores have a modest correlation with first-year grades and no correlation at all with what you do in the rest of your life."

It is generally agreed by the scientific world that IQ counts for about 30 percent of most success, with the rest dependent on other variables. University of Pennsylvania psychologist Martin Seligman says, "How people respond to set-backs—optimistically or pessimistically—is a fairly accurate indicator of how well they will succeed in school, in sports, and in certain kinds of work." Seligman's work is consistent with the "success imprint" thesis in this work, which relegates intelligence to a place far down the list in importance to great success in life.

An inordinately high number of these subjects did have a lot of formal education although they never used it to achieve success in their profession (see chapter 4). Education was more important to their parents than it was to them or to their later success in life. In Colin Powell's case, education was only a vehicle to an end. Powell was barely a C student in both high school and college, but while in college was fortunate to have become mesmerized with the ROTC, which turned out to fit his dreams and emotional needs. The military, with its control and organization, became Powell's savior and by his own admission the only reason he was able to make it through college. Intelligence played little part in Powell's ultimate success but he was able to use it to open some important doors on his way to the top. In his case, the labor of love became the most critical element in his success.

Another example of education as a door-opener but little else is Paul Robeson. Robeson desperately wanted to become a lawyer, but once he became one he turned to his private love and made his mark in the world as a Shakespearean actor. Shirley Chisholm had a master's degree in education but never used it in becoming America's first black U.S. congresswoman. Reginald Lewis had a Harvard law degree but actually had to quit practicing law to become one of America's greatest leveraged buyout specialists.

Michael Jackson never even made it to high school but insists on managing his own entertainment empire. The lack of formal education has not impaired his ability to manage his company but it certainly could have made him more of a conformist. More education may have proved counterproductive to Jackson's great success, as it may have demonstrated to him what he shouldn't have done. His ignorance in some sense contributed to his innovative dances and song writing. Could he have created the moon walk had he gone to dance school? Maybe, but probably not.

Lewis, Mandela, and Robeson all envisioned their law degrees as the elixir for later success. They worked diligently to obtain them but in the end the degrees were little or no use in their rise to the top. Education and intelligence are nice accoutrements at cocktail parties but certainly not prerequisites for greatness.

Success Imprints and Creativity

The thirteen subjects in this book were bright but not brilliant, which is important since research has shown that too much intelligence is counterproductive to successful achievement. Most were highly educated (much more so than the non-blacks studied in my previous books), but their formal education appears to have had little to do with their later success. Most important in their success were those experiences that contributed to the formation of their key success traits. It appears their personalities were formed by life experiences, family influences, traumatic imprints, or through metamorphoses that occurred at key points in their lives. It does appear that success does beget success and when an unexpected success occurs followed by great adulation from valued peers, that success becomes indelibly imprinted on the psyche.

Maria Montessori and Nurture/Nature Argument

Maria Montessori has never gained the acceptance in America she deserves for demonstrating that nurture, not nature, is the key determinate for success in school and life. This innovative woman changed forever the thought that uneducable children who, based on testing, are relegated to institutions (sounds strangely like *The Bell Curve*) cannot be taught like normal children. Montessori took children tested as "idiots" and had them reading within months, achieving at normalized levels within a year, merely by changing their impoverished environments into enhanced ones. Traditional educators have never accepted many of her findings, since they are in opposition to many of their revered dogmas. But much of this woman's pioneering work has now been authenticated with learning experiments on rats at the University of California at Los Angeles and Berkeley.

When Montessori was given uneducable children to teach in Rome, it was not her teaching skills the administrators saw but the fact that she was a medical doctor. Montessori didn't see uneducable children but children existing in despicable and horrid environments. How could anyone learn when their food was thrown at them and they were forced to fight for their very existence? These children had been treated as idiots and therefore fulfilled that self-image and functioned like idiots. Montessori refused to accept their sentence, changed their environment, and thereby altered their lives. By simply modifying their environment she hit on something that had been lost on the world of educators, psychologists, and sociologists. It is not the *nature* of the subjects but the *nurture* of them that will determine their success or failure in life.

Montessori's methods were simple but pragmatic and turned out to be revolutionary for the education of children. Her creative nurturing methods were immediately adopted throughout Europe and ultimately became documented as the "Montessori method" of teaching. Montessori was the first to clearly document the fact that genetics can be altered through change of the environmental conditions. She proved that children can improve their station in life by nurturing change into an "enriched environment" despite genetics.

Scientists at the University of California have recently performed many experiments with rats and found that, "Bright rats placed in 'enriched environments' double their brightness . . . and dull rats placed in an 'enriched environment' lose their dullness." An "enriched environment" can improve both bright and dull rats and an "impoverished environment" can inhibit the learning of both bright and dull rats. In other words, it is not the hand dealt but the way it is played and the playing field on which the player is nurtured that determines success. Nurture not nature is the critical factor in creating innovative and creative human beings, and these thirteen creative geniuses are living examples that success is bred not born.

Maria Montessori found that children aged three to seven have a similar learning propensity, as the American scientists have since found in rats. She initially took on the challenge of teaching children in the Rome Orthophrenic School and the children soon began performing like average children. Ten years later she was given uneducable ghetto children from the Casa de Bambino San Lorenzo tenement house. Using the innovative methods she had developed at the Orthophrenic School and refusing to hire any traditional educators, Montessori soon had these children reading and writing despite the fact that professional educators had labeled them retarded. Montessori accomplished her miraculous results by changing the environment and by adding motivational educational techniques. In the *Montessori Method* (1912) she wrote, "Education is acquired not by listening to words but by experiencing the environment." Her "retarded" children responded to the positive environment, personal attention, and freedom to perform without remorse and began achieving at normal levels within one year. Some even taught themselves to read and write at ages three and four, a feat beyond the capability of normal children. The educational world was flabbergasted.

Montessori called her method "scientific positivism" and her methodology "social engineering." She utilized "sense education," in contrast to the traditional systems taught at the time, and her fifty children were reading and writing in addition to functioning in accordance within societal rules. Montessori's approach is what this author calls "empirical pragmatism" based on "success imprints"—the identical methods used by these thirteen subjects to overcome any genetic deficiencies. Like Montessori's children they were not born with the key elements of creative genius but acquired them through motivation and freedom to learn and grow.

Metamorphoses into Success

Belief is a strong motivator, just as lack of confidence is sure to discourage one from success. We learn from our failures and are inspired by our successes and each are imprinted on our unconscious as victories of sort. Confidence and internal self-image can only be attained through trial-and-error experiences. These thirteen were never afraid to try and fail. They were internally motivated to try the difficult and when they failed would blame the failure on the elements, not on themselves. More importantly, they learned from their failures. Based on the findings on these subjects it appears that living on the edge is a formula for greatness. For those more interested in the status quo, success will reside in mediocrity, but for those who want to reach the gold ring, high risk is the only avenue for finding it. The only way to get to the top is to be willing to end up at the bottom. For great success one must go right to the very edge, making sure not to fall over, because it is at the edge where great success occurs. Of course, failure is the price paid by those who fall over.

These thirteen lived their lives on the edge and never fell over. However, success would not have been theirs had they not been willing to bet the farm. By risking and winning they were instilled with high self-esteem and "success imprints," which made them even more cocky. High self-esteem cannot be built without taking on great challenges and succeeding. That is where the great are separated from the mediocre. They believe because they climbed the mountain and were empowered by the experience.

Michael Jordan insists that his success as a basketball player began with one shot. He now believes he can make any shot with time running out, since he was empowered that time when he was just nineteen as a freshman at the University of North Carolina. Jordan was about to quit the team and had little confidence when he found himself with the ball and the biggest game in the history of North Carolina on the line. He sank that shot and won North Carolina's first-ever NCAA championship, creating a superman mystique that would follow him to the Chicago Bulls. He had been indelibly imprinted with success. He said, "My career started. . . . I was fearless after that shot."

Each of these creative visionaries experienced personal metamorphoses that instilled them with an awesome self-confidence. They became empowered; no one could persuade them that failure was possible, and therefore they often attempted and achieved the impossible. Most began to believe they were omnipotent and capable of overcoming any adversity. They came to believe they were special and when they reinforced their confidence with more successes, they were unstoppable. Some had experiences that were traumatic or highly negative but even these instilled them with a kind of survival instinct. Maya Angelou was raped at age seven and the trauma made her mute for two years. One day she was asked to recite some poetry and when she did she was transformed into a person with a destiny in literature.

Reginald Lewis was devastated when he went to camp as a ten-year-old and asked his mother to deliver his newspapers and she kept the money. He became so irate he threatened to sue her. Lewis wound up in Harvard Law School so that no one could ever take advantage of him again. After failing in three successive takeover bids Lewis was once again emotionally distraught and quit his law practice in order to become the greatest LBO specialist in America. He transformed himself into a raging manic at age thirty-eight and became the most knowledgeable LBO specialist on Wall Street making two of the biggest deals ever seen by that august avenue. Lewis became what he had envisioned for himself and succeeded beyond even his wildest expectations with the billion-dollar acquisition of TLC Beatrice Foods.

One of the more interesting transformations was that of Martin Luther King, Jr., who was baptized Michael King after his father, Michael King, pastor of Atlanta's Ebenezer Church. After his father visited Germany in 1934, when young

Michael was just five, he became inspired by Martin Luther's land and "Here I Stand" message. King's father returned home to rebaptize the boy into a change artist named Martin Luther King, Jr. Unknowingly, he had created a revolutionary dedicated to changing history. Henceforth, Martin Luther King, Jr., would see himself through the eyes of the Protestant Reformer, which encouraged the youth to become a renegade capable of instituting great change in the world.

Freud was convinced most changes occur in childhood, during the formative stages of development. I have found that most great inspirational changes occur between the ages of five and twelve and are often associated with some calamitous event or trauma. Walt Disney discovered cartoons at age eleven, Bill Gates became enamored of computers at age ten, Amelia Earhart decided to live on the edge at age six. Frank Lloyd Wright's mother placed Froebel blocks in his crib and then used them to teach him the importance of abstract thinking throughout his youth. Picasso's father placed pictures of the great masters over his crib in hopes that osmosis would take place.

Frederick Douglass chose his path to freedom when he was just eight and George Washington Carver left home at age ten to pursue a life of education. Both men lived to fulfill their childhood self-images. At age eight Berry Gordy was transformed by Joe Louis's great boxing victory and wrote sixty years later, "Joe Louis is the greatest hero in the universe . . . and in that moment a fire started deep inside me, a burning desire to be special, to win, to be somebody." Some of the more interesting metamorphoses that occurred in the lives of these thirteen subjects are listed in figure 4.

Superblacks Avoid Experts

Experts know all the reasons why any new idea or concept is unachievable, especially if it violates truisms in their area of expertise. Successful people never listen to them and in fact tend to avoid them at all costs. Michael Jordan is a classic example. He never listens to the coach and never has. He doesn't flaunt it, but says, "My mind is totally somewhere else." He thinks that if he allows someone else to control his mind he cannot function at optimum efficiency. This is a universal truth of highly successful and innovative people. John Johnson asked Roy Wilkens, the editor of America's most successful black magazine at the time, *The Crisis,* about his prospects in starting *Ebony.* Wilkens told him, "Save your money, young man. Save your energy. Save yourself a lot of disappointment." This is classic advice from an expert. My research on great entrepreneurs is rife with such ill-advised counsel. I suggest to anyone desirous of creativity or innovation to find out where the experts are operating in your profession and immediately go elsewhere. Since experts have such a psychological investment in what "is" they are oblivious of what "might be."

All great innovations and supersuccesses take place where others fear to tread. The erudite English professor and scientist Silvanus Thompson advised

FIGURE 4
METAMORPHOSES TO GREATNESS

Visionary	Metamorphosizing Experience
Maya Angelou	(Ages 7 and 15). Rape at seven ended in muteness and recovery with poems and Shakespeare that imprinted her with poems, success, and happiness, inspiring her to become a writer.
Shirley Chisholm	(Age 10) Seeing heroine Bethune on front page with President Roosevelt inspired her to want to be pictured with a president. She was, and then ran for the office herself.
Bill Cosby	(Age 8) His mother read him Mark Twain's *Tom Sawyer* at age eight and Twain became his hero and the inspiration for Cosby's streetwise humor.
Frederick Douglass	(Age 12) When slaveholder refused to allow him to read he had a "new and special revelation . . . and knew the pathway to freedom."
Berry Gordy	(Ages 9 and 20) Joe Louis's victory in 1938, when he was nine, was Gordy's first great inspiration. At twenty he wrote radio jingles for commercials and in his mind believed in himself, saying "I write songs" in describing his profession.
Michael Jackson	(Age 6) A first-grade teacher had him sing and when finished with "Climb Every Mountain" from *The Sound of Music* the adulation began that would make him great.
John Johnson	(Age 9) His family lost everything in a Mississippi flood. He wrote, "The boy on the levee was the father of the man and the publisher."
Michael Jordan	(Ages 15 and 20) Cut from team in tenth grade destroyed him. As freshman at the University of North Carolina he wanted to quit but hit the shot to win the NCAA championship. "I was fearless after that shot."
Martin Luther King, Jr.	(Age 6) Two white playmates forbidden to play with him and his name changed at age five to Martin Luther, a namesake he felt obligated to mimic.
Reginald Lewis	(Ages 8 and 38) His mother kept his newspaper money, which instilled in him the value of making your deal up front. As an adult he was destroyed by three successive takeover bid failures that forged his resolve.
Nelson Mandela	(Ages 16 and 32) As a boy he watched regent counsel and dreamed of one day becoming a lawyer. On Republic Day, May 31, 1950, eighteen blacks were killed when he called a national strike. "That day was a turning point in my life."
Thurgood Marshall	(Age 22) Denied entrance to University of Maryland Law School. "I never forgot and vowed to get even," the genesis of a career in civil rights activism
Colin Powell	(Ages 5 and 18) Named for war hero Colin Kelly and spent youth imagining himself in war. Order and structure of ROTC saved him from mediocre collegiate achievement.
Paul Robeson	(Ages 8 and 17) Dad's insistence on 100 percent effort imprinted on his psyche and he spent life being perfect. Rutgers entrance exam debacle instilled him with "inner resolve for life"; Robeson was forced to abandon a law career due to racial discrimination
Oprah Winfrey	(Age 25) Hit bottom in Baltimore in her early twenties and attempted suicide. She resolved, "I will overcome," and reached the top within two years.

young and inexperienced Thomas Edison, who was armed with but three months' formal education, to forget his stupid idea about inventing an incandescent light bulb. Thompson said it was "doomed to failure and showed the most airy ignorance of the fundamental principles of both electricity and dynamics." Six months later the ignorant but tenacious Edison exhibited his light bulb, which would soon illuminate the world. In a similar demonstration of expert arrogance, J. P. Morgan told Alexander Graham Bell that his telephone had "no commercial value." Bell ignored the sage advice from the financial wizard and the world has never been the same. Something even more ludicrous occurred in Chicago, when inventor Philo Farnsworth attempted to demonstrate his picture-radio (the first television) to Motorola. The receptionist called upstairs to the electronic experts and was told to "get rid of the kook but watch for knives or guns." New paradigms are always resisted by those afraid of the unknown.

What did Walt Disney know about amusement parks? Nothing, which is why he was able to create the greatest one—Disneyland—which the amusement park association predicted would fail miserably because it violated all the important principles of amusement parks—one entrance, free entertainment, one-priced gate, too many expensive attractions, and more—all the reasons for Disneyland's great success. Berry Gordy was told he didn't know anything about making movies when he made *Lady Sings the Blues.* He broke all the rules and that was the reason for the movie's great success. Experts always want to revert to market research to validate their concepts. The sad truth is that market research can never be done successfully on a truly innovative concept and a person must have total unconstrained belief in their dream in order to overcome the adverse opinion of the experts. J. Paul Getty lived by the principle, "If you want to make money, really big money, do what nobody else is doing. . . . Buy when everyone else is selling and hold until everyone else is buying."

Being Too Smart Is Sometimes Dumb

People who go into unknown territory often come out with surprising success. The greatest sales ever made were made by salespeople who had ventured into accounts the competitors "knew" were wrong. Those who venture into new areas are often shocked by the results as they stumble on unbelievable opportunities. The world's greatest breakthroughs have always been made by people unqualified or untrained. They were venturing into the unknown, where all great discoveries are to be found. One example is Galileo, who was a medical doctor not trained in science or astronomy. Maria Montessori revolutionized education because she was not a trained educator but a medical doctor. Had she been an educator she never would have achieved such success, because she would have been well steeped in the dogma of educators and wouldn't have questioned their most sacrosanct principles. Montessori didn't know enough not to have parent-teacher conferences so she created them, as she did numerous other innovative educational nuances.

Charles Darwin was an ordained minister awaiting assignment to a church when he took his historic *Beagle* voyage, later concocting the theories of evolution that resulted in the *Origin of Species*. Had Darwin been a trained biologist or anthropologist he would have had great difficulty propounding his earthshaking theory of evolution. IBM did not invent the personal computer because its mainframe experts knew that such a machine could never work since they expected all such devices to be hooked up to their precious mainframes. Steve Jobs wasn't so smart and created Apple Computer because of IBM's knowledge. Ted Turner created the Superstation and became the godfather of cable not because of any prescient technologic knowledge but because he wanted to transmit his TV signal to a broad area. He was innovating in areas that were not his expertise and consequently ended up creating CNN, which became the basis of the global village. Should Turner have been the one to have created CNN? No! The networks—ABC, NBC, and CBS—spent more in a week on producing a thirty-minute news program than Turner spent in a month on twenty-four-hour-a-day news. But the experts at the networks knew too much and predicted Turner's early demise. This same scenario can be repeated ad infinitum. Why didn't Gillete discover the disposable razor? They were too smart and some ignorant Frenchman by the name of Marcel Bich did it with the Bic shaver, becoming a billionaire in the process.

When Berry Gordy produced *Lady Sings the Blues* he violated every Hollywood principle and then invented some of his own. His eight Academy Award nominations were a direct result of making himself director—he had never directed a film—and hiring Diana Ross as the leading lady—she had no experience as an actress—and appointing Suzanne de Passe scriptwriter—she had never written anything but a college paper. Such successes could never occur listening to the experts, which these subjects were careful to avoid.

Paradoxical Intention

Trying too hard is often counterproductive. These thirteen visionaries set impossible goals, but then forgot them and concentrated on the fundamentals necessary to achieve the goals. They performed like the tennis player who concentrates on serving and groundstrokes instead of winning the match. If he concentrates on winning the match he will not be concentrating on the fundamentals required to win and therefore is destined to lose. These individuals never forgot where they were going but concentrated on the road to success, not the success itself. One of the axioms of great success is that virtually no rich man ever set out for riches. They set out with an obsession or dream and followed that in a tormented way. Money was always way down the list of important goals for many of these superstars, many of which are now superwealthy. They pursued perfection and excellence and relegated their larger goals to the background.

German psychiatrist Victor Frankl devised a psychoanalytic theory he called "logotherapy." In implementing this system of personal and emotional therapy he discovered a principle he labeled "paradoxical intention." Frankl came across this concept working with impotent patients and discovered that the harder they tried to have an erection the less they were able to. Frankl applied this principle to human dysfunctions like stuttering and handwriting. He was surprised to find that a stutterer who tried not to stutter couldn't stop stuttering, but one who attempted to stutter (the paradox) would not stutter. Frankl then applied the precept to simple handwriting and discovered that anyone attempting to perfectly replicate their handwriting could not do so unless they stopped trying to and then they could accomplish the objective. Just sign your name and attempt to copy it perfectly. It cannot be done until you relax and stop trying too hard. All things become more difficult when anxiety overrides a relaxed focus on the objective.

Relaxed concentration is the formula for all great success in life. In Frankl's words, "Fear brings about that which one is afraid of, and hyperintention makes impossible what one wishes." He added, "Don't aim for success—the more you aim at it and make it a target, the more you're going to miss it. For success, like happiness, cannot be pursued; it must ensue . . . as the unintended side-effect of one's personal dedication to a course greater than oneself." These thirteen subjects were exponents of Frankl's logic and approached all goals with intensity but never pressed too hard, since they intuitively knew his scientific principle. They were driven, but the drive was for perfection and to be the very best they could be, and not just to achieve a goal. Never once did any of these subjects confuse the map with the territory or their goal with their needs for perfection and excellence. And that is what made them great.

Summary—Born or Bred?

Great people are bred, not born. They learn to achieve and these thirteen are no exception. They also are unique in that they became successful while their siblings remained mediocre. Additionally, none had fathers or mothers who earned distinction outside their immediate families. Even Martin Luther King, Jr., and Malcolm X were considered very average individuals by author James Cone, who attributed their success to their personal contributions and great passion.

These thirteen could never meet Herrnstein and Murray's definition of the "cognitive elite," since they were not born with money, socioeconomic status, an inordinately high IQ, or were educated with the elite. In spite of their more average heritage they reached the very pinnacle of success and in so doing defied *The Bell Curve*'s thesis of a "cognitive elite" as the rulers of the world in the coming years. Even if *The Bell Curve* is correct in its hypothesis that blacks as a group have lower IQs than whites, the finding is without validity for success in the world. These thirteen are perfect examples of why *The Bell Curve*'s conclusions are invalid. Successful entrepreneurs, innovators, and creative geniuses are destined to become the movers and shakers in a dynamic world, not a cognitive elite.

I believe that most great people have experienced a metamorphosis during some critical period in their lives and that the positive effect of that experience imprinted them with strong self-esteem and an optimistic persona, which contributed to their later achievements. All of these black superstars experienced some such transformation and are prime examples of people living to fulfill their internal self-images. They learned not to listen to experts, were fortunate to not have been raised by overprotective parents, were careful not to become so arrogant as to know where not to go in life, and applied Victor Frankl's principles of paradoxical intention by avoiding trying too hard. Relaxed concentration was their path to success and they employed it with panache and precision. They were smart enough to "know" where they were "dumb."

3

Crisis and Creativity—
Discrimination: Crutch or Catalyst?

Dissipative structures of the mind—resilience, perseverance, matured defense, or transformational coping—are essential to survival if not creative achievement.

Mihaly Czikszentmihalyi, *Flow* (1990)

I have learned that success is to be measured not so much by the position that one has reached in life as by the obstacles which one has overcome while trying to succeed.

Booker T. Washington

Creative Destruction

Nothing new is possible without first destroying the old. It is impossible to build a new house on your lot without destroying the old one. Likewise it is impossible to launch a new product in the same market niche without destroying the old one or at least dramatically altering it to become more innovative or coveted. Think of a pizza shop that needs to change its pizza formula from bland to spicy. It can attempt to provide both products to its customers (prohibitively expensive for anyone who knows the pizza business) but it cannot do so for long. Buying into a new paradigm demands scrapping the old one just as touting capitalistic principles demanded that Mother Russia destroy all the old vestiges of communism. You cannot have both simultaneously. You must destroy your old paradigm in order to create a new one, whether it is a product, idea, or your own personality.

55

Security Is a Myth in Dynamic Societies

The only safe haven in a dynamic world is to change before you are changed. Most people are emotionally incapable of destroying a *safe known* for a *potentially dangerous unknown,* since the unknown is always frightening to the psyche. People are inclined to disdain changing an existing partner or product for a new one regardless of the intrigue of the new. Companies and people always wait until such time as they are forced to change by market conditions or the superior competitive mousetrap. This self-preservation and risk-averse mentality is why John Johnson was able to create *Ebony* and *Jet* magazines when they should have been created by *Life, Look,* or *Time.* It is why Famous Amos was so successful innovating with his cookies instead of industry leaders such as Nabisco. Those in command always take the safe road, which is why they virtually never create the truly great innovations in any industry. Unless some crisis occurs to force innovation and change, the change will never take place.

IBM had 60 percent market share in the computer industry and arrogantly disregarded the emerging personal computer business, allowing upstart Apple Computer to innovate with the hardware. Then when IBM jumped into the market late it was forced to turn to Microsoft to create the computer's operating software. These and other blunders made IBM an also-ran in the industry. What is truly amazing is that IBM had so thoroughly dominated this industry that few dared challenge it—until a couple of nineteen-year-olds—Steve Jobs and Bill Gates— changed the computer industry forever. These young visionaries had little to risk and were not emotionally and psychologically inclined to protect old products and concepts. They took on Big Blue and won. IBM now finds itself playing catchup and the little startup, Microsoft, in late 1995 finds itself with a stock market value, greater than IBM or General Motors. And Gates accomplished this in just fifteen years. Steve Jobs left Apple some years ago but left with a $250 million net worth.

Only those people and firms willing to destroy their own or others' products and traditions will succeed in a dynamic world. Those willing to take great risk and fail are destined to inherit the markets whether their innovations are in art (Angelou and Winfrey), business (Gordy and Johnson), politics (Chisholm and Mandela), entertainment (Cosby and Jackson), or sports (Jordan). In many cases it is preferable to have no products to protect or destroy, since it is easier to destroy someone else's products than your own. It gives you more options; no one fears losing something they don't have. These thirteen subjects innovated in new, fringe markets but were still able to destroy existing paradigms.

Dissipative Structures: Personal Transformations

Dr. Ilya Prigogine, a Russian-born chemist, won a Nobel Prize for his work on what he called "dissipative structures," which are instrumental in leading a person from chaos to success. He coined this phrase to describe systems in a state of disorder, what scientists call *entropy*. Entropy is the theory that all systems, including man, are in a continual state of running down or burning up in what the Second Law of Thermodynamics calls "heat death." This law asserts that all machines, including the universe, are perpetually moving toward decay and disorder. This is a nihilistic view of the world that the optimistic Prigogine revised with a positive hypothesis for the future. Prigogine agrees with the Second Law in that all systems are in a state of self-destruction, but he found that biological systems tend to either self-destruct when they reach the bottom (chaos state) or are capable of reemerging into something greater than before.

It is far easier to reach the top, in any endeavor, if you have visited the bottom. Reaching what Prigogine labeled the "bifurcation point," a person is either destroyed or reemerges much greater than before the crisis. People who stare mentality in the face become reenergized and more inclined to risk or pay the price necessary for greatness. Martin Luther King, Jr.'s stabbing on September 19, 1958, was the bifurcation point in his life. It catapulted him upward even faster than before the crisis. Having faced his own mortality, he found new energy and within five years had won the Nobel Peace Prize. Six years later he was instrumental in the passing of the Civil Rights Act of 1964.

Prigogine wrote: "It is out of chaos, turmoil, and disorder that higher levels of order and wisdom emerge, thus, if the creative thinkers have less mental stability . . . they also experience higher levels of mental connectedness, complexity, evolution." Prigogine predicted that when life becomes intolerable we reach the abyss or bifurcation point. It is at this time that all biological systems, including man, either self-destruct or become transformed into a higher form of effectiveness. History provides us many examples of individuals who rose from the ashes to change the world. Lord Byron was a cripple inspired to write *The Deformed Transformed* in cynical tribute to his affliction. Byron was introspective enough to have admitted that his personal defects were fundamental to his greatness. Beethoven was deaf when he composed his last great symphony and greatest masterpiece, the Ninth Symphony. Muhammad had a traumatic near-death experience and after a vision from the Angel Gabriel was transformed into a religious prophet. At age forty Mohammed changed from a humble and illiterate camel driver into a great sage, prophet, and conqueror. George Washington Carver of the Tuskegee Institute was kidnapped when only six weeks of age and lost his mother. He survived the experience and used the adversity to inspire himself to become the greatest black scientist in history. Ray Charles and Stevie Wonder have overcome blindness to become great recording stars and concert performers. All of these people reached their bifurcation point and reemerged stronger for having had the negative experience.

Figure 5 gives some detailed experiences of these thirteen who used their personal misfortunes to spur them on to greatness. Chaotic experiences appear to arm those who survive them with a greater resolve than they had prior to the adversity or trauma. Their imprints: resiliency, drive, an iron resolve, comfort with ambiguity, and tolerance for taking high risk are stronger after their crisis. As indicated

FIGURE 5
CRISIS AND CREATIVITY

INNOVATOR	LIFE CRISIS OR TRAUMA	CREATIVE SUCCESS
Maya Angelou	Rape and muteness at age 7. At 15 stabbed by father's girlfriend, homeless for month living in an abandoned car on a Los Angeles street.	Transformed with poetry, instilled self-sufficiency. Imprinted resiliency, survival instinct.
Shirley Chisholm	Fiancé's deportation for illegal activities almost destroyed her. Life-threatening tumor during U.S. Congress campaign.	Recovered, married, entered politics. Survived to win election.
Bill Cosby	Surviving N. Phila. "Jungle" project a miracle. One brother died, another incurable.	Used humor as antidote for social inequities and to get out of trouble.
Berry Gordy	Age 2 family on welfare, at 8 sleeping three to bed. Bankrupted record store business. Motown insolvent for many years.	Learned survival techniques, the ins and outs of the music industry.
Michael Jackson	Father's abuse and beatings as a child. Pepsi commercial hair fire in his twenties.	Rebellion and self-sufficiency. Turned into a media windfall.
John Johnson	Levee break at age 9 instilled survival instinct. 1947 *Ebony* insolvency came close to destroying his empire.	"Boy on levee father of publisher." Survival to even greater success.
Michael Jordan	Almost drowned at ages 7 and 12. Cut from high school sophomore basketball team: "I didn't want to ever have that feeling again."	Survival and fear of water. Obsessional drive instilled.
Reginald Lewis	Baltimore inner-city childhood. Loss of athletic scholarship at Virginia State College. In 1970s lost two huge LBOs, which made him quit law practice.	Created an obsessed overachiever. Forced to study and change career. Transformed LBOs.
Nelson Mandela	Father died at age 9. Arranged marriage at age 21. Spent 27 years in prison.	Learned independence and coping, groomed for mature leadership.
Thurgood Marshall	University of Maryland law school rejection. KKK mob in Tennessee attempted to lynch him.	Life's inspiration led to NAACP.
Colin Powell	Survived childhood in Ft. Apache, South Bronx. Two tours Vietnam, survived stick through foot and helicopter crash.	Survivor instincts.
Paul Robeson	Mother died tragically at age 5. Rutgers teammates broke his nose and shoulder to get him to quit.	Made him stronger and fiercer.
Oprah Winfrey	Raped from ages 9 to 12, runaway and had a baby by 14. Attempted suicide over man in Baltimore in her twenties.	Instilled independence and professional drive, creating disdain for marriage.

in figure 4, those reaching the "bifurcation point" were imprinted with the great drives and ambitions that often accompany such experiences. Anyone watching sports can identify with such resolve. Sick and injured athletes are constantly overreaching, reemerging with even greater intensity. Michael Chang did so to win the French Open, even though he could barely walk. Willis Reed hobbled onto the floor in the famous New York Knicks NBA championship victory. These subjects were able to use their great adversities to alter their personalities and instill the drive and risk-taking demeanor to reach the top. They have little expectation but tremendous focus, both critical to superachievement.

Many other examples of crisis inciting creativity abound in history. Martin Luther was walking home from school when he was suddenly struck by lightning, causing him to drop to his knees and appeal to St. Anne for assistance, promising to dedicate his life to Christ if saved. Two months later Luther quit school and became a cloistered monk. By the age of thirty-four he had revolutionized religion forever as the father of the Protestant Reformation. A similar traumatic experience occurred in the tumultuous life of Oral Roberts, who was stricken with tuberculosis as a teenager. He had already left home to become a lawyer and pursue his dream of becoming governor of Oklahoma. Roberts returned home in despair and to die when he was caught up in a mystical healing experience during one of his preacher father's tent revival meetings. During his conversion Roberts went through a personality change and was cured of his lifelong habit of stuttering. Surviving his life crisis Roberts went on to build a great ministry, including the Oral Roberts University.

One of the most inspirational stories of crisis becoming the catalyst for success is the story of black Olympic track gold medalist Wilma Rudolph, a classic example of how crisis can instill awesome drive and an indomitable will and then transform the subject into a superstar. Rudolph was born in the Tennessee mountains the twentieth of twenty-two children. She contracted double pneumonia, scarlet fever, and polio as a child and her prognosis was a lifetime on crutches. She couldn't walk without crutches until age nine but young Wilma was not one to accept such a sentence. As a child Rudolph struggled daily with her crutches and envisioned herself with normal legs that could run like those of a normal child. Her first goal was to walk alone without the benefit of her crutches. Running was merely a fantasy in her mind. When Rudolph finally mastered walking she was not satisfied and started running. It became an obsession. And once she could run, she wanted to run faster than anyone in history. And did she run. Rudolph amazed everyone who saw her. She ran like the wind.

As a sophomore in high school Rudolph was nicknamed "Skeeter" for her speed afoot. She established the high school girls' scoring record in basketball by scoring a record 803 points. Ed Temple, the Tennessee State track coach, was a basketball referee and witnessed Skeeter Rudolph flying down the basketball floor in front of her opponents. Temple was captivated by Rudolph's speed and recruited her to run for the Tennessee State track team. This poverty-stricken mountain girl who once could not even walk soon could not be caught. As a high school student she competed in the 50-, 75-, 100-, and 200-meter runs and the relay. She ran twenty different races one year and won every one. In 1956 she represented Tennessee State in the Melbourne Olympics and won the gold medal in the 100-meter dash. Four years later, at the Rome Olympics, Rudolph was unbeatable, realizing her lifelong dream when she became known as the fastest woman in the world. She won the 100-meter dash in the world record time of 11 seconds, the 200-meter dash in the world record time of 24 seconds. She combined with her Tennessee State teammates to win the 400-meter relay in 44.5 seconds. Had Rudolph had a normal childhood she probably would never have attained such high levels of achievement. Her infirmities were the catalyst for her overachievement and the reason she became the fastest woman on earth. Rudolph died of cancer in 1994 but remains a symbol of one who overcame great adversity to reach the top.

Insecurity Instills Greatness

The thirteen visionaries in this book experienced various insecurities that drove them to overachieve in much the same manner as Wilma Rudolph. Based on their stories it is apparent that the path to the top is easier to find after you have visited the bottom. When a person is totally stripped of everything, life's journey becomes more clearly defined and self-motivation becomes innate. With mortality on the line, great risk takes on a whole new perspective. The journey is less arduous. When there is little to lose, enormous gambles are easier options in life. Malcolm X told *Playboy* in 1963 that the black person from the big-city ghetto is "the most fearless. He will stand the longest. He has nothing to lose, not even his life, because he didn't have that in the first place."

Secure people are too content to make the great sacrifices or take the high risks necessary for supersuccess in life. Security-conscious people are not willing to jeopardize the status quo or violate societal norms, which are the essence of innovative success in any endeavor. Fear of failure is motivational and a greater cause of overachieving than more positive goals. The fear leads to higher-than-average risk behavior. These individuals are so scared that they take desperate steps. Desperate people do desperate things, and many blacks are experts at desperation. Many operate in a state of desperation in order not to fail. Insecurity therefore breeds greatness since it conditions a person with a fear of failure (returning to the inner city) and instills in them tremendous drive and a fearless demeanor.

Chaos and Inspiration

Prigogine found that "psychological suffering, anxiety, and collapse can lead to new emotional, intellectual, and spiritual strengths—confusion and doubt can lead to new scientific ideas." Just such a personality imprint happened to Maya

Angelou when she found herself stranded in Mexico at age fourteen with her drunken father and with no knowledge about how to drive a stick-shift automobile or get back home. At first she was traumatized but recovered, in the process teaching herself to drive in order to save herself from an uncertain fate. Her metamorphosis occurred and turned into a valuable learning experience. Chaos had led to inspiration. Fearful of being raped or worse, Angelou somehow got the car moving. When it stalled on a hill, she managed to get it restarted by rolling the car downhill and pumping the gas peddle. Maya feared death until she finally reached the border, and recalled: "I was controlling Mexico and night and aloneness and inexperienced youth and Bailey Johnson, Sr., and death and insecurity and even gravity. . . . No matter what happened after that I had won."

After Angelou returned to her father's Los Angeles house, things turned from bad to worse. His enraged girlfriend stabbed Angelou and would have killed her had Angelou not fled. She escaped by taking refuge in an abandoned car where she lived for a month. It was in this traumatic environment where Angelou honed her survival skills and was transformed into a woman who was capable of surviving virtually any calamity.

Oprah Winfrey experienced similar traumas during her youth. A cousin sexually abused her at age nine and then bought her ice cream cones and took her to the zoo to ensure her silence. Winfrey finally ran away from the degradation and lived in a hotel room for a month. Alone and broke, she finally returned home but found herself pregnant at age fourteen. Her furious mother placed her in a Milwaukee detention home. These traumas helped Winfrey form the resilient persona that is now seen on the "Oprah Winfrey Show." Although such crises are not desirable episodes in anyone's life, it appears from the research that such events are often the catalysts for transforming average people into overachieving visionaries.

Discrimination and Creativity

Dinesh D'Souza argues in *The End of Racism* that blacks' great struggle to gain power in the United States is not caused by discrimination as much as it is by the erroneously perpetuated dogma that "all cultures are equal." This author believes that inequality is preexistent in all races and creeds depending on the social setting. Blacks, at least during the period approaching the millennium, are discriminated against in approximately the same way as Indians, Asians, and whites themselves would be if they were dropped in the jungles of Brazil, New Guinea, or Tibet. Equality and opportunity are not mutually exclusive from the environment they exist in and cannot be legislated. Dropping anyone into a foreign environment who is armed with a Nietzschean will-to-power persona—like Mandela, Lewis, or Angelou—will not deter them from success. In other words, these thirteen succeeded because of their will power and insatiable drive, not because of or in spite of discrimination. This is axiomatic for any and all races.

The black man has to work harder to achieve the same degree of success and recognition as a nonblack. This is self-evident to many blacks, causing them to give up long before their white counterparts. This was not the case with these thirteen who refused to be denied success no matter the price. Not all people, black or white, are capable of dealing with the adversity or prejudices that they encounter on the road to the top. Willpower is the defining difference between the supersuccessful and the also-rans. Many people who are unsuccessful actually look for reasons for their ineptitudes and failures. They need a scapegoat to justify their lack of success, and discrimination can be used as a crutch for underachieving for blacks just as a white man's mother may take the brunt of his deficiencies.

Those people who use discrimination as a crutch instead of a catalyst are doing themselves a disservice. As shown in chapter 19 these thirteen superstars used prejudice as a catalyst and motivator. They didn't act defensive but were spurred on to become more offense-minded. Fairness doesn't exist in a dynamic world. Otherwise we wouldn't have horse races. It is just as difficult for a white Harvard graduate to find work in a redneck environment as a black. A Southern black is far more likely to be accepted in a University of Mississippi fraternity than a white kid from the Bronx. It is just as difficult for a Chinese to gain the top job at General Motors as a black—probably more so. It is imperative to recognize the strengths and weaknesses in any venue and to manage them instead of allowing them to manage you.

As previously discussed, sports and the performing arts are the easiest venues for blacks to gain supersuccess. It appears that black creativity and superstardom are most difficult in the sciences and technology. Some blacks have resorted to minority issues to make their mark in the world (see chapter 19). Others have elected to attack professions that have been the bastions of white supremacy. Oprah Winfrey and Bill Cosby have paved the way for blacks in this area, as did Colin Powell. Both Winfrey and Powell knew that they were tokens during their early years but took advantage of the opportunity and parlayed it into huge professional successes. Winfrey, as always, added levity to her role, telling a reporter, "Yes, I was a token, but I was a happy token." Powell learned the importance of patience and biting his tongue at times during his fight to get to the top. Arthur Ashe was so immersed in the white community with his tennis success that he apologized to the black community for not being a more vocal spokesman for black equality.

Most people who have made it pay a dear price for their success. There are no free lunches on the way to superachievement. Martin Luther King, Jr., saw this and said, "The children of darkness are frequently more determined and zealous." Hank Aaron gave the most simplistic but incisive description of what a black man must do to achieve. He said with uncharacteristic philosophic bent:

> Look, I don't have the vision or the voice of Martin Luther King or James Baldwin or Jesse Jackson or even of Jackie Robinson. I'm just an old ballplayer. But I learned a lot as a ballplayer. Among other things, I learned that if you manage to make a name for yourself—and if you're black, believe me, it has to be a big name—then people will start listening to what you have to say. That was

why it was so important for me to break the home run record. . . . I had to break that record. I had to do it for Jackie and my people and myself and for everybody who ever called me a nigger.

Unhappy and Lonely People at the Top

Those who grab the brass ring tend to have paid such a dear price that they often reflect back and question their decision and if the price was worth the spoils. They have reached the pinnacle of success but find themselves alone and a sacrificial lamb to that goddess called success. The word *crisis* has a double meaning in Chinese. It means both *danger* and *opportunity,* which we have already visited. In the same way the word *success* appears to lead to the dualism of loneliness and unhappiness. Both are the manifestations of the opportunity we call success. In fact, it appears that the greater the success, the greater the loneliness at the top. When you are out in front there are few support systems, including family and friends. And that is a price that few understand until it is experienced. I would be hard-pressed to find many superachievers of the hundreds I have studied who were happy or would admit to being contented, however, in the same light not one would live their life in any dramatically different way if given the opportunity.

Summary

Great crises and traumas, including discrimination, helped form the creative and entrepreneurial personalities of these visionaries. Looking tragedy in the face instills one with resilience and builds strong self-confidence and coping skills. Once the trauma has passed the individual is left in one of two states—either totally debilitated and ready to give up, or reenergized with drive and a need to overachieve. In other words, the person is destroyed or renewed, or, in Dr. Prigogine's words, "Many seeming systems of *breakdown,* are actually harbingers of *breakthrough.*" Discrimination or great crises can become a *crutch* or a *catalyst* depending on the individual's perspective.

Based on this research, it appears best to visit the bottom if you are interested in reaching the top. All of these thirteen visionaries did just that. Prigogine's work demonstrates that having experienced the degradation at the bottom, one becomes stronger than before the crisis. Just as a bone heals stronger at the break point, so it is for the psyche. Prigogine says, "Any organized system exists in dynamic tension between entropy and negentropy, between chaos and information." This is critical to anyone desirous of creative or entrepreneurial success. What appears to have happened to these individuals is that they were imprinted and molded by their traumatic experiences and those imprints are what developed the key behavioral characteristics that ultimately made them great.

Learning is magnified in the theta state, which is the state one is in as a child or when in any form of shock or trauma. That is where psychologists have discovered that "superlearning" takes place. Anything learned in this state is remembered far more readily than otherwise and in many cases lifelong imprints are formed in the psyche from such events. Our internal scripts are written when in traumatic states and surviving traumas instills the subject with great drive and initiative. These individuals became the greatest risk-takers, which adds credence to the aphorism that "Crisis is the mother of creativity."

4

Success Imprints—
The Psychological Armaments
of Greatness

When it comes to predicting people's success, brainpower as measured by IQ and standardized achievement tests may actually matter less than the qualities of mind once thought of as character.

Time, October 2, 1995, "The Emotional Intelligence Factor"

No human quality is beyond change!

Jerome Kagan, Harvard psychologist

Personality—The Key to Genius!

Personality is the key to creative genius and these great blacks validate that theory. The only difference between a woman growing up to become a prime minister or a prostitute or a male becoming a Nobel Prize winner or a bum is their attitude, which translates to their personality. All success is born of internal desire and a will to win, not by any latent talent. It comes from those unconscious reserves we all have buried inside that are looking for release. Madonna is a classic example of a person with very mediocre talent who rose to the pinnacle of success, breaking all records for top singles. With marginal talent she has accumulated $100 million in just ten years. How did someone with minimal talent become so rich and famous? The same way the slave Frederick Douglass became a great statesman, George Washington Carver became a renowned scientist, and Martin Luther King, Jr., the world's most distinguished civil rights leader. They were all molded by external experiences and driven by internal desires.

Most psychologists trained in the Freudian tradition believe personality is set in concrete by the mid-teens and those influenced by Erikson believe personality is set in stone by the mid-twenties. I am convinced that personality is set in putty, not concrete, that we can learn and grow far later in life, and that in crises or in the experience of "success imprints" we can be changed at virtually any age. If personality is not altered it becomes more rigid and far more difficult to change. My research indicates personality can be changed throughout life but changes become increasingly more difficult over time. Psychiatrist Clifford Anderson found that most people don't truly mature until their mid-thirties or -forties. In his 1995 book *The Stages of Life,* Anderson writes, "We continue to go through phases or stages much like a two-year-old." Others have shown that personality can be altered dramatically at any time in life when confronted with shock or great trauma. Daniel Goleman, author of *Emotional Intelligence,* writes, "It is not just IQ, but emotional intelligence that matters." He says, "The experiences that scare or thrill us the most in life are among our most indelible memories." Many of these subjects, especially Angelou, Jordan, Winfrey, Lewis, and Mandela, confirm these theory.

While Freud believed personality was fixed in concrete, his disciple Carl Jung believed all behavior was hard-wired and inherited as archetypes from a collective unconscious (innate fears passed down from ancestors as our key characteristics like drive and extroversion). Alfred Adler, another of Freud's disciples, concluded that we all have an innate drive to strive for excellence and superiority. I believe that personality is malleable and changeable throughout life, but at an ever-increasing price. After age forty the changes enacted become increasingly more difficult since the earlier imprints must be modified or removed prior to implementing the new you.

"Success Imprints" and "Failure Imprints"

These thirteen visionaries are examples of growing and changing throughout life. Most acquired their key traits early in life due to the factors discussed in this chapter, but many changed as a result of life-altering or threatening experiences, traumas, metamorphoses, or "success imprints." Michael Jackson became driven to succeed to spite his abusive father and then altered his behavior dramatically—both personally and professionally—due to the child-abuse allegations. Jackson was immature and asexual due to a dysfunctional adolescence and then turned into a more mature heterosexual, desperately striving to become an adult after his trauma. Paul Robeson went through a metamorphosis even later in life than Jackson. He was transformed in his thirties and forties when he went from a faithful follower with traditional values to a rebellious leader with revolutionary causes. Nelson Mandela admitted upon his release from prison after twenty-seven years that he was a changed man and had "now matured." It was his way of admitting he had changed from an emotionally driven revolutionary to a thinking reformer. The others went through similar experiences and changes, which became instrumental in their ultimate success.

How were they changed? By "success imprints" and "failure imprints," which we all endure throughout life. These "successful experiences" and "failure experiences" are continually encoded on our unconscious during our lives. People with more success than failure imprints become the movers and shakers in society. Those with mostly failure imprints are the losers in life and end up on skid row or in prison. Success begets success and failure begets failure. If one tries something new and succeeds, they are imprinted internally (unconsciously) and suddenly believe in themselves enough to try again. Failure has the opposite effect, causing the recipient to become convinced that they are incapable of success and will refuse to try again or often give up without trying. When Winfrey and Angelou survived life on city streets as teenagers, they became armed internally with a resilient belief system— an indomitable belief in their ability to survive against insurmountable odds. These two are examples of becoming internally scripted to survive adult crisis.

As discussed, Carl Jung believed we all are born with certain archetypes inherited from a collective unconscious, that if we are born an introvert we would not be able to change this trait during life since it is indelibly imprinted on what he called the *collective unconscious*. Even if Jung were right about how we acquire our key traits, it is my contention that an extrovert can and does change to an introvert if confronted with crisis, other traumatic events, or through success imprints. Scientists have now confirmed that a child who is born timid can be altered in the crib through various learning devices. Winfrey is such an example. It appears she was far more introverted early in life and lost herself in books to survive an abominable life. After her abuse, trauma, and thoughts of suicide in Baltimore, she has emerged an extroverted personality who is energized by others (the technical definition of an extrovert). Colin Powell certainly evolved from an insecure cadet to a highly confident general due to his experiences throughout his military career. He changed from a mediocre student to a highly educated and erudite leader, from a submissive youth to an assertive chief of staff who had the temerity to tell a national TV audience on January 23, 1991, "Our strategy for going after (Saddam Hussein's) army is very, very simple. First we are going to cut it off, and then we are going to kill it."

These kinds of imprints have been confirmed by recent research. Dr. T. Berry Brazelton, noted Harvard pediatrician, found children were able to learn "success" or "failure" while still in the crib. He utilized a simple diagnostic test on a baby's basic outlook on life by using blocks on eight-month-old children and found that the child who was "hopeful about life, who has confidence in her own abilities . . . looks up at you with a bright-eyed look of expectancy that says, 'Tell me how great I am!' " Contrasting children, however, come "from homes too bleak, chaotic, or neglectful [and] go about the same small task in a way that signals they already expect to fail." Brazelton says, "They already expect to fail" and their "demeanor is hangdog," which says, "I'm no good. See, I've failed."

These thirteen subjects were obviously imprinted with the "success imprint," which contributed to their successes later in life. Even those who started out with a negative life orientation were able to evolve and change their orientation to success by writing and rewriting scripts on the unconscious. Those with the strongest "positive images" or "success imprints" became the most successful adults.

Others, like many of the siblings of these thirteen, were the recipients of "negative" or "failure imprints" (see Angelou, Marshall, Cosby, Johnson). Their brothers and sisters often ended up in very subservient positions or worse. Bailey Johnson, Angelou's brother, ended up in San Quentin. Many others, like Thurgood Marshall's and Paul Robeson's brothers, died miserable failures. "Failure imprints" can prove as destructive as the "success imprints" can prove constructive. The secret is to strive for great success and then reinforce it with more success and suddenly a "success" imprint is written on your psyche just as it was for these thirteen.

Personality Imprints

Most scholars now believe that IQ is acquired by both genetics and experience. Some, like Thomas Buchard of the University of Minnesota's Center for Twin and Adoption Research, believe that IQ is 70 percent inherited and 30 percent acquired. Researchers like James Flynn believe that drive and work ethic can materially impact IQ scores. In any case, there is universal agreement that a symbiotic relationship exists between nature and nurture in molding the personality traits and intelligence of humans.

Positive and Negative Conditioning

Personality traits such as passion, confidence, risk taking, charisma, independence, drive, work ethic, and vision are learned through experiential interactions with the environment. *Passion* can be acquired as a result of frustrations, denials, and insecurities while growing up. A *competitive spirit* can emerge from sibling rivalry, father/son rivalry, or a need to prove oneself. *Confidence* is instilled through doting parents and relatives who imprint a messiah image, whether deserved or not. *Risk taking* is absorbed by watching parents operate as independent warriors (self-employed or entrepreneurs) and having parents who are indulgent and not overprotective. Whether otherwise advisable or not, parents who allow their five-year-old to walk to the store alone are instilling confidence, comfort with ambiguity, and self-sufficiency. Trying and succeeding is the essence of positive conditioning of those traits critical to great success in life. This is called *heuristic learning*. *Frequent travel or moving* also instills coping skills, temerity, and self-sufficiency. Such children learn to cope with new, unknown environments. *Charisma* grows out of a need for effective communications and enticing friends to follow. It is often acquired from valued role models and mentors who provide positive but incisive guidelines for leading (see Shirley Chisholm).

Positive interfaces with role models can instill assertiveness while negative feedback can instill submissiveness. *Independence* is often acquired when we are left to fend for ourselves at an impressionable age and surprise ourselves by succeeding. *Drive* emanates from trauma or crisis, which leaves us with a burning need to overachieve. *Intuitive vision* is molded through early training with jigsaw puzzles, Froebel blocks, or other abstractions that challenge one to envision the forest and not the trees of life. *Insecurity* can instill greatness through a "drive imprint" resulting from a fear of failure. *Risk taking* is engendered when a child is permitted to err and fail without retribution. A strong *work ethic* can be instilled when a ten-year-old is told he is industrious and then spends his life living up to that idealistic label. The reverse occurs when a twelve-year-old is told she is stupid and will never master math. Sure enough, she will grow up avoiding numbers like they are the plague. Valued teachers and role models are critical in the formation of positive or negative internal images which are then lived up to for a lifetime.

Modifying Personality Traits

Changing one's personality as an adult can be likened to altering the color of a large tumbler filled with red granules. Attempting to alter the color in the tumbler from red to blue (akin to a person changing from an introvert to an extrovert) by adding 50 percent blue granules will succeed only in changing the color of the tumbler to purple. Even adding 75 percent blue granules will achieve only partial success, as the tumbler will still appear bluish-red. The reason is the predisposition of the red granules, which are metaphorical examples of the thousands of experiential imprints that make up the human personality.

Changing the personality is possible, but, just as in the above tumbler example, modifying it can prove to be quite difficult due to the previous experiential inputs. The more experiential inputs creating a certain trait (fear, confidence, hard work, or laziness), the more difficult the change. Such changes take a lot of time and effort unless the individual experiences a trauma, brainwashing experience, or metamorphosis. Psychologists have shown that superlearning, permanently altering a personality instantaneously, can take place due to great trauma or crisis. Just as you could enact an immediate change by breaking the tumbler to remove all the red granules, so too can you change a personality if trauma intervenes.

History is filled with examples of traumatic changes. Martin Luther King, Jr., went though numerous changes. Changing his name from Mike to Martin Luther at age five altered his mission in life. Losing a white friend at six was another traumatic change that instilled a unique value system. Then he experienced having to stand on a bus for fifty miles at age sixteen because of his color which instilled great anger and drive. King's greatest trauma occurred in New York City in 1958 when he was stabbed and nearly died. From that point on King became more emotionally driven. Most of these subjects went through similar traumatic experiences which have molded their behavior (see figure 5).

FIGURE 6

DYNAMIC NATURE OF PERSONALITY

(PC AS HUMAN METAPHOR)

Personal Computer		Functional Characteristics	Human Personality
Systems Enhancements		Human Enhancements	
IBM PC/Apple Mac	Hardwired features	Gender and race, eye color, IQ (70%)	Genetic Qualities (RNA/DNA)
Board Upgrades	Modem/memory	IQ, drive, fears (Introversion/extroversion)	Hard-wired imprints (Collective unconscious)
Systems Software	MS-DOS	Will, vision, mania obsessions/compulsions	Cultural imprints (Crises/metamorphosis)
Operating Software	Windows	Self-esteem, charisma independence, rebellion	Experiential imprints (Parental and environmental conditioning)
Applications Software	WordPerfect Lotus 123	Resilience, temerity, competitiveness, energy	Cognitive experience (Success imprints from transience, books, etc.)

PC as Metaphor for Personality Change

The personal computer is an excellent metaphor for how a personality can be altered and improved by changing its operating style. The original personal computer box and the human body are similar in that they embody potential, but that potential is quite dormant until they are loaded with high-level programs. Until the basic units are programmed to perform at a high level of sophistication, neither is destined to become very effective in the real world.

Computers and people have the potential for upgrading and loading in higher level programs to enhance performance. These programs can alter their internal operating scripts to satisfy their psychological needs and positive performance. The PC is a fixed hardware machine with upper and lower limits of original architecture, not unlike humans, who cannot dramatically alter their color or stature but can alter their operating performance through drive and attitude.

An IBM-compatible or Apple Macintosh is purchased with certain hardwired characteristics like operating speed and memory capacity. This is not unlike a human born with preordained genetic qualities like race and gender. There is not much that can be done with the basic limitations of the original box. But within the given capacities of the box many changes and improvements can be made. The PC can be upgraded with extra memory boards or modems just like certain hardwired changes can be programmed into the human, like self-image and drive. Loading MS-DOS into a PC will endow it with certain unique operating characteristics just as cultural and parental imprints and crises, metamorphoses and other "success imprints" can predispose a human with unique characteristics like an indomitable spirit, obsessional drive, strong work ethic, high risk-taking propensity, and vision.

Loading a PC with Windows 95 or other such high-level operating software alters its operating style, just as experiential and success imprints can create an idyllic operating style for a human—one endowed with charisma, an extroverted-intuitive temperament, or high self-esteem. An introverted submissive person with little self-confidence and dominated by fear can also be scripted.

When the PC is loaded with applications software programs, like WordPerfect or Lotus 123, it can refine its operating style to a much higher level. Humans can also learn from various experiences and change their cognitive operating styles to survive and succeed. Resilience, temerity, and competitive behaviors are often formed from a desperate need to cope and survive in a dynamic and competitive world. Figure 6 gives a graphic illustration of how a personal computer can evolve into a very effective operating device by loading in more complex and sophisticated, higher-level programs. Humans can also go through a similar evolution of effectiveness by changing their internal scripts. Many of these occur without planning or can be altered consciously through concerted effort and training. Charisma is one of those key traits that has now been shown to be an acquired talent. Hitler was trained to be a mesmerizing speaker by Dietrich Eckart and there are now training centers to refine this trait. Winfrey, Angelou, and Mandela changed themselves into mesmerizing leaders through constant work and drive.

Variables in Forming Personality Traits

It appears from this research that many variables come together to mold a person into a creative genius or entrepreneurial power broker. The factors found most prevalent in forming the creative and entrepreneurial personality were: birth order, doting parents, early transience/travel, fantasy heroes from books and music, mythological mentors, real-life and parental role models (self-employed fathers), formal education, and early freedom to explore (latchkey environments). Let's analyze these critical factors.

BIRTH ORDER

Psychologists have long known that the first child in a family tends, on average, to have a higher IQ than those born later. Psychologist Alfred Adler did the pioneering research on birth order and personality development. He said, "The position in the family leaves an indelible stamp on his or her style of life." Later he wrote, "It is not . . . the child's number in the order of successive births which influences character, but the *situation* into which he is born and the way he interprets it." This gives some insight into the character traits found in Paul Robeson, who was the last born of eight children, but who acted like a firstborn due to being

FIGURE 7
BIRTH ORDER AND SIBLINGS

Subject	Birth Order	Siblings
Maya Angelou	Second born; 1st female	Brother, Bailey, one year older
Shirley Chisholm	First born of three	Sisters: Odessa, Muriel, Selma
Bill Cosby	First born of five	Russell, Robert, James (died at 6)
Berry Gordy, Jr.	Seventh born of eight	Namesake of two generations
Michael Jackson	Seventh child of nine	Two sisters and six brothers
John Johnson	First born	Half sister fourteen years older
Michael Jordan	Fourth of five siblings	James, Deloris, Larry, Roslyn
Reginald Lewis	Only child	Five half siblings
Nelson Mandela	Only child of parents	Polygamous father with four wives; foster brother, Justice, his best friend
Thurgood Marshall	Second born and last son	Older brother, William Aubrey
Colin Powell	First son of two	Sister, Marilyn, six years older
Paul Robeson	Youngest of eight	Siblings had left, raised as only child
Oprah Winfrey	Only child	Half sister and half brother

raised as an only child. All of Robeson's siblings had left the family home by the time he was four. Nelson Mandela had a similar situation. His father had many wives and children but he was doted on by his mother and then his father selected him as the chosen one. When he died—Mandela was nine at the time—the son was sent off to be mentored by the tribal chief.

The firstborn are more doted on and laden with great expectations to become family leaders. They are expected to carry on the family name and success, a stigma that has been handed down from centuries of indoctrination on primogeniture. Kenneth Leman, author of *The Birth Order Book,* maintains that firstborns are predestined for greatness. He says firstborns are instilled with a need to be "perfectionistic, reliable, conscientious, list makers, well organized, critical, serious, scholarly."

Eight of these thirteen subjects were firstborns or were raised as such (see figure 7). Robeson was actually the last born but, as mentioned, was raised like an only child and doted on by family and relatives. Maya Angelou was the second born but the first female. Her brother, Bailey, was a year older, her confidant and best friend, but she envisioned herself as carrying the mantle of the female name. Females had been the dominant role models in Angelou's family, a consistent finding in the thirteen, especially the males. Her grandmother Annie Henderson was an aggressive, self-sufficient shopowner and Angelou's mother, Vivian, was an icono-clastic entrepreneur. Angelou was instilled with the female power of these role models. She saw her absent and inept father only sporadically.

Only Children

Three of the thirteen subjects were only children and six were raised by doting grandparents. Psychologists have found that children with a separation of over six years were often treated more like only children than those who had siblings of similar age. Leman felt that only children were even more driven to succeed than firstborns due to their place of eminence within the family. Only children tend to be more prone to overachievement (or stress) and tend to become introverted, es-cape into books and fantasies, and become far more mature than their years. Such was the case for Winfrey, Lewis, and Mandela, all only children.

Doting Parents

Numerous examples of doting parents creating precocious children exist in history. Pablo Picasso, Frank Lloyd Wright, and Thomas Edison are prime examples of par-ents creating precocious, but arrogant, adults who grow up to become overachievers. Paul Robeson was a prime example of a person doted on by aunts, uncles, siblings, and a lonely and older father who looked on little Paul as a messiah. Reginald Lewis was another child doted on and spoiled by parents, maternal grandparents, un-cles, and aunts. He began thinking of himself as special at a very early age. The adults thought of Reggie as God's gift to the world and sure enough he bought into their dreams and grew up believing the truth of their predictions for him.

 The mothers of these subjects were often the dominant influence in their lives. They were usually the backbone of the family and the positive role models during their children's impressionable years. In Angelou's case it was her grand-mother Henderson who made her feel special. All the rest were most influenced by indulgent mothers, especially John Johnson and Bill Cosby. Chisholm, Powell, Marshall, Winfrey, and Mandela were those most influenced by their fathers.

Transience

Oprah Winfrey is an example of how childhood transience often molds adult self-sufficiency. She had moved five times by age fourteen and attended a dozen dif-ferent schools in Mississippi, Milwaukee, and Nashville. In the process she was forced to cope with new environments, make new friends, deal with unknown cul-tures, and learn to deal with ambiguity, all critical factors in the lives of adult cre-ative visionaries.

 Another subject so influenced was Shirley Chisholm. Chisholm was born in Brooklyn, moved to Barbados at age three, moved back to Brooklyn at age seven, and moved four more times within New York City by the time she started high

FIGURE 8
BIRTH LOCATION AND TRANSIENCE

Subject	City of Birth	Early Moves/Travel	Total Moves
Maya Angelou	St. Louis, Mo.	Los Angeles, Arkansas, St. Louis, San Francisco	7
Shirley Chisholm	Brooklyn, N.Y.	Barbados	4
Bill Cosby	Philadelphia, Pa.	Project to project	4
Berry Gordy, Jr.	Detroit, Mich.	East Side/West Side	3
Michael Jackson	Gary, Ind.	Louisiana and constant travel	3
John Johnson	Arkansas City, Ark.	Vicksburg, Chicago	3
Michael Jordan	Brooklyn, N.Y.	Wilmington, N.C.	2
Reginald Lewis	Baltimore, Md.	Four moves within city	4
Nelson Mandela	Umtata, Transkei, South Africa	Four moves within South Africa	4
Thurgood Marshall	Baltimore, Md.	Harlem, Baltimore & travel	3
Colin Powell	Harlem, N.Y.	South Bronx, two moves	3
Paul Robeson	Princeton, N.J.	Westfield, Somerville	3
Oprah Winfrey	Kosciusko, Miss.	Milwaukee, Nashville (twice)	6

school. This forced young Shirley to deal with a whole new culture in Barbados which had a British heritage, tropical climate, and agrarian economy all diametrically opposite to what she experienced in urban New York City. Consequently, Chisholm learned early that established traditions are transitory at best and change is always a viable alternative when the present is intolerable. The renegade congresswoman was definitely a by-product of her heritage and upbringing.

Figure 8 shows the extreme transience among these subjects. The average moved four times and some many more during their formative years. Those who didn't move extensively traveled a great deal. Chisholm not only moved a lot, she had visited Los Angeles and Washington, D.C., by her midteens. Michael Jackson had been to every major city in America before the age of ten and Thurgood Marshall had traveled on trains with his father at a formative age. Reginald Lewis was a traveling salesman as a teenager, working his way through school by traveling through three states.

Frequent moves and travel instilled resilience and self-sufficiency in these future superstars. Parents normally view physical moves as a debilitating influence on their children. This is incorrect. Children will often object to leaving their friends but are emotionally enhanced by the experience, and strong characters often result from the need to deal with new and unknown environments. While parents see the change as a loss in stability, it is this loss of external stability that forces one to become more stable internally. Lack of stability molded these individuals with more strength and resilience and their indomitable wills were a direct result of their being forced to deal with instability. Those children who never face ambiguity never learn to deal with it in the real world and consequently grow up to be followers, not leaders. Self-confidence is the benefit derived from early transience and these thirteen subjects are clear demonstrations of that principle at work. It is apparent that the key traits of self-confidence, temerity, and inner strength were acquired by early moves and travel.

Books—Sources of Fantasy Role Models

Joseph Campbell very insightfully recognized the source of most creative inspiration as an unconscious response to early myths and heroes from stories learned at a young age. In *The Power of Myth,* Campbell said, "The big problem of any young person's personal life is to have models to suggest possibilities." He concluded that, "All myths make heroes out of those who heed them since they are spontaneous predictions of the psyche." Campbell was convinced, as I am, that myths, both real and imagined, are the source of our unconscious dreams and wishes, which become the positive or negative driving forces in our lives.

These subjects certainly identified with superheroes at an impressionable age and their protagonists out of books, plays, and the Bible became inner scripts to draw on for later success. It is interesting that the majority of these subjects were voracious readers from a very young age. And it was their time spent in books and fantasizing about great heroes that kept them from succumbing to the ravages of street gangs, crime, drugs, and wasted lives. The world of make-believe that seduced the minds of these individuals instilled in them a vivid imagination that they never lost. Their imagination allowed them to wander intellectually and create an idealistic world to fit their inner fantasies. Winfrey said her character was molded by books. She told a 1994 American Booksellers Conference in Miami Beach, "I owe everything in my life to books." *Good Housekeeping* in 1991 quoted her as saying, "Books showed me there were possibilities in life, that there were actually people like me living in the world. I could not only aspire, but attain. . . . Reading gave me hope. For me it was the open door." While living in Milwaukee, Winfrey said she hid in the closet to read by flashlight so her half sisters would not make fun of her "trying to be somebody" (she was).

Maya Angelou lost herself in books to such an extent that they became her solace and fantasy reality. She told Shari Belafonte on national television in 1996 that success comes from books and her advice to everyone is: "Read copiously. Just read, read, read." She wrote of her own passion for books: "I spent most of my Saturdays at the library . . . breathing in the world of penniless shoeshine boys who, with goodness and perseverance, became rich, rich men, and gave baskets of goodies to the poor on holidays. The little princesses who were mistaken for maids . . . became more real to me than our house, our mother, our school."

Cosby's mother read to him about the misadventures of Tom Sawyer in books by his favorite author, Mark Twain. Cosby became so enamored with the honest humor of Twain that he turned to him for material for his bar act, resorting to the street ironies of the Jungle in North Philly, which were so Twainlike. John Johnson wrote in his autobiography that he spent all of his spare time as a teenager at the Chicago Public Library. He said, "I read all the self-help books I could find. I also read the great classics of black history and literature, including Booker T. Washington's autobiography, *Up from Slavery,* W. E. B. Du Bois's essays, and the poetry of Langston Hughes." Frederick Douglass and Dale Carnegie became his great heroes, influencing him into becoming what he called himself: a "success freak."

Books were a welcome diversion for most of these thirteen visionaries. Those who did not escape into the fantasy of books found inspiration in the Bible, black spirituals, Bible music, or jazz and blues. Many turned to the church for support and found redemption in spiritualism, using the church and its icons as fantasy role models. Biblical heroes and heroines become mythological mentors for many of the subjects, just as James Brown and Diana Ross were for Michael Jackson, Joe Louis and the Mills Brothers were for Berry Gordy, and Susan B. Anthony and Harriet Tubman were for Shirley Chisholm. These subjects became lost in their imaginations with books and music supplying the fictional heroes who became role models and people to emulate. Make-believe and imagination are great escapes for children who have little else to enhance their lives and are surely preferable to street gangs and drugs as substitute support systems.

Mythological Hero Mentors—"Follow Your Bliss"

Many of these individuals chose mythological mentors to emulate as children and some never totally escaped from their fantasy role-playing imagery. They were able to heed the sage advice of Joseph Campbell, who preached, "Follow your bliss"—enjoy a successful and satisfied life. Michael Jackson certainly heeded such advice. He so identified with his childhood hero Peter Pan that he was incapable of seeing himself as a normal person. Jackson worshiped and then mimicked Peter Pan and became fixated in that role. Psychologist Dan Kiley described the fixation in *Peter Pan Syndrome.* In the syndrome the male grows up to become a "man-child." Kiley wrote that these men are "out of touch with their true emotions, afraid to depend on even those closest to them, self-centered, and narcissistic, they hide behind masks of normalcy." He says, "Like the fairy tale hero, they resort to pretense, false gaiety, and 'magical thinking' in an effort to hide their failure from themselves and others." This is a truly incisive description of the man-child Michael Jackson who married his Tinkerbelle companion, Lisa Marie.

According to Freud, the unconscious is *acquired* as a young child ("The motive force of phantasies are unsatisfied wishes") as a result of repressed instincts

FIGURE 9
MYTHOLOGICAL HERO MENTORS

Visionary	Hero Mentor and Fantasy Role Model
Maya Angelou	Horatio Alger, Christ, Shakespeare, Poe, Dickens, Kipling, Frederick Douglass, W. E. B. Du Bois
Shirley Chisholm	Harriet Tubman, Susan B. Anthony, Mary McLeod Bethune, Marcus Garvey
Bill Cosby	The Shadow, the Lone Ranger, Mark Twain, Charlie Chaplin, Sugar Ray Robinson, Jackie Robinson
Berry Gordy	Rudyard Kipling's "IF," Joe Louis, Sugar Ray Robinson, Ink Spots, Mills Brothers, Billie Holiday
Michael Jackson	Peter Pan, Walt Disney, Elvis Presley, James Brown, Diana Ross, Fred Astaire, Gene Kelly, Berry Gordy
John Johnson	Horatio Alger, Dale Carnegie, teacher Mary Herrick, Harry Pace, and Earl Dickerson
Michael Jordan	Parents, David Thompson
Reginald Lewis	Superman, Batman, stepfather Jean Fugett
Nelson Mandela	Xhosa legendary heroes, Xhosa poet Mqhayi, Mao Tse Tung, Che Guevera, Marcus Garvey
Thurgood Marshall	W. E. B. Du Bois, Dr. Charles Houston, Paul Robeson, William Hastie
Colin Powell	Namesake WWII hero Capt. Kelly, General Charles Gettys, Frank Carlucci
Paul Robeson	Black spirituals, Bible music, Eugene O'Neill, W. E. B. Du Bois
Oprah Winfrey	Movie stars, 4th-grade teacher Mrs. Denvor, Barbara Walters, Maya Angelou, Diana Ross

molding a fixed cognitive behavior by the teens. According to Jung, all archetypes are inherited from a collective unconscious ("It is not Goethe who creates *Faust* but *Faust* who creates Goethe . . . *Faust* is but a symbol"). Life's experience then activates archetypes. According to Campbell, archetypes are *acquired* through identity with myths. The imagination develops symbolic experiences, recording them as mythical scripts on the unconscious. The emotions and actions in life allow the innate behaviors to be manifested from the hero imprints which have been recorded as archetypes ("Myths create heroes out of those who heed them"). The "will" of such people becomes inextricably tied to the metaphoric hero. Self-actualization emanates from "following your bliss." According to Landrum's mythological scripting theory, adults spend their lives fulfilling the internal images acquired during childhood. Strong internal images of mythical heroes are imprinted during childhood and become internalized as archetypes for successful behavior. Children with a "loser imprint" unconsciously strive to fulfill that negative image, just as those with a "hero imprint" strive to fulfill that image. Even deluded scripts become archetypical scripts. Children who are taught they are "little Messiah's" by indulgent/doting parents become arrogant, overachieving adults. *We all become as we think* (unconsciously) with positive imprints preordaining positive actions and negative imprints resulting in negative ones. Positive traits and attitudes like self-confidence, tenacity, indomitable will, and optimism often are the by-products of modeling one's life after a fantasy hero/mentor found in books, fairy tales, or spirituals. Mythical heroes like Superman, the Shadow, Peter Pan, or Batman can become inspirational images guiding one to great success. Real-life historical heroes such as Christ, Frederick Douglass, Harriet Tubman, Mark Twain, or Joe Louis can instill an unconscious belief system with few limits for success in the real world.

Michael Jackson's mythological hero Peter Pan was also responsible for other unlikely moves. This single recluse acquired a huge ranch in Santa Barbara, California, and then named it NeverLand Valley in tribute to Peter Pan's safe haven, Never Never Land. Jackson, like his real-life hero Walt Disney, preferred animals to people and acquired this 2,700-acre ranch to house a menagerie of animals who were safe and nonthreatening playmates for this man-child. Jackson has emulated his childhood hero in other ways as well. His mesmerizing moonwalk dance is as close as Jackson can get to flying away to happiness, safety, and freedom with hero Peter Pan.

My research has found that most superachievers have mythological heroes to emulate while young and their make-believe imagery becomes so entrenched in their psyche they are able to see themselves with limitless potential as adults. They identify with fictitious (sometimes historical, real-life) heroes from books, the Gospels, music, and fairy tales who are larger-than-life.

Maya Angelou utilized such fantasy imagery in overcoming her muteness. She spoke for the first time in two years when her real-life mentor, Mrs. Flowers, had her recite the poetry of Poe and Shakespeare. After this miraculous recovery Angelou became enamored of books, poetry, and the heroes from same and, not surprisingly, ended up as a writer and poet despite no training or college experience. She experienced her "success imprint" from a fantasy love affair with Shakespeare, who she admitted was her first great love.

At age eight Berry Gordy was mesmerized by Joe Louis's unexpected victory over Hitler's example of the master race, Max Schmeling. This was such a memorable experience for Berry that it was the first thing Berry wrote of in his autobiography almost sixty years later. Then Berry quit school in the tenth grade to become a boxer to emulate his great hero. He said Louis's victory was the inspiration he needed to succeed in life and that Louis's "phenomenal feats had opened my imagination to the possibility of being somebody in the world." Berry admitted, "At the moment of Joe's great victory a fire started deep inside me, a burning desire to be special."

It certainly isn't a coincidence that Nelson Mandela's real name, Rolihlahla, translates as "troublemaker." His destiny was further molded when he chose Mao Tse Tung as his fantasy political hero, which led him to fulfill the real meaning of his name. Think of John Johnson spending many hours as a teen dreaming of the great heroes out of Horatio Alger books and then spending the rest of his life emulating them. Johnson religiously followed Dale Carnegie's recipe for success in order to live out his rags-to-riches destiny. And consider Colin Powell totally identifying with World War II hero Colin Kelly and then pursuing a military career that allowed him to pattern his life after his childhood namesake. Powell grew up with headlines of war heroes and hearing stories of gallantry in the military in the early 1940s and then modeled his life after these unconscious imprints in Vietnam, Korea, Europe, Panama, and the Mideast. Aggrandizement of American military battles were unconscious scripts written on the psyche of an impressionable boy who then grew up to live out his fantasies.

Shirley Chisholm had three great heroines—Susan B. Anthony, Harriet Beecher, and Mary McLeod Bethune. She was inspired by the front-page photograph of Bethune pictured with President Franklin D. Roosevelt and his wife, Eleanor. Shirley grew up to not only have her picture taken with many presidents but actually took a shot at residing at 1600 Pennsylvania Avenue in 1972.

Joseph Campbell felt that, "Myths are models for understanding your own life" and fundamental "metaphors for realizing your personal vision." He was convinced an individual could only self-actualize by "following" their "bliss" which Campbell saw as buying into one's internalized fantasies. Campbell wrote, "Mythologies are symptoms of an unconscious need to survive to transcend life's adversities." They are masks of inspiration, tickets or passages to success in life.

Parental Role Models—Self-Employed Fathers

Parental influence is critical to instilling "success imprints" in children. Colin Powell, Michael Jordan, Berry Gordy, Nelson Mandela, Shirley Chisholm, and Thurgood Marshall all contended that they became successful because of positive parental role models. Powell and Jordan were the most ardent in crediting their parents for their great success in life. Jordan once told a sportswriter, "My heroes are and were my parents." "His Airness" asserts his superstardom resulted from the values instilled by his parents. He said, "My father's and mother's personalities . . . allowed me to become the person I am." Colin Powell had the same strong feelings toward his parents. When asked why he didn't succumb to the drugs of Fort Apache, he told Larry King without hesitation, "My mother would have killed me." He credits his family for his strong values and work ethic and says they were his "lifeline" and most responsible for his success in life.

John Johnson's mother instilled him with a herculean work ethic. She was the one who worked two jobs to get him out of Arkansas at age thirteen so he could go to school in Chicago where he would not be relegated to a one-room classroom for blacks only with inadequate teachers and curriculum. Her tenacity and pursuit of her dream for her son's education instilled in young John a fearless work ethic and tenacity that became the instruments of his later success in creating *Ebony* and *Jet*. Paul Robeson was molded in the image of his father, an escaped slave who worked his way through college to become a Princeton minister. Robeson adored his father and listened to every admonition of this self-made man. He worked very hard just to please his father and wrote in his autobiography, "I would have given my life for him." Robeson's father instilled in him the obsessional drive that would make him the greatest American Shakespearean actor of his era. Once when Paul brought home four As and one B, his father admonished him with, "Why didn't you get all As?" Paul was taken aback, saying nobody got 100 percent. His father explained to him that 100 percent was not only possible but necessary for a black man to effectively compete in a white-dominated society. From that day forward Paul worked diligently to get all As for his father and as an adult drove himself to achieve 100 percent at whatever task he attempted. It was this drive which contributed to Robeson's great success in life.

Thurgood Marshall told the *New York Times,* "My father turned me into a lawyer without ever telling me what he wanted me to be. He did it by teaching me to argue, challenged my logic on every point, by making me prove every statement I made." Reginald Lewis's stepfather, Jean Fugett, was a major influence on him. He worked all day and attended college at night, becoming an ideal role model for young Reginald, who became a workaholic himself. In Michael Jackson's case, his father Joe proved to be a motivation in a negative way. He beat Michael and abused him both mentally and physically, creating an internal drive in Michael and motivating him to strive to become the diametric opposite of his father. Jackson's bizarre dress and asexuality is openly defiant of his womanizing father, whom he hated with a passion. Bill Cosby was also negatively motivated by a father who was an alcoholic and absent from the family. Cosby doesn't drink alcohol because of this fatherly influence. He acquired his drive and work ethic from his mother whom he idolized for her tenacity and work ethic. Both Colin Powell and Shirley Chisholm were by-products of the West Indian work ethic, where they earned the appellation "black Jews." Chisholm became a renegade politician as a tribute to the Marcus Garvey philosophy preached by her father while Powell worked hard at everything he ever attempted in order to please his family.

Self-Employed Parents

Eight of these individuals were nurtured by entrepreneurially driven parents. Angelou's mother owned numerous businesses in San Francisco and was a true gambler both personally and professionally. Winfrey's father owned various businesses, including a barber shop and convenience store. Gordy's father was a plastering contractor while Lewis's father owned a Baltimore restaurant. Jackson's father formed his own band before organizing his sons into the Jackson Five. Thurgood Marshall's parents and grandparents operated grocery stores. Robeson's fa-

---

FIGURE 10
EDUCATIONAL ATTAINMENT OF BLACK VISIONARIES

Subject	Highest Education Attained	Educational Institution
Maya Angelou	High school diploma	San Francisco Mission High School (1945)
Shirley Chisholm	Master's in education	Columbia University (1952)
Bill Cosby	Doctorate in childhood education	University of Massachusetts (1976)
Berry Gordy	High school GED	Military (1952)
Michael Jackson	Middle school only	Tutoring (age fourteen)
John Johnson	High school diploma with honors	Chicago DuSable High (1936)
Michael Jordan	Bachelor's in geography	University of North Carolina (1986)
Reginald Lewis	LLB law degree	Harvard Law School (1968)
Nelson Mandela	Law examination (1952)	University of Witwatersrand
Thurgood Marshall	LLB law degree, magna cum laude	Howard University (1933)
Colin Powell	MBA and White House fellow (1973)	George Washington University (1971)
Paul Robeson	Rutgers prelaw; LLB law degree	Columbia University (1923)
Oprah Winfrey	Bachelor's degree in drama	Tennessee State (1987)

Graduate degrees: 7 (54 percent); bachelor's degrees: 2 (15 percent); high school diploma: 3 (23 percent); less than high school: 1 (8 percent).

---

ther was the head of his own Episcopalian ministry and Nelson Mandela grew up with a father and stepfather who were tribal chiefs.

Two of the subjects had mothers who were teachers (Marshall and Robeson) and five had mothers who were self-employed domestics (Chisholm, Cosby, Johnson, Powell, and Winfrey). Watching parents cope with life as independent business people is highly instructive to young minds. They learn early that one doesn't have to depend on the corporate womb for existence. This makes them independent and resilient. Strong-willed parents tend to instill strong wills in their children if only by osmosis. If nothing else the children have a strong tendency to become renegades. They learn very early in life not to depend on others to make it in the world. They learn coping skills, independence, risk taking, and self-sufficiency from watching their parents earn a living without punching a time clock or depending on a weekly dole called a paycheck. The reverse is found in welfare parents, who tend to wean children with the same propensity as themselves.

Formal Education

Formal education can open doors. These thirteen knew that and were more highly educated than any group I have ever studied. In their case it worked, which is a real contrast to the findings on nonblacks, whose success was not nearly so dependent on formal education. Knowledge is critical to all success no matter the race, creed, or gender. However, it appears that minorities are far more dependent on formal education to gain access to the industrial inner sanctums or to open doors critical to great success. In my research, successful blacks have the most formal education, successful females, second, and nonblack males, third.

For nonminorities too much formal education can often prove detrimental to great success since it can place a person in the box of mediocrity. Highly educated people can be less motivated or have expectations that are too high or unrealistic. They often become conditioned to their station in life (MBAs expect to start in middle management) or to that level of achievement that is "possible." Such people can learn too much—like what is possible and what is impossible in life. Most of the great nonblack entrepreneurs I have studied had little formal education but great knowledge in their area of expertise (Bill Gates, Ted Turner, Bill Lear, Howard Hughes, Walt Disney, Liz Claiborne, Estée Lauder, and Mary Kay). Howard Hughes, Walt Disney, Liz Claiborne, and Frank Lloyd Wright never graduated from high school. They had immense knowledge but little formal education. Too much education tends to lead such people into middle-management positions in a corporate hierarchy that is *not* where great success originates. Great success only starts at the bottom, where Bill Cosby debuted, where John Johnson and Berry Gordy honed their skills, and where Oprah Winfrey and Reginald Lewis began.

In fact, all of these individuals had a great deal of formal education, but due to various reasons were forced to start at the very bottom. Robeson was a lawyer who never practiced law due to discrimination, while Lewis launched a successful law practice in New York City but never made it until he closed his law practice to become a takeover specialist. In fact, Lewis admitted that had he not quit his law practice he would never have been able to pull off his multimillion-dollar coups with McCall Pattern and Beatrice Foods. Gordy and Johnson, this book's two whiz-kid entrepreneurs, and poet Maya Angelou never spent one day in college. Others such as Bill Cosby, Michael Jordan, Oprah Winfrey, Nelson Mandela, and Colin Powell received their formal education coincident with pursuing their careers.

Seven earned graduate degrees (four in law), two earned bachelor's degrees, and three graduated from high school, leaving only Michael Jackson as the subject without a high school education (see figure 10). Bill Cosby earned a doctorate in childhood education, but was fortunate that the University of Massachusetts allowed him to use his screenplays and creative entertainment scripts as the material for both his master's and doctoral degrees. The Weird Harold and Fat Albert cartoon series were truly educational vehicles for both the public and their creator. Winfrey was also finally awarded her bachelor's degree from Tennessee State in 1987 after demonstrating professional experience in television, since she had left only a few credits shy of earning her degree. It is quite telling that not one of these individuals used formal education as the direct route to success and power but utilized the pedigrees as door openers and validation of their talent. Their formal educations certainly made them more erudite, better communicators, and more acceptable to a suspect leadership, but it was not the prime contributor to their great success in life.

Street Smarts, Not Classroom Knowledge

Reginald Lewis knew more about leveraged buyouts than anyone in America. But his knowledge never came from books. He was self-taught. He wrote a paper at Harvard titled "Defenses to Takeover Bids" that first piqued his interest in what would ultimately make him one of the richest men in America, but it was his need to "devour every piece of MESBIC [minority enterprise small business investment companies]" that made him into a superstar. None of his expertise came from his Harvard education.

Integrated Educations

Maya Angelou, Shirley Chisholm, Bill Cosby, Michael Jackson, John Johnson, Reggie Lewis, Colin Powell, and Paul Robeson all attended integrated high schools. Only Angelou, Jordan, Johnson, and Winfrey experienced segregated primary schools with Jordan, Marshall, and Mandela the only subjects who attended segregated schools throughout their formative years. Those who attended integrated schools were for the most part oblivious to educational discrimination during their early years. Only later did they become acutely aware of the overt discrimination that ran rampant in society and didn't appear to be quite as bitter as those blacks who faced personal discrimination daily while growing up. An example is Colin Powell, who told reporters in late 1995 that, "Race has probably helped me more than it has hurt me." He told *Time* in 1995, "I was lucky to be born black" in referring to his fast rise in the ranks of the military. When asked how he coped with racism issues in the military, he responded, "I am not going to carry this burden of racism. I'm going to destroy your stereotype," which was his way of getting it off his back and into the lap of those who saw race as an issue.

FIGURE 11
KEY VARIABLES OF PERSONALITY FORMATION

The key to molding a success-oriented personality is not money, an Ivy League education, a pedigreed name like Rockefeller, or an exceptional IQ. Creative geniuses and great entrepreneurs are fulfilling their own internal self-images, acquired in childhood through the following factors.

Variable	Personality Effect
Birth Order '	Being firstborn or raised as such grooms one for a life of perfectionism, leadership, and overachievement and often causes a higher IQ.
Indulgent Parents	Creating "special" or "messiah" imagery on the child's psyche, which instills strong self-esteem, resulting in "arrogant believers" or "overachieving egocentrics" who see few limitations to their potential.
Transience/Travel	Frequent moving and travel instill self-sufficiency, independence, temerity, and coping skills. These subjects never feared the unknown or ambiguity due to their extensive early travel and transience.
Books/Music	Voracious reading helps children escape into a fantasy world where their imagination identifies with larger-than-life fictional characters who they adopt as their hero/mentors and role models.
Mythological Mentors	Great heroes arm children with fantasy mentors who they emulate as adults. Such heroes tend to remove limitations to potential or motivates one to live out their fantasies.
Parental Role Models	Self-employed parents who work outside the mainstream instill in children autonomy, independence, and self-confidence. Most never feel required to buy into the corporate womb to make it in the adult world.
Formal Education	Formal education imprints some children with self-confidence and independence and opens important doors or established credibility. It was not the formula for these subjects' success but important to their mental attitude.
Integrated Educations	Being raised and educated in an enhanced environment devoid of discrimination and rejection is critical to success. Most of these subjects were schooled in the North and all achieved their success in the North.
Freedom to Explore	Latchkey children learn to cope on their own and to try and fail without feeling rejection. Unrestrained freedom to explore and get lost molds indomitable wills, strong self-esteem, and temerity.
Crisis/Trauma	Traumatic experiences imprint children with great resolve and drive and those who emerge unscathed find themselves emotionally stronger than before the experience. Visiting the bottom grooms one for the top.

Freedom and Permissive Parents

Psychiatrist Anthony Storr in *The Dynamics of Creation* writes about the "divine discontent" of children who were left alone and used the experience to over-achieve later in life. He says a child's "prolonged and unsatisfactory infancy" tends to "spur him on to creative achievement." Teresa Amabile in *Growing Up Creative* agrees, writing, "Give children choice wherever possible." Freedom is critical to grooming a child for later success and these subjects benefited by the experience of freedom and latchkey environments. Colin Powell writes of his latchkey early years where he was allowed to roam the streets of the South Bronx playing stick-ball and learning to cope. Bill Cosby and Shirley Chisholm grew up in virtually identical environments, due to working mothers who had little time to establish rigorous schedules, which turn out to be restrictive to the creative process.

All thirteen of these visionaries learned self-sufficiency early in life. Most were latchkey kids who were left to their own devices at a very early age. Such freedom to explore life and learn survival builds character early and teaches coping skills while instilling temerity, independence, and self-sufficiency. In such environments children learn to cope or are destroyed by the experience. These thirteen learned to cope. The prisons and drug wards are occupied by those who didn't. Shirley Chisholm learned to cope by playing mother to her younger brothers and sisters on the streets of Brooklyn when she herself was under age ten. Chisholm's mother worked and had little choice but to give young Shirley far more responsibility than would be prudent, but the training proved worthwhile as she became far more competent and self-assured due to the experience. Training such as this instills great temerity and self-sufficiency later in life. Some of the subjects did not fare as well, or as in Winfrey's case, were not molded for quite the same reasons.

Overprotective mothers and authoritative fathers are the bane of creativity. The unemployment rolls are rife with children who were raised in overprotected environments where "security" and "risk adversity" were of paramount importance. Locking your child in a room is guaranteed to keep them out of harm's way but is also guaranteed to make them totally incapable of functioning in a dynamic world. The street is where most of these thirteen were nurtured and that is where great coping skills are honed. The overprotective parent is counterproductive to molding creative and entrepreneurial offspring and fortunately these children were raised in nonthreatening households where freedom prevailed. Researchers are now finding evidence of this principle. Harvard psychologist Jerome Kagan says, "It appears that mothers who protect their highly reactive infants from frustration and anxiety in the hope of effecting a benevolent outcome seem to exacerbate the infant's uncertainty and produce the opposite effect."

Summary—Success Imprints

As many psychologists have shown, we become as we think. Even more apparent is that we tend to grow up fulfilling our internal self-images, which were formed when we were quite young. Valued role models and mentors who tell us we are "bright" are arming us with a positive self-image or "success imprint," while those who say we are "dumb" are indoctrinating us with a "failure imprint," which forms a negative self-image. From the data in this chapter it is clearly apparent that these subjects were more positively impacted by their role models and mentors. They were molded with positive self-images, which endowed them with a success motivation. And even when they failed they saw their failures as due to external influences, not due to their own inabilities. Stanford psychologist Albert Bandura found that, "People who have a sense of self-efficacy bounce back from failures; they approach things in terms of how to handle rather than worrying about what can go wrong." He was talking about these visionary spirits.

Early experiences and parental influences have a lifelong impact on who we are and what we will become. "Success imprints" or "failure imprints" will determine our future. Neither imprint is set in concrete, but the longer we reinforce them the more difficult they are to change. Modifying our internal scripts can be difficult unless we encounter some great tragedy or go through some metamorphosis that changes the unconscious failure imprints into successful ones. The factors involved in such an evolution can be summarized in a statement of the intrinsic profile covered in this chapter: The black creative genius tends to be a firstborn child with above-average intelligence who is highly educated. He/she has been reared by parents who were doting, self-employed, and permissive and who moved or traveled a lot, which instilled them with coping skills and caused loneliness and a need to escape in books or music. Mythological, fictional, or real-life hero/mentors became inspirational and positive influences to their later success. Early life experiences or crises armed them with "success imprints" that led to the key behavior traits critical to their later success.

A summary of those success patterns and key experiential factors in molding their strong characters are shown in figure 11.

5

Personality: The Key to Genius— Ten Key Traits of Black Success

Many business tycoons, entrepreneurs, speculators, stockbrokers, politicians, etc., belong to the [personality] type—extroverted intuitives.

Carl Jung

Only those who see the invisible can do the impossible. . . . I reached for the sky, but I missed so I grabbed a few stars.

Wally (Famous) Amos, *Man with No Name*

What defines success? The answer differs for each person. Is becoming a creative genius the same as success? Not for everyone. But for those willing to pay the price the road is accessible, and with effort they are able to tap into those key attributes necessary for creative genius. Most of these visionaries were quite different but exhibited many similar qualities. Their differences were more in magnitude than in style although they differed from nonblacks in many ways (see chapter 19). This chapter will discuss only the key personality traits found pervasive in all of these black superstars. Many theories have been propounded by some of the world's great psychologists and a few of these should be discussed before proceeding to the key traits.

Differing Personality Theories

Freud saw repressed sexual energy at the base of great creative success and spent much time proving his hypothesis with Leonardo da Vinci's need to sublimate his sexual appetites in order to create. Freud's disciple Alfred Adler believed that all men are imbued with the need for perfection and are perpetually "striving for superiority," which he said was "innate." Adler said, "In people who lead, one can

---

FIGURE 12
KIRTON'S BEHAVIOR STYLES

Adaptors	Innovators
Efficient	Unique ideas
Predictable and stable	Flexible and ingenious
Good manager of time and money	Unconstrained by limited resources
Organized	Spontaneous
Thorough, comprehensive planners	Enthusiastic and insightful
Apply structure to ideas and innovations	Break new ground
Creative in productive ways	Productive in creative ways
Cautious risk-takers	Capricious risk-takers
Appear close-minded	Appear open-minded
Avoid "rocking the boat"	May seek change for the sake of change

---

find that they have developed the leader complex already in childhood. . . . Such children do not like to be losers in a game, or to be the horse rather than the coachman. All geniuses have this complex."

In the above theories the personality rises to center stage as the critical factor in all great success in life. It is the one common denominator in creative and entrepreneurial genius and this was never more true than in the lives and successes of these thirteen black wunderkinds. In addition, I found a high correlation between the findings of some of the more contemporary theories on creative genius and these thirteen subjects. David Kirton's "behavioral styles," Carl Jung's archetypes," Myers-Briggs's "MBTI personality types," David Kiersey's "personality preferences and temperaments," David McClelland's "needs (motivation) theory," and Frank Farley's "Big T" thrill-seeking personalities are all pertinent to this discussion.

Michael Kirton's "Innovator Style" Behavior

Two styles of behavior were concocted by David Kirton, which he labeled "adaptor" and "innovator" styles of behavior (see figure 12). Kirton concluded that adaptors prefer "doing things perfectly" and tend to be "organized and cautious risk-takers," whereas innovators prefer "doing things differently" and tend to be "spontaneous and capricious risk-takers." The innovator style is consistent with the findings in these thirteen subjects. They exuded the traits Kirton used to describe the innovator-style personality. All but Colin Powell were classified as innovator styles and it is important to note that Kirton's innovator personality type correlates very well with Kiersey's intuitive-thinkers and Farley's "Big T" thrill-seeker personalities.

Jung's Archetypes and Myers-Briggs's Preferences

Carl Jung coined the term "archetypes," which he used synonymously with "instinct." In his system, archetypes are the cognitive manifestations of man's unconscious. Jung's description of the archetypes was that, "All experiences are represented (in the archetype) which have happened on this planet since primeval times. The more frequent and the more intense they were, the more clearly focused they became in the archetype." From this Jung built a foundation of "psychological types" from the archetypes, which were either male behavior characteristics (animus) or female (anima) and determined our preference for interfacing with the world and people. Jung classified these unconscious drives into a personal unconscious and a collective unconscious. Jung believed the personal unconscious was "acquired during the individual's lifetime" while the archetypes were "present from the beginning." These unconscious preferences for operating in the real world vary, with everyone operating as extroverts or introverts, sensors or intuitors, thinkers or feelers, and judgers or perceivers. Jung went on to say that, "Everyone has in him something of the criminal, the genius, and the saint," which gives credence to the nurture/nature argument in this book. In other words, those who become geniuses have been able to effectively tap into their "genius" unconscious side in order to overachieve.

Jung's psychological types were refined even more by the mother-daughter team of Katherine Briggs and Isabel Briggs Myers, who just after World War II developed the Myers-Briggs Test Indicator Test (MBTI). This test has since become the most widely used psychological test in the world and offers some insight into the creative personality. The eight dimensions into which all people fall are:

EXTROVERSION	People who are energized by others (9 subjects were Es)
INTROVERSION	People who are energized internally (4 were Is)
SENSING:	People who are "facts" oriented (2 were Ss)
INTUITING:	People who are "possibilities" oriented (11 were Ns)
THINKING:	People who are "logical problem solvers" (10 were Ts)
FEELING:	People who are "personal and compassionate decision makers" (3 were Fs)
JUDGING:	People who are "structured and organized" (10 were Js)
PERCEIVING:	People who are "spontaneous" (3 of subjects were Ps)

See figure 13 for the summaries of the above personality preferences. Notice that eleven of these thirteen subjects (85 percent) were intuitive-thinker or intuitive-feeler types. These types correlate well with Kirton's innovator styles and have been found dominant in entrepreneurial and creative personalities. Intuitives have "vision" and thinkers have a "rational perspective" for implementing their dreams, which is why they tend to become the movers and shakers of the business and entertainment worlds. They see the opportunities and possibilities in life, in contrast to those who are sensors. Long-range planners should be tested to make

FIGURE 13
JUNGIAN ARCHETYPES AND KIERSEY'S TEMPERAMENTS

Subjects	Jung's Archetypes			Kiersey's Temperament Preferences
	Extroverts/Introverts	Intuitive/Thinkers	Thinkers/Feelers	
Maya Angelou	Extrovert	Intuitive	Feeler	Apollonian NF Catalyst
Shirley Chisholm	Extrovert	Intuitive	Thinker	Promethean NT Visionary
Bill Cosby	Extrovert	Intuitive	Thinker	Promethean NT Visionary
Berry Gordy	Extrovert	Intuitive	Thinker	Promethean NT Visionary
Michael Jackson	Introvert	Intuitive	Feeler	Apollonian NF Catalyst
John Johnson	Introvert	Intuitive	Thinker	Promethean NT Visionary
Michael Jordan	Introvert	Intuitive	Thinker	Promethean NT Visionary
Reginald Lewis	Introvert	Intuitive	Thinker	Promethean NT Visionary
Nelson Mandela	Extrovert	Intuitive	Thinker	Promethean NT Visionary
Thurgood Marshall	Extrovert	Sensor	Thinker	Dionysian SP Trouble Shooter
Colin Powell	Extrovert	Sensor	Thinker	Epimethean SJ Traditionalist
Paul Robeson	Extrovert	Intuitive	Thinker	Promethean NT Visionary
Oprah Winfrey	Extrovert	Intuitive	Feeler	Apollonian NF Catalyst
TOTALS	9 Extroverts 4 Introverts	11 Intuitive 2 Sensors	10 Thinkers 3 Feelers	8 Prometheans 3 Apollonians 1 Dionysian 1 Epimethean

sure they are intuitive-thinkers, just as accountants should be tested to make sure they are sensor-judgers, as both are destined to fail in the wrong position. Sensors will invariably fail as the head of long-range planning, where the possibilities are more important to success than the facts, which the sensor prefers. And intuitors will invariably fail in positions where detail is critical to success since they are more prone to ignoring the details and facts in deference to opportunities. Women who are strong feelers and refuse to make anything but emotionally based decisions are unable to survive in a male-dominated organization where rational "thinking" decisions predominate, just as a "rational thinker" type would make a terrible nurse. Likewise male extroverts should not become nightwatchmen and female introverts should not become hostesses.

Kiersey's Temperaments

David Kiersey expanded on the Jungian archetypes and Myers-Briggs personality types. He gave them order and a metaphorical Greek god to better describe the person's interaction with the world.

Personality Type	Metaphor	Label	Strength	% of Population
Intuitive-Feeling	Apollo	Spirit	Idealist	12
Intuitive-Thinking	Prometheus	Science	Visionary	12
Sensing-Perceiving	Dionysus	Joy	Artisan	38
Sensing-Judging	Epimetheus	Duty	Guardian	38

The Promethean temperaments dominated this group, with eight of the thirteen subjects classified intuitive-thinkers with a preference for pursuing the opportunities and possibilities in life. Kiersey considered these types "the architects of change" but found they represented only 12 percent of the general population. Eight of the thirteen subjects—62 percent—were Promethean, making them unique in the world. The Prometheans are considered visionaries who constantly pursue knowledge and truth and prefer to operate with ingenuity and logic. Shirley Chisholm, Bill Cosby, Berry Gordy, John Johnson, Michael Jordan, Reginald Lewis, Nelson Mandela, and Paul Robeson were Promethean temperaments.

The only other temperament well represented among these thirteen wunderkinds was the Apollonian. These types are intuitive-feelers, preferring idealism to logic. Martin Luther King, Frederick Douglass, Maya Angelou, Oprah Winfrey, and Michael Jackson were this type personality. According to Kiersey, these types prefer to operate as "catalysts" and are often found as the spokesperson. Winfrey and Angelou are excellent examples of such a person in their professional endeavors as talk-show host and well-known poet. These types are imaginative and sensitive but not typically great entrepreneurs.

Farley's "Big T" Thrill-Seeking Personalities

Frank Farley, former president of the American Psychological Association, originated a theory based on high testosterone that he believes is responsible for cre-

---

FIGURE 14
FARLEY'S PERSONALITY TYPES

Big Ts (High Arousal Value)	Little Ts (Low Arousal Value)
High variety	Low variety
Complexity	Simplicity
Bright colors	Soft colors
High activity	Low activity
Noisy	Quiet
Extrovert	Introvert
Satyriasis	Erotophobic
Uncertainty	Certainty
Unpredictability	Predictability
High risk	Low risk
Ambiguity	Clarity
Flexibility	Rigidity
Low structure	High structure
High intensity	Low intensity
High conflict	Low conflict

---

ativity, risk-taking behavior, and competitiveness, all key traits found in these thirteen subjects. In May 1986 Farley told *Psychology Today,* "The Type T personality as a group tend to be more creative, and more extroverted, take more risks, have more experimental artistic preferences, and prefer more variety in their sex lives." He added, "They have a tendency to seek the novel, unknown and uncertain, combined with their risk-taking characteristic, further enhancing their likelihood of being creative."

Farley classified everyone as either a Big T or a little t, with the Big Ts high in testosterone and thrill-seeking behavior and the little ts low in testosterone and thrill-seeking behavior. All but one of these thirteen subjects were Big Ts to a lesser or greater degree, as virtually all of them lived on the edge and fit Farley's "high arousal values" illustrated in figure 14. Notice from the chart how the Big Ts prefer uncertainty, while the little ts opt for certainty. The "word traits" Farley assigned to the Big Ts are strikingly similar to Kirton's traits for the innovator personality and Kiersey's Promethean temperaments.

All of these subjects fit Farley's definition of a Big T with the exception of Colin Powell, who, despite growing up in the South Bronx, spent most of his life in a bureaucratic environment where high risk and change are antithetical to the reigning dogma. All government institutions dictate "rigidity," "certainty," and "high structure," in contrast to the world of Big Ts, where "flexibility," "uncertainty," and "low structure" are revered.

FIGURE 15
MCCLELLAND'S "NEEDS" THEORY

Harvard University researcher David McClelland used projective testing methods to isolate three different types of personality needs in people. He concluded that everyone is motivated toward "achievement," "power," and "affiliation." The two motivations especially pertinent to this work are achievement and power. This matrix represents McClelland's behavioral findings on these two personality types. I have listed the thirteen subjects in the category that best fits their personality characteristics. These categorizations are based on the data from the subject chapters in this book and an exacting fit could only come from taking the projective test, although that in itself is a subject analysis of behavioral characteristics.

Needs	Achievement Types	Power Types
Drive	To excel and achieve to a set of standards	To persuade others to change their behavior
Strives	To succeed	To control
Ideal Profession	Entrepreneurs and innovators	Leaders, managers, charismatics
Seeks	Efficiency and personal status	Impact and control
Enjoys	Unique challenges	Competition
Types	Perfectionists	Control freaks
Passion	To excel	To influence
Wants	Excellence	Status orientation
Subjects	Maya Angelou Michael Jackson John Johnson Thurgood Marshall Oprah Winfrey	Shirley Chisholm Bill Cosby Berry Gordy Michael Jordan Reginald Lewis Nelson Mandela Colin Powell Paul Robeson

Source: *The Achieving Society* (1961)

McClelland's "Motivation Needs" Theory

Harvard University's David McClelland developed a theory of "achievement" and "power" that has a high correlation to the operating behaviors of these thirteen subjects. McClelland also developed a third element that he labeled "affiliation," an innate need to build alliances and gain acceptance, but this factor was not relevant in the lives of these overachievers and power brokers. McClelland described the need for achievement as the "drive to excel" and power as the "need to make others behave in a way they would not have behaved otherwise." He said achievement is "the need to do something better than it has been done before" and power is "the need to strive for influence—to feel powerful." McClelland believed, as I do, that "achievement can be developed" and gave great credence to the findings in this book with this prediction on the creative personality: "Motivated people are more likely to be developed in families in which parents hold different expectations from normal families. They expect their children to start showing some independence between ages six and eight, making choices and doing things without help, such as knowing the way around the neighborhood and taking care of themselves around the house."

McClelland's definition fits the early life profiles found in the chapters on Cosby, Angelou, Chisholm, Winfrey, Gordy, Johnson, and Lewis. All of these children were nurtured in families with unique expectations and tremendous freedom to roam and learn. They were latchkey children with tremendous responsibility at a very early age, which molded them with self-sufficiency and high motivation to achieve. Most were mature far beyond their years due to the early freedom to explore and survive on their own. Figure 15 groups these subjects into achiever or power types and shows the needs of each.

Ten Key Success Traits of Creative Genius

Superior behavior comes in ten flavors, all of which are critical to great success in any profession. A person does not have to be endowed with them all, but most of these subjects were to a greater or lesser degree. Three subjects have been selected to represent each of the ten traits and each subject personifies one of the traits far more than the others, although it appears from this research that anyone who utilizes these traits in their life are destined for success in almost any venue.

Charisma	Nelson Mandela, Paul Robeson, Oprah Winfrey
Competitive	Michael Jordan, Reginald Lewis, Paul Robeson
Confidence	Bill Cosby, Reginald Lewis, Thurgood Marshall
Energy/Work Ethic	Shirley Chisholm, John Johnson, Colin Powell
Independence	Shirley Chisholm, Nelson Mandela, Paul Robeson
Passion	Berry Gordy, Michael Jackson, Michael Jordan
Perfectionism	Bill Cosby, Berry Gordy, Reginald Lewis
Temerity (Risk Taking)	Maya Angelou, Berry Gordy, John Johnson
Tenacity	Maya Angelou, Nelson Mandela, Thurgood Marshall
Vision (Intuitiveness)	Maya Angelou, Michael Jackson, Oprah Winfrey

CHARISMA

This trait can become a source of great power. It is unique in that it can not only enhance personal performance but can also be used to empower others. The word *charisma* comes from the Greek, meaning "gift of divine grace." It has become synonymous with the words "magical," "mystical," and "mesmerizing." Leaders with this quality can move mountains, as has been seen throughout history, starting with Jesus and Mohammed and followed by some nefarious characters such as Napoleon, Hitler, Jim Jones, and David Koresh. These individuals were able to mesmerize disciples to the point that they were willing to follow them anywhere, including to their death. Such leaders are able to use the power of speech to gain great power and influence. It can arm them with a captivating dialogue that instills passion in their disciples, convincing them of their invincibility. Messianic personalities can become dangerous with such power as they are able to convince their followers to subjugate their wills to them. These thirteen used their charisma for the positive and it was an important instrument in their ultimate success. Winfrey, Angelou, Mandela, Robeson, Jordan, Lewis, and Gordy were the most charismatic, but the rest were well steeped in this important trait. Winfrey is our model for charismatic power. She has become America's daytime psychiatrist by identifying with the problems and hopes of her audience. She has a unique sense of just what the audience wants to hear and she says it. She is "everywoman," who exudes the passion of a Sunday morning evangelist. Winfrey, Robeson, Angelou, and Gordy had a mesmerizing influence over their associates and fans that at times bordered on the supernatural and superhuman. They were mesmerizing speakers capable of influencing their audience to follow their lead. Jordan's charisma is on a par with Babe Ruth and Elvis Presley. He can electrify a crowd like an evangelist.

Even one of the least charismatic of these thirteen, Colin Powell, proved capable of motivating strong individuals and diverse groups. Political analyst David Broder characterized Powell's captivating presence and influence during the fall of 1995, when Powell was considering entering the political arena as a presidential candidate. Broder wrote of Powell, "I've never seen anyone who has so mesmerized the political world." A military associate of Powell said, "When he walks into the room all the eyes turn towards him."

COMPETITIVE

Aggression and assertiveness defined these subjects. Most were highly competitive and were able to make their mark in the world because they were determined to fight to the death for their dreams. They had an awesome need to win, regardless of the casualties along the way. No one better symbolizes a fierce competitive spirit than Michael Jordan. He wrote in 1995, "I love to compete." The Chicago Bulls coaches tell rookies, "Don't play cards with Mike." Even Jordan's father was concerned about his son's competitive fire and just before he died told the press, "Michael has a competition problem," causing Mike to respond, "I don't believe I've ever heard of Competitors Anonymous." Charles Barkley confirmed Jordan's competitive spirit saying, "Michael Jordan is the only person in the entire world that I've ever met who is as competitive as I am." An anonymous teammate said, "He's the most viciously competitive player I've ever seen. That's what makes him, I think, the greatest player ever."

Reginald Lewis was not as competitive as Jordan but still owed much of his success to a highly competitive spirit. He was intensely competitive in anything he ever did, including playing tennis matches for pleasure. A law partner once said of him, "It was warfare all the time with Reg." Two of the subjects—Berry Gordy and Nelson Mandela—actually took up boxing, which is probably the most intensely competitive one-on-one sport in the world. Paul Robeson once took on a whole professional football team led by Olympic champion Jim Thorpe. Robeson's competitive spirit caused Chicago fight promoters to offer to back him against Jack Dempsey for the heavyweight championship of boxing.

Competitive people win. They are not always the best loved but they are usually there at the end. Competitiveness is a key element in the success of many of these subjects. Even Winfrey and Angelou were highly competitive, leading Winfrey to admit to Larry King in a 1995 CNN interview, "I am far more competitive than I ever thought I was." John Johnson conceded in his autobiography that much of his success was due to "the dare, it was the gamble, it was the deal that captivated me." Even Supreme Court Justice Thurgood Marshall regularly played poker and admitted, "I enjoy a fight."

CONFIDENCE

This trait represents the difference between feeling superior or inferior. It is probably the most important ingredient for success in any venue. Self-esteem is the stuff dreams are made of and without it few dreams are realized. Superstars believe. In fact, they have an awesome and at times deluded belief in their ability and their chances for success. They are so optimistic and positive that they are able to overcome the worst adversities through mental strength. Even when the whole world is burning, they believe. When their parents and friends thought them crazy, they had the self-confidence to pursue their dreams.

Most psychologists have found optimism to be highly correlated to self-worth. According to University of Pennsylvania psychologist Martin Seligman, "Optimism . . . is a fairly accurate indicator of how well [people] will succeed." Seligman found that when optimists fail, "they attribute the failure to something they can change, not some innate weakness that they are helpless to overcome." In other words, they do not blame others. They assume the responsibility for their destiny. Seligman found that insurance salespeople who were optimistic "sold 37 percent more insurance . . . than did pessimists" who had everything else in common. Albert Bandura, a Stanford research psychologist on "self-efficacy," found that, "People's beliefs about their abilities have a profound effect on those abilities." These types spend their energies pursuing success and never worry about their failures.

Well-known psychologist Eric Erikson said, "Study after study has shown that children with superior intelligence but low self-esteem may do poorly in school while children of average intelligence but high self-esteem can be unusually successful." Many of these subjects fit Erikson's model, namely, Colin Powell, Reginald Lewis, Shirley Chisholm, and Bill Cosby. Martin Luther King, Jr., and George Washington Carver were similar examples of an optimistic attitude leading to eminent success. They believed in themselves to such a degree that they excelled in school and life.

High self-esteem is pivotal to high achievement in any venue in life because it shapes our self-image, which in turns manifests itself in what the world sees as our self-confidence. Optimism and a positive attitude are the inevitable by-products, which result in great success. Many of the "success imprints" discussed in the previous chapter were instrumental in instilling a strong self-esteem in these subjects. They attempted difficult tasks and when successful were suddenly imprinted with a positive self-image. Many even began believing they were infallible.

Sports Illustrated characterized Michael Jordan in 1993 as having "an unreasonably high level of optimism." This was never better illustrated than in his mesmerizing performance against Portland in the 1992 NBA playoffs, when he made six consecutive three-point shots, some of which were shot from another time zone. Jordan suddenly believed that any shot he took would go in, grabbed the ball and shot without any preparation. The ball just kept swishing through the net and Jordan was as amazed as his teammates and coach, Phil Jackson. Jordan looked at Magic Johnson in the press box and just shook his head in disbelief at his unbelievable performance.

Many of these subjects had optimistic internal scripts instilled by doting parents and relatives. The result was an indomitable self-esteem that at times bordered on arrogance, as in the cases of Thurgood Marshall, Reginald Lewis, Bill Cosby, and Paul Robeson. The positive attitudes of these men became their instrument of success even though they were sometimes seen as arrogant and suffering from what psychologists describe as egomania. Reginald Lewis's associates all concurred that he had an "air of confidence" that defied logic and once caused one of his employers in high school to say, "What are you trying to do, conquer the world?" A Harvard classmate said, "Whatever he had it was powerful. . . . It was some kind of magnetism or power or something that I couldn't understand." It was this positive attitude that allowed him to "break down the doors of Harvard Law School" and become the only student ever who never filled out an application. He got in on pure moxie (see chapter 13).

John Johnson also gave much credit for his success to an optimistic demeanor. He relied on what he called "PMA"—positive mental attitude—and said, "I believed in the plastic power of the possible." One of the most audacious acts of optimism by any of these individuals was Berry Gordy's placing the sign on his first Detroit studio that read HITSVILLE. He was predicting hits within the inner-city ghetto of East Detroit and he hadn't even had one yet, but internally knew he would. All of these subjects were blessed with an irrepressible self-esteem but no one personified self-confidence more than did Thurgood Marshall. Marshall's biographer and friend, Carl Rowan, called him "overly optimistic." Humility was never one of Marshall's attributes as he bullied his way through life with positive expectations even when nothing looked possible. His positive attitude in the face of the worst adversities is what made him so successful. Nelson Mandela was another optimist who never lost hope even though he was being hunted like an animal for years and then relegated to prison for twenty-seven years. This tenacious man never lost hope or the confidence that his work would be rewarded and his dreams realized.

ENERGY INCARNATE—WORKAHOLICS

Virtually every subject was a Type A workaholic, led by Colin Powell, Reginald Lewis, Shirley Chisholm, John Johnson, and Berry Gordy. Powell biographer Howard Means (1992) said, "He simply outworks the opposition." Powell said of himself, "I decided to be the very best" and spent whatever time and energy it took to achieve that noble goal. He worked diligently in every military post until he had reached the very top. A law associate of Lewis said, "Practically everything Lewis achieved was extracted through hard work and titanic struggle." Tom Lamia, an associate of Lewis, attempted to keep up with the manic Lewis and became exhausted from the experience of flying nonstop between dozens of countries in Europe with meetings taking place two and three times each day. Lamia could not understand how Lewis could withstand such a grind. He described Lewis as having a "demon work ethic" with a "megawatt intensity." He said that "his incredible stamina" is what made Lewis so successful.

Shirley Chisholm admitted to her intensity in pursuit of the U.S. congressional seat she won in 1968 and said her toil was "beyond reason." She said, "I almost killed myself," but that was her style in everything she did. Berry Gordy wrote of his all-night sessions, but he considered music "pleasure not work," which is why he could work eighty-hour weeks most of his life without fatigue or regret. Michael Jackson learned well from his mentor, and says, "I work all the time." John Johnson was even more driven than Gordy and Jackson. He said, "Work is my vacation," and outlined his formula for success by saying, "I set goals and work night and day to achieve them."

Type A personalities often confuse self-worth with achievement. They are incapable of separating the two and consequently feel personally inadequate if they don't win in every venture they pursue. These personality types refuse to quit until they win, so they can feel emotionally sated. Twelve of these thirteen (92 percent) were classified Type As, with Gordy, Jordan, and Lewis Type A+++ and Chisholm and Robeson right behind in intensity. Type As have what I have labeled a "rushing sickness." They were always in a hurry as if double-parked on the highway of life. They talked fast, walked fast, ate fast, thought fast, and worked fast. They perpetually scheduled more work than could physically be accomplished and then flagellated themselves or their associates when it was not completed. Lewis was the most guilty of this and even after he had pulled off the coup of the decade with McCall Pattern, an acquisition in which he made $90 million in three years, the driven Lewis admonished himself with, "Why didn't I accomplish more?" It is no accident that none of these individuals were overweight. Type As with this kind of rushing sickness never are. In fact, most were slim. They were excessively impatient and intolerant classic traits of the Type A personality. Michael Jordan's coaches with the Chicago Bulls, Phil Jackson and Doug Collins, both have said that Jordan is the most intensely driven basketball player they had ever seen. *Sports Illustrated* (June 1993) reported that Jordan has a "high level of energy and friends say he rarely sleeps. If he stops at 18 holes in a day, a typhoon is coming." As a group they lived fast, thought fast, played fast, ate fast, and drove fast. Speed was their friend.

INDEPENDENT RENEGADES—REBELS WITH A CAUSE

All of these thirteen were considered renegades in their professions and often personally. Colin Powell is the only subject who was not. He could never have succeeded in the military without complying with that institution's rigorous authoritarian style and pyramidal approach to organizational behavior. The rest followed Nietzsche's sage philosophy, "And whoever wants to be a creator in good and evil, must first be an annihilator and break values." Sam Walton, the late founder of Wal-Mart, was more direct on the subject when he said, "I always prided myself on breaking everybody else's rules, and I always favored the mavericks who challenged my rules." Most successful entrepreneurs and creative geniuses follow his advice. They find out where the pack is and go elsewhere.

Michael Jackson is the most flagrant maverick of these subjects. He refused to conform to any of the music industry's rules of decorum or even societal rules in his personal life. Never satisfied with his past successes, Jackson would look for ways to be different in order to achieve greater and greater success. He is truly an independent iconoclast of the first order. His crotch-grabbing stage persona, one white glove, and bizarre clothing have been the subject of much controversy and ridicule. Jackson finds inspiration in his rebellion. His response to critics about his dress was, "My attitude is if fashion says it's forbidden, I'm going to do it." David Weeks, a British neuropsychologist, spent ten years studying eccentrics and published his results in *Eccentrics,* listing Michael Jackson as one of the examples for his book on the eccentric personality. Weeks defines an eccentric as a "permanent nonconformist who is creative, curious, idealistic, and obsessive about some special interest." Weeks concluded that these individuals suffer less stress "because they are not worried about conforming." Michael Jackson and some of his peers in this book prove Weeks's theory. Jackson impulsively marrying the nurse Debbie Rowe months after his divorce from Lisa Marie is further testimony to a renegade nature. When Rowe was queried by her father about her impromptu marriage, she responded, "Michael doesn't do anything like anyone else."

John Johnson, the founder of *Ebony* and *Jet* magazines, said, "I was driven to succeed by the whip of social disapproval." All the experts said his idea of a black entertainment magazine was stupid and doomed to failure. He ignored them and became rich and famous by daring to be different. Michael Jordan admits that his success on the basketball court comes from his refusal to listen to anything the coach says. He told a sportswriter, "I never listened to the coach. . . . My whole life I never did . . . my mind was totally somewhere else." Bill Cosby said, "I joined the Navy . . . because I didn't want to be like everybody else." Shirley Chisholm quickly earned the ire of the United States congressmen and was immediately labeled the "troublemaking maverick" due to her refusal to adhere to their rules. She then wrote a book titled *Unbought and Unbossed* to further demonstrate her defiance of the "good ole boy" system that she had pledged to fight and destroy. Nelson Mandela has lived up to the literal translation of his name Rolihlahla, which means "troublemaker" in English. Paul Robeson was by far the most rebellious and nonconforming visionary in this book. He best exemplifies a person who rose to prominence by opposing the system. He defied all established traditions in work, political ideology, and actions and wrote in his autobiography, "I am a radical and I am going to stay one until my people get free to walk the earth." Defiance defined his creative genius. He would often change the lyrics to the song he made famous—"Ol' Man River"—from "I'm tired of livin' and feared of dyin' " to "I must keep on fightin' until I'm dyin'." The height of Robeson's rebellion came during the mid-thirties when he sent his only son at age eight to school in Moscow to show his total disdain for the American way of life. He then defied the U.S. Congress by pleading the Fifth Amendment during the McCarthy hearings, moving to England to support socialism in open defiance of the government.

PASSIONATE DRIVE

Passion is an essential element of success. Think about the persona of Martin Luther King, Jr., Jesse Jackson, Malcolm X, or Louis Farrakhan. All are passionate and driven men as was Frederick Douglass. Visit a black church and see the emotional energy that pervades their every move. Or witness the emotional energy permeating the work of Oprah Winfrey or Maya Angelou. King's "I Have a Dream" speech is one more testimony to the pure ecstasy and energy incarnate that emanates from the soul of those impassioned leaders. One of King's aphorisms sums up passion as an important trait for achievement. King wrote, "If a man hasn't discovered something that he will die for, he isn't fit to live." Daniel Goleman in his 1995 book, *Emotional Intelligence,* offers some scientific evidence for this, saying, "The emotional mind is far quicker than the rational mind," which he believes makes it the causal element in great and continued achievement in life. Too much focus on the numbers (the left brain) often stymies creativity and innovation since it venerates structure and the status quo, while those with a right-brain spontaneity can evoke great creative output since they can allow free rein to the imagination and uninhibited passion that bears innovative fruit. Reginald Lewis exuded passion in everything he did. A McCall Pattern executive characterized his style: "It was fun for me to watch this African American intimidate these very senior, established Caucasian businessmen. . . . He could generate incredible passion."

Buddha and Jesus both resorted to passion in delivering their message to the people and contemporary psychologists have now found that emotional words and messages are the most memorable ones. Goleman is convinced that a person's "emotional intelligence" is the driving force for his or her creative success. He writes, "The emotional mind . . . takes its beliefs to be absolutely true, and so discounts any evidence to the contrary . . . feelings are self-justifying." He is saying that we buy into emotional ideas much more strongly than rational ones. This is hardly a revelation. Just watch any argument where one is defending an emotional versus a rational position. The emotional argument is by far the most heated and is the reason for the wise man's admonition, "Never discuss politics or religion on a date."

Michael Hutchison said in *Sex and Power*, "Sex and Power are inextricably intertwined." He was convinced sex drive was the force that made people strive for power. Freud believed the same thing but for different reasons. Freud felt unfulfilled sexual gratification was redirected into professional drive, as in the case of Leonardo da Vinci, and that anyone totally sated would atrophy professionally. He concluded that success in sex would prove counterproductive to success in a profession. This and other studies on creative geniuses would indicate otherwise. Supersuccessful people can have both a ravenous sexual appetite while producing a prodigious amount of creative activity as well. Freud believed the two to be a zero-sum game. These individuals had both in abundance.

Michael Jackson is one subject who fits Freud's theory. Michael is quite asexual, having sublimated a great deal of sexual energy into his work instead of spending it on sexual conquests. Jackson has made the headlines for his exploits with children, but these are a function of his arrested youth. Just look at the back cover of the "Scream" single, where he has depicted himself as a little boy in a fetal position scribbling on the walls with his crayon, "Before you Judge Me, Try Hard to Love me, Look within your heart, Then ask, Have you seen my childhood." Jackson is quite introspective in this promotional act, admitting that he lost his childhood and that his love of young boys is his passionate need to be allowed to be one now even though he is in his late thirties. Jackson's highly passionate nature has caused him as many problems as it has contributed to his great success. Psychologists have found that the best way to become creative is to think as a child. This child-man has all the tools for creative success.

Frank Farley's theory on the "Big T"—testosterone and thrill-seeking—personality is consistent with the findings on these subjects. Their creativity, risk taking, competitiveness, and high sex drive were a factor in their success and most probably a result of higher-than-normal testosterone levels. All of these subjects were classified as Big Ts with four—Gordy, Jordan, Mandela, and Robeson—labeled as T+++, with Johnson, Lewis, Marshall, and Winfrey not far behind. These Big T attributes were the cause of their high kinetic energy and led them to outperform, outwork, and outhustle their competition.

Berry Gordy used his gargantuan sexual energies to overachieve both professional and personally. His appetite for passion was enormous. He undoubtedly had the highest level of testosterone of any subject in this book. Not many individuals, in this or any other book, exceed Gordy's passion at work or in bed. Passion was fundamental in Berry Gordy's extraordinary success. It also came close to destroying him, which is classic for those who are driven and live on the edge. Gordy had eight children by four different women, only two of which he married, and seldom did he separate work from pleasure. From the tales told by his ex-wife Ray Liles Gordy, and stories from ex-girlfriends like superstar Diana Ross, Gordy was an insatiable man. They talked of the inordinate amount of time and energy he spent on his passions. When a friend asked him about his obsession with blondes, he responded with typical candor, "I just can't resist 'em," which sums up his passionate life.

PERFECTIONISTS

A need for perfection and control pervaded the lives of these individuals. Most were control freaks who were impatient with anything but the best, which they had to have *right now!* Martin Luther King, Bill Cosby, Berry Gordy, and Reginald Lewis exceeded all norms for demanding excellence and impeccable performance from themselves and those around them. These perfectionists led lives of precision and were so finicky that many people were unable to work for them. They demanded exactness both professionally and personally. Everything they did had to meet the most precise standards, which could drive their associates nuts. Consequently they were viewed as very difficult bosses.

Martin Luther King, Jr., said, "I had a tendency to overdress, to keep my room spotless, my shoes perfectly shined, and my clothes immaculately pressed." He was not alone in this, as many blacks are considered models of sartorial splendor. To people who have little, personal grooming and appearance can make life more bearable, and these subjects were no exception, although a few were incomparable paragons of perfection. Bill Cosby once wrote a script that he felt was perfect and said, "I thought it was the most brilliant thing I'd ever seen." He then sat down with his associates and while reading it through became increasingly disgusted with the mediocrity of his work, and later said, "I tore out all of it." Cosby destroyed many scriptwriters who had toiled furiously to create a masterpiece only to have it torn to shreds by Cosby, who had to have every word impeccable.

Berry Gordy matched Cosby's passion for perfection. He referred to it in his autobiography as "my obsession with perfection." He would recut a record hundreds of times, even if it took all night. He said, "Time was never a factor in achieving perfection." Gordy was incapable of releasing a record for shipment until it met his impeccable scrutiny. Reginald Lewis's need for flawless work exceeded even Gordy's. Everything Lewis touched had to be perfect. A college roommate said, "He was an exacting person . . . and could be very hard on people if he felt they weren't giving 110 percent." He valued excellence in everything he did or touched and was referred to as a "neat freak" by his associates. He rated the magazine articles he read in terms of their quality and usefulness. The ultimate control freak, he insisted on scrupulous perfection, which most of his employees were unable to achieve, making him a very tough employer. When asked about his need for exactness and pristine surroundings, he responded, "The quest for perfection was its own reward." In a final tribute to his need for perfection, his pilots scrubbed and polished his private jet in order to fly his body back to Baltimore for his 1993 funeral. It was their way of saying thanks and wishing him a perfect goodbye.

TEMERITY

Most of these subjects were successful because of their ability to live on the edge in everything they attempted in life. Risk was their god and one of the most important factors in their ultimate success. Academics will tell you that the word *entrepreneur* is synonymous with risk and the three great entrepreneurs in this book—Johnson, Lewis, and Gordy—all worshiped at the altar of risk. The bigger the risk the more exciting for superstars since they instinctively know that there can be no great wins in life without taking big risks. John Johnson is a classic entrepreneur who has fathered many new ventures, including *Ebony* and *Jet.* Both of these publications were high-risk products that turned into great wins after passing through the critical mass period of growth. Johnson loved risk and wrote, "I believe in risk and daring." He was convinced that his success was based on "living on the edge," which he called the "summit of life." Johnson loved to use metaphors as instructive philosophies of life and said, "If you want to get a lion's cub you must go into the lion's lair." This great entrepreneur was convinced his ability to take large risks was fundamental to his business success. He said, "I'm convinced the only way to get ahead in this world is to live and sell dangerously. . . . It was the dare, the gamble, the deal which captivated me."

Risk and reward are inextricably intertwined in life and business, which these visionaries understood better than most. There are only three kinds of people: risk-takers, care-takers, and under-takers, which equate to those who *innovate,* those who *vegetate,* and those who *irritate* (see figure 16). The care-takers always attempt to eliminate all the risk from every venture, which the entrepreneurs view as the "adventure" or fun of business. Eliminating all the risk—personal or professional—is guaranteed to eliminate all the potential. It is axiomatic that, "There are no great rewards in life without great risk." You can only hit a home run by swinging for the fences and when you do there is a strong likelihood of striking out. All great innovators, entrepreneurs, and creative geniuses understand this intuitively, and it is the reason for their great success. All bureaucrats refuse to believe, which is the reason for their great ineptitude at innovation. Risk-takers always sacrifice the present for the future; others tend to sacrifice the future for the present.

Risk taking slows with age and accumulation of assets for normal people. For these subjects and most creative artists and entrepreneurs, risk taking does not wane with age and money, since they understand that those are not the reasons for risking in the first place. Bureaucrats never understand that principle and consequently never change their risk-averse behavior despite age or accumulation of assets. Average people who have accumulated a lot of wealth are reticent to bet that wealth on some risky new venture, regardless of its potential. Those who are

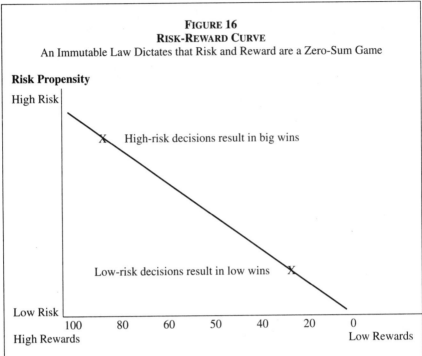

FIGURE 16
RISK-REWARD CURVE
An Immutable Law Dictates that Risk and Reward are a Zero-Sum Game

Risk Propensity

High Risk

High-risk decisions result in big wins

Low-risk decisions result in low wins

Low Risk

| 100 | 80 | 60 | 50 | 40 | 20 | 0 |

High Rewards   Low Rewards

Risk-Taking Axioms for People and Organizations

- Elimination of risk simultaneously eliminates potential opportunity.
- Development of employees and children is a function of taking risk.
- Success imprints result from trying the impossible and succeeding.
- Greatness emanates from living on the precipice and surviving the experience.
- Locate the greatest risk you can find and manage that risk.
- Risk taking is highly correlated to creativity, assertiveness, and sex drive.
- All managers fall into one of three categories:
  Risk-takers = People who innovate
  Care-takers = People who vegetate
  Undertakers = People who bury (themselves or their firms).

older also tend to become more risk-averse than younger people. That is why eighteen-year-olds and not forty-year-olds are found in foxholes.

Berry Gordy's ex-wife Ramona described him as a "high stakes gambler." She wrote that he would bet on anything that moved. She said he would win or lose $100,000 in one night, which baffled her. It is the nature of the temperament, and Gordy's Promethean temperament is conducive to seeking the possibilities and opportunities in life. An associate said that Gordy was willing to bet on the time it would take a raindrop to reach the bottom of the window at Hitsville in Detroit. Gordy admitted in his autobiography, "I made a game out of everything," which was his method of self-motivation. Cosby was also steeped with a gambling spirit. He said, "I've often won more at the tables than what I was earning per week on stage." He, like Gordy, spent a great deal of time in Las Vegas and Lake Tahoe.

Maya Angelou was also a fearless risk-taker who lived much of her life on the edge. She once faced a young gang leader in Harlem who had put out a contract on her teenage son. She walked in on him and his girlfriend, pulled a .38 pistol from her purse, and, pointing the gun at his head, said, "If you so much as touch my son, I will come over here and shoot Susie's [his girlfriend] grandmother, her mother, then I'll blow her away. You understand? I will then find your house and kill everything that moves including the rats and cockroaches." She never had another problem with street gangs.

TENACITY

Despite great adversity, these subjects persevered and became rich and famous in the process. In the book *Emotional Intelligence,* Daniel Goleman wrote, "What seems to set apart those at the very top of competitive pursuits from others of roughly equal ability is the degree to which . . . they can pursue an arduous practice routine for years and years . . . doggedness depends on . . . enthusiasm and persistence." Stanford University researcher Sanford Dorenbusch researched ten thousand students of all nationalities and found that Asian Americans "spent 40 percent more time doing homework than did other students," which was the major contributing factor on their higher test scores and career success. These subjects all fit Goleman's and Dorenbusch's prescription for success. They persevered despite great adversity. However, none exemplifies such tenacity of character as Nelson Mandela.

Mandela spent twenty-seven years in prison in pursuit of his great dream of destroying apartheid. He first pioneered as an underground freedom fighter and when caught refused to capitulate to the wills of the South African white supremacists. Even while in prison he continued to write articles and lead his rebellion constituency from behind bars. After twenty-two years behind bars the white government led by P. W. Botha attempted to defuse his power and offered him a conditional release. This man of fierce will and determination thumbed his nose at the offer and remained in prison another five years rather than capitulate to the enemy. It worked. Upon his release Mandela become South Africa's symbol of freedom and equality; within two years he had won the Nobel Peace Prize; in another year he was elected president of his country. Apartheid died in part because of Nelson Mandela, but his success was due to a tenacious spirit that would not be denied.

VISION

Intuitive right-brain visionaries such as Michael Jackson see the big picture in life. They have a macrovision that gives them a huge advantage over the microvisionaries who are mesmerized with the "now" and the details and never the essence of any opportunity. Visionaries see the qualitative in life while the left-brain types are obsessed with the quantitative. Researcher Daniel Cappon told *Psychology Today* in June 1993, "Intuition is the 'secret' of survival and success in all human endeavors." Cappon says that, "Intuition is . . . holistic, mosaic, big picture, insight-oriented intellect favoring inductive reasoning." Those destined to lead and become power brokers must be able to see the grand scope in any new concept or venture. They must not be misled by the number crunchers who insist on "analysis paralysis" prior to proceeding and any new venture as an adventure. In contrast, Michael Jackson told a reporter, "If I can see it, I can do it. My success is due to my inner vision." He told a judge in Chicago, "People don't see what I see. I rely on instinct."

Any new concept can be proven to be invalid by playing the MBA financial analysis game. Visionaries refuse to bow to such a dogmatic approach to any new venture, which has evolved out of the Western obsession with science and numbers. However, even a scientist of Einstein's genius was convinced that his true genius was based on intuitive (right-brain) powers, not rational (left-brain) ones. He became famous and infamous within the scientific community for his intuitive revelations and was often referred to as the "artist of science." Rationalists hated him and his methods while visionaries idolized him. He was convinced that: "The really valuable thing is intuition," and wrote, "When I examine myself and my methods of thought I come to the conclusion that the gift of 'fantasy' has meant more to me than my talent for absorbing positive knowledge."

Scientific philosopher Robert Anton Wilson has given an eloquent definition of genius pertinent to success through vision. He said, "A genius is one who, by some internal process, breaks through by painting a new somatic map, builds a new model of experience . . . this is always a profound shock to those still trapped in the old robot-imprints, and is generally considered a threat to territory. The long list of martyrs to free enquiry, from Socrates onward, shows how mechanical this neophobia is."

The world is qualitative, not quantitative, and people are analog, not digital. Creative genius must see the big picture and pursue it methodically. That was the approach of these thirteen.

Summary of Success—Personality Traits

Personality is the root for all success or failure in life. Strong personalities succeed while weak personalities fail. This is the eternal struggle we all face. It is apparent from this research that certain key personality traits are fundamental to success. The psychological theories propounded by Freud, Adler, Jung, Kirton, Kiersey, Farley, and McClelland all have contributed to our understanding of what makes the great tick. But in the final analysis it is individuals and their internal drives and needs which are the ultimate arbiter of success or failure in life. The ten key success traits that appear to be critical to supersuccess in entrepreneurship and creativity were acquired by these subjects while quite young and were fundamental to their later success in life. They ultimately lived to fulfill their internal self-images, which were formed by "success imprints," metamorphoses, key role models, and mythological hero mentors.

Carl Jung developed a theory of archetypes that he felt were products of a personal and collective unconscious. These he called "psychological types" which were then further refined by Myers and Briggs and by David Kiersey, who ultimately labeled them with the names of Greek gods—Apollo, Prometheus, Dionysus, and Epimetheus. Prometheus is the metaphorical god who best fit the intuitive-thinking nature and is the one most commonly found in these great entrepreneurs and creative geniuses. Frank Farley came up with a theory of testosterone as a key factor in creativity, risk taking, and competitiveness. He labeled the high-testosterone types as "Big Ts" to describe their thrill-seeking and high-testosterone behaviors. All these subjects qualified as Big Ts with the exception of Colin Powell, who lasted in the armed services through a "little t" style of behavior. David McClelland concocted a theory of motivation that he called a "needs theory," where achievement, power, and affiliation are the motivating factors driving all people. Five subjects were achievement-oriented and eight were power-oriented. There was a high correlation between both the achievement and power types and the innovator styles of Kirton, the intuitive-thinking personalities of Jung, and the Big T thrill-seekers of Farley.

To summarize the above theories relative to these creative geniuses: they have an innovator-style personality with an intuitive-thinking preference for dealing with life, most likely a Promethean temperament with a propensity for extroversion, a preference for living on the edge as thrill-seekers, and a need for power and overachieving that motivates them to self-actualize more than most people.

The research ferreted out ten key success traits that appear to have been critical to these subjects' success later in life. These traits were consistently found in all of the subjects although some were more steeped in one trait than another. The key traits found were: charisma, competition, confidence, energy, independence, passion, perfection, temerity, tenacity, and intuitive vision. These became the foundation on which they built their personal and professional success. Little else played such a material part in their great success.

6

Maya Angelou—Assertive

Author, Actress, Educator

"You may encounter many defeats, but you must not be defeated."

Maya Angelou is a survivor of the first magnitude. She is an accomplished poet, celebrated author of twelve books, writer of screenplays and television scripts, actress, dancer, singer, social activist, and tenured professor at Wake Forest University. The term *Renaissance woman* is not broad enough to encompass her vast accomplishments. Angelou began life at the bottom and used her ingenuity and innate drive to get to the top. And this visionary did it the old-fashioned way—through hard work and tenacity.

Two of Angelou's celebrated autobiographical works, *I Know Why the Caged Bird Sings* (1970) and *All God's Children Need Traveling Shoes* (1986), chronicle her unique history and add credence to her enormous contributions to the arts and life. *Caged Bird* is an exorcism of a black woman trapped in a white, male-dominated society. Her first book is an incisive, at times cynical, and above all an honest, soul-searching portrayal of her heartrending, sometimes tragic, journey from Arkansas to motherhood. *Traveling Shoes* is a journey depicting her emotional need to flee American racism. It was the story of her mid-thirties attempting to cope with an adolescent son and maintain sanity in a world in turmoil. It is about a woman searching desperately for her true heritage by moving to Africa in a futile attempt to discover her African roots. She attempted unsuccessfully to flee the bigotry, subjugation, and discrimination of a country she unconsciously loved and hated but couldn't live without. It is about the psychological isolation of a perceptive and talented black woman in twentieth-century America. Her last lines in the book give insight into her dilemma over racism and the love of America when she writes, "Through the centuries of despair and dislocation we had been creative, because we faced down death by daring to hope." That is when she returned to America and began to write seriously.

Maya Angelou is a paradox. She was an accomplished singer who never had a singing lesson and couldn't even read music. She became one of America's most acclaimed authors without taking any writing courses or having ever learned to type. In the seventies she became a college professor without ever having atteneded college. Then she became a universally sought after lecturer even though she had no training in the art of speech making. Angelou then became a tenured professor of American Studies at Wake Forest University in 1981 with no educational credentials. Later she would be asked to read a poem at President Bill Clinton's inauguration, the first such reading by a black. This Renaissance woman has never allowed reality to interfere with her vision. Angelou is fluent in French, Spanish, Italian, Arabic, and Fanti—all self-taught. When she visited a new country, she made it her duty to study the language of that culture and learn to speak it without benefit of training. Additionally, Angelou mastered many diverse professions while working as a social activist and becoming the northern director for Martin Luther King, Jr.'s Southern Christian Leadership Conference (SCLC).

Angelou receive a Yale Fellowship in 1970 at age forty-two and was made a Rockefeller Foundation Scholar in 1975 at forty-seven. Annie Gottlieb wrote in the *New York Times Book Review*: "Angelou writes like a song, and like the truth. The wisdom, rue, and humor of her storytelling are borne on a lilting rhythm completely her own." Angelou's twelve books and poetry have earned her honorary degrees from Smith College (1975), Mills College (1975), and Lawrence University (1976). The *Ladies Home Journal* named her Communications Woman of the Year in 1976. In 1977 she was nominated for an Emmy Award for best supporting actress in "Roots." She was the recipient of the Horatio Alger Award in 1992, and in 1994 won a Grammy for her recording of the poem written for Clinton's inauguration, "On the Pulse of the Morning."

Innovative Contribution

Writing was Angelou's catharsis for survival. She began writing to exorcise past ghosts that had occupied her past. She spent much of her life escaping from some abyss of insecurity where rape, drugs, discrimination, abuse, infidelity, inferiority, and rejection had molded her an indomitable spirit. Angelou was able to successfully resurrect those past experiences out of her fertile mind and transfer them onto paper with sensitivity and passion. She was able to transform an unfortunate past into a productive writing career or, as Joseph Campbell so eloquently said, "Changed vice into virtue."

Angelou's innovative contribution to the world was her ability to illustrate how one can utilize personal introspection and spiritual integrity for creative production in the visual arts. She bared her soul in her books and the world could sense her pain through her own unique style of communication. Her style has been eulogized as a novel approach for that genre—almost a collective unconscious of the genesis of a black female. Her use of black colloquialisms and dialogue, homilies, and racial aphorisms transformed her from a struggling single mother into America's autobiographical martyr. Biographer Nancy Shuker writes, "Not since the days of my childhood, when the people in books were more real than the people one saw ever day, have I found myself so moved. . . . Her portrait [in *Caged Bird*] is a biblical study of life in the midst of death." Houston A. Baker, writing for the *New York Times Book Review* in 1986, called Angelou one of the "geniuses of Afro-American serial autobiography." Sidonie Ann Smith in *Southern Humanities Review* writes, "Her genius as a writer is her ability to recapture the texture of the way of life in the texture of its idioms, its idiosyncratic vocabulary and especially in its process of image-making."

Angelou admittedly mixed fact with fantasy in her autobiographies. She justifies her methodology saying, "There's a world of difference between 'truth' and 'facts'. Facts can obscure the truth. You can tell so many facts that you fill the stage but haven't got one iota of truth." Critic Eugenia Collier offers insight into Angelou's innovation in the world of autobiography and more importantly, to her metamorphosis from mediocrity to superstardom: "The pervasive theme, naturally developed in all the autobiographies, is the strength of the black woman, her ability to prevail despite the awful hurting put upon by the world, even by her own black man, who often assuages his own hurt by oppressing her. Yet there is no blatant preaching, no anti-male rhetoric."

Personal History

Marguerite Annie Johnson was born in St. Louis, Missouri, on April 4, 1928, the second child of Vivian Baxter and Bailey Johnson. Her brother, Bailey, was one year older and her soulmate for much of her anguished youth. He accompanied her from St. Louis to Long Beach, California, when they were both toddlers. Her name Marguerite was a bit much for Bailey to handle as a child and he would refer to her as "mya-sister," which she later adopted as a stage name during her early days as an entertainer in San Francisco.

With their parents' marriage breaking up, Maya (age three) and Bailey (age 4) were put on a train alone in Long Beach, California, for a long trip across the United States to Stamps, Arkansas, which was the home of their paternal grandmother, Annie Henderson. Henderson owned and operated a general store in this rural agrarian town and was a huge influence on Angelou's values and philosophy of life. Henderson became Angelou's role model and her substitute mother. She instilled in the girl the aggressive behavior and fighting spirit that characterizes the adult Angelou.

Angelou's father, Bailey Sr., was a doorman and navy dietician who lived most of his life in southern California and had little positive influence on her development. Her mother, Vivian, was a registered nurse, card dealer, professional gambler, and boardinghouse proprietor and a huge influence on Maya's growth.

Both parents were itinerant free spirits who chased the American dream and went wherever destiny led them. During her early years there was no time for the kids, so the parents remained in Arkansas until Angelou was seven. Then the children relocated back to St. Louis to live with Vivian.

A few months after their arrival in St. Louis Angelou was raped by her mother's new boyfriend, a man named Freeman. Her mother learned of the assault and pressed charges, which resulted in Angelou's testifying against Freeman. Freeman had told Maya he would kill her beloved brother, Bailey, if she ever told and she was traumatized at the thought and was hesitant to testify. When Freeman was found guilty and then murdered by Angelou's uncles, Angelou became mute and didn't talk publicly for the next five years. Within a few months she and her brother were sent back to Stamps; Vivian had come to realize her lifestyle was not conducive to raising two young children.

Angelou told reporters of her mute period, saying, "I thought he was killed because I spoke his name. That was the only logic I was able to employ. So I thought if I spoke, anybody might die." Angelou was only seven when she had been assaulted and for the next five years she escaped into books as solace from a cruel world where people were killed if one spoke. She speaks of "language" becoming important for her during this period. While not speaking, "language" became synonymous with the written word and Angelou saw it as very powerful, as it is "written, spoken and sung." She retreated into a safe world of books where her imagination became her life, since it was suave and exciting.

A woman named Bertha Flowers came into Angelou's life as she got older and would become her mentor and savior. This woman was the aristocratic black woman of Stamps, Arkansas. She enticed Angelou to recite passages from the Bible and from the works of black poets like Paul Lawrence Dunbar, James Weldon Johnson, and Langston Hughes. Angelou soon graduated to William Shakespeare, Edgar Allan Poe, Matthew Arnold, and Charles Dickens. By the time she reached high school she was not only speaking but writing and reciting poetry as a redemption for her lonely soul.

Angelou graduated from the eighth grade in 1940 in segregated Sparks and not only had begun to speak but adults called her "precocious and eloquent." She had become a voracious reader of classics and inspirational books, and had a photographic memory that allowed her to quote whole passages from Shakespeare. At age twelve Angelou and her brother left Stamps for the West Coast. They lived briefly with their father and other relatives in Los Angeles. They finally moved to Oakland and then to San Francisco, where they moved in with Vivian, who was by now living with a new husband. Angelou's teen years were spent in San Francisco, where she enrolled in Mission High School, winning a two-year scholarship to study dance and drama at the California Labor School.

Angelou was a latchkey kid and learned many important lessons on the streets of San Francisco. She worked at various jobs while Bailey hung out with gangs and became involved with drugs. School was of little interest. She dropped out for awhile but then decided it was important and went back and studied hard to make sure she would graduate. She spent the summer before her senior year with her father in Long Beach, which proved to be a disastrous but educational experience. After returning with her father from a Mexican trip, to which his girlfriend Dolores had not been invited, the girlfriend took out her frustrations and jealousy on Angelou, stabbing her during the heat of an argument. Distraught, afraid, and with nowhere to turn, Angelou ran away from her father's apartment and lived for a month with black, whites, and Mexican street urchins. She slept in a car and became extremely self-sufficient in the process. Finally she decided she had better return to San Francisco, where her mother never learned the truth of her summer of leisure in Los Angeles.

When Angelou returned to San Francisco at age fifteen, she lied about her age and became the first black ever hired to operate a cable car. Big for her age, she was aggressive and able to open doors through moxie and intimidation. She had grown to be six feet tall and often survived through sheer guts and audacity, which is the way she had gotten the job as a cable car operator. Bailey became a delinquent during this period and ended up in San Quentin as a result of drug dealing. Her teen years were solitary and she soon became worried over her lack of breasts and sexuality, causing her to ask a boy to have sex with her just to prove that she wasn't a lesbian, a term she had learned in books. She graduated from Mission High School at age sixteen in 1946, just two months before giving birth to her only son, Clyde Johnson.

By age eighteen Angelou had become a renegade searching for her true calling in life. Calling herself Rita, she was a belligerent and untamed youth who found work as a cook in a creole restaurant, a nightclub waitress, a madam for two San Diego lesbians, and other less-than-redeeming professions. This distasteful life caused her to reflect on the tranquil life with her beloved grandmother, Annie Henderson, in Stamps, and one day she jumped on a train with her young son and ended up in Stamps to start life anew in the South. The sociocultural contrast of racist Stamps and ultraliberal San Francisco was shocking to her. After just two months she came running back to her mother in San Francisco, where she really hit bottom. Angelou then began experimenting with drugs and got caught up with a pimp who sold her services as a prostitute for a short time. With the help of her now-free brother she weaned herself from this nefarious lifestyle and found herself a job in a record store. This is where, at age twenty-two, she met and married Tosh Angelos, a Greek immigrant who had just been released from the navy.

Angelou's marriage to Angelos was ill-fated from the start, since Angelou had learned self-sufficiency from all her early freedom and Tosh, who was a good father, was well steeped in European chauvinism, which was incompatible with this renegade's lifestyle. When the marriage ended, Angelou was forced into economic survival and in classic fashion bluffed her way into a job as a dancer and singer in a North Beach strip joint even though she knew little of singing or dancing. Whatever she lacked in talent she made up for in stage presence, charisma, moxie, and emotional expression. The owners of the famous Purple Onion, the star-making emporium in San Francisco, saw this statuesque women dance and offered her a legitimate entertainment job dancing and singing calypso in their club. This was her first authentic job as an entertainer and helped launch her career, as it had numerous others, including the likes of Mort Sahl and Phyllis Diller.

Dancing at the avant-garde Purple Onion not only legitimatized Angelou's dancing career, it brought her into contact with many show business professionals. It was here she came into contact with white entertainers and executives who were different from those she had known in the past, whom she had seen as dominant whites exploiting needy blacks. Of the Purple Onion, Maya wrote, "There, whites were treating me as an equal, as if I could do whatever they could do. They did not consider that race, height, gender, or lack of education might have crippled me and that I should be regarded as someone invalid." This indomitable spirit was finally on her way professionally.

Professional History

Angelou's first professional success came as a dancer and singer of calypso songs. Her timing was impeccable, since the calypso craze coincided with her Purple Onion routines which became the impetus of her burgeoning show business career. She perfected her song-and-dance routine and in addition to performing at the Purple Onion in San Francisco, she took her act on the road to Chicago's Mr. Kelly's and New York's Blue Angel and Village Vanguard. During this time the State Department sponsored a twenty-two-nation production of Gershwin's *Porgy and Bess*. Angelou accepted a key role and visited many countries from 1954 to 1955, which contributed to her education in global affairs and fluency in different languages.

After Angelou's return she took her cabaret act to various cities, appeared in an off-Broadway play *Calypso Heat Wave* (1957) and the Columbia picture of the same name, and cut a record titled *Miss Calypso*. During this period she met Billie Holiday, who jolted her into reality with a cynical, albeit optimistic observation that, "You can't sing all that good. But you're going to be real famous" (*Heart of a Woman*, 1981). A few months before Holiday died of a drug overdose she confided in Angelou, "Remember, you can't get too high for somebody to bring you down." This caused the thirty-year-old vagabond to reflect on her future and she decided to pursue her true love—writing. She had met writer John Killens in Los Angeles and told him of her passion for writing and he convinced her to move to New York. In New York she became an active member of the Harlem Writer's Guild and met some of the great black writers of the time: James Baldwin, John Killens, Paule Marshall, and John Henrik Clarke. She became inspired enough to quit her show business career in deference to her writing, but the necessities of paying the rent delayed her writing career for another decade.

The sixties were a period of social unrest and black militancy and Angelou became a protagonist in the movement. She sang rebellious "Black Power" songs at Harlem's Apollo Theater and wrote much of Godfrey Cambridge's dialogue in the off-Broadway play *Freedom Cabaret* (1960). This work brought Angelou to the attention of Martin Luther King's Southern Christian Leadership Conference and King appointed her his northern director. Social activism began dominating her life and energies. She met many of the world's great leaders, especially those from Africa and Europe. One of these was the charismatic Vusumzi Make, a South African dissident who proceeded to sweep Angelou off her feet despite her engagement to a very stable postal worker Tom Allen. The wedding was one month off and the invitations were in the mail when she impulsively agreed to marry Make and move with him and her son to Cairo, Egypt.

Make was a mesmerizing speaker and brilliant social activist in northern Africa, both traits Angelou had a hard time resisting. The couple moved to Cairo with Maya's son and she was forced to resort to her wits to survive as Make's public brilliance kept him away for weeks at a time and left no money to buy even the barest of essentials. Angelou had to go to work to put food on the table. Her survival instincts intact, she was able to get hired as an assistant editor of the English-speaking *Arab Observer* in 1962, which proved providential for her writing career. She was asked to write editorials on social activism and the experience helped develop her writing skills. When she broke up with Make she was still not prepared to return to America and decided to get better acquainted with her African roots. She and her son moved to Accra, Ghana, where he enrolled in the University of Ghana in 1964 and his mother took a job working in university administration, a tough position for a woman without formal education who didn't even type.

This tenacious woman returned from Africa in the mid-sixties and took residence in Harlem, where friends in the Harlem Writers Guild helped her get started in a writing career. Jules and Judy Feiffer were intrigued by Angelou and became instrumental figures in her success. The Feiffers introduced Angelou to a friend at Random House and strongly recommended that the company consider publishing an autobiography of the mesmerizing life of this frenetic woman. Angelou spent the next few years writing and rewriting her first book, *I Know Why the Caged Bird Sings,* which was finally published in 1970 to overwhelming critical acclaim. Within a decade Angelou had written several sequels about her hectic but intriguing life attempting to succeed—*Gather Together in My Name* (1974), *Singin' and Swingin' and Getting Merry Like Christmas* (1976), and *The Heart of a Woman* (1981).

She completed her series of autobiographies in 1986 with the release of *All God's Children Need Traveling Shoes.* In addition to these books Maya has written six volumes of verse, which is her first love. David Streitfeld wrote of the unfavorable reviews of her poetry, saying, "She's a people's poet rather than a poet's poet, which means she has a much bigger audience but doesn't win awards." During this period Maya's workaholic nature found many outlets in the movies, screenwriting, and television. In 1977 she appeared as Kunta Kinte's grandmother in the acclaimed television miniseries "Roots." She also wrote the musical score and script for the TV adaptation of *I Know Why the Caged Bird Sings,* which was broadcast in 1979. In 1993 Angelou read a poem at President Bill Clinton's inauguration. In 1994 she was asked to read a new poem, "Still I Rise," for an upbeat advertising campaign for the United Negro College Fund. She now lives in an eighteen-room mansion in North Carolina and lectures at Wake Forest University as a tenured professor.

What Makes Angelou Tick?

Maya Angelou has what psychologists call an Apollonian temperament—she is a spokeswoman and energizer who works by interacting with people about values. As such she prefers to operate and interact with society through a right-brain, emotional style of behavior. She is imaginative, nurturing, and secretly would like to save the world. The Jungian description of this temperament type is "intuitive-feeler," one who sees the world with a macrovision and operates with a personal style. Angelou is an assertive extrovert who is highly spiritual. The motto of such personality types is "grace under pressure," which describes Angelou's tenacity quite accurately.

This woman's success has been a function of her ability to meet adversity head-on and defeat it. She has persevered through much and admits her whole life has been about survival. Her mother and grandmother both instilled in her the axioms: "Never back down from a bully" and "Strength is power." They practiced what they preached, as her mother once killed a lover who dared to call her a "bitch" even after she had warned him of the dire consequences of such a confrontation. Once, when Vivian and Maya met in a segregated Fresno, California, hotel lobby her mother brought along a German Luger and "dared anyone to stop them" as they checked into this previously "white only" motel. The young, uninitiated Angelou was in shock at the fearless nature of her combative mother. Vivian told her, "Never, never let a person know you're frightened." The sage advice was not lost on this iron-willed woman who once accosted a Harlem gang leader who had put out a contract on her teenage son. This young thug was the head of a street gang known as the Savages and the fearless Angelou tracked him down, pulled a loaded revolver, and told him she would wipe out him and his family. Jerry, the gang leader, looked at her and meekly said, "O.K. I understand. But for a mother, I must say you're a mean motherfucker." Her assertive style was due to the early training from her black female role models, who refused to be used or abused by anyone.

MYTHOLOGICAL HERO MENTORS

Much of Angelou's great success in life, writing, and poetry can be traced back to early imprints with Shakespeare, Poe, Dickens, Kipling, and the Brontë sisters, which her friend and mentor Bertha Flowers used to make her read and then speak. This woman was the aristocrat of Sparks, Arkansas, and in Angelou's words, was "one of the few gentlewomen I have ever known, and has remained throughout my life the measure of what a human being can be." Flowers used poetry to relieve the great trauma that had caused Angelou to go silent years earlier. Flowers inspired her by telling her, "Words mean more than what is set down on paper. It takes the human voice to infuse them with shades of deeper meaning." And suddenly the mute little girl began to speak the words of the great poets and literary geniuses.

Angelou was captivated by the books, saying, "When I read Shakespeare and heard that music, I couldn't believe it, that a white man could write so musically. I already . . . had an affection for Poe, because I like his rhythm." Later she would discover Dostoevsky when she was in another great turmoil as a nineteen-year-old in San Diego. After reading *Crime and Punishment,* she was transformed by the experience and fled her distasteful lifestyle since she saw the analogy between her tragic lifestyle and that of Dostoevsky's protagonist, Raskolnikov. Biographer Nancy Shuker wrote in *Genius—The Artist and the Process,* "Her fantasizing and her impulsiveness would mature into a vivid imagination and the strength to take both personal and artistic risks."

Angelou admits to having escaped into books and the fantasy of make-believe where Shakespeare and Kipling became her fantasy mentors and their fictional characters her heroes. She often dreamed of becoming white in order to flee the perpetual misery of being a black girl in a white world. She wrote of a passionate desire to wake up as a blond to avoid the misery of being black in the Deep South. Black spirituals sung at her grandmother's house in Stamps, Arkansas, also proved influential in her move into entertainment and her need to write verse. Angelou said, "I had a heritage, rich and nearer than the tongue which gave it voice. My mind resounded with the words and my blood raced to the rhythms." She admitted to drawing strength as an adult from the wisdom of these old songs of worship and their influence can be readily seen in her adult poetry.

Angelou told *Parade* in 1995, "A hero/shero encourages people to see the good inside themselves and to expand it." She listed Eleanor Roosevelt, Pearl Buck, and Frederick Douglass as her heroes, saying, "They confronted societies that did not believe in their ideas and faced hostile adversaries. . . . I try to act as I would want my hero/shero to act."

INSECURITY BREEDS GREATNESS

This indomitable spirit encountered adversity at every major crossroad in her life and viewed each simply as a roadblock to overcome. She admits to being driven by her fears but says, "To those who would try to diminish me, I say you cannot cripple my spirit. . . . I have nothing but my spirit, and I will not allow anyone to trample on it." Nevertheless, Angelou is motivated by fear of failure. Her self-doubts erupt every time she picks up her yellow pad to write. She says, "I look at the yellow pad, I am absolutely terrified. I think: I have talked a good talk. I have fooled everybody. Everybody thinks I can write." Angelou has said, "Writing in itself instills fear and insecurity." She told *USA Today* in 1995, "My knees knock, my throat gets dry, my eyes wander," but in the end the negativity motivates her to greater achievement.

LIFE CRISES AND TRAUMAS—METAMORPHOSES

Angelou's life was a series of crises. Raped at seven, mute until eleven, stabbed by her father's girlfriend at fifteen, pregnant at sixteen, madam for lesbians at eighteen followed by a period of drugs and prostitution at nineteen all add up to a life of survival against enormous odds. Her first metamorphosis occurred after the trauma of her rape and subsequent murder of her assailant when she was eight.

Angelou's most frightening trauma and resultant metamorphosis occurred during a summer vacation with her insensitive father. Bailey Johnson took his fourteen-year-old daughter deep into Mexico and then partied into drunken oblivion, leaving a frightened Maya alone with strange but lecherous Mexican males who intimidated her. In abject fear, and with absolutely no knowledge of the language or how to extricate herself from the innards of Mexico, Angelou jumped into her father's car and started driving without ever having a lesson. This might not seem a big thing with automatic shifts in the nineties, but with a 1940s stick-shift car, it was a terrifying experience.

Angelou propped her inebriated father in the back seat and started driving toward the United States border. She was able to get the car moving by trial and error and drove away from what she envisioned as inevitable molestation or worse at the hands of drunken Mexicans. Through sheer power of will she made the car move forward but it suddenly stalled on a hill due to her ineptitude with the clutch. Without knowledge of starting a car on a hill she kept pumping the pedals and miraculously the car started and lurched forward. She drove toward the border with her father still fast asleep in his drunken stupor and later wrote of the horrid experience: "The challenge was exhilarating. It was me, Marguerite, against the elemental opposition. As I trusted the steering wheel and forced the accelerator to the floor I was controlling Mexico and night and aloneness and inexperienced youth, and Bailey Johnson, Sr., and death, and insecurity, and even gravity. . . . No matter what happened after that I had won.

Charisma

Angelou exudes an aura that is hypnotic to audiences and for those whom she has been a mentor, like Oprah Winfrey. This woman is a gigantic intellect and overwhelming presence who is extremely articulate and at six feet tall presents an intimidating persona to the world. She has deep, penetrating eyes; a dominating persona; and a photographic memory that has made her fluent in seven languages. Her spiritual nature borders on the occult. At President Clinton's 1992 inauguration Angelou spoke with eloquent deliberateness in delivering a passionate and spiritual poem written for the occasion. Her delivery elicited varying responses from the media. One such critique came from novelist Louise Erdich, who said, "I felt that this woman could have read the side of a cereal box. Her presence was so powerful and momentous, she made a statement that I was personally longing to see and hear."

This mesmerizing woman has succeeded in numerous venues due to her moxie and charisma where her talent was less than outstanding. As a singer and dancer she was able to elicit rousing applause. At age twenty-six in Africa she once performed for four thousand Moroccans who jumped to their feet screaming and shouting. They were not applauding some great musical talent but her onstage passion, her moxie, and her entertainer personality, which transcended the performance. Further testimony to her wide-ranging charismatic influence is Oprah Winfrey's comment to Larry King in a 1995 CNN interview, "Maya Angelou has been the greatest influence on my life as an adult."

Assertiveness

Angelou wrote in *All God's Children Need Traveling Shoes*, "I always knew that fury was my natural enemy." She was speaking of her competitive juices, which caused her to unceremoniously lose her temper and thus lose control of the situation. This highly competitive woman never saw a challenge that was too great. She went after whatever she wanted without fear of the consequences, saying, "Ask for what you want and be prepared to pay for what you get."

Confidence

This consummate optimist wrote, "You can't use up creativity. The more you use, the more you have." Angelou learned life from her mother and grandmother, who had instilled her with streetwise aphorisms like, "Can't do is like don't care. Neither have a home." She understands the importance of molding children with strong self-esteems so they may be armed to cope with the "struggles" later in life. She said, "Black mothers give their sons contrived arrogance in order to cope." She prophetically added in *Heart of a Woman* (1981), "We were meant for great things. The size and power of our adversaries were not greater than our capabilities."

Angelou's positive self-assurance is what made her a great success in many different professions. It was her awesome self-esteem which armed her with the willpower to ignore all those who saw fit to deride and ridicule her due to race or gender. Angelou had an awe-inspiring confidence that refused to be denied, as indicated by her quote from *All God's Children Need Traveling Shoes,* "Although I was born of slaves, I was descended from kings." Such a belief system is the cornerstone of genius.

Passion and Drive

When this intransigent lady found herself broke and without a job in faraway Cairo, Egypt, she wrote, "I challenged myself to do whatever job assigned to me with intense commitment." Her obsessive drive and psychic energy contributed greatly to her success in life. Highly passionate people have an ability to move mountains. They see the possibilities and are usually very spiritual. Angelou was such a person. She relied on a kind of mystical sixth sense in making career moves and turned to what some people refer to as extrasensory perception. Once in Ghana she was riding down a road with four other people in the car when she suddenly became short of breath, and with her heart racing, screamed at the driver, "Stop the car, stop the car." The car had been approaching the Keta Bridge, which had a mystical reputation in the community for collapsing when vehicles crossed it. Natives often stopped their cars and walked across rather than upset the gods of the mysterious bridge. When Angelou ordered the driver to stop, she was unaware of this local superstition. Without knowing it she had stopped the car in order for the passengers to walk across the mythical bridge, to the surprise of those in the car who knew of the bridge's legend. Angelou had always been highly steeped in a mysterious psychic energy and in 1993 told the *New York Times,* "My life could be credited to miraculous experiences."

Psychosexual energy was pervasive within her. Angelou told *USA Today* in 1985, "What I would really like said about me is that I dared to love," which in her words was "spirit." She told *Essence* in 1992, "I think spirit is the energy of life." Angelou credits her spirituality with much of her success in life, adding credibility to the thesis that high energy and passion are critical traits for achieving supercreativity and power. She said, "Spirit is an invisible force made visible." Philosophizing to the media in 1993, she said, "I have tried many things, failed at many, and succeeded at many. I will try anything that I think is good, because I find myself surrounded by spirits in front of me."

Such a free spirit and uninhibited energy defined much of her early life. During one period she lived on a communal Sausalito houseboat with her son and four white men—two musicians, an inventor, plus an ichthyologist. She was a renegade who dared have a child out of wedlock; spent time as a madam, a prostitute, and strip club dancer; and proceeded to marry three men of different nationalities. This is not the style of a suburban housewife. Angelou was a sensual women with strong drives, which she acknowledged with her philosophy on the passion of black women: "Black women . . . really love sex. Love to enjoy it, love to give it. . . . We are sensual people and do not decry or deny it."

Hypomania

A tribute to Maya Angelou's maniacal work ethic is her habit of getting up every day at 4:00 A.M. to write, even while in her sixties. When she was sixty-three she told the *New York Times* that she "used work as therapy for her soul." Work had been an integral part of Angelou's life since she was a teenager. Work was her means of self-actualization, and a way to use up her immense psychic energy and satiate her passions. Angelou, like most Type A workaholics, was famous for taking on far more work than she could possibly accomplish. Therefore she was forced to juggle many projects, but in her mind the more the better, as it gave impetus to her great spirit and energy. Hard work was ingrained in her psyche by her paternal grandmother, who told her, "If you can't change it, change the way you think about it. Don't complain." Angelou told the *Ladies Home Journal* in 1993 that the essence of writing is that, "You've got to work. Write each sentence over and over again, then write it again." But since writing was her passion, she never saw it as work but as fun, and therefore was willing to work much longer hours than those who envision their profession as work.

Independence

Angelou is a classic renegade who refuses to listen to so-called experts. She pioneers in her writing just as she did in singing, dancing, screenwriting, on the stage, and as a social activist. She has always been a maverick, which was never so apparent as when she decided to have sex as a teenager to prove she wasn't a lesbian—a term learned from a book. Struggling with the internal conflict, she made a conscious decision to resolve it by very rationally seducing a boy she found appealing. She nonchalantly walked up to the unsuspecting youth and said, "Hey! Would you like to have sexual intercourse?" Needless to say, with her luck, she turned up pregnant after this one-time seductive experience.

When she returned to Sparks, Arkansas, at age nineteen she was forced to leave town due to what she said was "insubordination." Returning to San Francisco she then married a man who appealed to her sense of right rather than any sense of love. Her chosen mate was not black but a white macho immigrant of Greek extraction. This was not the most "normal decision" for a passionate young woman. She had married out of her race and culture almost in defiance of the establishment. She had married like she had gotten pregnant, not out of any well-planned and articulated strategy, but as an impulsive act of rebellion. When she ran off to Cairo, Egypt, with freedom fighter Vusumzi Make, she was making the same kind of statement of nonconformity, as if it was an impulsive search for freedom and vitality. Angelou justified her eccentric actions by saying, "Intelligence always had a pornographic influence on me."

This maverick always sang to her own philosophical tune, which was never more true than at the Apollo Theater in Harlem in 1959, when she abjectly ignored the management's policy of "no audience participation" and sang the Swahili freedom song "Uh Uhuru." The audience went wild when she asked for their participation even though the management was livid over her iconoclastic move— *verboten* at the Apollo during this era of social turbulence and black power. Her defiance almost caused a riot, which only reinforced her image as a free spirit and rebel who loved to defy the establishment.

Perfectionist

Who but a perfectionist would set a goal to learn the language of every country she visited on a tour with *Porgy and Bess*? Angelou was still in her twenties when she toured Europe and the Middle East and learned to speak seven languages without so much as a lesson. Another testimony to her perfectionism is her flawless dedication to detail in her writing. Her approach borders on obsessiveness. Angelou rents a motel room near her residence and uses the setting for the necessary seclusion demanded by the total dedication to writing and freeing of the imagination. Angelou walks into her motel room equipped with nothing more than a yellow pad of paper, a dictionary, a thesaurus, the Bible, and a bottle of sherry. She stays ensconced in this environment until she has achieved some personal goal set prior to arriving. Such an intensity and demand for excellence is what has made her a successful superstar in every venue undertaken.

Temerity

Gambler Angelou says, "I try to live my life as a poetic adventure." She was always a free-spirited wanderer who felt comfort in some unknown territory or in pioneering with a new song, dance, or poetic expression. This comfort with ambiguity was learned early in life from her grandmother and mother, who taught her fearlessness and transformed her into a vagabond spirit through the transience experienced from seven moves encompassing the Midwest, South, and West. Without such a childhood Angelou would not have been as comfortable with risk taking and wandering the world to seek fame and fortune. She adds credence to this theory with her statement, "It is the desperate traveler who teaches us the most profound lessons and affords us the most exquisite thrills."

Angelou's very first encounter with the unknown was at age three, when she and her brother crossed the United States with a "To Whom It May Concern" wrist tag on. Angelou moved repeatedly, which instilled such comfort with the unfamiliar that she spent much of the rest of her life living on the edge in unknown habitats and somehow was able to find comfort in them. She wrote, "Difficult encounters may be the very experience which creates the vitality and the power to endure. . . . Belief in a power larger than myself . . . allows me to venture into the unknown." Her personality was initially nurtured in the bigoted South, reinforced in St. Louis and Los Angeles, and ultimately formed on the streets of San Francisco. Angelou learned early to take risks and live with the consequences. She always operated just on the edge where live creativity or crisis, genius or madness, wins or losses, success or failure. She was very careful to never go over that edge, and, like the others in this book, ended up wearing the gold ring known as success.

Tenacity

If nothing else, this visionary has persevered. When everything looked forlorn or when she could not pay the rent or buy food, she found a way to survive. In fact, she told the *New York Times* in 1993 that, "My life is about survival." She always refused to believe that she would lose in any endeavor.

Dolly McPherson said of her writing style, "The themes of Angelou's autobiographies are courage, perseverance, the persistence or renewal of innocence against overwhelming obstacles." In a statement written for *The Black One Hundred* in 1993, Angelou said her success in life was a function of her struggles and adversities, without which there would have been no fun or success: "All my work, my life, is about survival. . . . You may encounter many defeats, but you must not be defeated. In fact, the encountering may be the very experience which creates the vitality and the power to endure."

Vision

Angelou is one of those macrovisionaries who sees the big picture in all things. She is a right-brain-driven individual who never sweats the little things but keeps focused on the larger goals in life. Her female intuition borders on precognition, a power she touches on in some of her works. Poets are famous or infamous for anticipating the future and attempting to define it for posterity. This intuitive woman is no exception. Her imagination and pursuit of the possibilities in life are what have made her great. She could well be viewed by history as an amateur philosopher with her pulse on the streetwise nature of life.

Will to Power

Angelou grew up around extremely strong-willed people who were her role models for living and surviving in a dynamic world. Both her mother and grandmother were strong women who depended on no one, including their men. Angelou inherited those traits and in some ways expanded on them. She wrote, "The word 'can't' didn't exist for me." She had learned that axiom from a strong-willed mother who once went to sea because a man told her she couldn't. Her daughter didn't fall too far from the tree. Her strong "will" was molded during a transient childhood, where she learned to cope with the unknown and the foreign. Growing up in four diverse cities in three diverse areas of the country before age fifteen imprinted her with an implacable will to overcome any adversity. A latchkey child, she learned to cope due to the freedom to explore and learn, try and fail. These experiences reinforced her strong sense of self, transforming her into an iron-willed personality who relied on no one but herself to succeed. Angelou wrote: "I was a loose kite in a gentle wind floating with only my 'will' for an anchor." Her grandmother was a major influence in the development of her indomitable will. Angelou wrote, "My grandmother had no use for whiners. Her constant theme was, 'If you can't change it, change the way you think about it.' "

Summary

Maya Angelou is an assertive, independent woman who marches to no one's tune but her own. Once at age twenty she refused her mother's help and told her, "I have to own myself." Her mother looked at her and said, "You know, baby, I think you are the greatest woman I have ever met." This moved her beyond words and in a moment of introspection about her mother's words wrote: "She's very intelligent and she's too mean to lie. So just suppose she's right? Suppose I really am somebody? And it was the first time I ever remember being on the earth as opposed to being a part of the earth. I was aware, at that moment, of being on a hill. It's almost as if at times like that, the whole earth holds its breath."

This story was told to reporter Catherine Mangold on the eve of her poem "On the Pulse of Morning" at President Clinton's inaugural. Angelou had remembered her mother's words forty years after the event that proved to be a kind of metamorphosis from a young woman in turmoil to one governed by her "intransigent will." This proved instrumental to her future writing and her success in life. Angelou said of the experience, "These are the times that are really the essence and the origin of poetry . . . because whether one knows it or not, one goes to those watersheds, those times when you are moved to write."

Maya Angelou has had a worldwide influence in autobiographical writing. This vagabond spirit has lived in London, New York, Cairo, Accra, San Francisco, and Los Angeles and now calls the hills of North Carolina home. She married men of two races from three continents and along the way found time to be an accomplished dancer, singer, playwright, poet, award-winning actress, and tenured professor. Now in her late sixties she still exudes confidence and vitality. This assertive, almost aggressive, woman of the world is a self-made creative genius and admits to being a survivor who is "nobody's creature" but a "child of God's."

Maya Angelou is highly spiritual and exemplifies the quintessential rags-to-riches story. This was confirmed in 1992, when she was presented the Horatio Alger Award, although riches might be stretching the point relative to her financial success. It might be better said that she "read" and "wrote" herself from the proverbial "playhouse" into the intellectual penthouse. Without one course in college and no money or social influence, this woman worked her way from an impoverished existence to become a world-renowned poet. And she did it the old-fashioned way—through hard work and an indomitable will that would not accept defeat. Maya Angelou is a consummate creative genius who changed the world by daring to be assertive and different. This is best expressed in her words in *Maya Angelou—Genius! The Artist and the Process*: "It is the desperate traveler who teaches us the most profound lesson and affords us the most exquisite thrills. She touches us with her boldness and vulnerability, for her sole preparation is the fierce determination to leave where she is, and her only certain destination is somewhere other than where she has been."

MARGUERITE ANNIE JOHNSON (MAYA ANGELOU)
Apollonian Temperament (NF)
Entertainer—Playwright—Actress—Author—Poet—Scholar—Activist—Educator
born April 4, 1928, St. Louis, Missouri

Dominant trait: Aggressive, assertive, and extroverted with an indomitable will and tenacity
Motto: "You may encounter many defeats, but you must not be defeated"
Religion: Fundamentalist Christian
Philosophy: "We are more alike than unlike"; "Ask for what you want and be prepared to pay for what you get"
Nicknames: Maya, Ritie, Sugar, Rita
Creation/innovation: *Caged Bird* became standard for autobiographical insight—"collective unconscious of black female"
Successes: 12 books (4 autobiographies; Emmy for "Roots" performance)
Vices/Hobbies: Books, wine, cigarettes, partying, dancing
Romantic Liaisons: Married men from 3 continents: Greek Tosh Angelos, African Vusumzi Make, European Paul de Feu
Self-Description: "I dare to love"; "All my work, my life, everything is about survival"; "I'm a child of God"

Birth order: One older brother, Bailey
Parental influence: Named for paternal grandmother Annie Henderson; Vivian positive influence, father negative
Early transience: Seven moves at early age between Midwest, South, and West ending in San Francisco
Parents' occupations: Grandmother owned general store; mother was a gambler, nurse, realtor, hotelier; father was a doorman
Role models: "Momma" Henderson, teacher Bertha Flowers, John Killens, Pearl Buck, Eleanor Roosevelt
Hero mentors: Horatio Alger and authors Shakespeare, Poe, Dickens, Brontë sisters, Frederick Douglass, and Kipling
Formal education: Mission H.S. San Francisco, 1945, with some drama and dance classes as teenager
Life crises: Raped at 7 and mute until 11; stabbed and street person at 15; pregnant at 16; drugs at 19
Metamorphoses: Escaped emotional silence at 11 through poetry; used wits to survive Mexico fiasco at age 14

Charismatic: Overwhelming personality, size, and intellect; "Her presence was so powerful and momentous"
Competitive: No challenge too great. first black cable car attendant; first black to have screen-play produced
Hypomanic: Energy incarnate; learned to speak language of every country visited; speaks seven fluently
Independent rebel: Maverick who follows heart; "I have nothing but my spirit, I will not allow anyone to trample on it"
Indomitable "will": Intransigent inner strength; "You cannot cripple my spirit . . . it is not yours. . . . I alone am responsible"
Intuitive vision: A right-brain visionary who always sees the forest, not the trees
Libidinal drive: Madame, prostitute, strip club dancer; "Intelligence always had a pornographic influence on me"
Perfectionist: Exacting precision in all things
Risk-taker: Fearless: a singer who couldn't read music; an educator with no college; a writer without training; a mother without a husband. Never afraid to attack any problem and live on the edge
Self-confident: Said, "I would have the job . . . I would!" at age 15. She lied about age and got it
Tenacious: "My life is about survival"
Workaholic: Multitasking Type A energy
Honors: Horatio Alger Award (1992), Reynolds lifetime professor; 50 honorary degrees

7

Shirley Chisholm—Indomitable Will

Iconoclastic Political Leader

"Unbought and unbossed—I won office without selling out!"

Shirley Chisholm was a political anomaly and an absolute paradox to other politicians, including members of her own party and race. She steadfastly defied the system with all her energy and power, refusing to capitulate to machine politics or any other force that attempted to corral her. Shirley was warned that she was committing political suicide in every race she ever ran since she insisted on doing it "my way." She refused to conform or kowtow to any political machine or power. Her resilience in the face of strong adversaries certainly took its toll on this petite but strong voice for honesty and truth, but it never succeeded in changing her. She was so proud of her success in the face of the establishment that she titled her 1970 autobiography, *Unbought and Unbossed*. In this book she proudly contended, "I won public office without selling out to anyone."

Presidential Bid

Chisholm was the first female and first black ever to run for the office of president of the United States, in 1972. She recognized her renegade nature when she wrote, "I started out as a freak candidate, a kind of political sideshow." Chisholm was always candid with herself and her constituency, which is what made her such a shining star on the university speaking circuit during the turbulent sixties. It was the young, the minorities, and the gay community that were the foundation of her support. The young and rebellious could totally identify with this defiant fighter for the oppressed and little people. She gained much notoriety during the mid-sixties traveling the college circuit and reviling the establishment.

This human dynamo insisted on taking up residence at 1600 Pennsylvania

Avenue in 1972 was simply to make the statement that, "It can be done." It is remarkable, indeed, for a relatively unknown black woman without a law degree, money, socioeconomic status, or party backing to have made such a strong national run for the United States presidency. Without money or backing she resolutely plowed forward against unimaginable odds and adversaries. Will alone drove her. She would not be denied even though she was opposed by every powerful political force in the country. The white-dominated political machines attempted to destroy her, and, as expected, the Southern power brokers did everything in their power to discredit her, but strangely the congressional Black Caucus, Jesse Jackson, Ralph Abernathy, Julian Bond, and Carl Stokes also rejected her. This rejection by her own people hurt Chisholm worst because she was looking for their political and emotional support if for no other reason than to make a philosophical statement to the establishment. They had refused allegiance because of her virulent nonconformity and iconoclastic behavior. They were not sure that she would be controlled and the black males became more of a problem for her than the whites.

Reverse Racism

Despite being ignored by the groups that one would have thought were behind her, this strong-willed woman put together a coalition of blacks, feminists, gays, and other minority groups who succeeded in getting her twenty-four delegates in the primaries. Chisholm desperately wanted to show that minorities could command power in national politics. But her inability to get blacks to support her platform or candidacy destroyed any chances of making that statement. Furious with black males, she wrote, "They are prisoners of their traditional attitudes and some of them are just plain jealous." She went further, saying, "If anyone thinks white men are sexists, let them check out black men sometime." Not playing the game had cost her dearly within her own ethnic group. She would blame the good ole boy clubs saying, "Of my two handicaps, being female put many more obstacles in my path than being black."

Teacher Turned Politician

Shirley Chisholm was intellectually a teacher and emotionally a politician. She craved the chance to make a philosophical statement on freedom and equality, and politics was the only venue where a philosophical intellectual could be heard. She dedicated her life to gaining freedom of opportunity for the underprivileged and for those blacks willing to work their way out of the inner city. She would become a model for anyone from a poor neighborhood who dared buck the system and achieve prominence. And she did so at age forty, further evidence that Horatio Alger opportunities still exist in America.

As a politician this visionary was able to break down many barriers and make inroads into arenas that no other black female had dared to attempt. When she arrived in Congress as a freshman legislator, the powers that be placed her on the Agriculture Committee, but this strong-willed and irascible personality refused to accept such a ludicrous assignment, telling House powerhouse Wilbur Mills that there were few agricultural problems in Brooklyn, but many social problems. She told House Speaker John McCormack, "I vehemently object to my committee assignment. . . . I think it would be hard to imagine an assignment that is less relevant to my background or to the needs of the predominantly black and Puerto Rican people who elected me, many of whom are unemployed, hungry, and badly housed, than the one I was given."

Chisholm spent her time in Congress as a fearless supporter of justice for the average working person regardless of race, creed, or religion, which enabled her to be elected to two terms in the New York Legislature followed by seven as a congresswoman representing the twelfth congressional district in Brooklyn. She quit to go back to her first love, teaching, in 1983, and was appointed ambassador to Jamaica in 1993 by newly elected President Bill Clinton. This was her reward for many years of dedicated service to the Democratic party.

Shirley Chisholm is an ideal role model for anyone desirous of achieving great success even thought they are the products of a black inner city. This petite but tenacious woman grew up in the Bedford-Stuyvesant district of Brooklyn and worked her way through college and graduate school with a dedication to self-improvement and success that is inspirational. She then made a dramatic impact on the world of politics, changing forever the idea that females or minorities without money, cultural status, or a Mensa IQ could not make it to the top. Chisholm's creative genius was due to her will, temerity, and tenacity, which she adroitly used to overcome the huge obstacles she confronted on the road to fulfilling her childhood dreams. Those traits were born of an intransigent "will" that became the cornerstone of her great resolve. Chisholm has received worldwide acclaim for her many achievements and been awarded many honorary degrees. Her consummate success in life should be a model for the poor and disadvantaged everywhere.

Innovative Contributions

This unassuming school teacher was an elementary school teacher in 1960. Chisholm taught in Harlem but was not satisfied with the politics of her black neighborhoods, where white political machines controlled black lives and opportunities. She decided to do something other than just talk and became an avid and passionate political activist. This interest propelled her into the leadership of the Unity Democratic Club in Brooklyn, where she was instrumental in the overthrow of the seventeenth assembly district political machine that had dominated elections in Brooklyn for decades. You either paid off the machine or were unable to play the game. You joined the power elite and blindly followed their rules or died a political death. One had to pay homage to city hall or resign oneself to never participate in local, state, or national politics which stifled all change other than that subscribed to by the corrupt, powerful, white reigning machine.

Such a system infuriated this petite woman, who was intent on providing new opportunities for her people. Her Unity Democratic Club failed miserably at first but started making gradual inroads into the power structure and by 1964 had gained enough grassroots strength to elect Tom Jones to the New York legislature. Jones was then appointed to the judiciary by the manipulating political powers, who attempted to place their own man in his place. Chisholm would not be defeated and decided to campaign for the vacant assembly seat herself. She won it handily. This was her baptism of fire into politics and proved to her that one could buck the system and win. Chisholm also clearly demonstrated that a black female schoolteacher with few credentials for political leadership could challenge the system and win. Even more important, she had shown that the "machine" could be beaten with little more than moxie, common sense, hard work, and an indomitable willpower.

Personal History

Shirley Anita St. Hill was born in Brooklyn, New York, on November, 20, 1924. She was the firstborn daughter of Charles St. Hill of Guyana and Ruby Seale of Barbados. At age three she and her two younger sisters, Muriel and Odessa, were sent to Barbados to live with their maternal grandmother, Emily Seale. This proved to be a valuable experience, where Chisholm learned a new culture highly influenced by Great Britain where self-sufficiency is important to development. She was driven to learn and said in her autobiography, "I learned to read and write before I was five." Later she would write, "I have always believed that many teachers underestimate the powers of children." Chisholm believes that children have enormous untapped potential.

Chisholm wrote that her early training in Barbados was instrumental to much of her later success in life. She spent seven years in Barbados, where she became a by-product of the British authoritarian school system and an agrarian work ethic. These traits are what would cause less motivated New Yorkers to label her and her fellow West Indians "black Jews." The agrarian work ethic stuck, as did the highly structured schooling, of which she would write, "Years later I would know what an important gift my parents had given me by seeing to it that I had my early education in the strict traditional, British-style schools. . . . If I speak and write easily now, that early education is the reason."

The family moved one time while they were in Barbados but life was far slower than the frenetic New York life that Chisholm had left. It was slow and deliberate, and she grew to love the balmy island in the South Atlantic, but her parents in New York decided it was time to reunite the family and the children returned to Brooklyn in March 1934, during the height of the Great Depression. Shirley almost froze to death that first winter, when the only heat available in their little apartment was from the kitchen stove. The family would move two more times between Chisholm's return and her entry into high school. They finally ended up in the highly ethnic Bedford-Stuyvesant area, which became a notorious crime area in subsequent years. Chisholm's friends and schoolmates were a diverse mixture of Jews, blacks, Puerto Ricans, and Italian immigrants. There were no majorities, only minorities, but they were not aware of such labels, as they were all accepting of being different as a way of life.

As the oldest child in their close-knit family, Chisholm was given a great deal of responsibility for watching over her younger sisters. She was still a child but was responsible for grocery shopping, picking up her sisters from school, watching over them, and fixing their lunch. She was sent to the store alone and many times was rescued by a policeman when she would get lost in a city that changed daily—quite unlike Barbados, where nothing ever changed. Susan Brownmiller wrote, "How could a store in Brooklyn be there one week and gone the next? Easy, during the Depression in New York City, where change was the order of the day." With both parents working Shirley was given an inordinate amount of responsibility and her latchkey (the term was coined from the New York City Depression children who had apartment keys hanging around their necks) environment instilled in her the freedom, temerity, resilience, and self-sufficiency that such children learn from being alone and responsible for their own welfare. According to her younger sisters, Chisholm was a strict disciplinarian.

Chisholm's father worked in a factory and was a voracious reader and an amateur political philosopher who was well steeped in the teachings of Marcus Garvey. He had an enormous influence on his oldest child, telling her, "If it's the last thing I do, my girls are going to get a good education so they can do better in life than I did." Chisholm idolized her father and later wrote, "We had always been the closest." She bought into his "black is beautiful" ideology long before it became popular in the sixties. Her mother was a domestic seamstress who had a profound affect on Shirley since she was dedicated to fashioning them into renaissance women with strong self-images. During the middle of the Depression there was barely money for food but the family had a piano and there was never any question that all of the girls would become educated and successful.

Early Role Models

An overachiever, Chisholm became a voracious reader like her father. She often read a book a night throughout her school years. During her childhood she became fascinated with American history and was inspired by many of the female political leaders of the time. Three of these women had a profound influence on the young Shirley Chisholm. They became her fantasy heroes. The three—Harriet Tubman, Susan B. Anthony, and Mary McLeod Bethune—were all highly assertive and driven fighters for female equality and freedom. Her absolute favorite was Harriet Tubman, a diminutive black woman and escaped slave who risked her life bringing slaves North prior to the Civil War. Tubman's code name was "Moses" and many newspapers wrote editorials about her being a man since no woman could be so daring. Chisholm totally identified with the renegade and resilient Tubman and ultimately fashioned much of her own life after this woman who had such an indomitable will to power.

Education

Chisholm was an excellent and overachieving student and graduated from Brooklyn's All Girls High School in 1942. She led a very ascetic life, however, due to the Victorian rules set down by her very strict and overprotective parents. She never had a date in high school or in college, as her mother thought it would detract from her studies and was not conducive to success in life. Sublimating her energies, Chisholm graduated with honors and was offered academic scholarships to Vassar, Barnard, Hofstra, and Oberlin. Finances dictated that she enroll at Brooklyn College, where she graduated cum laude in 1946, majoring in psychology and sociology while minoring in Spanish.

At Brooklyn College Chisholm decided to become a teacher. She joined the Harriet Tubman Society in her sophomore year since sororities were off-limits to blacks at the time. This social activism experience had a powerful impact on her as she became highly sensitized to "black consciousness." She also joined the Debating Society and became an instant success. Her strong intuitive sense and verbal proficiency impressed Professor Louis Warsoff, who become her mentor during her school years. He convinced her that "white people were not really different from me" and that we should be treated equally if we were equal.

Warsoff was blind and white. He was a political science professor at Columbia who not only became her favorite teacher but was her biggest admirer. He asked her, "I wonder if you've ever thought of going into politics. . . . I happen to think you're a natural for it. I think you might be able to make quite a contribution in the political field." Surprised at such praise and support, Chisholm responded, "Proffy, you forget two things. I'm black, and I'm a woman." After further reflection, and some years later, she would take his sage advice and follow the career path of her two female role models who had made such a political contribution to society—Harriet Tubman and Susan B. Anthony.

Chisholm received her B.S. from Brooklyn College in 1946 at age twenty-one. She still looked seventeen and consequently was unable to get a teaching position because she looked so young. After many months of trying she finally was put on at Mount Calvary Child Care Center in Harlem. With a perpetual interest in pursuing knowledge and education, she immediately enrolled in Columbia night school to seek her master's degree in childhood education, which she finally received in 1952. While at Columbia Shirley met Conrad Chisholm, who was a private detective for a security company, and they married that same year. Conrad attempted to change Shirley from her workaholic nature, but it proved futile and he finally gave up trying and grew content with her "organized mania." He said, "I agreed to work behind the scenes and let her be the star in our family."

Professional History

The little warrior became involved in politics when she first met her political mentor Mac Holder. She helped him elect Lewis Flagg, a black lawyer, to a municipal judgeship in 1953. It was considered an unprecedented upset. In 1958 she and Holder had a falling out when her mentor created the Bedford-Stuyvesant Political League and the two fought over its presidency. He proved the stronger and won it. Chisholm dropped out of politics for two years. By 1960 Chisholm returned to help form the Unity Democratic Club. This political action group was successful in electing Tom Jones to the state assembly. When Jones was appointed to the bench, Chisholm ignored opposing forces and ran for his seat against the machine. She won the election despite intense male opposition to a female running for what was presumed to be a male office. Chisholm had resolved her differences with Holder and he became her campaign manager, press agent, and administrative manager.

During the race for the New York State Assembly, chauvinist adversaries decided to use gender as a campaign issue. They claimed that a female would make emotional decisions and should stay home and cook for her husband. The gender issue only made Shirley more motivated to defeat the machine and she responded by rallying women to her cause. She said, "When someone tries to use my sex against me, I delight in being able to turn the tables on him." Her adversaries used arguments like, "Women talk too much . . . are illogical and take everything too seriously. This isn't a game for women." One male confronted her while campaigning and told her, "You ought to be home, not out here politicking." Chisholm wrote, "They underestimated me, and they underestimated the women like me," who helped her to win the race. Chisholm went to the PTAs and the women's groups and elicited the help of those whose husbands were against her. Chisholm demonstrated that black women are often the strength in unstable communities and organized these women and they in turn helped her defeat her male opponent.

When Chisholm entered the New York State House of Representatives in Albany, she was forty years old. But she was just getting started as a force in politics. During her four years in Albany her simple but honest approach to government caused her to vote her conscience and follow her gut feel for what was right. This was not the way of the political animals who become part of the system or fail to stay in office. Her blatant honesty and integrity would cost her much turmoil and heartache throughout her years in office, but she always refused to capitulate to the political pressures. She was the only black female in the New York State Legislature in 1964 and it proved to be a boon since her uniqueness made her highly visible to the media. The Associated Press called her and Percy Sutton "two of the most militant and effective black members of the Assembly."

Realignment of the United States congressional districts by the Supreme Court during the mid-sixties created a primarily black twelfth congressional district. Chisholm became the favorite daughter of the citizens committee to run for this new office and she became a whirlwind of activity. Alan Duckworth said in *Notable Black Women,* "She was chosen for her independent and indomitable spirit." Chisholm's opposition in the primary was party machine candidate William Thompson. She needed a miracle, but her old mentor Mac Holder once again came to the rescue and promised her, "I'm going to organize the campaign and sell you." And sell he did despite the impossible odds of electing someone to the United States Congress without money, a law degree, or political influence.

Chisholm wrote, "I didn't have the money for a conventional campaign. I had to make up for it with hard work." She won the Democratic primary by one thousand votes despite having major surgery right in the middle of the campaign. Her Republican opponent was James Farmer, a national chairman of the Congress on Racial Equality, and he was well staffed and financed. Just months prior to the election Chisholm was diagnosed with a massive tumor requiring surgery immediately. Chisholm resolutely refused. She told her doctor, "I am running for Congress and don't have the time for it." When her husband and doctor insisted that her life was at stake, she agreed but still refused to be sidetracked. After the surgery she immediately resumed work on the campaign and went back out on the street despite her doctor's orders to the contrary. Her doctor said of her iron will and resolve, "Any other woman would have collapsed." This dynamo once again turned to the female electorate to gain support, since her opponent attempted to use her gender as a weapon in the race. She won the election with 34,885 votes against Farmer's 13,777 and was off to Washington as the first black congresswoman in history.

An Innovative Renegade

Shirley began her first term with rebelliousness and controversy. As mentioned, the leaders of the House treated her like any other freshman congresswoman, and placed her on a meaningless subcommittee dealing with forestry. This infuriated Chisholm, who was told to "just be a good soldier and wait your turn." Conformity and patience were not her style. She had waited for years to be in a position to help her people and to influence national legislation that would make women and blacks equal in all ways. She told Speaker John McCormack to place her on a committee where she could be of some service to her black and Puerto Rican constituency. She said, "It does not make sense to put a black woman representative on a subcommittee dealing with forestry" and proved her mettle by telling these men in a semithreatening manner, "I will do what I have to, regardless of the consequences." With the feminist movement in full bloom her moxie worked and they capitulated by placing her on the Veterans committee. She cynically quipped about the change, "There are a lot more veterans in my district than there are trees." Within three years she won her stripes and was elevated to the prestigious

Education and Labor Committee, which proved providential for both her district and the country. Even this victory had strings attached, however, since Chisholm was forced into what politicians refer to as "strange bedfellows." She had supported Hale Boggs of Louisiana on one of his important issues and he in turn used his enormous influence to have her placed on the Education Committee.

Presidential Candidate

By this time, 1972, Chisholm was on a roll and decided to take a shot at the highest office in the land. This coincided with her larger plan of making a national impact while in Washington as a social activist with the issues of change, equality, freedom, and social acceptance for all. Her plea was, "I am your instrument for change. . . . Give your vote to me. I belong to you." Desperately lacking in funds, Shirley literally and figuratively ran the race on her American Express Card. The campaign ended up costing a total of $300,000, much of which was paid out of her personal checkbook. It actually contributed to her insolvency and ultimately to the break up of her marriage (her husband, Conrad, had been her campaign manager and turned out to be a terrible financial manager). Conrad's incompetent management of the campaign funds led to her being investigated for violation of campaign fund laws, which was overturned a few years later.

At the Democratic National Convention held in Miami during the summer of 1972 Chisholm garnered 151 votes, which she would later release to Hubert Humphrey. She had run a good race considering her lack of funds and support and felt the campaign was worth the effort. She said, "What I hope most is that now there will be others who will feel themselves as capable of running for high office as any wealthy good-looking white male." This valiant soldier's effort had broken the ground and set the stage for Jesse Jackson's Rainbow Coalition candidacy in 1984 and 1988. Newark Mayor Sharpe James said, "If there had been no Shirley Chisholm, there would have been no 'Run, Jesse, Run' in 1984 and no 'Win, Jesse, Win' in 1988."

By 1977 Shirley Chisholm had moved up the power ladder and was appointed to the powerful House Rules Committee and then elected secretary of the Democratic Caucus. She had learned to operate within the system although she would never be seen as someone who was predictable in her voting. During her first two years she backed the party on only 97 of 127 bills. In 1979 and 1980 she voted the party line on 154 of 163 bills. But this resilient and iconoclastic woman always said her piece if she did not agree with the content. Chisholm divorced her husband of twenty years and married a black New York businessman, Arthur Hardwick, Jr., in the spring of 1977.

Back to Teaching

When her new husband was nearly killed in a bad car accident in 1979, Chisholm reevaluated her priorities. She started reviewing career opportunities at various colleges around the nation. By 1982 she had made up her mind to return to the teaching profession that she loved with a passion, intending to give sage guidance to the nation's youth on political philosophy. She announced her retirement as a congresswoman in February 1982 and embarked on a teaching career as a professor at Mount Holyoke College in the spring session of 1983. She taught a course on "Congress, Power, Politics, and Policy." She moved on to a teaching assignment at Atlanta's Spelman College. In 1987 Arthur Hardwick died unexpectedly and Chisholm retired from teaching. She once again became caught up in the passion of a presidential race in 1988 and assisted Jesse Jackson in his unsuccessful run for the Oval Office. During this period she helped organize the National Political Congress for Black Women and served as its first president. Bill Clinton recognized her many years of dedicated service to the Democratic party and appointed her ambassador to Jamaica in 1993, a position she still holds.

What Makes Shirley Tick?

Shirley Chisholm was a maverick politician who got to the top by daring to challenge the establishment and relying on her indomitable will in going for the gold. She was a human dynamo who refused to be defeated, driven by an insatiable desire to show that one could win without having to capitulate to male power brokers. This petite workaholic was never motivated to become a traditional wife and mother. She spent most of her life fighting the "good ole boy network" to insure equality for women and blacks. Her battles were not in vain. Shirley Chisholm has made the world an easier place for both because of her need to fight the establishment and traditional roles for women and minorities. Nonconformity is her most dominant personal characteristic although she is probably best known for her energy, a strong work ethic, and integrity. This dynamo was an extrovert and intuitive visionary—a superb role model for young inner-city females.

Mythological Hero Mentors

Shirley emulated her father's political philosophy that had been nurtured from Marcus Garvey's "black is beautiful" philosophy. This ideological background helped hone her interest in social activism, which ultimately led to her political posture on most major issues. She was in fact the spokesman for her father's dreams of social activism and he and his own hero Marcus Garvey became the source of many of this visionary's most deep-seated beliefs.

Chisholm's mythical heroes came from books about great female leaders who were unafraid to violate the existing norms of society. She fell in love with these fantasy stories of greatness and fashioned her own image in their likeness. As a teenager she became inspired by Harriet Tubman, Susan B. Anthony, and Mary McLeod Bethune. Tubman's gutsy creation of what became known as the "Underground Railroad" inspired Chisholm as did Anthony's fight for female equality and the cause of antislavery. Susan Brownmiller offers some insight into Chisholm's early fantasies over these heroine mentors: "It made her dizzy to think of such powerful, independent women who by organization, speeches, and courageous action overcame fearful odds and helped to change the course of events of the nation."

Insecurity Breeds Greatness

Being black and female was a constant source of irritation for Chisholm as it permeated her writings and speeches like no other topic. It was the basis of some fundamental insecurities in Chisholm that she refused to acknowledge, turning them into a motivation for achievement. Chisholm saw her gender and color as accidents of birth, limitations she was driven to overcome. Her feelings on her gender and color were constantly reinforced during her school years. Once in the midst of a heated argument a boy told her "Negroes don't go to college" and "Girls never do anything. They just become housewives. When I grow up I can be the president of the United States."Young Shirley shot back, "This girl is going to do something when she grows up."

Metamorphoses

Chisholm experienced many crises during her life. Her earliest ones occurred as a result of her being the eldest child in her family and continually finding herself lost on the streets of Brooklyn. She would be brought home by the neighborhood policeman but the experience molded her with the knowledge that she could go to strange places and survive the experience, which tends to transform a child from being "security-based" to "risk taking."

Chisholm's parents would not allow her to date as a teen. Lacking in experiences of the heart almost proved disastrous during her early twenties when she met and fell in love with a sophisticated Jamaican living in the United States. He turned out to be married with a family in Jamaica but had proposed to her. When he was deported on illegal immigration charges, the truth came out. It almost destroyed Chisholm, who said, "I couldn't sleep or eat. I became a skeleton. I considered suicide." She emerged from the debacle and became even more determined to become an advocate for integrity and social change.

Crisis entered her life just as she was considering running for the U.S. Congress. First her father died unexpectedly and she said, "I collapsed screaming." He was her everything and his death had a terrible impact on her, but Chisholm became even more determined to fulfill his dreams for her as a politician. Shortly after recovering from this tragedy she decided to run for Congress but became seriously ill during the campaign with the previously mentioned tumor. When told she could no longer campaign she told the doctor, "Look Doc, I've had it for two years. Can't I carry it a little longer, until after November?" The doctor and her husband forced her to have the operation and even then the resilient Chisholm insisted on working until the doctor had to anesthetize her to keep her in bed. Staring mortality in the face, this near-death experience inspired her to a herculean effort and Chisholm won the election handily.

Charisma

Chisholm was an inspirational speaker who could bring audiences to tears. She discovered this talent while on the debating team in college and wrote, "I can really persuade people when I speak." Much of her charismatic charm was due to her simple honesty. She spoke to people in simple but honest terms that they could understand and never resorted to what she called "jiving" in her book *The Good Fight*. She wrote, "I never tailor what I say . . . they can tell that I'm not jiving." She disdained using notes to make speeches, including her address to the 1972 Democratic Convention in Miami. Chisholm's strength is an unabashed integrity and the ability to communicate it through the power of speech. Her disciples would become so stimulated they were often willing to follow her anywhere.

Competitiveness

Chisholm's campaign slogans were "I'm Fighting Shirley Chisholm" and "Join Me on the Chisholm Trail," both testimony to her competitive spirit. She never avoided any confrontation, whether it was politically correct or not. Aggressiveness and assertiveness defined her. She was able to tap into her male qualities like few females and use the competitive aggression to win her fights. During the turbulent sixties this dynamo became a dove and fought against the Vietnam War effort when such a stance was not politically correct. The college students were against the war but not United States congressmen. Chisholm never let such things deter her and she became the darling of the university set. She supported a woman's right to abortion during the sixties and attracted supporters because they knew she would never back off from what she believed in. They always knew where she stood on any issue and that she would fight to her death rather than capitulate.

Confidence

Optimism permeated Shirley Chisholm from her days as a teacher into the United States Congress. She always believed she could succeed in any venture and behaved in that positive fashion. She knew this about herself and wrote in her autobiography, "I am not often charged with false modesty." She loved to tell students to follow their dreams and never listen to the pessimists and skeptics who can find something wrong in anything. At her Mount Holyoke retirement speech in 1987 she advised students to "pay absolutely no attention to doomsday criers around you." She implored them to be "open" and "enthusiastic even when things look dark."

By fantasizing about great heroes she had molded her own psyche with an optimistic vision of the possible in life. Tubman, Bethune, and Anthony had instilled her with an awesome self-confidence that would not be denied. Chisholm was convinced that a person should have the right to gravitate to whatever level their talents allowed despite the accidents of their birth. This proved to be her cause in life and she was so confident that she was right that she was able to overcome unbelievable obstacles to reach the top. Chisholm was able to achieve more with less than most of her male and white adversaries, who always felt she would have been more useful staying in the kitchen.

Passion and Drive

At Brooklyn College Shirley formed an organization called IPOTHIA—In Pursuit of the Highest in All. This is testimony to her passionate need to be the very best she could be. When diagnosed with the tumor in the middle of campaigning for Congress she resorted to her psychic energy and refused to let herself become bedridden like ordinary mortals. On leaving the hospital she said, "Look, the stitches aren't in my mouth, I'm going out." She told her husband, "You walk in front so if I fall, I'll fall on you." Her doctor was so miffed he told her, "If anything happens to you, don't call me." Her resilience paid off as it did in everything she attempted. Her passion and intransigent drive to overachieve and self-actualize are at the root of Shirley Chisholm's great success in life.

Hypomania

Shirley Chisholm had all the qualities of Type A personalities who see their self-worth inextricably tied up in their success. A workaholic, she was always in a hurry, slept little, and was impatient with those who were not. During her first campaign she said she almost worked herself to death to win the seat in the New York Assembly. She said, "I almost killed myself because I wanted to show the machine that a little black woman was going to beat it." She wrote in *Unbought and Unbossed*, "I didn't have the money for a conventional congressional campaign: I had to make up for it with hard work." A manic work ethic was a critically important vehicle that led this visionary from being a local Democratic Club supporter into the United States Congress. Hard work separated her from the pack.

Independence

Shirley Chisholm had the courage of her convictions and defied the machine politicians and establishment in making her mark in the world. From the very beginning she refused to conform to the "good ole boy" political system, a stance that became her political platform. Susan Brownmiller characterized Chisholm as "true grit" for her renegade nature. Shirley named her book *Unbought and Unbossed* in an attempt to politely let the world know that politicians are seldom "unbought" or "unbossed"—but Shirley Chisholm was above and beyond such submissive behavior. One congressional leader said, "Shirley is a nice person, but she doesn't play by the rules."

Because of such a nonconformist attitude congressmen labeled her "the troublemaking maverick" who "bucked the system." They would say, "There is that little black matriarch who goes around messing things up." She wrote, "I horrify them," but never allowed their nicknames or attitudes to dissuade her from pursuing her own agenda. This renegade was proud of always breaking the rules of the antiquated "ole boys club" and refused to vote for anything but that which fit her sense of values, which is not the way to succeed in Washington. Even her 1972 run for the presidency was made "to shake up our system." The old-line politicians hated her while the dissenting students loved her because of her unpopular anti-Vietnam and prochoice stances. Chisholm identified with minorities of all kinds due to her "femaleness" and "blackness." Independence defined her platform.

Temerity

Susan Brownmiller called Chisholm a "fearless rebel" due to her willingness to jump into any fray, some of which had the potential to destroy her political career. Such considerations never affected Chisholm's decisions, which is what made her unique as a politician. She had the risk-taking mentality of the entrepreneur, not the politician, infamous for avoiding all risk. Not so with Shirley Chisholm, who probably understood that the greatest risk is often the one not taken and that those who take the bigger risks are those who enjoy the biggest victories. Only big challenges result in big wins and this adventuresome spirit was willing to bet the farm in politics.

Tenacity

Testimony to Chisholm's perseverance was her decision to live in different Brooklyn apartment complexes for much of her adult life in order that the machine politicians could not change the lines of the voting district to remove her from office. She became known as a "persistent rabblerouser" by her adversaries, who knew she would never give up on any important program. When she was humiliated by male politicians, many of her own race, during the 1972 presidential campaign, she wrote, "I can handle them. That's been the story of my life." Chisholm finally had had enough and told them, "Get off my back!" as reported by the *Chicago Tribune.* The presidential race was the culmination of Chisholm's philosophical need for social action. She told one writer, "I do not want to be remembered as the first woman who happened to be black and make a serious bid for the presidency. I'd like to be known as a catalyst for change, a woman who had the determination and [a] woman who had the perseverance to fight on behalf of the female population and the black population."

Vision

Shirley Chisholm is a political visionary who was always looking at the possibilities and opportunities for her race and gender through the legislative process. She is a true Promethean spirit who was an architect for change in the world. When she backed John Lindsay for mayor of New York City, her friends and associates said she had committed "political suicide." He had been a turncoat to his own party and now she was backing him, to the chagrin of her Democratic supporters. A pragmatic visionary, she considered not the party but the man and was convinced Lindsay was the best man for the job. She turned out to be intuitive when Lindsay won the mayoral job and they became close political allies for years until she opposed him in the 1972 presidential race. Quality and the possibilities were far more important to this woman than quantity and the status quo. These are the traits of a creative visionary.

Will to Power

Shirley Chisholm became a national figure by sheer force of her indomitable will. She was certainly not born with any positional pedigree, such as the Kennedys, who appear to be preordained for Congress. This indomitable spirit relied on an internal drive and will to work her way out of Bedford-Stuyvesant to the regal parlors of Washington, D.C. In her second book, *The Good Fight* (1973), Chisholm admitted, "I ran for the Presidency, despite hopeless odds, to demonstrate *sheer will* and refusal to accept the status quo." An introspective woman, Chisholm was telling the world that "will" was a critical factor in her success. A further example was the time she became exasperated with Gloria Steinem, who would not make up her mind between her candidacy and George McGovern's. She told Steinem "to stop equivocating between me and George." Chisholm very candidly told Gloria to make a choice, even if it was McGovern, since she was unable to deal with not knowing who was in her corner.

Summary

Newark Mayor Sharpe James said there would never have been a "Run, Jesse, Run" had there not been a Shirley Chisholm in the 1972 election. That is just a part of the magnificent heritage left by this woman who grew up with an insatiable need to be somebody. This self-made woman has been the recipient of numerous awards and honors, a few of which include winning the Clairol 1973 "Woman of the Year" Award for Outstanding Achievement in Public Affairs. Another was being voted one of the Gallup Poll's ten most-admired women in the world for three straight years during the early seventies. Chisholm is the recipient of more than a dozen honorary doctorates from many credible educational institutions including North Carolina Central University (1969), Wilmington College (1970), LaSalle College (1971), Pratt Institute (1972), Kenyon College (1973), Aquinas College (1974), Smith College (1975), Mount Holyoke College (1981), and Spelman College (1982).

After Chisholm retired from Congress in 1983 she spent her time spreading her gospel of integrity with an emphasis on freedom of expression and achievement for either gender and all races. This led her to found the National Women's Political Caucus, which kept her in the limelight and active until Bill Clinton rewarded her for years of dedicated service to the Democratic party by naming her ambassador to Jamaica in 1993.

This pioneering visionary prefers to be remembered more for her many contributions to female and black equality than to having been the first black congresswoman in the United States. Based on her many accomplishments, her wish will surely be granted. This product of the Great Depression and one of America's most infamous inner-city ghettos, this petite bundle of energy, was successful in overcoming numerous hostile adversaries, overt chauvinism, and rampant bigotry to catch the brass ring. Shirley Chisholm is living proof that a resilient willpower can overcome all else, professionally and personally. By any standard Shirley Chisholm is a creative genius who helped change the world for the better by becoming the quintessential role model for black women everywhere.

SHIRLEY CHISHOLM
Promethean Temperament (NT)
First Black Female Congresswoman
born November 20, 1924, Brooklyn, New York

Dominant trait: Strong-willed nonconformist with high energy and integrity
Motto: "Unbought and Unbossed" campaign slogan and book title
Religion: Methodist
Philosophy: "Men always underestimate women"; "My role is that of a catalyst"
Politics: Democratic congresswoman
Nickname: "Fighting Shirley Chisholm"; "Hard-to-Handle Chisholm"
Creation/innovation: First black woman elected to U.S. Congress, 1968, or to run for president, 1972
Successes: N.Y. State assemblywoman, 1964; U.S. congresswoman, 1968; ambassador to Jamaica, 1993
Vices/hobbies: Voracious reader
Romantic liaisons: Never had a date in high school or college; 5-year romance with married man and two marriages
Self-description: "I am a pragmatist"; "My significance is that I won public office without selling out"

Birth order: Firstborn of Charles St. Hill and Ruby Seale; sisters Odessa, Muriel, Selma
Parental influence: Grandmother in Barbados instilled work ethic as "black Jews"; father's political ideology
Early transience: Six moves prior to high school between Brooklyn and Barbados
Parents' occupations: Father a factory laborer, mother a domestic seamstress
Role models: Mother, father, Harriet Tubman, Susan B. Anthony, Mary McLeod Bethune, Eleanor Roosevelt
Hero mentors: Father, Marcus Garvey, blind professor Louis Warsoff, politician Mac Holder
Formal education: All Girls High School, 1942; Brooklyn College Education cum laude, 1946; Columbia M.A., 1952
Life crises: Deportation of Jamaican fiancé; BSPL political fight; tumor during campaign inspired her to victory
Metamorphoses: Seeing Ms. Bethune with Roosevelts moved her to belief that blacks could achieve greatness

---

Charismatic: "Charming congresswoman"
Competitive: "I do my own thing"; "I Am Fighting Shirley Chisholm—Unbought and Unbossed" campaign slogan
Hypomanic: A woman in a hurry who never had time to have a family; slept little in drive to succeed
Independent rebel: "Troublemaking maverick" who bucked the system and "broke the rules"
Indomitable "will": Voted her mind despite controversy; "I horrify them, they never could predict what I would do"
Intuitive vision: A visionary who violated all logic in backing Republican John Lindsay and won
Drive: Once postponed tumor operation to campaign; her doctor said, "Anyone else would have collapsed"
Risk-taker: Temerity and conviction seldom found in females, let alone politicos, who always follow rules or die
Self-confident: "I am not often charged with false modesty"; power was integrity, belief, and strong sense of self
Tenacious: Persevered by constantly moving residences to maintain district integrity
Workaholic: "I almost killed myself. I wanted to show the machine that a little black woman was going to beat it"
Honors: Gallup's 1973 woman of the year and one of the ten most-admired women in the world for three years

8

Bill Cosby—Perfectionist

Preeminent Comedian and Innovator of TV Sitcoms

"Strive for excellence. . . . Comedy with roots in truth."

Bill Cosby grew up in the North Philadelphia projects known disparagingly as "The Jungle" because of its likeness to survival in mid-Africa. From that humble beginning he has become America's wealthiest black according to *Forbes* magazine in 1993, which claimed he had a net worth of $315 million. Oprah Winfrey has since passed him as America's wealthiest black, just as he had replaced Reginald Lewis after Lewis's death in 1993. *Forbes* also named Cosby the top-earning entertainer in the United States in 1991 and 1992, another title he has since lost to Winfrey. Some success for a man who says he tells jokes only because "I wanted to be accepted." While working as a bartender to finance his way through Temple University, he found that he always got bigger tips when he told better jokes, which motivated him to become ever funnier. During this time Cosby began working on his street humor and ever-broadening his repertoire of off-the-wall stories in order to pay the rent. His humor became so bizarre and weird the management offered this ex-jock bartender with the graphic imagination an opportunity to substitute for the regular comedian. The rest is history.

Cosby had the ability to tell stories of childhood debacles that most people could relate to as they had experienced many of the same stupid situations. His ability to relate to the audience was his great appeal during those bar comedy days. Spoofing about street football huddles where the kid is asked to run to the fireplug, turn right, hide behind the Chevy, and catch the ball before getting hit by the bus is classic Cosby. It was his formula for success prior to revolutionizing the family situation comedy. After paying his dues in the Philadelphia and Greenwich Village coffee houses, Cosby became an overnight sensation on the cabaret circuit, appearing at the Hungry I in San Francisco and Mr. Lucky's in Chicago. Cosby had a knack for transforming simple childhood experiences like "stickball," "spin the bottle," and "God's conversations with Noah" into "ludicrous and absurdly in-congruous" stories that broke up early sixties audiences.

Weird Harold and Fat Albert were actual reincarnations of Cosby's childhood on the streets of North Philadelphia. He was a street kid whose mother worked and he enjoyed the freedom that helped form his survival techniques but also molded his vivid imagination of street shenanigans. Cosby's genius was a unique ability to verbalize "vivid imagery" as if it were reenacted right there on stage. Cosby was able to transform negative experiences into fun-loving episodes that had a positive connotation. He was able make the complex simple through words and facial expression, endowing him with the reputation as the Electronic Twain. Marrying fantasy with schtick became Cosby's tool for success and led to great fame and a vast fortune. Weird Harold and Fat Albert became the mythical heroes from his vivid imagination, which he parlayed into a fortune.

A Successful Humorist

Cosby's first major success was a starring role in "I Spy," followed shortly by his first Cosby TV special and millions in record sales. Five books (26 million sold in hardback alone), twelve movies, countless nightclub appearances, Saturday morning cartoons, "The Cosby Show," and a nonstop cabaret tour through the years made Bill Cosby into a household name throughout America. He even utilized his two characters Weird Harold and Fat Albert in qualifying for master's and doctoral degrees from the University of Massachusetts during the height of his popularity. Not a bad payback for an apprenticeship in the Jungle projects of North Philadelphia where he learned to use humor to avoid punishment as a compulsive prankster.

Cosby's success has been nothing short of extraordinary. In his first show, "I Spy," Cosby was a smash hit, which catapulted him into the venues where he could showcase his real talent. He was the first black to play a nonstereotypical role and his partner, Robert Culp, became one of his best friends, joking that his part was that of the intellectual and it should have been Cosby's, since he saw Cosby as far smarter. The 1964 show received great acclaim and he was extolled in *Daily Variety* as "TV's Jackie Robinson." Cosby then topped that success by winning eight Grammy Awards for best comedy album from the National Society of Recording Arts and Sciences. Cosby has for years had one of the highest "Q score ratings" (a barometer used to evaluate TV viewership), an achievement he shares with Michael Jordan. Cosby's Jell-O commercials were extraordinarily successful.

In spite of his great success Cosby has remained just plain "Bill" or "Cos" to his millions of fans. The Gallup Poll ran a 1992 poll on the most "regular guy" in America. Cosby was listed as number one, garnering 42 percent of the total votes. When he launched "The Cosby Show" in September 1984 it quickly became the most successful television show in history and had an influence far beyond Cosby's personal success. The show was such a phenomenon that it was able to catapult NBC from the very bottom as the number-three network behind ABC and

CBS to number one. And it took just one year. During the 1985–1986 and 1986–1987 seasons of "The Cosby Show" over 50 percent of viewers watched the show, an achievement that will probably never be equalled. The January 22, 1987, episode was watched by 82 million homes—equivalent to Super Bowl viewership—making it the most-watched TV sitcom in history. "The Cosby Show" was voted the top-rated series for the decade of the eighties. Cosby's biographer, Bill Adler, wrote, "Cosby is one of the all-time greats" and also "the most talented exponent of comedy in the entertainment world."

Innovative Contribution

Bill Cosby was infamous for ignoring the industry experts and pundits who constantly told him he was wrong. These bureaucrats were never able to identify with his innovative approach and were afraid of his black role reversals. "The Cosby Show" was turned down by two networks before NBC picked it up. Their reasoning was that "a family comedy—particularly one featuring a black family—could not succeed on modern television." As usual, the experts were wrong and Cosby was right. He ignored their advice and followed his own vision of what the world wanted to see and hear in comedy and made sure the "family" and the "black roles" in it were nonethnic in nature. Cosby's innovative power was based on his ability to "creatively destroy" the past while developing the new. Few people have that vision or the temerity to see it through to fruition.

Cosby, like anyone who innovates, has had some bombs. But his vision has been on target more times than not. His rating success and financial windfalls are testimony to the correctness of his insights. Cosby not only has been proclaimed the king of family humor by the industry and ratings wars, he has been universally acclaimed as the one person who made black sitcoms viable network fare. Before Cosby, television gurus still preferred taking the safe route and projecting blacks in Amos and Andy roles. None was willing to take the economic gamble until Cosby showed them the way.

In his very first role on network TV Cosby played a role that was previously verboten by the networks. When he portrayed Alexander Scott as Robert Culp's sidekick in the "I Spy" series he was not only portrayed as the equal of Culp, but in many ways as his superior. Scott was depicted as a dashing CIA agent and Rhodes Scholar and tennis pro who spoke seven languages including Chinese. Both Cosby and NBC took considerable flack over such a portrayal but it was pure Cosby that pulled it off. Cosby never talked, acted, or appeared like the black stereotypes most whites envisioned. He was an anomaly and it worked. What is strange is that it was just Cosby playing his normal self as a tennis-playing intellectual. There is a remarkable likeness between Cosby and his "I Spy" character. Cosby was a superb athlete (captain of Temple University's football and track teams), was tested in high school as a "gifted" student, and would ultimately earn his doctorate in childhood education. In addition, Cosby is a world-traveled raconteur who is as daring as any CIA agent in producing and creating comedy for the masses on tape, television, and in the movies. The truth was far closer to reality than the "I Spy" script actually called for and few saw this except Robert Culp, who said, "The character he's playing is very close to the real Bill Cosby. He's taken off all the veils."

The family sitcom is Cosby's innovative contribution to the world of television. And his dedication to portraying blacks in nonsubservient roles is his personal contribution because without Cosby this would have been a long time coming. He pioneered the way for others, which is now acknowledged by the industry. Cosby says of his work, "I'm trying to bring out the similarities in all of us—not the differences." He first accomplished this objective with "I Spy," then with the Cosby specials, by producing the "Electric Company" cartoons featuring Fat Albert and the Cosby Kids, and finally with the award-winning "Cosby Show." This effort proved to be the crowning achievement to his artistic genius where he reversed the stereotypical roles by playing a medical doctor with a lawyer wife where both parents were in the home, employed, and black. By his own admission the show was not a far departure from his own family situation, as both had five kids with the same number of boys and girls with similar names.

Cosby's motto is "Comedy has its roots in truth." This encapsulates his true innovative genius. He showed the way by depicting the irony and ludicrousness common in all our lives and was able to paint vivid mental images in the audience's minds like no one before him. Like all creative geniuses, Cosby was able to make the complex and bizarre seem simple and innocent. He was able to make us all reminisce about disastrous situations that in retrospect can be seen as comical. Cosby liked to say he wanted to portray comedy relative to the "human condition" and not the "black condition." Cosby's lifelong ambition was to educate— to mix humor with metaphor, comedy with knowledge, not unlike his fantasy mentor Mark Twain. He exclaimed, "I want to use this tube to educate," which earned him the nickname "The Electronic Mark Twain." Making people laugh in a learning environment is not any easy task, but Cosby has proved more than equal to the task and has changed the world of situation comedy in the process.

Personal History

Cosby was born in Philadelphia on July 12, 1937, the first child of William Cosby and Anna Hite. He had three younger brothers and one younger sister. His brother James died of rheumatic fever at age six, when young Bill was eight. Cosby's mother was the major influence in his life. She told a reporter, "The only thing I had to give him was plenty of love, and oh, dear God, I gave him all I had. But success comes from within, and Bill was determined to be something." His childhood turned out to be a motivating force to a man who resorted to comedy to survive the dire poverty and escape the denigration of the Philadelphia projects. He and his younger brother James shared the same bed for most of his youth and they worshiped their mother and were scared of their father. Cosby later said, "The word *father* still spells disappointment to my brother and me."

CRISIS TO CREATIVITY

Onstage Cosby liked to joke that he was born the same year and month as Superman and sure enough, he learned to leap over metaphoric tall buildings and in turn brought comedy relief to Metropolitans who could easily identify with his witticisms about life growing up on the street. Cosby's father was a navy steward-turned-welder who disappeared whenever the rent was due, causing Anna Cosby to move the family from apartment to apartment. Cosby's friends commented about how poor the Cosbys were when they saw the eviction notices on the door of their "project" home. The boys referred to their father as the "giant." He was either drunk or absent, which thrust young Bill into the role of substitute father to his three younger brothers. When asked about Christmas, Cosby said "We didn't have enough socks for our feet let alone any spare ones to hang." Cosby sidesteps references to this period in his life, preferring to joke about it, but confides that many aspects are "too painful to even think about." Instead, Cosby created a mythical childhood adorned with laughter and jokes. His younger brother Robert said, "Bill could turn painful situations around and make them funny. You laughed to keep from crying."

Anna Cosby earned her living as a domestic but was strong on authority, education, and nurturing. The family was so poor that they never had a phone, but Anna was a hardworking taskmaster who constantly read to the children from the Bible. It was Mark Twain that Cosby would learn to identify with early in life, but he also escaped into radio serials featuring the Lone Ranger, the Green Hornet, Superman, the Shadow, Jack Benny, Jimmy Durante, and George Burns and Gracie Allen. This was a unique marriage of fantasy heroes and comedy, both of which became indelibly imprinted on Cosby's subconscious imagination.

MYTHICAL ESCAPE

Anna's stories from the Bible and Mark Twain were Cosby's favorites, especially Twain's comical routines of Noah and the Ark and Tom Sawyer's adventures on the Mississippi. Twain's books served as solace for the despicable life in the "Jungle" and Bill came to identify with the master of American humor. He so identified with Twain that he became a clown to mask the true reality of his life. Miss Forchic, a sixth-grade teacher, wrote on his report card, "He would rather be a clown than a student and feels it is his mission to amuse his classmates in and out of school," but added that he was "a boy's boy, an all-around fellow, and he should grow up to do great things." Life in the Philadelphia projects was eased by these Twain stories and it appears they turned out to cause Cosby's phone booth metamorphosis, not unlike Superman's transformation from a reporter to a super-being. He was transformed into a Comedian of Steel by mimicking Twain's river-boat buffoonery—a Krypton power of the mind and spirit.

This visionary escaped into books, becoming a voracious reader, which contributed to his being tested as a gifted student in middle school. He was always in trouble due to swapping textbooks for comic books, which were more to his liking since they had fantasy heroes who won out over the bad guys. His real-life childhood idols were Jackie Robinson and Sugar Ray Robinson, in addition to radio comedians. Even though he had tested as gifted in school, Cosby became known as the class clown rather than for his academic achievements. He was perpetually in trouble for his pranks, but learned to use humor to ease the ensuing punishments. He figured people who were laughing could not be too severe in their retribution. He used this ploy on all authority figures: adults, parents, and teachers.

Cosby acquired his work ethic from his mother. He told the *Los Angeles Times*, "I think one of the most important things to understand is that my mother, as a domestic, worked 12 hours a day, and then she would do the laundry, and cook the meals and serve them and clean them up, and for this she got $7 a day. So 12 hours a day or whatever I do is as easy as eating Jell-O Pudding Pie." Cosby emulated his mother's work ethic by taking his first part-time job at age eight in a local delicatessen. When not in school he was always working or playing street stickball, football, baseball, and basketball. Always the prankster, he once painted butterflies on his father's underwear and another time placed a frog in his milk to get a laugh. He liked to joke that as a kid he was a member of the Asphalt Athletic Club. He said, "When I was a kid I always used to pay attention to things that other people didn't even think about. I'd remember funny happenings, just trivial things, and then tell stories about them later. I found I could make people laugh." His mental transformation into a comedian came one day in his teenage years when he was sitting in a diner watching a group of six kids breaking up over another kid's joke. He told himself, "That's what life is all about."

Cosby's interest in sports and disinterest in schoolwork caused him to fail the tenth grade. Instead of repeating the grade, he quit school and joined the navy for a four-year hitch. Within a week he knew he had made a terrible mistake and said, "I knew I was committing a mental sin" by not pursuing my education. His mother was furious and Cosby began immediately to rectify his error by passing a high school equivalency test while playing football and basketball in the service. Upon his release from the navy in 1961, at age twenty-three, Cosby was offered an athletic scholarship to Temple University for football and track. He participated in the discus, javelin, broad and high jump, and 220 low hurdles events in track and played right halfback on the football team. Many people, including some pros, suggested Cosby was good enough to have played professional football. Cosby's response to such statements was, "I wasn't going to let them kill me for $13,000 a year."

While attending Temple, Cosby tended bar at five dollars a night at the Cellar—a local Philadelphia coffeehouse popular in those beatnik days—and learned to joke to supplement his meager income. He then moved on to the Underground Cafe, earning the huge stipend of twenty-five dollars a night. Then a friend secured him an engagement at the Gaslight Cafe in Greenwich Village during a summer break from college that included his room and board. This gig proved providential, as Cosby never returned to Temple. He had decided that comedy, not education, was his ticket to success. This decision almost destroyed his mother, who revered education and told her oldest son that he had made a grievous mistake. She spent a week in bed over his horrendous decision and never got over it until he became a star and finally made her proud when he received his degree in the early seventies.

The Cosby mystique began with a cabaret career where demeaning racial material was used to gain identity. He got caught up in the traditions of Dick Gregory and Flip Wilson, who always used ethnic jokes in their acts. Reflecting on this approach, Cosby quickly changed his act to aracial. Never again would race be the butt of his jokes and Black Power leaders were never able to recruit him to take up their cause. Cosby decided in the sixties to take the low-key approach and changed the way blacks were portrayed in the entertainment medium instead of white-bashing.

Cosby turned to down-home homily humor that he had learned at his mother's knee. He borrowed from Mark Twain's "common sense" style of American satire, utilizing the absurd, bizarre, and preposterous real-life situations he remembered from his days in the Jungle. He began by telling Bible stories with ironic twists, borrowing these initially from his fantasy hero Mark Twain. The most notable material was lifted from Twain's "Adam's Soliloquy" and God's conversations with Noah. He began fabricating stories around two childhood friends, Fat Albert and Weird Harold.

During this period Cosby was a struggling comedian and didn't even own a car, even though he was now twenty-four. He was making $60 a week at the Gaslight Club but by 1962 had worked his was up to a staggering $175 week. He began getting calls from Chicago and other cities around the United States as his act was gaining notoriety. He was on his way professionally. It was at this time that he took a job in Washington, D.C., and went on a blind date with a University of Maryland sophomore who was majoring in psychology. Camille Hanks was a very attractive nineteen-year-old when they first met. She was from a distinguished family whose father was a research chemist at Walter Reed Hospital. Camille was immediately caught up in Cosby's humor even if her family was not. They saw little future in a college dropout working as a stand-up comedian. It took much wooing on his part to finally convince Camille to marry him and even after they were engaged her father convinced her to call it off until the itinerant Cosby was more stable. The couple married on January 25, 1964, and neither have ever regretted the decision. They have five children and an idyllic, loving relationship. He wrote in *Love and Marriage* (1989), "Marrying Camille is the best thing I ever did."

Professional History

Cosby's first comedy record, *I Started Out as a Child,* won a Grammy in 1964 and spawned over twenty albums. In 1967 Cosby sold over seven million albums. He

won rave reviews for his recording *Bill Cosby Is a Very Funny Fellow . . . Right!*
Within a year of his marriage, he proved his father-in-law wrong when he landed
the "I Spy" role and never looked back.

POLYPHASIC/MULTITASKING

Consistent with the findings on the eminent, Cosby constantly dabbled in various
venues. Never during his career did he limit himself to working in just one entertainment discipline. When on television, he worked the Tahoe and Vegas nightclub
circuits. While making records, he also made movies. Working on "Fat Albert and
the Cosby Kids" program, he completed his doctorate. A mania for work dominated his life and his fear of failure drove him to produce beyond any economic
need to push himself to such lengths.

AN EDUCATOR OF TRUTH!

Cosby's professional life has been an amalgam of comedic routines aimed primarily at educating and enlightening through the vehicle of humor. Comedy is his
antidote for societal ills and he has been eminently successful in providing the
most incisive medicine for our ills. He said, "I think I have a talent for teaching"
and "My lone rule is to be true rather than funny." He wrote, "Entertainment is my
elixir to change people's thoughts" and to do that effectively he resorted to the
basic issues of life that all people could understand. He honed in on life's incon-
gruities and perversities, childhood frailties and insecurities, family idiosyncrasies
and dysfunctions, but most importantly insisted on depicting blacks as average,
mainstream people.

A SELF-SUFFICIENT CREATIVE GENIUS

Cosby insisted on writing his own material. He never got caught up in following traditional methodologies in entertainment—the true mark of any creative innovator.
His early routines included a childhood game of street football that all kids and
grownups could relate to. One of his great talents was the ability to paint absurd pictures of an inner-city street football game to a multicultural audience. He would tell
them, "Weird Harold you go down to Third street, catch the J bus, have him open
the doors at 19th Street, and I'll fake her to ya." His use of such neighborhood ver-
nacular added color and reality to his routines and his outlandish imagery would
crack up the most staid fans. Noah's conversations with God were classic parodies
of man talking to an almighty being, especially when God told Noah to build the Ark
and Noah asks God, "What's an ark?" "Get some wood. Build it three hundred cubits by eighty cubit by forty cubits." "Right. What's a cubit?"

Cosby was able to meld a rare combination of slapstick, reality, and facial expression to pull off a believable but outrageous routine that audiences of all backgrounds could enjoy. He was able to crack up the most austere customers. Cosby's

big break came when he was asked to costar with Robert Culp in the "I Spy" series in September 1965. It was a show about international intrigue that became an instant success. This led to a "Bill Cosby Special" in March 1968, which allowed Cosby the opportunity to delve into his deeper imagery. Sudden success allowed him to dabble in some of his own, deep-seated fantasies about life in the Jungle, which materialized in his creation of an inane but funny radio program he named the "Brown Hornet"—a takeoff on his childhood hero the Green Hornet. The Brown Hornet did not have the wealthy man-about-town theme of Batman or Superman but was characterized as an average Joe who lived in a fifth-floor walk-up with the only phone five flights down. Cosby's perverse imagination had the Brown Hornet driving a 1957 Plymouth with an assistant with the unlikely name of Leroy. This Cosby creation included dashes of absurdity, humor, and reality to make it superb entertainment.

The first Cosby special aired in 1968 and was hailed as "simply marvelous." It was the first time he introduced his childhood fantasy characters Weird Harold and Fat Albert to a national TV audience. In the late sixties NBC signed Cosby to a $15 million contract for five Cosby specials, two cartoon specials, and the first "Bill Cosby Show," where he played an alter-ego type character named Chet Kincaid, a high school teacher and coach.

EDUCATOR EXTRAORDINAIRE

Cosby was never idle. When not appearing in a TV special he was recording, working the club circuit, or writing a new sitcom or children's cartoon series. While working on the children's cartoon series "Fat Albert and the Cosby Kids," Cosby took advantage of the opportunity to further his own education. Due to his lifetime achievements Temple University granted him his bachelor's degree, which motivated Cosby to further his formal education through his work on children's educational programming. He approached Dwight Allen of the University of Massachusetts about using a nationally syndicated educational program to qualify as work toward graduate study. He employed educators and psychiatrists as consultants in the writing of his cartoon scripts and convinced Allen to apply his comedy script work towards both master's and doctoral programs. Cosby's scripts were credited as term papers toward curriculum requirements and his doctoral thesis—"An Integration of the Visual Media Via 'Fat Albert and the Cosby Kids' into the Elementary School Curriculum as a Teaching Aid and Vehicle to Achieve Increased Learning"—was reformatted material from his syndicated programming. Cosby realized his greatest dream on May 23, 1976, when he was awarded a doctorate in childhood education.

INNOVATIVE SOCIAL ACTIVIST

By the early eighties Cosby was tired of what he called "blaxploitation" on network television. He said, "I got tired of seeing television shows that consist of a car crash, a gunman, and a hooker talking to a black pimp." Always the joker, he said, "It was cheaper to do a new series than throw out my family's television sets." He cynically commented on the deplorable state of network programming with this statement on their motives: "Give them some sex, some guns, and some cocaine to capture the black audience. It is a proven formula, man! . . . It is easier to throw some dude five hundred thousand dollars and tell him to give with the sex, tits, and coke." Cosby's futility over this state of affairs motivated him to look for a venue that could become the outlet for his personal creative energies while refuting the racial inequities being fostered on TV.

This became the genesis of "The Cosby Show," which he launched in 1984 but only after having been rejected by two of the three networks. Cosby played the lead role in this series. He played his alter-ego—a harassed father of five named Dr. Huxtable—with a lawyer wife played by Phylicia Ayers-Allen (later Rashad). Cosby often resorted to subtle and at times not-so-subtle subliminal messages on the set to impart his philosophical feelings about discrimination. One such incident was posting a sign in the background which read "Abolish Apartheid." Often he resorted to artwork by black artists and even named the show's twins—born of his oldest daughter—after Winnie and Nelson Mandela.

"The Cosby Show" has proven to be the culmination of Cosby's artistic genius. It eulogized "family" and "children" in real-life situations that were humorous but always real. Quincy Jones commented on this, saying the show "destroyed a lot of stereotypes." Cosby had at long last realized his dream of "using the tube to educate." He finally outdid his childhood idol Mark Twain by creating humor that emulated humanity and truth. The show debuted on September 20, 1984, and ended its epic run on April 30, 1992. It proved to be the most popular and highest-rated show during the eighties and achieved this despite the decade's reputation for conspicuous consumption. The family was of paramount importance to Cosby and this award-winning show is testimony to his creative genius. It is ironic that Cosby's only serious competition toward the end of the decade was the absolute antithesis of him and his show—"The Simpsons." But like "The Simpsons" producer—Rupert Murdoch—the characters emulated the philosophical values of the "big cheese." Cosby was proudest of a quote appearing in *USA Today,* where a consumer wrote in saying they were going to start watching "The Simpsons" because you learn too much watching Cosby.

NEW ENTERPRISES

During the nineties two of Cosby's ventures flopped. Both "You Bet Your Life" and "The Cosby Mysteries" were less than successful and short-lived. Nevertheless CBS was looking for a miracle to dig themselves out of the ratings grave in late 1995 and gave Bill Cosby an unprecedented two-year contract to launch a new show in the fall of 1996 based on the British series "One Foot in the Grave." On this show Cosby was cast as an Archie Bunker–type character without the racism and sexism. As the curmudgeon named Hilton Cosby "is a bit more apt to rant."

At age fifty-nine Bill Cosby is still in the hunt and this show proves that he is a man driven not by money—although CBS paid him dearly for the opportunity—but for the chance to further family values in an innovative and creative format.

What Makes Cos Tick?

Bill Cosby strove for excellence in all things, which gave him a well-earned reputation as a perfectionist and workaholic among his fellow performers and family. Cosby was so intensely serious about excellence for himself and those he loved that he made sure each of his five children were given names beginning with the letter "E for excellence and education"—Erika, Erinne, Ensa, Ennis, Evin. Cosby believed, as I do, that we all live to fulfill our inner images of ourselves and one's name is the personification of internal imagery.

Cosby is an extroverted, intuitive-thinking personality. He is perpetually looking for the opportunities to communicate and educate through the medium of television. Bill Cosby is the classic Promethean personality who is a visionary who prefers to work on ideas with ingenuity and logic. Such individuals view the world as "qualitative," not "quantitative," and seek knowledge as a personal growth vehicle rather than for utilitarian value. The Promethean is an architect of change and Bill Cosby truly qualifies.

Mythological Hero Mentors

Bill Cosby has a vivid imagination molded while quite young by a mother who read to him of fictional heroes out of the Bible and other books. Mark Twain was his favorite author. His "warm, gentle humor" became indelibly imprinted on Cosby's psyche, causing him to spend the rest of his life attempting to emulate the master. Cosby saw Twain as a man able to take the average absurdities of life and tell them simply. He, like Twain, learned to raid the Bible for ideas for his material. His first great comedic routines were copied from Twain's "Adam's Soliloquy." Cosby cast Noah as a typical American male in a desperate fight for survival against greater forces. He started refining the Noah routine at the Gaslight Club in the early sixties and broke up the hip crowds with his ability to play God's and Noah's voices in both straight and street dialects. As Noah he tells God, "Okay, Lord. Me and you—right?" just as a couple of street-smart hippies would have said it.

Cosby adopted many fictional heroes as role models during his youth. He escaped into the heroic machinations of the Lone Ranger, Batman, Superman, the Shadow, and the Green Hornet and their conquests became his escape into a positive hero worship. In real life he chose Jackie Robinson and Sugar Ray Robinson as idols. In comedy his chose Charlie Chaplin, W. C. Fields, Jack Benny, Jimmy Durante, Burns and Allen, and Laurel and Hardy. All of these larger-than-life characters inspired him to big things. He saw few, if any, limitations to his own greatness due to adoption of these superhuman heroes. These fantasy heroes were all omnipotent overachievers, which is what it takes to make a child believe that anything is possible in life. Cosby's fantasy heroes gave him the incentive to reach the top but it appears none was quite the influence of the pragmatic realist and comedian Mark Twain.

INSECURITY BREEDS GREATNESS

Cosby often jested, "I'm a frightened atheist" to describe his fear of failure. He said, "I found I could make people laugh, and I enjoyed doing it because it gave me a sense of security. I thought that if people laughed at what you said, that meant they liked you." Being raised in the "Jungle" was always deeply imbedded in his mind and he was determined never to go back. He wrote, "You know it's all because I wanted to be accepted. That's why I tell jokes."

Cosby had been urged to get an education by his mother, who felt it was the way out of the Jungle. She instilled in him the values necessary for greatness, but in so doing, never let him forget where he came from. He believed blacks were in a "life and death struggle for real identity" and told an audience at Harlem's Apollo Theater, "In show business you can be rich today and back in the projects tomorrow." That inner fear drove Cosby to become a perfectionist and workaholic, which helped catapult him to the very top of his profession.

METAMORPHOSES

Cosby's true metamorphoses occurred during his abominable early life, when he and his family were evicted from one apartment after another until they ended up in the North Philadelphia housing project euphemistically known as the "Jungle." Cosby's transformation occurred as the result of books, which were first read to him by his mother and then those he read or the radio programs he listened to as an escape from the realities of the Jungle environment. The Mark Twain stories helped mold his sense of humor and sense of reality from a fantasy medium. He was highly impressionable at the time and Twain's perverse sense of humor appealed to Cosby's depraved sense of value in being able to con another boy to paint a picket fence. Forever after, Cosby yearned to emulate the master he so admired as a child. This "success imprint" proved critically important to Cosby's later success since it instilled in him the larger nature of the world and that the Jungle was only a temporary interlude in a larger life.

Charisma

Bill Cosby is a mesmerizing storyteller who has an intuitive feel for an audience's "hot button." As Shakespeare said so eloquently, "imitation is the ultimate compliment." Cosby has been given huge compliments by the repeated imitation of his scripts and television portrayals. It is hard not to relate to Bill Cosby on any level, as he has honed his image and material into "everyman," which is his great strength. His charismatic charm onstage is contagious and audiences never forget his shows, which has proven critically important to his success in life.

Competitiveness

Cosby's coach at Temple said, "Bill Cosby is a real competitor." His competitive spirit contributed to his becoming a great athlete in school and what has since made him an accomplished tennis player, actor, bridge player, and producer. He does not back down from any confrontation and always holds his ground in any fight. Surviving the projects and college athletics is testimony to his competitiveness. Even as an amateur tennis player Cosby's reputation precedes him, especially after he won a number of celebrity tennis tournaments. When he first appeared on the "I Spy" series he was somewhat combative, which led costar Robert Culp to refer to him as an angry man. Culp commented on Cosby's fearlessness. The racial epithets by producer Sheldon Leonard instigated Cosby's competitive comment, "If you make a joke about my color, then I'm going to make a joke about your color!" It is always instructive to look at one's idols to discern their own nature. Cosby's teenage idols were Jackie Robinson and Sugar Ray Robinson, both highly combative personalities, and he followed their tact of aggressiveness in all confrontations.

Confidence

Cosby says, "My life is generally optimistic." He is a man who approaches all new concepts with an air of positive optimism. He is a true Promethean who believes in himself to such a degree that he is able to ignore those experts who always disdain anyone who dares question the status quo or established values. He told a reporter, "I may not know the exact formula for success. I do know the exact formula for failure; and that is trying to please everybody." This was Cosby's way of saying one must believe in oneself and have the guts to pursue one's own beliefs. Seldom did the industry experts or even other blacks agree with his approach toward humor, but Cosby never capitulated to their way until he was positively sure his way would not work.

Passion and Drive

Cosby was a man who lived life as a maniac on a mission. He had intense determination and as biographer Bill Adler wrote in 1986, "There is no way to confine him. He is protean." Many of his show business peers were amazed at the sheer energy of Cosby, who was driven to be the very best he could be and demanding perfection from himself and his associates at all times. Passion and drive are at the seat of much of Cosby's great success both personally and professionally. He is well steeped in a kind of psychic energy that drives him to be the very best he can be.

Hypomania

Cosby is a workaholic who started working at age eight and continued his strong work ethic throughout his life. A comment in his 1988 book, *Time Flies,* gives some testimony to his work ethic while a student at Temple. He says, "I was a perpetual motion machine. I would start playing basketball at eight o'clock in the morning, play touch football all afternoon . . . and find a pick-up triathlon for the evening." Cosby's wife, Camille, acknowledges his passion for work, saying that he often spends eighteen-hour days working on a new project. What motivates an individual who in 1993 was listed by *Forbes* as the richest black person in America? Psychologist Alfred Adler said that all mankind has one defining need and that is to "strive for excellence." Cosby sure confirms Adler's hypothesis since he has this drive in abundance. Sheldon Leonard, producer of "I Spy," called him a "tireless worker" and biographer Bill Adler described him as "a workaholic." Cosby defends this, saying, "In this business if you stand still you disappear." Well no one ever accused Cosby of standing still, so he is still the preeminent television comedian in the United States after three decades of breaking up audiences with his preposterous, common sense stories.

Independence

Cosby never listened to an expert in his life. He is proud of offering unique and off-the-wall solutions to difficult problems. He loves to be different and often resorts to shock to elicit a laugh from an austere audience. A classic example of Cosby's need to be different is a story he likes to tell about his teen years when he worked as an apprentice shoemaker. He described himself "going crazy" in such a slow-paced business and as a distraction he said, "I started destroying the shoes." His diabolical nature took precedence over any innate rationality and he said, "I loved putting two-inch heels instead of half-inch heels on some guy's shoes" and "couldn't wait till he came to pick them up!"

The culmination of Cosby's perverse sense of adventure occurred when he failed the tenth grade in high school and joined the navy to avoid repeating the grade. Later he wrote of his reasoning, saying, "I joined the Navy because . . . I didn't want to be like everybody else."

Perfectionist

Cosby always insisted that everything produced met his meticulous stamp of approval. He had to have it just right and would change scripts continually to meet his fanatic need for excellence. Such is the mark of one who becomes supersuccessful. Cosby was a tough but fair taskmaster who demanded precision and excellence from anyone who worked for him but he also demanded the same of himself. He once wrote a script he believed to be perfect and said, "I thought it was the most brilliant thing I'd ever seen. After we sat down at the table and read it through, I tore out all of it." One time Cosby also read a finished script and proceeded to take out thirty-two pages. Needless to say, this thoroughly destroyed the scriptwriter, who had assumed his job was acceptable. That is Cosby's style and a major reason for his eminent success. He is the consummate perfectionist who is driven to be the very best he can be and damned be the cost in time or casualties in the rewrite.

Temerity

Cosby was always a high-stakes gambler and risk-taker who loved to live on the edge in any venture. He was never afraid to take any large risk and intuitively knew great wins were the result of taking great risks. He once told a reporter questioning his time spent at the tables in Lake Tahoe that, "I've often won more at the tables than what I was earning per week on stage." When the social activists got on his case about not using Black Power and other racial issues in his act, he ignored their entreaties, refusing to bow to their pressure.

One classic example of the entrepreneurial personality is its love for fast sports cars. Cosby fits this mold, having owned many fast cars, including a Ferrari, plus his own airplane. Another demonstration of an innate need to take large risks occurred when Cosby turned down an offer by Doubleday of $4 million for the publishing rights to a fourth book. Cosby refused this offer in order to make his own deal with Putnam Books which included no advance but 50 percent of the profits. Cosby had sacrificed the safe present for a great future, which is the principle motivating force of the great entrepreneurs of the world. This is the mentality that separates Cosby from the pack. The pack mentality would have taken the $4 million and gone to the beach.

Tenacity

This one-time shoeshine boy persevered to become America's richest black man. Cosby was tenacious and his resilience proved worth the price. He overcame some of life's greatest adversities which he experienced by surviving life in the projects of North Philadelphia. His persistence paid huge dividends. This boy who was raised without a telephone or many of the most basic amenities of life learned to survive through hard work and tenacity. Further evidence of his persevering nature is the fact that he was a high school dropout, who upon realizing his error, passed the GED, and then went on to earn master's and doctoral degrees in childhood education from the prestigious University of Massachusetts. This is the mark of a driven man who will not give up despite any obstacles or roadblocks.

Vision

Bill Cosby had an unfailing instinct for what people wanted to hear, like that of Oprah Winfrey interviewing a guest. Cosby can paint word images that audiences are able to see in their mind's eye. Cosby once told executives at Capitol Records, "While I'm up on stage I can actually put myself into the people in the audience and adjust my pace and timing to them. I can get into their heads through my ears and through their eyes. Only through this total communication can I really achieve what I'm trying to do." This is a unique ability and Cosby and Winfrey both have it. He is a right-brain-driven individual who always sees the forest in contrast to the trees in any real-life situation. Cosby has a "knowing" without knowing why but "feels it," which is a street smarts that makes him special.

Will to Power

Biographer Marianne Ruuth says Cosby has a "determination and will of iron." She was quite close to the truth, as Cosby's great success is a by-product of his will to power. His superman persona was born of his Nietzschean nature where "will" is at the seat of all success in the world. Cosby, like Superman, was born in 1937, one in the projects, the other in the comics. Cosby's whirlwind creative energy is fueled by an indomitable will. This indefatigable and multifaceted man won numerous celebrity tennis tournaments and as an accomplished athlete could have played football for the New York Giants. Within a few years he was earning $50,000 a week on the night club circuit, winning Emmys for his starring role in "I Spy," being paid $5 million for television specials, making a dozen movies, and selling millions of comedy records. Through all this Cosby was able to maintain a rational perspective as a faithful husband and father of five children. That takes some doing! It is the stuff of which "supermen" are made, where "will" is the driving force for all success.

Summary

Cosby was a product of the projects who rose from shoeshine boy with a playhouse imagination to the penthouse in fifteen short years. He had every reason to fail but didn't because he was different than most. He rebounded from early debacles to pursue success with a passion.

Cosby is an idyllic role model for all those people who were taught to believe that money, socioeconomic status, and formal education are needed to make it big in the world. Bill Cosby is the consummate example of someone who had all the reasons to fail but persevered and became greater than his dreams could have imagined. Always a giving man, Cosby and Sammy Davis, Jr., paid the funeral expenses for Cornell Gunter, singer for the Coasters, who died broke. By 1990 Cosby had become a true philanthropist when he and his wife donated $20 million to Morehouse College. He was given the YMCA's "Humanitarian Services Award" and in 1990 George Bush presented him with NBC's "Lifetime Achievement Award" along with Bob Hope, Milton Berle, and Michael Landon.

Helen Dudar wrote in the *New York Post* in 1964, "Cosby's view of the world suggests a cracked funny-house mirror, offering a deranged reflection of the world in good, clean, friendly fun. He seems incapable of malice." That is a very accurate caricature of a man who used a diabolical sense of humor to open doors. Once the doors were opened, he walked in and took over. He utilized perfectionism and a strong work ethic in getting to the top and is proof that great entertainers are bred, not born.

Bill Cosby is the quintessential creative genius who changed the world of entertainment by daring to be different. He created the instrument of his own success. He was not born a genius and few in his early life considered him such. When asked how he made his living, his mother told friends, "Oh, he makes a fool of himself and gets paid for it." She could have added that if you do anything in life better than anyone else in the world, you get paid very well.

WILLIAM HENRY COSBY, JR.
Promethean (NT)
Protean Entertainer—Comedian—Actor—TV Specials—Night Club Performer—Recording Artist
born July 12, 1937, Philadelphia, Pennsylvania

Dominant trait: Extroverted perfectionist with intuitive feel for audience desires
Motto: "Strive for excellence"; "Comedy is exaggeration"; "Comedy with roots in truth"
Religion: Religious pragmatist: "I believe there is a Supreme Being"
Philosophy: "I want to use the tube to educate"; "I'm trying to bring out the similarities in all of us"
Politics: Democrat with libertarian tendencies who dislikes politicians as untrustworthy
Nickname: Cos; Silver Throat (stage name as singer); Bill; "The Electronic Mark Twain"
Creation/innovation: Comedy of "human condition," not "black condition"; pioneered blacks as
hero in sitcoms
Successes: 20 recordings, 4 books, 12 movies, "The Cosby Show" (#1 all time); $315 million in
1992, U.S.'s richest black
Vices/hobbies: Cuban cigars, tennis, sports cars; classic comedy film collector: Chaplin, Fields, etc.
Romantic liaisons: Learned drums to be jazz musician since "those cats got all the chicks";
Camille Hanks true love
Self-description: "I assumed responsibility for my life"; "I think I have a talent for teaching"

Birth order: Firstborn of five (one died) of Bill Sr. and Anna Hite Cosby; he and brother Russell
slept together
Parental influence: Idolized hardworking mother who had been left by his alcoholic father
(Cosby doesn't drink)
Early transience: Moved constantly as child fleeing irate landlords, ending in North Philadelphia
projects called the "Jungle"
Parents' occupations: Mother a domestic; father a welder and navy steward
Role models: Mark Twain, Jack Benny, Charlie Chaplin, Jimmy Durante, Laurel and Hardy,
Sugar Ray Robinson his idol
Hero mentors: Commonsense humor of Mark Twain; the Lone Ranger, the Shadow, emulated the
walk of Jackie Robinson
Formal education: High school dropout at 16; Temple 2.5 years; B.A., M.S. (1974), and Ph.D
(1976) degrees U. Mass.
Life crises: Eight when brother died, another had epilepsy; raised in "Jungle" project; father left
when 10
Metamorphoses: Mother read him *Tom Sawyer*; learned to joke to avoid punishment as prankster;
jokes got bigger tips

Charismatic: A mesmerizing storyteller who has visionary feel for audiences' "hot button"
Competitive: Robert Culp said, "The angriest man I ever met"; aggressive track, football, tennis,
and bridge player
Hypomanic: "Special vitality"; new ideas were "constantly springing from his active mind"; "he
is mercurial"
Independent rebel: Loves to break rules; "I joined the Navy because . . . I didn't want to be like
everybody else"
Indomitable "will": Biographer: "He has determination and will of iron"
Intuitive vision: "While I'm up on stage I can actually put myself into the people . . . paint im-
ages in audiences' heads"
Passionate drive: Man with a mission and intense determination; "There is no way to confine him.
He is protean"
Perfectionist: Strives for excellence in all things
Risk-taker: Gambler who will risk for beliefs; "I've often won more at the tables than I was
earning on stage"
Self-confident: A supreme optimist who believes and is willing to bet on his ideas; "My life is gen-
erally optimistic"
Tenacious: Raised in projects, high school dropout who persevered to become Ph.D. and U.S.'s
wealthiest black
Workaholic: 1st producer ("I Spy"); "tireless worker"; "many years working 18-hour days—TV,
concerts, recordings"
Honors: "He has outrated, outsold, and outranked every other entertainer in history"

9

Berry Gordy—Driven

Motown Founder and Star Maker Extraordinaire

"My obsession with perfection was a driving force."

Berry Gordy was the energy that created the Motown Sound—a sound that rocked the world and changed music forever everywhere. This driven man had the intuitive vision to transform black gospel music into mainline pop. But how could a man revolutionize popular music when he was unable to read music and whose sum training included one high school clarinet lesson and teaching himself to play "Chopsticks" on the piano as a child? Gordy's secret was innate in that he resorted to a "gut street sense" of what people wanted to hear and proceeded to give it to them. He was able to integrate the emotional, ethereal sound of the spiritual in gospel music—which he referred to as "basic feelings"—with lyrics expressive of the turbulent sixties.

The Motown Sound was able to blend mental word pictures with passionate music and the mixture proved to be provocative and impelling for a rebellious generation looking to be different and for an identity in sound. Gordy's music was inextricably tied up in the sixties cultural revolution, which demanded words and music that told the story of life. "To Be Loved," "Lonely Teardrops," "Bad Girl," "Money," "Please Mister Postman," "Do You Love Me?" "My Guy," "Love Child," "I Heard It Through the Grapevine," "My Girl," "Cloud Nine," "He's So Fine," and "For Once in My Life" were just a few of the hits that made Motown a monumental success. They were hits because they told of the passion and the problems of daily life in the sixties. It was the marriage of an passionate beat with emotional words that in the end made Berry Gordy a genius. Simplicity, like in most all great success, is the genius in innovative endeavors. Most people pursue the complex, but Berry Gordy was never so smart nor steeped in traditional values to be a conformist. He had the vision to ignore the nuances of musical dogma to follow his own intuitive feel for the "beat" and the "words." If a song felt good to him, he went with it. If it didn't, he scrapped it.

The Motown Sound appealed to multicultural audiences. It transcended all cultural or social bounds and finally forced white radio stations to take heed of its enormous appeal. It soon became the heartbeat of the sixties. Hitsville was a company buried in hits and began topping the pop music charts like no other firm in history. The Motown Sound became the soundtrack for millions of young Americans and the list of stars created by this phenomenon was truly amazing.

Gordy rode a similar vehicle to the top as was taken by the other superstars in this book. He was oblivious of race during his trek to the top but always sensitive to what worked for the masses, regardless of their heritage. Gordy was successful in marrying the ethnic music of black America to the needs of a society in social revolution. The renegade mentality so pervasive between 1960 and 1975 was waiting for a beat and words that could be used as personal motivation. Gordy gave this in one place—Motown. His sound struck a sensitive cord with the rebellious generation and the Motown Sound became the basic communications medium for people attempting to deal emotionally with the assassinations of President Kennedy and his brother Robert Kennedy and the black social activists Dr. King and Malcolm X. A generation reeling from chaos and destruction of ideals was in dire need of a common bond. Gordy supplied the solace in the form of a common music bond. Singing and dancing in the sixties and seventies were an experience in Motown music. Oprah Winfrey wrote in 1995 that one Sunday night, December 27, 1964, was "a night that changed my life forever" when she saw the Supremes on the "Ed Sullivan Show" and said, "I was inspired by the possibilities of what I could be." The subtle philosophical messages of the Motown Sound provided an emotional outlet for a society searching for truth and spiritual enlightenment. Winfrey is not the only one who was so inspired.

A Grassroots Approach to Innovation

Once his magic formula was in the process of being implemented, Gordy created a business environment that was unique. He first put up an audacious sign—Hitsville, USA—and then deluged the world with a whirlwind of music and black stars to present it. The Motown Sound became a common bond of the young and the average people. And it appealed to a very broad sector of the socioeconomic community because it was born of the streets and tapped the innermost emotions of people's souls. Berry was the genius behind this as he implored his songwriters to "write a song like it's happening right then, so people can associate with it." He extorted his artists to deliver it in a venue which had universal acceptability so that it would appeal to black, whites, and Hispanics, as well as other cultural audiences. In one stroke of instinctive genius Gordy brought in high school kids to judge the songs and allowed these kids to become the supreme arbiters of the record's release. Such a "grassroots" validation of the "realness" of the words and music was a fundamental factor in Motown's ultimate success. Gordy always played dictator in these product release forums. He asked the critical question on any new record release: "Would you buy this record for a dollar or would you buy a sandwich?" Such was the simplistic but effective business approach that made Motown a mega-success and Gordy an extraordinarily wealthy man.

To put Gordy's success in perspective during the mid-sixties, one should look only at the songs he released that rose to number one on the charts. The average song released during the period had a one in ten chance of appearing on a popular chart like that of *Billboard* magazine. Motown's success rate was a staggering 75 percent—three-quarters of the company's records hit *Billboard*. Another amazing statistic shows that over 86 percent of all new releases never earned back their initial investment, which equates to a .140 batting average in baseball. In contrast, Motown's releases enjoyed well over a 65 percent success rate for a .650 batting average, which would have qualified for anyone's record Hall of Fame.

Gordy not only revolutionized the sound of the sixties and seventies, the stars he created would have made any Hollywood mogul drool. Smokey Robinson, Marvin Gaye, Diana Ross, Stevie Wonder, Gladys Knight, Michael Jackson, and Lionel Richie are only a few of the superstars he discovered. Even more astonishing were the groups he groomed into megastars, including: the Supremes, Temptations, Commodores, Miracles, Martha and the Vandellas, Four Tops, Gladys Knight and the Pips, Spinners, and the Jackson Five. The Hollywood star-making studios of the heyday thirties and forties pale in comparison to Gordy's achievements. Gordy's influence and mentoring of his stars was such that it motivated Michael Jackson to say, "I love Berry Gordy. I think he's a genius." It is also why Diana Ross was mesmerized by him.

Despite Berry's many detractors, his contribution to the music industry has been enormous. *Current Biography* described Motown in 1975 as "the most successful black enterprise in the United States." When others attempted to denigrate his influence, Gordy told *Rolling Stone,* "I earned $367 million in sixteen years. I must be doing something right." *Rolling Stone* went on to say without equivocation that "Gordy's impact on popular music cannot be overstated." Berry's comment on the $367 million was the amount he realized from the sale of Motown Records and only a pittance of the monies he actually earned during his reign as record *star maker* and *hit maker.* He sold Motown Records to MCI in 1988 for a cool $61 million cash and then sold Jobete to Polygram, a division of Philips, for an astounding $301 million. The $800 loan from his family in 1958 had paid huge dividends.

Innovative Contribution

Gordy's great insight into star making was never more apparent than his making of the Supremes. First he had to coerce them into singing old standards that these inner-city teenagers detested. He had to force them to sing "Make Someone Happy," "You're Nobody Until Somebody Loves You," and "Put on a Happy Face"—all Broadway tunes accepted by the white stations and the audiences who could afford to attend their performances at the Copacabana in New York City.

Gordy intuitively knew the Supremes were good but would never gain acceptance with hard rock from the inner city. Gordy signed them to what he referred to as a "slave contract" at the world famous Copacabana for three years at a ridiculously low $3,000 per week. This was their baptism of fire and carefully orchestrated to make them credible so they could gain acceptance to the white television shows like Ed Sullivan's and the white disc jockeys who could make or break them. They thought the Copa deal was "stupid," never quite understanding the subtle nuances of his moves, which were always aimed at the big-picture wins in life. He said, "I was always willing to lose money if it meant building stars," and many of his stars would later leave him because they did not have his vision. New York critics wrote that the Supremes' Copa show was one of the "most dramatic openings the Copa had ever seen." Gordy's vision proved 20/20. The Supremes became an overnight sensation commanding huge contracts and numerous television appearances. They became international celebrities because of Gordy's intuitive genius. The cost of the Copa contract was a small price to pay for their later success and Berry Gordy suddenly became known as the "star maker" and "Magic Man."

Vertical Integration of Star Making

Berry Gordy will one day be recognized as the one man who contributed more to marrying gospel, soul, and rhythm and blues (R&B) than any other. His artistic creation—the Motown Sound—became the industry standard within one decade, an unprecedented accomplishment tantamount to a cultural revolution. His innovation was creating a full-service talent agency and music production warehouse where an aspiring young star could be groomed and molded from "cradle to creative culmination." Once they were molded into the Motown likeness he promoted them right into superstardom. No other company, before or since, has had the audacity to attempt such vertical integration in the entertainment industry. Gordy created a star-making enterprise encompassing: songwriting, record production, distribution, artist promotion, record advertising, sales, and total artistic management. In this masterful undertaking Gordy had gone beyond the industry norms and thereby created his own Frankenstein monster that would attempt to destroy him later when the stars resisted such total control.

Gordy's obsessive dream was launched with virtually no operating capital or experience—the classic sign of the obsessive entrepreneurial personality. When queried about his "gutsy" approach to the creation of Motown, he responded: "I didn't know any better. . . . If somebody told me today, 'Okay, you're gonna go into business, and you've gotta make a profit every year for the first five years or you'll be out of business,' I'd say that's not a good gamble. . . . Motown was a freak."

Personal History

Berry Gordy was born on Thanksgiving Day, November 28, 1928, the seventh child of Bertha Fuller and Berry Gordy II, who he always referred to as Pops. Born later was his younger brother Robert, who would play a material role in the management of Motown, as would many of his other siblings. Berry Gordy was the last of three generations of Berry Gordys. He came from a stock of steel-willed Southern-bred males who were self-reliant and very industrious. Gordy was highly influenced by his third-generation inheritance of the name Berry and wrote in his 1995 autobiography, *To Be Loved*, "A name is something we wear throughout our lives. It has it's own power. The sound, the personality and the meaning all affect both our perception of ourselves and others' perception of us." When he was two, the Depression hit and the family lost its home and Pops was forced to accept welfare. There were now eight kids—four boys and four girls—all of whom lived in the squalor of Detroit's inner city.

Always superstitious, Gordy was highly influenced by his astrological sign, Sagittarius. He was convinced that he was born to fulfill the Sagittarian traits and appears to have lived his life fulfilling those traits, writing in his autobiography: "Sagittarians shot straight like an arrow, were honest, and couldn't be contained easily. They also had a good sense of humor, were philosophical, competitive, and adored women." In compliance to his sign Gordy always had a great sense of humor, was highly competitive, and approached all new ventures with a philosophical vision. He wrote that he had acquired his gambling spirit at age six playing the kids' card game War and later graduated into a full-fledged high-stakes gambler and risk-taker. He said that by his teens "I was a gambler. Craps, blackjack, poker, anything." His idols in life were all gambling spirits who lived their life on the edge—Joe Louis, Sugar Ray Robinson, Pops, and Billie Holiday. By any standard Gordy was a womanizer, a behavior he began early and continued throughout his adult life. He loved to read and discovered Rudyard Kipling's poem "If" as a teenager and was moved by the potential it showed him.

Gordy's father fit the profile of others in this book. He was always self-employed, owning a small grocery store and then starting a plaster contracting business where Berry III worked part-time as a teenager. During Gordy's youth the family moved to a better part of town, which inspired him to write some fifty years later, "Pops bringing us to the Westside was a major factor in who I became." Although poor beyond belief the family invested in a piano and his uncle B.A. taught him to play "Clair de Lune" and the Prelude in C# Minor. He then taught himself to play by ear, learning such black classics as "Boogie Woogie," which he would modify years later into a published tune "Berry's Boogie." When he was six and a half the family moved to the Eastside of Detroit, a block from Hastings Street, where young Berry was "scared to death."

In school Gordy became the class clown and displayed no interest in formal education. He said, "I was always so far behind the rest of the class, I just knew I had to be dumb," adding, "I was considered the black sheep of the family—mischievous, terrible in school, always in trouble." But young Berry III went through a kind of metamorphosis when Joe Louis won the heavyweight boxing championship in 1937. Gordy was eight at the time and wrote of the memorable experience of this Detroit black man who made the headlines everywhere in the world. He said, "Joe was the greatest hero in the universe . . . and at that moment a fire started deep inside me, a burning desire to be special, to win, to be somebody. I stood up from the curb and headed back into the house, a new certainty to my eight-year-old stride."

Gordy dropped out of high school in the eleventh grade to pursue his first love, boxing, and to become famous like his hero Joe Louis. He knew he didn't want to work as hard as his father to become rich and famous and decided boxing was his ticket to the big time. Gordy fought as a welterweight and had fifteen fights in all with ten wins, two draws, and three losses. By August 1950 he came to the realization that he was not going to become another Joe Louis and was smart enough to realized the terrible toll this sport could have on one's body and mind. One day he was looking at posters of one of his music heroes, Duke Ellington, and next to it was one of a boxer. He immediately discerned "the fighters were about twenty-three and looked fifty; the band leaders about fifty and looked twenty-three. . . . I took off my gloves for good." When he quit boxing he decided to pursue his other great love—music.

Professional History

This visionary wrote, "Songwriting was my love, and . . . in many ways the motivation of everything." He continued to drum out songs on the family piano without so much as a piano lesson or any formal knowledge of music. Gordy's sisters had a printing business that was in dire need of promotion to increase sales. In an attempt to help his sisters Gordy suddenly had his first "success imprint," which proved to be his emotional metamorphosis into songwriting. He wrote them a commercial song that was used on the local black station WJLB. As soon as it was broadcast this cocky twenty-year-old started telling everyone his profession was songwriting. This experience gave him the temerity to write a song for Doris Day and send it to her in California. His letter was never answered but he was mentally on his way, as he was now convinced of his destiny as a great songwriter.

Gordy was then drafted to fight in the Korean War and during his hitch there was able to get his GED. On his release the aspiring entrepreneur decided to use his money to open a record shop featuring jazz and blues. This turned out to be a disastrous undertaking and the store failed after just one year of operation. Gordy worked at various jobs, including the production line at a Lincoln-Mercury plant, in a Chrysler plant, as a cookware salesman, insurance salesman, sometime gambler, and oftentimes bum. These were unhappy years where Gordy was barely able to pay the rent and provide for his new family since he had met and married during his early twenties and had three children. Throughout this period Gordy wrote songs and attempted to have them published without success. In the late fifties he finally experienced some success when he wrote "Reet Petite" and "Lonely Teardrops" for Jackie Wilson. Both songs became smash hits and were soon followed by "To Be Loved." Berry Gordy was on his way.

CREATIVE COMPETITOR

Gordy approached the music business like entering the boxing ring. He formed creative commando teams to attack each facet of the recording business—song creation, artist development, music production, distribution, tours, management—and soloists and then put family or friends in charge of each. The Tamla label was created exclusively for the solo artists and Motown for the groups. Jobete Music Company was originally founded to produce and market the songs the young upstart intended to write himself but this enterprise became the cash cow that owned and controlled the publication rights to all the Motown songs. Later the International Talent Management company was formed to "act as personal manager to the artists." In other words, this visionary had vertically integrated, like a conglomerate. He would write the songs, mold the artists, produce the records, distribute them, and manage the careers of the artists. A bold move, but it worked.

A FAMILY AFFAIR

Gordy very adroitly appointed faithful family members to the key executive positions within the company, but, as a control freak, was careful to maintain complete command of every nuance of the creation and production of the music. Jobete actually owned the publishing rights to the Motown songs, which turned out to be a financial coup as this company would be sold in the late eighties for $301 million to Philips. Jobete was named for the first letters of his first three children, Joy, Berry, and Terry. Gordy was still struggling at age twenty-nine and his sister Esther told him, "You're twenty-nine years old and what have you done with your life?" He was not deterred, saying, "That's what's wrong with people; they give up their dreams too soon. I'm never going to give up mine." This recognition, however, motivated him to go to his family for the $800 he would need to start Motown. After much hassling over the repayment, his mother and father took the $800 out of their savings on January 12, 1959, and gave it to Berry Gordy to embark on his dream.

A GRANDIOSE VISION

Berry's first move was to audaciously place a huge sign which read Hitsville, U.S.A. on the lawn of the house from which he launched Motown. This sign was so incongruent inasmuch as the company had no organization, income, or successes and the corporate headquarters were located in the middle of Detroit's inner-city ghetto area. The company was located at 26648 West Grand Boulevard, which was, in fact, a home owned by Raynoma Singleton, Gordy's girlfriend and roommate since he was unable to afford an apartment let alone a corporate headquarters. Such was the grandiose dream of an entrepreneur with a clear vision for success.

Raynoma would later become his second wife and partner-turned-adversary. She said, "When I met Berry he had no car, no clothes, no money." The first recording they produced was "Come to Me" and it soon became a national hit. Gordy had met and befriended William "Smokey" Robinson in 1957, when he was just a teenager who wanted to write songs. Robinson would become Gordy's closest confidant and highly instrumental in the success of Motown, plus a major contributor to the firm's music. He wrote "Bad Girl," one of their first huge hits, and the Miracles performed the number to great acclaim. "Bad Girl" (1959) proved to be Motown's first big hit that was totally written, recorded, and produced by the company. Success came quickly as the Marvelettes recorded a huge hit called "Please Mr. Postman" (1961) followed by Stevie Wonder's "Fingertips, Part 2" (1963), Marvin Gaye's "How Sweet It Is to Be Loved by You" (1964). By 1964 Mary Wells had lit up the charts with the hit "My Guy," soon followed by Martha and the Vandellas' "Dancing in the Street" (1964) and the Temptations' "My Girl" (1965). These back-to-back successes ensured the company's survival despite virtually no working capital. The company succeeded only because Gordy didn't know enough to realize that he couldn't start a conglomerate without seed capital.

RAGS TO RICHES IN ONE DECADE

The Supremes would become one the most successful female singing groups of all time and were pivotal in Gordy's professional and personal life. The group had auditioned for Motown while in high school and although impressed, Gordy refused to hire the group until they graduated. In the interim he employed Diana Ross as a secretary, a penchant he would continue throughout his career. He would often put people on the payroll who he felt contributed to his personal needs or his vision for the future. He said later that Ross was as "bad as a secretary as she was good at singing." The group's first big hit was "Where Did Our Love Go?" (1964) followed by five consecutive chart-topping releases in 1965 and 1966. Not long after their great success the Motown reputation for building superstars was rampant within the industry and artists and groups came flocking to its doors. One such group was the Jackson Five, who were living and working in nearby Gary, Indiana. This group was really discovered by one of Motown's female stars, Gladys Knight, not by Diana Ross as people thought, since Gordy had used Ross as a promotional gimmick to kick off the careers of the Jackson Five. The Jackson Five would soon become Gordy's most lucrative property and started the seventies with three consecutive number-one hits: "I Want You Back," "ABC," and "I'll Be There." At the same time Gordy was becoming a producer of disco hits and Gladys Knight and the Pips hit the top of the charts with "The Way We Were" (1975).

DIANA IN LAS VEGAS

An example of Gordy's risk-taking propensity took place at Diana Ross's sixties debut in Las Vegas at the Frontier Hotel and Casino. Five hours before show time only 5 percent of the seats were booked, which had all the signs of disaster for her debut. The Magic Man took charge, instructing his confidants: "I want some people there. . . . I don't care how we do it." When no one came up with an acceptable solution, Gordy came up with a plan to tear five hundred twenty-dollar bills in half and pass one set of halfs out on the strip, promising attendees the other half as a free bonus for appearing at the performance. The promotional ploy worked, but almost turned into a riot just prior to showtime. A mob assembled outside the entrance demanding the other half of the twenty-dollar bills. Attempting to match five hundred serial numbers proved an impossible task and the angry mob became disruptive. Gordy demonstrated his moxie and vision when he took advantage of his casino gambling credit and gave out five hundred fresh bills totalling $10,000 to calm the crowd before Ross's performance. The show went on but Ross never knew the lengths her manager and lover had gone to ensure her a successful opening night.

HOLLYWOOD RISK-TAKER

The Magic Man relocated his corporate headquarters to Hollywood in the late sixties since he now believed himself to be infallible and wanted to prove that he could make movies with the same degree of success that he had achieved with recording stars. Berry's first film was a black musical that he personally financed and produced, not all by design. He embarked on this project to produce a movie about his early idol Billie Holiday titled *Lady Sings the Blues* with Holiday played by his protégée and lover, Diana Ross. Despite enormous problems and predictions of his failure by Hollywood moguls, he was finally exonerated, winning five Academy Award nominations and grossing in excess of $8.5 million. The Hollywood experts predicted Berry's demise in Hollywood, saying "Gordy really screwed up this time." These Hollywood experts were appalled by his moxie, especially when he insisted on Diana as the leading lady, considering she had never had an acting lesson. Paramount Pictures executives couldn't believe someone would bet millions on a movie with an untested star. They said, "She has never acted before!" causing the gambling man to say, "Of course she has. She's been acting all her life—as most black people have to do just to survive."

Paramount finally pulled out of the deal, leaving Gordy to survive on his own. He became so entrenched in the project that he got into an argument and replaced the director with himself. Then he gave the job as screenwriter to his assistant, Suzanne de Plesse, who had never written anything but a college paper. She was now given the responsibility to write a movie script. Gordy had a leading lady who had never acted, a director who had never directed, and a screenwriter who had never written anything.

Then the gutsy and flamboyant Motown leader showed his true gambling spirit when the financial backers decided to pull out due to the above moves and the constant delays in production. When the movie began exceeding its $2 million budget they finally revolted and canceled the movie production. Gordy, in his inimitable style, walked in and handed Frank Yablans of Paramount a check for $2 million and the movie was his. He was ecstatic but also concerned over the potential gamble, which had grown to titanic proportions. He wrote, "Creative people many times do dumb things. Business people watch for the budget, creative people only go for the magic." This time he had actually bet Motown on the magic and fortunately rolled a seven.

MAGIC AT THE MOUNTAINTOP

The most-watched TV special of 1975 proved to be "Motown 25: Yesterday, Today, Forever," which was a celebration of the twenty-fifth anniversary of the start of Motown. It featured most of the artists Gordy had either discovered or fashioned into megastars. The stars who came back that night to pay tribute to their mentor and friend included Stevie Wonder, Richard Pryor, Diana Ross, Marvin Gaye, Mary Wells, Michael Jackson, Smokey Robinson, Gladys Knight, and eighties sensation Lionel Richie. They paid tribute to the man who was most responsible for their huge success in the industry. It was a historic homage to the Motown Sound, through what Gordy liked to characterize as "camaraderie, creativity, competition."

What Makes Berry Gordy Tick?

Gordy's ex-wife and one-time business partner, Raynoma Singleton, said, "Berry was both feared and revered at Motown." She went on to say he was "humorous, a little bit of a tease, a lot of mystery, an artist at disguising whatever more serious thoughts he was having." She characterized him as a "raggedy bum and part-time pimp" when she first met him but later admitted that he was a "born leader." Gordy's energy and charisma "charged everyone." He was a "latter-day Socrates, an inveterate philosopher." He often rationalized his own behavior, saying, "a big ego is necessary in our competitive ranks."

As most entrepreneurial superstars, Berry Gordy was a high roller, perfectionist, and libidinally driven overachiever. He had a compulsive need to win at all costs that was behind his high-stakes gambling. He was a regular at Hugh Hefner's backgammon games at the Versailles Palace in Los Angeles. Singleton said he would start with $15,000 as pocket change for his weekly soirees at Hefner's palace.

Gordy is an extrovert with an intuitive-thinking approach to life. He became very successful because of his vision and big-picture view of the opportunities in the recording industry. He is a Type A, driven man who was always impatient with himself and others and made impulsive decisions based on his intuitive feel for the situation.

MYTHOLOGICAL HERO MENTORS

Joe Louis knocked out Max Schmeling when Berry Gordy was an eight-year-old. Louis's victory proved a memorable experience for a child mired in the inner city of Detroit. Gordy wrote fifty years later, "How could I ever do anything in my life that could make this many people happy?" and proceeded to use Louis as a hero mentor for the rest of his life, writing in his memoirs, "Joe Louis is the greatest hero in the universe." Gordy went so far as to say, "In that moment a fire started deep inside me, a burning desire to be special, to win, to be somebody. . . . Joe Louis was the first person who made me know what the word *hero* meant. His phenomenal feats had opened my imagination to the possibility of being somebody in this world." Based on this nostalgia, it is not an accident that the hero-worshiping teen quit school in the tenth grade to become a boxer. He had had his first "success imprint" and Joe Louis had inspired him to go for the gold.

A few years later Berry become enamored of the Mills Brothers, followed by the Ink Spots, Billie Holiday, and later Sugar Ray Robinson. These people became his mythological heroes and they gave him the impetus to believe there were no limits if one tried very hard. He said, "My biggest hero of all in the end turned out to be my father, Pop." The heroes out of books and music were the motivating forces behind much of Gordy's success and one poem would prove to have the most profound effect on him. He read Rudyard Kipling's poem "If" while still a teenager and the words became deeply imprinted on his psyche. He would reprint this poem in full fifty years later in his autobiography, saying, "I learned 'If' by heart (at age fifteen), picking apart each verse and finding ways to apply its philosophies to my own life." Berry lived his life governed by those last memorable lines:

> If you can fill the unforgiving minute
> With sixty seconds worth of distance run,
> Yours is the Earth and everything that's in it,
> And—which is more—you'll be a man, my son!

INSECURITY BREEDS GREATNESS

Raynoma Singleton, Gordy's second wife, wrote that he "suffered from a black inferiority complex" due to his "lack of formal education." She was convinced that "insecurity" was his "greatest weakness." Whether she was right or wrong, it is evident that Gordy was driven from some inner need to succeed and feared failure with a passion. Such is the power of the great as they turn the negative into a positive force. Gordy's rampant insecurity was in evidence when the Hollywood gurus questioned his use of a nonactress, Diana Ross, as Billie Holiday in *Lady Sings the Blues.* He ultimately paid them off rather than fail in his dream to successfully produce the movie of his heroine's life. This is the trait of a Type A personality who confuses self-worth with success and therefore will go to any length to succeed rather than suffer personal mortification.

Randy Taraborrelli wrote in *Call Her Miss Ross* that one of Gordy's Motown employees said, "Berry had this intense paranoia that someone was after him. No one really knew why he was so scared, but all of us in the inner circle knew something was very wrong in his life." Gordy's publicist said he "encouraged people to spy on each other" and reported that "for years he had two bodyguards at his side." Some of these stories incited rumors that Motown was going to be taken over by the Mafia. Other allegations kept the company in constant turmoil but also functioned as motivation for a man afraid to fail. Motown attorney Ralph Seiter called him "a ruthless gambler." Marvin Gaye told of him betting on the time it would take a raindrop to hit the window and reach the bottom.

LIFE CRISES AND TRAUMAS

The founder of Motown never quite forgot whence he came. A child of the Depression, welfare, and the repugnant environment of East Detroit, he would work to never return to those days. The family lost its home when he was two and was forced to go on welfare, which was a terrible thing for a proud family who felt they were above such travail. Gordy and seven siblings shared three beds, which helped hone his survival instincts. Being raised near Detroit's rough-and-tumble Hastings Street provided nostalgic memories of crime and degradation where "you could easily be killed by drunk people." Gordy wrote, "I was raised near the Detroit River, where you would just disappear and never be heard from again." This early chaos became a motivation to achieve and strive for perfection as an adult. Like most creative geniuses, Gordy's failures exceeded his successes. He never gave up despite continual failures beginning with his boring career as record store owner, pot and pan salesman, assembly worker, and insurance salesman.

Charisma

James Jones of *USA Today* interviewed Gordy regarding his autobiography, *To Be Loved*, in 1994. Writing about the interview, Jones characterized Gordy as a man "waving his arms in dramatic gestures. He exudes the charisma and magnetism of a Baptist preacher. It's easy to see why so many were enraptured by his dream of building a recording empire." Marvin Gaye added credence to this appraisal, saying, "Berry could make you think what he wanted was what you wanted, when actually what he wanted was what he wanted and not even in your best interest." Even those who didn't like his style admitted that he was very charismatic. Taraborrelli wrote, "Diana Ross was mesmerized by him." He added, "Sometimes he got cooperation as a result of his great charisma." One of Motown's early songwriters said, "Gordy's best talent was that he set fire to people around him." Part of Gordy's charismatic charm was creating a positive belief system. When a *Rolling Stone* reporter called Gordy "arrogant," in reference to one of his promotions, which said he intended to "revolutionize the record business," Gordy corrected the reporter, saying it wasn't arrogant: "That's what I'm gonna do." And he did! When Gordy purchased a palatial mansion in Detroit and named it Gordy Manor, it just added to his allure and charismatic persona.

Competitiveness

The Magic Man's favorite motto was, "Camaraderie, Creativity, and Competition." He wrote, "I believed competition breeds champions" and called his approach to develop stars in the early days "the survival of the fittest." He formed what he called "creative commando teams" to battle it out in "Battles of the Bands," where he pitted one against the other to bring out the best in them. Unfortunately, he found it also brought out the worst as well and had to stop his competition. "Battles" were sensational hits with the public where the Supremes battled the Velvettes, Martha and the Vandellas were pitted against the Marvelettes, and the Temptations went up against the Contours. The competition of this Motown Review made his blossoming stars perform better and gave the audiences a real variety show of enormous vitality. Gordy used the audience responses to gauge which groups he would promote and which he would table. Competition was Gordy's most motivating quality. It was his driving competitive spirit that made Motown a success.

Confidence

Gordy's self-esteem was so great that his employees saw him as dictator. It is this level of confidence, whether deluded or real, that becomes the cornerstone of all great achievement. Gordy was always a people person who loved to use motivational games to inspire his artists and employees. He created his own individual style and labeled it "People Over Structure." He said, "I built the structure around the person." He went so far as to have his friend Smokey Robinson write a company song to be sung at company events and meetings. Always the perennial optimist, he wrote, "We treated setbacks the same as success. They were both opportunities." One of the things which made this visionary so great was his consummate optimism for new ventures or artists. When he first met Michael Jackson he told him, "I'm gonna make you the biggest thing in the world and you're gonna be written about in history books." As Muhammad Ali said, "It ain't bragging if you do it," which validates Gordy's statement to Jackson. The Gloved One would write of Gordy years later, "He's the man who told the Jackson Five they would become a part of history and that is exactly what happened." Gordy went even further and predicted they would have three straight number one hits, which also proved true, but not until he worked feverishly to ensure that it happened.

Passion and Drive

Gordy wrote in his autobiography, "I was obsessed. I couldn't wait to get to work in the morning and hated to leave it at night." He was a Type A personality giving credence to Freud's hypothesis on achievement. High achievement emanates from within and according to Freud is a result of sublimated sex drive. It has now been shown that people with high testosterone are excessively driven, creative risk-takers and pursue sex with unabated passion. Berry Gordy could be the model for this definition of the "Big T" (high testosterone) personality. He was a driven man and apparently motivated by some mystical internal need for sex, power, and creative achievement. As a teenager, Gordy admitted, "Romance and love were always on my mind." It is a strange coincidence that a man from a family of eight children would have eight of his own and these eight would come from six different women only two of which he would marry. Gordy always had a penchant for blondes, whom, he said, he couldn't resist. Even his second wife, Raynoma, although black, was a blonde. Chris Clark was an extremely attractive California blonde woman who Berry put on the payroll and when on the road would arrange to have her in a room on one side of him with Diana Ross on the other side. Chris knew of Diana's personal role in his life but Diana never knew of Chris's.

Margaret Norton was a beautiful teenager when he met her and she ultimately became the mother of one of his eight children. She became one of Gordy's fantasy extravagances: "I always dreamed of Cinderella. When I saw the girl I knew she was my Cinderella." According to Raynoma, Gordy spent their honeymoon with Norton instead of with her. Gordy's psychosexually driven nature confirms one of Napoleon Hill's hypotheses in *Think and Grow Rich* that, "Sex energy is the creative energy of all geniuses." Hill believed, "There never has been, and never will be a great leader, builder, or artist lacking in this driving force of sex." Berry Gordy is the personification of Hill's findings, and achieved much of his success through a libidinal drive that knew few bounds.

Mixing work with pleasure was one of Gordy's weaknesses. Two of his wives were executives at Motown, in addition to his lovers who were placed on the payroll, such as Chris Clark, Margaret Norton, and Jeana Jackson, or those artists and professionals like Diana Ross and Suzanne de Passe. Gordy's enormous libidinal drive prompted Ross to say, "Berry is like nothing I have ever experienced. He's as demanding in our private lives as he is in business. . . . He's a terrific lover, but also a mean-minded one because he uses sex more as a tool to keep a woman in line than as an expression of true love." A Motown colleague said, "Berry Gordy was the freakiest man I'd ever known. He could make love to five different women a night and if Diana was one of them that was okay. But if she wasn't that was okay, too."

Hypomania

Gordy admitted to being "obsessed" with work and gambling, writing, "Work was the thing that brought me the most pleasure. Music was never work. It was like my hobby." Music had always been a labor of love for this hypomanic, which is what allowed him to be such a Type A workaholic. He was able to spend countless hours in the studio, and often the whole night, because it was the joy of his life. Gordy was always in a hurry and his impatience required him to stay and complete a mix or solve a problem instead of leaving it for tomorrow. He had what I have labeled "rushing sickness," which saw him driving fast cars and living life in the fast lane. He was an animated, almost manic personality who ate fast, talked fast, thought fast, and worked fast. Berry was a classic Type A personality who always scheduled more than could be accomplished. He said, "I was unaware of the realities of time and space. People I worked with often had to move mountains or create miracles to meet the challenges I presented."

Perfectionist

"I had a maddening need for perfection" in all things Gordy said after torturing Smokey Robinson with over one hundred mixes on one song. This maddening experience caused the more laid-back Robinson to call him a "madman." Berry Gordy was a perfectionist in everything he attempted as well as a control freak. He was incapable of allowing any record to be shipped without meeting his impeccable standards. Nothing short of excellence was tolerated at Motown and that ideology was born in the head of Berry Gordy. He admitted that success was to a great degree a function of "my obsession with perfection." It appears perfection was a critical and driving force in both Gordy's and Motown's success.

Independence

Berry Gordy was the "black sheep" of his family and certainly would have been persona non grata in any establishment-type organization. He rebelled against school and all traditional values. He delighted in being different. When he produced *Lady Sings the Blues* he violated every Hollywood maxim when he hired Diana Ross to be the leading lady and Suzanne de Passe as the screenwriter, two women who had no experience in either profession. Gordy was then considered totally off-the-wall when he made himself producer and director of the film. Hollywood and Paramount Pictures executives were in shock at Gordy's audacity. But the ever-confident renegade thumbed his nose at industry protocol and said, "I will use the same unconventional team approach we had always used in music, TV, and stage shows."

Temerity

Whether it was Ping-Pong in the office or $10,000 bets at the crap tables in Las Vegas, Gordy was the consummate gambler who often won or lost hundreds of thousands of dollars in one night. Gordy was highly introspective about his need for thrill-seeking and living on the edge. He wrote, "Whether sports, cards, math or history lessons, I made a game out of everything." Gordy loved to gamble, owned race horses, engaged in futures trading, and generally lived life as a high-roller both professionally and personally. He prided himself on allowing the people at Motown to "experiment creatively" and prodded them to risk without remorse and have "the courage not to be afraid to make mistakes."

Tenacity

When Gordy turned twenty-nine and was unemployed and still pursuing a dream his family saw as futile, they told him to grow up and get a job. The constant harping did not deter Gordy from his dream and he persevered to become rich and famous. He remained persistent even when he was close to insolvency, which occurred every few years until he sold out in the late eighties. Nothing ever deterred Gordy from his larger vision and goals in life and that is what ultimately made him great. After his sister's admonition at age twenty-nine to get serious, Gordy started Motown Records and within five years he was chairman of a highly successful enterprise. Within twenty years he had a net worth in excess of $300 million.

During one period in the mid-seventies Berry was dissolute when Diana Ross walked out on him in the middle of filming the movie *Mahogany,* which almost ruined him. She left him both professionally and personally, which was devastating to a man with his ego. A few months later the Jackson Five signed with CBS. Simultaneous with these tragic events Gordy's mother died and Gordy was close to losing everything. He had reached the very bottom of what scientists call *chaos* and only persevered by recalling the immortal words in Kipling's poem "If." That was his strength and power. No matter what happened or how long it took to get back on top, Gordy would persist. In the long run his determination paid big dividends.

Vision

Randy Taraborrelli writes that, "Berry's greatest asset would always be his musical intuition." He resorted to a right-brain, qualitative approach when marrying the black gospel sound with the more trendy pop music. The Motown Sound was born of his macrovision and whenever in doubt Gordy would turn to his "gut" rather than more objective solutions.

Will to Power

Berry Gordy was infused with an internalized will that was at the root of all his great success. Taraborrelli describes him as a man "intoxicated by great power," which is testimony to his compulsive need to control and infuse his will into his actions. Gordy's power was taken from whatever source he could find and became part of his personal arsenal for use in creating an empire. It appeared that he often willed success out of certain calamity, like when he lost both Diana Ross and the Jackson Five within months and was virtually insolvent. He came precariously close to losing the company but refused to capitulate, relying on his volition to make it.

Summary

Berry Gordy is now retired, living in Beverly Hills in a ten-acre, multimillion-dollar Tudor mansion previously owned by Red Skelton. His influence has been pervasive, with early influences on the Beatles and the Rolling Stones and more recently on Janet Jackson, Paula Abdul, and Madonna. It is difficult to list the many top artists, songs, and groups Gordy created at Motown. Part of Gordy's genius was positioning his work into the transitory movement he called "the Sound of Young America." He told *Rolling Stone* in 1990 that this strategy helped turn Motown into "a general-market company. . . . Whether you were black, white, green, or blue, you could relate to our music."

Berry Gordy relied on his risk taking, drive, vision, and need for perfection to achieve great success both personally and professionally. Those who take the greatest risks and live closest to the edge are those who experience the biggest wins in life and the Magic Man is living proof of that maxim. He was always willing to bet the farm, which is the reason he now lives in a palatial mansion. Berry Gordy is the classic Promethean personality who sought opportunity and possibilities and became an architect of change for the music world. Such success seldom comes without toil or torment. In Gordy's case he first had to fail as a boxer, salesman, foundry worker, and assembler before seeing the light and starting Motown. He even failed personally at writing songs for others, since he had to be his own person and in control of his own destiny. This is stuff of creative success.

Berry Gordy is a true creative genius and the Motown Sound is testimony to that genius. It will live on long past the time when his enormous contributions have been forgotten.

BERRY GORDY
Promethean Temperament (NT)
Songwriter—Motown founder
born November 28, 1928, Detroit, Michigan

Dominant trait: Risk-taking perfectionist with extroverted, intuitive personality
Motto: "If" by Kipling; "Communication breeds understanding"; "Camaraderie, creativity, competition"
Religion: Methodist
Philosophy: "Be direct, decisive, deliberate but not dumb"; "Only 3 kind of people: dumb, smart and super-smart . . . the super-smart don't care and the dumb don't know"; "We build careers, not hit records"
Nickname: "Junior"—family; "Black"—Diana Ross; "Fearless"—entertainers; "Magic Man"
Creation/innovation: Motown Sound, the sound that rocked the world, transforming black gospel music into pop
Successes: Hitsville—the world's most successful black enterprise; $800 loan in 1958 to $376 million in two decades
Vices: Books—a voracious reader; gambling (dice, cards, horses, commodities); golf; women
Romantic liaisons: Married four times with eight children by six different women; libidinal energy incarnate
Self-description: "Be yourself"; "My system was . . . doing it again and again until it was right"

Birth order: Six older siblings, one younger, of Bertha and Berry, Sr.; Namesake of father and grandfather
Parental influence: Strong family bonds with philosophical messages from tenacious father
Early transience: Moved at ages 2, 4, and 6, ending up on Detroit's rough East Side Hastings neighborhood
Father's occupation: Plaster contractor after a time on welfare during the Depression
Role models: Pop, Joe Louis—"the first person that made me know what 'hero' meant"
Hero mentors: Joe Louis, Sugar Ray Robinson, Mills Brothers, Billie Holiday, Ink Spots, Doris Day
Formal education: High school dropout, tenth grade; terrible student; taught himself to play piano by ear
Life crises: Welfare Depression childhood in East Detroit; 8 children shared 3 beds
Metamorphoses: Wrote and produced singing commercial for Gordy Printing at age 20, miraculously: "I write songs"

Charismatic: Marvin Gaye: "Berry could make you think what he wanted was what you wanted"; "great charisma"
Competitive: Taraborrelli: "He was a reckless gambler," "On any given day he could lose $50,000–$100,000"
Hypomanic: Smokey Robinson: "You're a madman" for hyperkinetic energy in all things
Independent rebel: Black sheep of family; unconventional in music, TV, stage, movies
Indomitable "will": "Obsessed—I couldn't wait to get to work in the morning and hated to leave at night"
Intuitive vision: "Musical intuition" his greatest asset; "innovative improvisation" his style—"opportunities"
Libidinal energy: "Romance and love were always on my mind"; womanizer with penchant for blondes
Perfectionist: "My obsession with perfection" a driving force
Risk-taker: "I had gambled since childhood"; high-roller in dice, poker, horses, commodities, women, and music
Self-confident: Sheer audacity of Hitsville USA sign; believed in himself when the experts decried his moves
Tenacious: Most people give up on their dreams, "I'm never going to give up mine"
Workaholic: "Loved work"; time never important, often "I worked all night"; "music was pleasure not work"
Honors: *Rolling Stone*: "Gordy's impact on popular music cannot be overstated"

10

Michael Jackson—Intuitive Vision

Entertainment Superstar Extraordinaire

"I must achieve. I must seek truth in all things."

The Peter Pan of Pop is the quintessential entertainer of this era if not all time. When Arsenio Hall officially inducted him into Soul Train's Hall of Fame on November 22, 1995, he told a national television audience, "Michael is undoubtedly the greatest entertainer to grace any stage, ever!" Arsenio's observations are confirmed by Jackson's millions of adoring fans, and even older adults, who are mesmerized by his ability to moonwalk across the stage of life. Jackson is an entertainment superstar with energy incarnate and has a unique ability to incite fans to emotional freneticism. For that reason the King of Pop has been included in this book as one of the world's creative superstars.

Jackson is an emotional man-child who emulates his mythological hero Peter Pan and adamantly refuses to grow up to face an adult world in which he finds little comfort. Jackson's fixation with childhood fantasy has contributed immensely to his success, since it has painted him with a persona of innocence and purity that appeals to the younger generation that dominates the record-buying industry. Many of Jackson's older fans are women who are attracted to his innocence and sensitivity. The King of Pop has an emotional need to be a perpetual teenager where innocence and truth prevail.

Being armed with the vivid imagination of a child has contributed greatly to Jackson's creative success, allowing him to push the envelope of fantasy and tradition. Psychologists have learned that creativity and innovation are the exclusive province of individuals capable of reverting to their "childhood imagination." Einstein was convinced he had few fertile thoughts or ideas after the age of thirteen and delighted in resorting to his childhood fantasies in concocting his theories on relativity. One of America's foremost authorities on creativity, Dr. Paul Torrance of the University of Minnesota, says: "Don't discourage fantasy. One of the qualities of the creative person, young or old, is his ability to move freely between the world of facts and reason, and the vast realms of the mind that lie just below the surface of consciousness." Torrance went on to denigrate qualification for the "gifted" category through the use of intelligence tests, saying, "No fallacy has done more harm to children or to rob society of creative talent." Jackson's ability to resort to childhood fantasies has been a great asset creatively.

It appears Michael Jackson was frozen in an emotional time warp due to a bizarre early life that robbed him of his childhood. His 1995 single "Scream" depicts Jackson on the back cover in a self-portrait that is very telling indeed. He is shown cowering in a fetal position with crayon scribblings on the wall in his handwriting: "Before you judge me, try hard to love me, look within your heart then ask, have you seen my childhood. Signed M. J." This gives great insight into Jackson's complex psyche, that of a thirty-eight-year-old man who is still desperately searching for a lost youth and crying out for acceptance. He is a man desirous of reliving a childhood, which is an impossible undertaking, and who is adamantly resisting the dog-eat-dog world of adulthood. He is a man perpetually frustrated by people who will not allow him to live life his way, as a perpetual teenager with youthful friends. He is virtually begging for the right to live life on his terms, a life in complete opposition to societal rules and mores of acceptance. He is a man who, like most children, constantly feeds his emotional needs, in ways like creating his own amusement park, building his own zoo, and marrying his idol's daughter as a way to escape into the fantasyland of his dreams.

Carl Jung gave us some insight into Jackson's great entertainment genius when he said, "The debt we owe to the play of the imagination is incalculable." By refusing to grow up, Jackson has in many respects become the Peter Pan of his imagination. He attempted to marry his fantasy heroine Tinkerbelle—the daughter of the King—Lisa Marie Presley, but when that failed he immediately sought to create his own child by nurse Debbie Rowe. Their baby is due in the spring of 1997.

Jackson and Walt Disney have many similar characteristics. Like Disney, Jackson dislikes and fears adults, preferring the company of children and animals, who are nonthreatening, honest, and love unconditionally. It is not surprising that Walt Disney was always one of the King of Pop's fantasy heroes. Both men continually regressed into their own subconscious havens of emotional safety where they were able to live out their wildest dreams of creative illusion.

Because one of Jackson's most endearing fantasies has been Peter Pan, he also is attempting "to never grow up" and would prefer to fly away to other mysterious lands where no one can harm him. His home in Santa Barbara, California, was called Never Land, but that proved insufficient to protect him so Michael now lives and travels outside the United States much of the time. This has caused Steven Spielberg to comment, "Michael is one of the last living innocents. . . . I've never seen anybody like Michael. He is an emotional child-star."

Michael Jackson sold in excess of one hundred million records during the eighties, including the largest-selling album in history, *Thriller.* No one person has ever been able to spawn the same degree of adulation as this man. He combined the media drawing power and mesmerizing charisma of a Babe Ruth and Elvis Presley with the bizarre iconoclasm of Greta Garbo. His bizarre friendship with a monkey, attempting to physically make himself into a white Diana Ross, buying the Elephant Man's bones, and having a personal sleeping chamber all add to his bizarre persona. These eccentricities have also contributed to a business acumen that makes Jackson creatively astute, which was never more apparent than when he acquired the right to the Beatles songs.

Michael Jackson is without question a consummate creative genius who has been able to transform emotional retardation into artistic success. Consequently, his enormous financial successes have allowed him to live out his wildest fantasies, both professionally and personally. Michael Jackson is arguably the world's most enigmatic and spellbinding superstar. The Wizard of Odd has few peers onstage, where he can mesmerize the most callous of critics. Every move he makes is a media event and when he dances the truly great stop and watch. When Fred Astaire saw him perform the moonwalk dance to the song "Billie Jean" on the "Motown 25" TV special in the mid-eighties, he called Jackson and told him, "You're a hell of a mover. . . . You're an angry dancer. I'm the same way." Jackson said, "It was the greatest compliment I had ever received in my life."

Innovative Contributions

The innovative contributions of the King of Pop are a function of his renegade approach to creativity, which is manifested by his refusal to follow tradition and by his total reliance on his mystical vision. Jackson intuitively knew that success in show business is fleeting at best and that one must remain fresh and, when necessary, bizarre; he found those qualities in characters like P. T. Barnum, Greta Garbo, and the Three Stooges. The Peter Pan of Pop came to the realization that uniqueness would prove critical to his remaining on top and he began fashioning his image as an iconoclastic megastar while still a teen. He adopted the single white glove, white socks, and sunglasses as one of many signature looks that were not only bizarre but in synch with some of his own personal needs. He once told a reporter who questioned his attire, "My attitude is if fashion says it's forbidden, I'm going to do it." Such a defiant stance against tradition and establishment values is the true mark of the innovative creative genius. Joseph Schumpeter long ago defined "innovation" as "creative destruction" and those wanting to become creative must adhere to this fundamental principle. Jackson not only has adhered to it, he has improved upon it, as his nickname Wizard of Odd testifies.

Jackson's true creative contribution, however, is immersed in his unique ability to innovate on stage. Jackson admits that he never preprograms any performance and allows himself freedom to innovate throughout. Instead of staging his performance like most entertainers, he prefers extemporaneous innovation where he can move to the feel of the audience and his own energy. That is his strength and his genius and the origin of his most famous dance, the moonwalk.

When asked about the new genre of dance, Jackson says the dance emanates from his inner soul and is "spontaneous." He said he decided "I was going to walk backward and forward at the same time, like walking on the moon." His innovations are an irreverent respect for tradition and his defiant acts onstage, like grabbing his crotch, to prove his artistic iconoclasm.

Early Personal History

Michael Jackson was born in Gary, Indiana, on August 29, 1958, as the seventh child of a family of nine. He was the son of Katherine Scruse, a Sears cashier, and Joe Jackson, a steel mill worker and sometime guitarist. Nothing in the family history would have indicated that young Michael or any of his siblings would be destined for show business greatness. The family lived in a house built for three or four people. In the Jacksons' case it housed two adults and nine children, requiring Michael to sleep with his brother Marlon in a triple bunkbed with older brothers both above and below.

Young Michael demonstrated signs of rhythmic talent when he would gyrate to the washing machine at eighteen months. Joe worked as a laborer in a steel mill and managed his own rhythm and blues band at night, which caused him to be overworked and overwrought. Joe proved to be a tyrannical and authoritarian parent who took out his own frustrations on the children while the ever-submissive Katherine watched but never interfered. Joe was abusive and constantly used psychological threats to maintain control over his large brood of children. He would terrorize them with such bizarre behavior as pointing a .38 revolver at their heads and pulling the trigger and laughing if they flinched. Anyone who misbehaved bore the brunt of his masochistic nature and Michael was not only the smallest but the most independent and bore the brunt of Joe's perverse wrath.

Katherine was a Jehovah's Witness who instilled that faith's strong, dogmatic beliefs in her children and especially in Michael, who she would take along on her door-to-door crusades. Since Michael was the child most influenced by his mother's devout religious beliefs, he was destroyed when Christmas was canceled the first year after his mother's conversion. Jehovah's Witnesses do not believe in Christmas, swearing, smoking, drinking, fishing, or even hunting. Young Michael was so indoctrinated that he follows these religious doctrines to this day. His mother loved to sing to him. His favorites were "Danny Boy" and "You Are My Sunshine." When Joe found any musical inclination in any of his children he insisted they become part of the family's performing Jacksons, who became known as the Jackson Five. In the first grade Michael was asked to sing "Climb Any Mountain" from *The Sound of Music,* and his performance brought the house down. The teachers and student body gave him a standing ovation, which made a lasting impression on young Michael. Hearing of the event, Joe made sure that Michael became a permanent fixture in the Jackson Five.

Joe was a tough taskmaster and young Michael was just rebellious and defiant enough to become the target of his terrible wrath. Jackson wrote in his memoirs about how he would run until caught and then "I'd try to get back at him, or I'd just fight back swinging my fists." Jackson's lightning-like quickness proved advantageous, but also a detriment, since Joe would become furious when he was unable to catch the fleet Michael. Once caught, Michael would receive the brunt of Joe's wrath. Joe quickly booked the popular Jackson Five into any club that paid well, regardless of the environment. During these early engagements the Jackson Five found themselves working hoodlum hangouts, strip clubs, and gambling joints. At the Guys and Dolls in Chicago, the children performed between strip acts while young Michael watched the men throw money after the women for a moment of sexual excitement.

Jackson remembers little else as a child but these tours and wrote, "The majority of the time we spent working." By the time Jackson was eight the group was performing five sets a night six nights a week at Mr. Lucky's in Gary, Indiana. By the time he was nine they had appeared at the Apollo in Harlem in addition to gigs in Philadelphia, Kansas City, St. Louis, Cleveland, Boston, Phoenix, and Washington, D.C. It was not the most idyllic life for nurturing a young boy into adulthood. Jackson was a man-child during this era, which became the fundamental cause of him later becoming a child-man attempting to relive his lost childhood. He would spend years desperately searching for that lost childhood and, like most people, looking in all the wrong places, which caused him further pain. Of this period in his life Jackson has written, "I can remember looking at those kids playing games. I'd just stare in wonder. I couldn't imagine such freedom."

The King of Pop was a cute kid and the youngest of the Jackson Five. His nurturing in strip joints began having subtle but lasting effects. One night "stripper Mary Rose . . . took off her panties and threw them to the audience. The men would pick them up and sniff them. I was blown away." Jackson soon became enamored of fairy tales and became a voracious reader while his older brothers reveled in the provocative education surrounding them. Jackson's favorite books were the Bible and *Peter Pan,* although he said, "I read everything I could get my hands on." Later when they were in California and touring the country to masses of groupies, his older brothers would bring women from the audience into the room they shared, since Joe insisted on saving money and made the boys live together for many years. A shocked Jackson told of his brothers performing the wildest sex acts in front of him when he was thirteen, which totally destroyed his image of women and sex. He said they would often awaken him with their sexual gymnastics and "degrading acts." He attempted to forget these despicable acts and would "bury himself in his faith" and act as if they never occurred. Even his father would display his sexual powers by bringing women by young Michael's room to show them off before taking them to bed, which really destroyed a boy who adored his ever-faithful mother. Katherine would turn her head to Joe's philandering, which only added to the confusion in Jackson's head over the morality involved in adult relationships.

One of Joe's most despicable acts of masochism was related by Jackson in his memoirs, *Moonwalk.* He was asleep in his room and woke up to the smell of smoke and started screaming when he saw his foot smoking from a match held by Joe, who was hysterically laughing at Michael's discomfort. Such was the early life of a superstar who grew up with an identity crisis due to the unnatural circumstances of his early success but more so due to a father who enjoyed torturing what he couldn't control.

Professional History

Jackson's future, as well as that of the Jackson Five, was secured after they were auditioned by Berry Gordy in early 1969 when Michael was nine years old, his brother Marlon, eleven, Jermaine, fourteen, and Tito and Jackie, fifteen and seventeen, respectively. Gordy was already being hailed as the "Magic Man," since he had become a star maker for Diana Ross and the Supremes, Gladys Knight and the Pips, Stevie Wonder, Marvin Gaye, and Smokey Robinson and the Miracles, among others. The founder of Motown was extremely impressed with Michael and said after that first meeting "he had an unknown quality that I didn't completely understand but I knew was special. Somehow at that first meeting he let me know of his hunger to learn, and how willing he was to work as hard as necessary to be great, to go to the top."

Gordy said after the first audition, "The little kid had an incredible *knowingness* about him," and he told Jackson, "I'm going to make you the biggest thing in the world." He later told Jackson, "You're going to be written about in history books," which had a mesmerizing effect on this nine-year-old. Gordy would become his substitute father and professional mentor from that day forward. Then Gordy very adroitly assigned Diana Ross the task of grooming him in the nuances of stage presence, moving the group to California so they could be close to him and his mistress. Jackson moved in with Diana in preparation for their national debut at the Hollywood Palace on October 18, 1969, where they were introduced by Ross and Sammy Davis, Jr. Their first song, "I Want You Back," became an instant hit and by December had shot up to number one on the charts. Living with Ross, Jackson fell madly in love and began mimicking her actions. After all, she was an international superstar who had taken on the responsibility of mentoring his career.

Gordy proved to be very prophetic when he told the boys, "You'll hit the charts just as Diana Ross and [the] Supremes did," referring to their three straight number one hits. True to his prediction, the first recording, "I Want You Back," went to number one. Jackson was eleven. Soon it was followed by two more number-one hits, "ABC" (Jackson's favorite) and "I'll Be There." Gordy wrote some years later, "The Jackson Five had gone from anonymity to a household name. . . . They would be the last big stars to come rolling off my assembly line."

JACKSON BECOMES A SUPERSTAR

By this time Jackson was emulating James Brown, Jackie Wilson, and Sammy Davis, Jr., but he was under Diana Ross's emotional spell. He said, "I was crazy about her. She was my mother, my [platonic] lover, and my sister all combined in one amazing person." Jackson began emulating her and desperately wanted to become a little male Diana Ross in looks, actions, and as an entertainer. He actually asked people if he looked like her and attempted to make his voice sound like hers.

Within a couple of years, Smelly, as his brothers called him, had become the dominant Jackson and the one who had the economic clout to call the shots. However, Jackson remained passive and capitulated to the iron will of his father, if only to placate his mother, who asked that he not break up the family by going on his own. During this period Jackson was used as the heavy to break from their Motown contract. Joe had made a more favorable deal for them with CBS's Epic label. Joe and Michael's brothers knew that he was the one CBS was after and persuaded the teenager to tell Gordy they were leaving. By this time Jackson had become a megastar.

Despite his soft voice and effeminate looks, Jackson was strong-willed and admitted that the day he terminated Gordy's contract "I was a lion." It would take a few more years for him to gain the courage to fire his father, but when the time came, he did it with the same indomitable will. Contrary to popular belief, Michael Jackson is a strong decision maker and firmly in control of his professional destiny. He wrote in his memoirs, "I am a person who is very much in control of his life."

Jackie Kennedy, who interviewed Jackson during the late seventies, once characterized him as "a perfectionist who is constantly challenging himself." This was never so true as when he won just one Grammy for his *Off the Wall* album in 1979 and was devastated by this abject rejection of his work. He construed the critics' assessment of his work as the ultimate rejection and vowed to make them kneel in subjugation to his genius, saying, "Wait until next time, next time! . . . That experience lit a fire in my soul." True to his prediction, this driven man pushed himself like never before in producing what would become the album titled *Thriller*—the largest-selling album in history, released in November 1982. This record-setting album spawned three number-one hit songs and three music videos: "Billie Jean," "Beat It," and "Thriller." The album not only exceeded the record-breaking eight million sales of *Off the Wall,* it eventually sold an unprecedented forty-six million copies, a feat that has never been topped. This work catapulted Jackson to the pinnacle of show business success and made him a very wealthy young man who was still just twenty-five years old and purportedly still a virgin. Jackson was not merely one-dimensional. He not only performed "Billie Jean," he had written and produced it.

THE KING OF POP IS BORN

February 28, 1984, was Grammy Awards night and above all, this night was Michael Jackson's night. He wasn't interested in the politics of the Grammys like many artists, but said, "I just want as many of 'em as I can get." That night he received an unprecedented twelve nominations. He dazzled the audience by showing up for his coronation as King of Pop in a spangled uniform with epaulets, his signature rhinestoned glove on the right hand, and Brooke Shields on his arm. The eighteen-year-old Brooke was not his first choice for a date on his night of nights as he chose to sit between her and Emmanuel Lewis, his twelve-year-old playmate. That night Jackson won Best Record ("Beat It"), Best Vocalist for Pop ("Beat It"), Rock ("Thriller"), and Blues ("Billie Jean"). He also won Best Children's Album (*E.T.*), Best Rhythm and Blues Song ("Billie Jean"), and Best Record Producer, an award he shared with his new musical mentor, Quincy Jones. Jones gave the ultimate tribute to Jackson that evening by telling the audience, "I've seen four phenomena in my lifetime: Frank Sinatra, Elvis Presley, The Beatles, and Michael Jackson." One of the first indications of the megastar's desperate search for a lost youth through an identification with children was seen that night. He not only had Emmanuel Lewis sitting on his lap most of the evening to the chagrin of his date, Brooke Shields, he told the audience, when asked, that his favorite song was "My Favorite Things."

INNOVATIVE ENTREPRENEUR

In March 1985 the savvy twenty-seven-year-old acquired the ATV Publishing library for $47.5 million. It included such all-time hits as the Beatles' "A Hard Day's Night," "Yesterday," "Ticket to Ride," and "All You Need is Love." When that library is coupled with the Jackson megahits, it is awe-inspiring indeed. When he married the King's daughter, Lisa Marie, Jackson added copyrights to the Presley library of hits, which could make him the musical potentate for the twenty-first century. Jackson made a deal in the fall of 1995 with Sony that adds other potential assets to his repertoire. He received a $95 million stipend and ended up with access to Elvis and the Three Stooges.

CHILD ABUSE ALLEGATIONS

Jackson spent the balance of the eighties producing, writing, and performing on tour and in the studio. He was slow to realize the great price of fame and fortune, as he no longer had a personal life and often went out in disguise. Jackson was no longer able to go to his favorite haunts like Disneyland or other children's amusement parks. He had the money and was able to spend time in amusement parks in Europe. His adamant refusal to grow up became the focus of the media, which found great delight in exposing his bizarre and childish needs. By the late eighties rumors had begun within the industry and within the Jackson family about

Jackson's preference for the company of young children, especially boys. These rumors became rampant and child abuse claims began surfacing in the early nineties.

Jackson's affinity for children and a juvenile lifestyle was a by-product of a lost childhood, which he was desperately attempting to reclaim. One CBS executive gave some insight into his obsession, saying, "Michael is totally, absolutely obsessed with retaining a teenage figure . . . the secret of eternal youth." His conflicting emotions over his sexuality were not helped by his father and brothers, who were worried over his lack of sexual desire as a teenager and once locked him in a hotel room with two prostitutes to ensure that he lost his virginity. In classic Michael Jackson style he grabbed the Bible off the bedstand and began quoting Scripture until the hookers finally became frustrated and left him with his Bible.

The superstar was forced to cancel his "Dangerous" tour prematurely in 1993 because of the Joey Randall child abuse allegations, which he purportedly settled with the boy's parents for $26 million rather than face an interminable trial and negative publicity. It was probably a cheap alternative and one that was critical to his mental health. He ultimately appeared on national television for the sole purpose of squelching rumors of his sexual preferences and other more serious allegations about his abuse of children. Both Oprah Winfrey and Diane Sawyer interviewed him on national prime-time shows—some indication of the power of this megastar—to answer the media's questions about his sexuality. In the interim he had married Lisa Marie Presley, which the media interpreted as a ruse to divert attention from his sexual abuse legal problems. After their sudden divorce was announced in mid-January 1996, music insider Jamie Foster Brown, publisher of *Sister 2 Sister*, said, "They were two superstar kids who got together to help each other out. I thought she was being a friend to him and I don't think he was really in love with her." He then created a furor in the media by paying his long-term nurse, Debbie Rowe, to have his child via artificial insemination. The resulting hysteria caused him to marry her in November 1996.

The couple married in the Dominican Republic so as not to create a carnival-like atmosphere, as would have occurred in the United States. Jackson told Diane Sawyer that he intended to have a family and would adopt the two Presley children. He also called the sexual child abuse allegations pure hype, reiterating that he "*Never, ever*" had touched a child. He implied the accusations were motivated by money. I am convinced that Michael is asexual and prefers the company of teen males, not as sexual objects, but, sadly, as playmates.

COMEBACK

In 1995 Jackson released a new album, *HIStory—Past, Present and Future*. This appears to have been a cathartic exorcising of his innermost monsters relative to the previous years, where his image and ego were devastated. In this album he attempts to assuage those allegations and give some insight into the psyche of Michael Jackson. In "Scream" he resorts to bizarre, rebellious, and oft-described bigoted lyrics. He utilized stereotypical imagery and lyrics to portray his innocence to the world. But once again his eccentricities backfired when he wrote lyrics like "Jew/me, sue/me, kick/me, kike/me" which were intended as a philosophical message but were viewed by the media as bigoted statements. He went back into the studio and changed the offensive words but justified his lyrics as ideological statements of defiance which he was unable to speak but could sing. His words "The whole system sucks" and "I'm taking no shit" would not have played well in media statements but prove to be acceptable in lyrics where artists typically attempt to communicate their innermost feelings. Jackson was obviously an angry man in late 1995, and attempting to tell his story to the world.

What Makes Jackson Tick?

Jackson is an interesting combination of a man who, like Walt Disney, was emotionally arrested in childhood due to fatherly abuse. The real world was far too demanding and scary, so he refused to be part of it. Animals and children pose little threat and the fantasyland of amusement parks and movies meet his need for innocence and purity.

Michael is a committed vegetarian and teetotaler who disdains all drugs other than tranquilizers. One of Michael's problems resulting from his passionate need for remaining perpetually young was a bout with anorexia. He became so obsessed with his weight and figure that he went to great lengths to maintain a teenage figure that resulted in hospitalization a number of times. At one time he weighed only 103 pounds and has experienced many panic and anxiety attacks often compounded by his spartan diet.

Michael Jackson has what behavioral psychologists label an *Apollonian temperament.* He is highly "intuitive" with a "feeling" approach to problem resolution. These personality types prefer a life as catalyst and spokesperson or energizer. They work by interacting with people and values. They are idealistic and imaginative enablers who would prefer to nurture the world than own it. They see the big picture and are sensitive to the possibilities of themselves and others. Michael Jackson certainly fits this profile.

As with everyone, Jackson's greatest assets often proved to be his biggest problems. His total fixation with childhood has made him a man who is truly pure of heart and an artist capable of producing wonderfully fresh and original entertainment. This highly sensitive nature has also been at the seat of the constant sexual abuse allegations. Jackson is a shy, highly introverted, and intuitive artist who is a perfectionist and recluse. He likes structure and makes decisions very rationally even though he is a very sensitive, polite, and compassionate artist. He is far more comfortable onstage than off but the stage he prefers is one steeped in fantasy and make-believe.

Mythological Hero Mentors

Jackson began escaping in books while very young and adopted their fictional heroes as his own. The fantasy hero who became imprinted on his psyche was Peter Pan. Jackson went so far in emulating his hero that he attempted to fly. He became so caught up in this fantasy fairy tale that he told reporters during his teen years, "We can fly, you know. We just don't know how to think the right thoughts and levitate ourselves off the ground." In that inner world of the subconscious Jackson was Peter Pan and that image became the "success imprint" which manifested itself in the child/man megastar who flies across the stage doing the moonwalk. It is also the reclusive eccentric who lives in Neverland in Santa Barbara, California. Michael Jackson has so identified with his mythological hero/mentor that he has reincarnated himself into that image.

Mythical role models were responsible for many "success imprints" in this megastar's early life. Real-life role models then replaced Peter Pan. Diana Ross was the first major entertainment influence on him, soon followed by singer James Brown and dancers Gene Kelly and Fred Astaire. Professionally, Berry Gordy and Quincy Jones have proven to be the greatest influence on him other than his mother.

INSECURITY BREEDS GREATNESS

The King of Pop wrote in *Moonwalk,* "I am one of the loneliest people in the world." His inability to cope with a grown-up world has left him emotionally retarded with symptoms ranging from anxiety and panic attacks to addiction to Valium and Percodan. Jackson even considered suicide during his 1993 child abuse debacle. Life's adversities have contributed to his fear of failure, which has manifested itself in a desperate need to be perfect in everything he does. Highly introspective, Jackson once said, "The biggest struggle is right there in the mirror. To a great degree my identity as a person was tied to my identity as a celebrity."

Like most Type A personalities Jackson is most comfortable when enmeshed in activity onstage. He is never satisfied unless his performances are perfect and the resultant adulation is overwhelming. The bottom line is that much of his enormous success can be attributed to his terrible fear of failure. He wrote, "My father made me feel worthless," which in his case has led him to overachieving to compensate for his emotional loss. In his case insecurity has been the father of greatness, although it can prove destructive for weaker individuals. Jackson biographer Christopher Anderson confirms this with his conclusion, "Michael channeled into his work all his pent-up anxiety and rage over what his parents had done to him. Every soul-wrenching performance was an unspoken indictment of Joe."

CRISES AND TRAUMAS

This tragic superstar was first traumatized at age five, when his mother went through conversion to the rigorous dogma of the Jehovah's Witnesses religion. This Christian sect does not believe in celebrating Christmas as a holiday and suddenly canceling Christmas can be truly devastating to a five-year-old who is not so steeped in religious dogma as he is the fun and presents under a brightly lit Christmas tree. That first Christmas without presents was an unhappy experience for Jackson. He responded by pouring his soul into song and dance.

During these years Michael was abused, threatened, and beaten by an overbearing and authoritarian father. This drove young Michael to rebel against everything his father stood for and to make himself as unlike his father as possible. He hated his father with a passion and loved his mother unconditionally. Then he grew up and faced the teen trauma of pimples. His whole face became covered with acne, causing him to become a virtual recluse who refused to leave his room for fear of being seen by anyone, including his family. He was delighted when he began working with Quincy Jones, who covered his face with makeup. This introduced him to the world of physical change and plastic surgery. He refused to remove the makeup and would go home with the makeup still on his face in order to mask the ugly pimples. Jackson wrote in his autobiography, "I became subconsciously scarred by this experience."

Jackson's most serious crisis occurred while shooting a Pepsi commercial in January 1984. The pyrotechnics used to shoot the commercial ignited his hair. A crew member said, "It was horrifying. For a moment he looked like a walking inferno." One of his friends, Miko Brando, raced up and doused the flames, but Jackson understandably panicked from the burns on his head and face. Jackson wrote that the doctor in attendance said that "it was a miracle I was alive." Jackson was at the peak of his popularity in 1984 and this crisis turned into a publicity boon that could not have been better planned by Madison Avenue. The hospital was bombarded with calls and the King of Pop's face was plastered on every front page in America due to the near-tragedy. When Pepsi awarded Jackson $1.5 million in damages he donated it to charity, gaining even more publicity from what could have been a disaster.

By far Jackson's greatest tragedy was the child abuse charges by Joey Randall in 1993, which were finally resolved when he paid an estimated $26 million to forego a long media circus trial. The payoff gave the appearance of a man who is guilty, but, in this child-man's defense, he is highly sensitive and was probably emotionally incapable of withstanding such a trial. It would have been a debilitating ordeal and the price was probably very cheap relative to a trial, which would have potentially ruined his ability to earn megabucks that can dwarf the payoff amount. He probably earned back these monies within one year of the payment. Jackson was rich enough to avoid the trauma—he had the luxury of buying off his adversaries. The *HIStory* album is a direct result of this trauma in Jackson's life and once again proves that crisis is the mother of creativity.

Charisma

The King of Pop has a mesmerizing stage presence that can bring audiences to tears or passionate adulation. When young, his angelic look caused teens and pre-teens to scream hysterically. Teenage girls loved his sensitive nature and when in his twenties he said, "I haven't slept with a woman. I don't believe in sex before marriage. I am still a virgin," it only incited them to greater hero worship. Later, many would throw themselves at him in a mad attempt to save him from his apparent gayness. An icon had been born. He was the idol of the teenage set and even such strong personalities as Tatum O'Neal and Brooke Shields threw themselves at him with total abandon.

Jackson's charismatic power is that of Elvis and Babe Ruth that can captivate audiences and make his fans do strange things. Many young girls have begged him to father their children and gone to inordinate lengths to feast at the king's table. The *Village Voice* said in 1983, after the release of the "Beat It" rock video, that Jackson had an "astonishing sexuality." Further evidence of Jackson's enormous charismatic appeal is the mass imitation of his dress and dance.

Competitiveness

Contrary to his submissive persona, Jackson is highly competitive. Despite his soprano voice, feminine attire, and ascetic behavioral style, this seemingly submissive man is quite aggressive in battle. He adamantly fought harassment suits and repeatedly appeared in court in Chicago and Cleveland to defend against plagiarism suits. Each time he won, which demonstrated his competitive nature and proved his willingness to fight when pushed to the wall. When his agent Freddie Demann advised him not to do "Motown 25," Jackson impulsively fired him for such stupid advice. He had been resilient enough as a teenager to do the same with Berry Gordy and his manager father. It is this indomitable competitive spirit that has saved him from being destroyed by the continual child abuse charges brought against him by enterprising and mercenary individuals. Jackson's competitive juices came to the forefront in 1979 when he was devastated over winning just one Grammy Award for his *Off the Wall* album and vowed to get even. He said, "All I could think of was the next album." This rejection led to the creation of *Thriller*—the best-selling album of all time. This time Jackson was placated after receiving an unprecedented eight Grammys.

Confidence

"I am very self-confident" and "I aim to be the very best I can be," says Michael Jackson. An internally inspired optimism pervades his every move onstage. He exudes the self-confidence of someone who "knows" he is right. Jackson admits to being "very self-confident" and adds, "I'm an instrument for the expression of ecstasy." Producers have been awed by his positive demeanor, causing one to say, "Michael is totally self-assured. . . . He told his brothers where to stand, how to move, how to sing" even though he was much younger. Jackson told the *Los Angeles Times,* "Onstage . . . I feel so free, so unlimited . . . like I can do anything." During a moment of philosophical introspection in his autobiography, he said, "Often people don't see what I see. They have too much doubt. . . . You can't do your best when you're doubting yourself. If you don't believe in yourself who will?"

Hypomania

Jackson has boundless energy. He would often wear out twenty different dancers in rehearsals and then go home and practice. No one could keep up with him. He wrote, "I work all the time. There's so much I want to do and so much work to be done." Reminiscing about the past, he said, "I remember my childhood as mostly work. . . . The majority of the time was spent working." He is a Type A personality who suffers from what I call "rushing sickness." He is manic and always in a hurry. He talks fast, walks fast, thinks fast, eats fast, and works fast. Such is the nature of the great and powerful. Speed wins in both sports and life. Jackson is quick as a cat, which is obvious in watching him dance and his quickness has become synonymous with his persona.

When he collapsed onstage while preparing for an HBO concert in late 1995, it was attributed to a virus, but the bottom line is that Michael Jackson had once again pushed himself far beyond the limits of human tolerance. His nephews Taj, Taryll, and TJ (Tito's children) told TV's "Day and Date" they weren't surprised when he collapsed. They said: "He's a workaholic. He had a lot of pressure going into this concert. He knew that everyone was going to be watching this. He works day and night, night and day, sometimes missing meals . . . sometimes without sleep for three or four days."

Independence

Innovative and creative geniuses tend to be renegades who refuse to listen to experts. In Jackson's case he literally and figuratively dances to his own tune. Jackson delights in being different, which is such a contrast to mediocre entertainers who prefer following the lead of others and always avoid being too unique. Jackson is so different that most people see him as an eccentric at best and bizarre at worst. His own lyric said it best, "Life isn't so bad after all, if you live it off the wall." The *HIStory* album is further testimony to Jackson's rebellious nature. He wrote and produced the lyrics as a contentious response to the media who he sees characterizing him in a negative light just because he dares to be different. *HIStory*'s lyrics and graphic illustrations were originally written to overcome prejudice, ignorance, and bigotry but only served to highlight Jackson's idiosyncratic hangups. Jackson changed some of the lyrics in response to media criticism but insisted on doing it his way. Jackson's defiance is a direct result of an autocratic father who he refused to acknowledge as his superior. He suffered many physical and emotional bruises by daring to resist his father, and the struggle made him far stronger for the experience. He has not changed and his renegade nature has made him into an innovative adult.

Passion and Drive

Michael Jackson is a driven man. *Rolling Stone* said in 1983, "He was so energetic that at five years old he was like a leader—a dance monster." According to biographer Christopher Anderson, he has a "superhuman drive." The truth is that Michael Jackson is determined to be the very best he can be, which he confirmed in his autobiography, saying, "My goal is to do the best in every area," adding, "When I perform I lose myself. I'm in total control of that stage." In a 1995 interview on "Prime Time Live" Jackson told Diane Sawyer, "I am obsessed with perfection." Such is the mentality of the creative genius. Jackson admitted that he became an entertainer, not because of his parents, but because "I was compelled to do it . . . by my own inner life." The enormous psychic energy of Michael Jackson is the driving force behind his greatness.

Perfectionist

Quincy Jones calls Michael Jackson "a headstrong perfectionist." The world's greatest entertainer didn't get that way by accepting anything less than the best. Jackson proved his dedication to perfection in 1979 when he received what he thought was grossly inadequate recognition for his first solo album, *Off the Wall*. He was so devastated he dedicated the next two years to becoming the dominant force within the industry. He succeeded when *Thriller* became the largest-selling album in history. Jackson approaches everything with the same resolve and that is what has made him great. He accepts nothing but the very best from his associates or himself and often suffers from severe panic or anxiety attacks when he falls short of his objectives. Perfectionism and control are classic symptoms of the Type A personality and Jackson fits the model well.

Temerity

While onstage the King of Pop lives on the very edge of acceptance. That is his modus operandi. He is always willing to gamble that he is right even when the majority of experts disagree. Most people thought his staging of *Thriller* was wrong.

His mentor and soulmate Quincy Jones thought it would fail, saying that "it was a mistake" to produce such a number. Michael refused to be dissuaded and went against the experts and through sheer guts and temerity succeeded even beyond his own wildest imagination. He was proved right and, as in all things, won big because he had been willing to bet big.

When Jackson's brothers jointly agreed to hire Don King to promote their "Victory" tour, Jackson was the only one who saw through this shallow promoter. Only Jackson had the guts to stand up and tell them, "This guy is a joke. I don't like him. I don't trust him." Jackson turned out to be accurate in his appraisal and took it on himself to terminate King's services.

When Pepsi offered the Jackson Five $5 million to sponsor their "Victory" tour with a $700,000 bonus to each of the brothers, Jackson had the guts to tell them, "I don't drink that crap and I'm sure not going to tell other people to drink it—especially kids." Jackson was adamant and refused to be part of the contract, which then jeopardized the whole "Victory" tour. He finally capitulated in deference to his mother, who pleaded with him not to break up the family. While shooting the commercial for the sponsorship, his hair caught fire, which almost ended his career, if not his life. Ever the showman, Jackson was rushed to the hospital waving to the cameras with third-degree burns on his head. The King of Pop has a fearless side that is often lost in his bizarre actions and attire but in the end it has led him to the top of his profession and kept him there for over twenty-five years.

Tenacity

Jackson is tenacious. When he was ridiculed for his outlandish dress, badmouthed for his desire to be with kids, and ridiculed for his music and lyrics, he never gave up or capitulated to the establishment. He accepted the wrath of the media and resolved the child abuse allegations by doing what most experts predicted was the kiss of death by paying off his accuser. He resolved the issue with a $26 million settlement, which took enormous courage since the payoff had the taint of guilt written all over it. But Jackson refused to listen to counsel and persistently moved on to another phase of his life. The Wizard of Odd never succumbed to societal pressures and lived life on his terms no matter the price. He told Diana Sawyer, "I will remain in this country if I can just be myself. If I can't I will leave." For much of 1996 he was gone but he has shown no signs of giving up his reign as the King of Pop.

Vision

When a Chicago judge asked if he had plagiarized the lyrics and music for his recording of "The Girl Is Mine," Jackson told him emphatically, "I woke up from my sleep and wrote the song." This might seem unusual to some people but it was the way Jackson created. He relied on his special vision for the words and music of most of his hit songs. He was convinced he had what he called a special "spontaneous vision." He said, "People don't see what I see. I rely on instinct." He was referring to his work on *Thriller,* which was spawned from his inner imagination and vision. He said, "A certain force tells me what works" and *"Thriller* transformed many of my dreams into reality." Jackson has a very mythical view of the world and a fantasy sense of what works on the stage. He never depends on rational approaches but relies on his intuitive macrovision. Evidence of this is how he can wake up with a song completely finished as by "magic." He says, "I wake up from dreams and go, 'Wow!' put this on paper." He wrote in *Moonwalk,* "Often people don't see what I see.They have too much doubt. If I can see it, I can do it."

The King of Pop is convinced he is precognitive due to the numerous times he has had a premonition of impending disaster, such as the ill-famed Pepsi commercial. Just prior to the commercial he was nowhere in sight and after searching for Jackson producer Bob Giraldi found him in the bathroom staring down at his white sequined glove floating in the toilet bowl. He told Giraldi, "I've got a bad feeling about this." Jackson said that during the days just prior to the filming he would awake "sweaty, panicky, and with a bad premonition." Jackson has always believed in "magic" and, like his fantasy hero Peter Pan, was convinced if you wish hard enough, anything is possible.

Will to Power

Jackson's real power is a Nietzschean type willpower that has Superman-like characteristics. His "will" has been instrumental in helping him maintain sanity in the face of enormous adversity. Unending legal skirmishes, screaming fans who invade his privacy, interminable attacks on his manhood, and zero family life are adversities that the King of Pop has been able to overcome. He has maintained his composure primarily due to an indomitable will that refuses to be overwhelmed. It is a sad commentary that superstars such as Michael Jackson and Michael Jordan are destined to pay such a dear price for their fame and fortune. Both have said their greatest wish in life is to be able to walk through Disneyland without the need of bodyguards to protect their very being. Such is the price of becoming an icon. Only those with an intransigent willpower are capable of coping with such pressures. Living life as a recluse is the only alternative to one of chaos—one that Michael Jackson has chosen.

Summary

The world's most enigmatic pop icon is also the world's most famous eccentric entertainer. Michael Jackson's unconventional histrionics make Madonna's shock tactics appear bland, even though her actions are by intent while Jackson's emanate from a natural tendency to be different. This megastar has never danced, sung, or written music for money. He told *USA Today* in 1995, "Everything in life is about growth" and it "has nothing to do with needing funds." That is a true entrepreneurial approach to life and what success is all about. Jackson is only driven to perform as an emotional catharsis or release which happens when he is turned-on while onstage.

According to biographer Randy Taraborrelli, Jackson's net worth in 1990 was $300 million and estimated to be up to $500 million by mid-decade. If he continues to work he will approach billionaire status by the millennium. But success in show business is fleeting. Jackson recently has been outdone by sister Janet and is in danger of losing his superstar status, or even his life, if he does not gain control over his insatiable need to look and act like a teenager. He was hospitalized in December 1995 due to anorexia, anxiety, and excess work. His breakup with Lisa Marie didn't help. The loss of a passionate relationship will not prove as great as his image loss. His *HIStory* album was not the supersuccess he had envisioned even though it was successful. It sold 391,000 copies in the first week and helped assuage the pain of the child molestation charges that had enveloped him for the better part of three years. However, his 1996 divorce from Lisa Marie has opened him up to further confrontations over his alternative lifestyle and unusual choice of close friends. Maybe his 1996 marriage to Debbie Rowe will prove to be more than a ruse to sidetrack all those child abuse lawsuits.

Whatever one thinks of Michael Jackson, the man is the consummate creative genius as an entertainer. When Jane Fonda told him he was the personification of Peter Pan—"the symbol of youth, joy and freedom"—Jackson started crying and told Fonda, "You know . . . I totally identify with Peter Pan . . . the lost boy of Never Never Land." This child-man's need to escape into fantasy and to relive his lost childhood caused him to dream of flying away to a fantasyland in the likeness of his mythical hero. His desperate need to escape into the innocence of childhood has groomed him for becoming a superstar without peer. The King of Pop is arguably the greatest entertainer in history and he got there by playing himself as protagonist in one of life's great passion plays.

MICHAEL JACKSON
Apollonian Temperament (NF)
Entertainment Superstar and Media Icon
born August 29, 1958

Dominant trait: Driven perfectionist and recluse; highly intuitive introvert with feminine politeness and compassion

Motto: "I must achieve. I must seek truth in all things"

Religion: Jehovah's Witness dropout due to extreme limitations for entertainer. Very spiritual and devout.

Philosophy: "I believe in wishes and in a person's ability to make a wish come true"

Politics: Apolitical

Nicknames: Big Nose (dad); Smelly (Quincy Jones); Peter Pan of Pop; Joker; Wizard of Odd; Wacko Jacko

Creation/innovation: Moonwalk a "spontaneous" creation of breakdancing fad "from black ghettos . . . like walking on moon"

Successes: First 3 recordings went to #1; *Thriller* #1 album ever with 46 million sales

Vices/hobbies: Fantasizing in Disneyland with children; Monopoly; toys; amusement parks; Valium

Romantic liaisons: At age 10 Diana Ross; Tatum O'Neal and Brooke Shields as teen; Lisa Marie Presley at 35; Debbie Rowe at 37

Self-description: "I'm a stage addict"; "I am one of the loneliest people in the world"; "I'm a perfectionist"

Birth order: Seventh child of Katherine Scruse and Joe Jackson, one younger brother and sister

Parental influence: Father, Joe, abusive and tyrannical, whom he hates; mother loving and doting, whom he loves passionately

Early transience: On the road to Chicago nightspots ages 7–9; after age nine constantly on road

Parents' occupations: Joe steel mill crane operator and part-time R&B guitar player; mother cashier at Sears

Role models: James Brown, Diana Ross, Fred Astaire, and Gene Kelly

Hero mentors: Peter Pan, Walt Disney, Greta Garbo, Howard Hughes, P. T. Barnum, Berry Gordy, Quincy Jones

Formal education: Tutored by Rose Fine until 15; "the greatest education in the world is watching the masters at work"

Life crises: Father's abuse; acne at 15; Pepsi hair fire; anorexic by 20s and panic attacks

Metamorphoses: 1st grade "Climb Every Mountain" to acclaim; *Thriller* transformed many of my dreams into reality"

Charismatic: White glove, socks, and sunglasses signature of a mesmerizing icon who can move mountains

Competitive: "Most people don't think of me as tough or strong-willed . . . that's just because they don't know me"

Hypomanic: "Boundless energy"; "I work all the time"; "I must achieve"; "I'm obsessed with perfection"

Independent rebel: "Bizarre" crotch grabbing iconoclast who created monster with PR stunts Elephant Man, hyperbaric chamber; "My attitude is if fashion says it's forbidden; I'm going to do it"

Indomitable "will": Strong-willed: "I don't do many things until a certain 'force' tells me to do them"

Intuitive vision: "If I see it, I can do it"; "Thinking too much" is bad, an artist should be "naturally spontaneous"

Drive: "My goal is to do the best I can in every area"

Risk-taker: Fired Berry Gordy at 17 and father when 21; fearless under fire

Self-confident: "I'm really very self-confident"; "I'm an instrument for the expression of ecstasy"

Tenacious: After *Off the Wall,* he vowed to come back; child abuse case launched *HIStory*

Workaholic: "I work all the time"; Quincy Jones: "Headstrong perfectionist"; Gordy: "willing to work hard"

Honors: Artist with simultaneous #1 hits: pop single, pop album, R&B album, R&B single; #1 all-time album

11

John Johnson—
Risk-Taking Entrepreneur

America's Most Successful Black Businessman

"I believe in the silent power of the possible."

John Johnson started out with a dream of becoming a journalist and used mass consumer magazines to achieve his objective of depicting blacks in a positive light. Along the way he expected to educate and communicate with the black masses in much the same way as magazines like *Look* and *Life* did. His breakthrough creations were *Ebony* and *Jet* magazines, the preeminent entertainment mediums for the black community for over half a century. John Johnson was successful in achieving his mission in life through the medium of advertising, of which he knew nothing when he began. No magazine can succeed without the financial support of national advertisers, who happen to be almost all white. Johnson effectively made his magazines enormously successful because he was able to educate white advertisers about the enormous potential opportunity of the *Ebony* subscriber.

Johnson's genius was in making the black person "the marketing and advertising agenda of corporate America." He was the first black ever to successfully attract Fortune 500 advertising dollars to a black publication. This ingenuity then became a self-fulfilling prophecy as he was able to educate and motivate black consumers to buy the products and services of his advertisers. The resulting media clout helped him create a niche readership that became more culturally aware—all aimed at leveling the playing field for ethnic groups. John Johnson will go down in history as the first magazine publisher, of any persuasion, to portray blacks in a positive and accurate light.

Johnson launched his business empire with the *Negro Digest* in 1942, "dedicated to the development of interracial understanding and the promotion of national unity." From that innocuous beginning this entrepreneurial genius was quick to launch *Ebony* (1945), *Tan* (1950), and *Jet* (1951), all aimed at fulfilling a void in black readership. Then Johnson saw an opportunity in black beauty and launched the internationally successful Ebony Fashion Show in 1958. Once on a roll he was not to be stopped. He entered the highly competitive cosmetics market in the 1970s with what would become the largest such black enterprise in America—Fashion Fair Cosmetics. Johnson's business empire became a corporate conglomerate in the seventies when he acquired the company where it all started, the Supreme Life Insurance Company.

Testimony to the success of Johnson's empire is the approximately $300 million in annual revenues produced by the Johnson Publishing Company, Supreme Life Insurance, and Fashion Fair Cosmetics, plus various radio stations and other subsidiaries. Johnson's enterprises now employ 2,600 people, mostly in Chicago. Johnson's true contribution to society and his people is in the creation of a desperately needed product, but in the end business success is a numbers game. In 1984 Johnson was listed by *Forbes* magazine as America's richest black and one of America's four hundred richest people, with a net worth of $200 million. This number has now grown to approximately $300 million, according to industry sources. Not bad for a poor Mississippi River boy who was raised in a town with no newspaper or radio and who did not see indoor plumbing or mechanical heating until he arrived in Chicago at age fifteen.

Johnson became the second black man, after Ralph Bunche, to receive the Horatio Alger Award in 1965. He certainly qualified for the award of "pulling oneself up by his own bootstraps." In 1987, a competitive black publication, *Black Enterprise,* saw fit to name Johnson Entrepreneur of the Decade. This pales in comparison to the ultimate compliment paid him by corporate America, which invited him into their inner sanctum as a corporate board member. Johnson has sat on some of the country's most prestigious boards of directors, not the least of which were those of Zenith, Bell and Howell, Continental Bank of Chicago, Dillards department stores, and Greyhound. The culmination of these honors came in the eighties, when Johnson became a board member of Chrysler and 20th Century-Fox. The boy who grew up with no shoes now sat in his grey flannel suit giving sage advice to an Ivy League cognitive elite.

John Johnson, the son of an Arkansas domestic, struggled to survive the denigration of being raised in the Jim Crow South, but adamantly refused to become molded in that tradition. He very astutely groomed himself for success. He became a multimillionaire by age thirty-one and a tycoon by his fifties. He accomplished all this by living by a philosophy of equality and truth and wrote of this philosophy in his autobiography: "I believe that black, brown, and white Americans are chained together by tradition, history, and a common market and that what helps one group of Americans helps all Americans."

John Johnson is a creative genius who changed the world by daring to believe in himself and his dreams. He got to the very top by living on the edge in everything, as is the case with all great entrepreneurs. Risking and gambling on untried ventures made him very successful. His commitment to excellence was supported by the motto of this consummate salesman who had the highest integrity: "I believe finally in the power of persuasion, in the power of truth. I believe the word is mightier than the sword and, in the end, will prevail."

Innovative Contributions

Johnson modeled his first publication, the *Negro Digest,* after the universally acclaimed *Reader's Digest.* He was just twenty-four years old on November 26, 1942,
when he launched this breakthrough magazine to fill the void he saw in communi-
cating news and entertainment to blacks hungry for positive information about
themselves. He had seen what so many others had not. There was a desperate need
to communicate the positives on black people in mass consumer magazines while
leaving the muckraking negatives to the masters of that medium—the newspapers.

Johnson was a trainee at Supreme Life Insurance in Chicago working for the
president and founder. He was given a "keep busy" assignment of reading magazines and newspapers to keep his executive boss up-to-date on the happenings in
the black community since Supreme Life was founded to sell insurance to blacks.
This assignment would change John Johnson's life forever. Most people would not
have benefited from such an assignment, but in reading all the articles written
about blacks Johnson immediately recognized the serious void that existed in the
black media for positive pictorial material on blacks. He wrote, "There was an almost total white-out on positive black news in white-oriented media." During this
era there was an unwritten rule that "a black's picture could not appear in the press
unless connected with a crime." Johnson saw this problem as an opportunity and
immediately set out to change a gross miscarriage of information and justice. He
created a magazine which became the genesis of an empire.

He soon became aware after his research effort that he, John Johnson, was one
of the most knowledgeable persons in Chicago on the subject of black culture and
news. He said, "I started telling my friends about the amazing things I'd read . . .
and I was usually the center of attention at social gatherings." When Johnson attempted to enlist interest in his idea with friends and acquaintances he was told
No! Emphatically no! Even such a renowned black leader as Roy Wilkins, the editor of the most successful black magazine of the time, *The Crisis,* told him, "Save
your money, young man. Save your energy. Save yourself a lot of disappointment."
That was the first rejection of many, none of which deterred Johnson's enthusiasm
for the project.

Johnson's first innovation was to utilize the mailing list of twenty thousand
blacks that he was responsible for keeping updated in his job at Supreme Life. Unable to find backers or partners, he had the brilliant idea to send these black customers a letter asking for a prepaid subscription of $2 each for a magazine on black
news. When he found he had no money to mail the promotions, he talked his
mother into putting up her new furniture for a $500 loan for stamps. He then
showed his true entrepreneurial genius in creating the distribution for the *Negro
Digest.* He printed the first edition and when a newsstand proprietor told him he
only bought through a distributor, this naive businessman suddenly realized he had
to create a demand for his product beyond the Supreme Life customer list. He met
with Joseph Levy, a dominant distributor of magazines in Chicago, who refused
to stock the *Negro Digest* since it had no demand. Levy told Johnson "colored

books don't sell" and explained to him that he was Jewish and it was not his race but market demand which kept him from stocking Johnson's magazine.

The enterprising Johnson then had all his friends go to every Chicago newsstand and make an impassioned request for the magazine and offer to pay cash in advance. The ploy worked and Levy agreed to stock a thousand copies. This obstacle behind him, Johnson showed the tenacity and temerity of all great entrepreneurs by taking all of his remaining cash and buying up the thousand magazines and giving them away in black neighborhoods. Levy immediately ordered another two thousand magazines and the *Negro Digest* was an overnight success soon finding its way into New York City, Los Angeles, and Washington, D.C. Johnson said, "Circulation begat circulation." He was now in business. This innovative wunderkind had singlehandedly created his own market demand, without which the magazine would have died at birth.

Personal History

John Johnson was born on January 19, 1918, the only child of Gertrude Jenkins and Leroy Johnson in Arkansas City, Arkansas. This Mississippi River town was rife with all of the tragic history of such southern cities. His mother had a daughter named Beulah from a previous marriage, but she was fourteen years older than John and had left the roost prior to his arrival. Leroy Johnson was an itinerant levee camp worker and Gertrude a domestic who cleaned homes, ironed clothes, and cooked meals for wealthy white families. Of his father, Johnson said, "I never really knew him." Leroy Johnson was always gone and was killed in a sawmill accident when John was just eight. His mother then married James Williams, who became the dominant male influence in Johnson's life. While he was young, the family never experienced a stable life, moving often along the levees and at one time relocating to Vicksburg, Mississippi. Arkansas City became Johnson's permanent residence after age eight. The town had no radio or newspaper.

Johnson wrote in his autobiography that his first sharp memory of life on the Mississippi took place when he was nine. He wrote emotional passages saying, "We were running for our lives" due to a break in an upriver levee. The whole town was on the verge of perishing and was forced to run en masse for their lives seeking the higher ground of the Arkansas City levee. Johnson wrote, "I remember the hands—black, white, brown, yellow hands—reaching out to us, pulling us to safety. And I remember, as if it were yesterday, the shock as I opened my eyes on a scene of interracial bedlam." This horrible experience permeated Johnson's young mind as the family lost everything—clothes, furniture, and money and was forced to live on the snake-infested levee for six weeks until the Mississippi River subsided.

Johnson attended an all-black elementary school in Arkansas City, but the Jim Crow South did not provide a black high school for him to attend. This, he said, was his "greatest gift," since it forced the family to relocate to another town because his mother was adamant that he receive a first-class education. His mother was so bent on moving to Chicago with Johnson that she went to unbelievable ends to make it happen. She wanted him to have the education she never had and refused to be denied. When Johnson graduated from the eighth grade in Arkansas City in June 1932, it was the height of the Great Depression and his mother still did not have quite enough money to finance their move north. They were poor as "church mice" according to Johnson, and his mother couldn't even afford the price of a train ticket. So Gertrude Johnson told her son to retake the eighth grade while she took on two jobs to buy the precious train ticket to Chicago and freedom. The Johnsons viewed Chicago as a mecca where blacks could achieve based on their talent, not their color. Johnson was already fifteen in July 1933 when he and his resilient mother got on the train. He chronicled the experience with the self-fulfilling prophecy: "Nothing would ever be the same again."

Chicago

John Johnson became the perpetual optimist and grew to know a grandiose lifestyle. But his early life was not a bed of roses. He wrote, "For twenty-three years, I slept on couches and rollaway beds. In fact, I never had a bedroom of my own until I got married." During his early years in Chicago, Johnson became a voracious reader in a valiant attempt to help the family off the welfare dole that had become their destiny. The family spent much of the mid-thirties on welfare, causing Johnson to write, "Something of the shame and terror of those days remain with me to this day. If I don't feel like getting up in the morning, all I have to do to motivate myself is to recall the government truck stopping in front of my house—and I jump up and go to work."

Johnson read voraciously of the rags-to-riches success stories and identified with the fictional and real heroes. Horatio Alger led the list of his favorites but the shame of receiving a dole after reading of these stalwart Alger protagonists left a lasting mark on his psyche. Johnson constantly dreamed of success until it finally became his passion. Then Dale Carnegie became his fantasy hero, to be followed by Frederick Douglass and others who had made it from the very bottom to the top. One of Johnson's favorite books became Napoleon Hill's *Think and Grow Rich*. Johnson wrote, "Faith, self-confidence, and a positive mental attitude: These three were the basic messages of the self-help books that changed my life." He said, "I read all the self-help books I could find. I also read the great classics of black history and literature. . . . I used to hang out in the Chicago Public Library . . . reading books on Frederick Douglass and other blacks who had succeeded against the odds."

Education and Journalism

Johnson wrote, "I wanted to be a journalist," and so became the editor-in-chief of the DuSable High School paper. He was elected senior class president and admitted, "The food and drink of my life is trying to succeed." Even as a man in his seventies Johnson says, "Success is still my hobby." He was a compulsive reader of magazines and newspapers, both denied him as a child, and said he was unable "to pass a newsstand without stopping." He graduated from DuSable High in 1936 and immediately changed his name from Johnny Johnson to John Harold Johnson at the suggestion of his civics teacher and white mentor, Mary Herrick. She thought that Johnny was far too juvenile sounding for a young adult with such serious ambitions. The commencement speaker at Johnson's graduation was Harry Pace, president of Supreme Liberty Life Insurance Company, the biggest black employer in Chicago. Johnson was selected to speak as well and did such a commendable job that Pace offered him a position at Supreme Life. Pace became Johnson's business mentor and lifelong friend. Johnson had to make a decision between the job and a scholarship he had received from the prestigious University of Chicago, but the job won out since he never had the money to accept the college scholarship even though that was his first choice.

Johnson's Loves

John Johnson met and married Eunice Walker, a graduate student at Loyola University, just as his professional career was beginning. They married in 1941 and have been a dedicated and loving couple throughout his long career. They were unable to have children and adopted two: Selma, who is now the president of Johnson Publishing, and John Jr., who was unfortunately afflicted with sickle cell anemia and died in his twenties. Johnson's mother, Gertrude Johnson, was by far the most influential person in his life and he never forgot her enormous sacrifices which allowed him to make his mark in the world. Johnson made it his duty to call his mother every day of his life, even those times when he was in Russia or on board a ship. He once even climbed a telegraph pole in Haiti so that he could make his daily call to his beloved mother. Gertrude Johnson had her very own office in the Johnson headquarters in Chicago's Loop and Johnson has left instructions that her office will remain untouched as long as Johnson Publishing exists.

Professional History

Whenever asked about his success Johnson responds, "I was lucky, the timing was right, and I worked hard." Harry Pace became a valued mentor and made him his assistant at Supreme Life. It was 1942 and the world was in chaos, affording Johnson the opportunity to give blacks news on blacks that was not biased or misconstrued by whites. After hatching the innovative idea for selling presubscriptions to the Supreme Life customer list, he needed the $500 loan for stamps.

He first went to the local banks and requested a loan. They just laughed at this young black with a dream but no assets, experience, customers, or collateral. Johnson then turned to friends and acquaintances, who were not interested either. After hundreds of rejections Johnson turned to his beloved mother, who had just bought the first new furniture in her life. It took some months before Johnson was able to convince her to pledge her furniture for a $500 bank loan. Using her furniture as collateral, he was given a loan for the $500 and implemented his mailing plan. He was overjoyed when three thousand individuals responded with prepaid subscriptions and sent in $6,000 in checks and cash.

Johnson had been turned down by everyone and would later write that he was glad, since they would "today be multimillionaires." Johnson printed five thousand copies of his first issue and went out and created his own demand. He refused to leave the sales to chance and took his last dollars and gave them to his friends to buy up the magazines. The distributor called him and ordered more, proving that success often needs a jump start. Johnson had created his own demand.

EBONY

Once the *Negro Digest* was financially sound and on its way to nationwide distribution, Johnson was asked to become a partner in a new enterprise by two of his freelance writers on the *Negro Digest.* Jay Jackson and Ben Burns had the initial idea for a pictorial spread in the likeness of *Look* and *Life.* This would be an entertainment-oriented magazine and they proposed a three-way partnership for the venture. Johnson accepted and turned out to be the only one of the three willing to take the financial risk. He put up the start-up funding for *Ebony,* which was launched on November 1, 1945, a date of the year that would become a superstitious launch date for every one of his future enterprises. Jackson and Burns proved critical to the early success of this slick magazine. Their work helped build circulation to more than two million within a few years. The magazine grew to be the very backbone of the publishing empire and proved there was an inherent demand in the market for black entertainment and pictorial news. Johnson wrote years later, "I will forever be grateful to them. If they had invested then I wouldn't be the sole owner of Johnson Publishing today."

After just one year the success of *Ebony* almost destroyed the firm and Johnson. Between 1946 and 1948 *Ebony* teetered on the verge of bankruptcy due to a lack of cash flow to sustain its burgeoning operations. Circulation was great and the retail price was adequate, but there was never sufficient revenues from advertising to cover costs and profits. Johnson wrote of the trauma of this period, "I walked a tightrope without a net, pyramiding creditors, postponing bills, stalling, improvising, selling." What created this dilemma was that the magazine sales had taken off like a rocket and the firm was never adequately financed for such growth. In addition, Johnson did not have the experience for managing such growth nor did he have sufficient internal cash flow to sustain the higher level of sales. Bankruptcy was an imminent possibility every day for a period of two years. He said, "*Ebony* was like a runaway horse, hurtling down the streets and pulling me behind."

Crisis is a catalyst to great achievement and Johnson's ultimate success turned out to be greater because of this early trauma. When all appeared lost he refused to capitulate and worked passionately to make his runaway publishing empire solvent. He wrote of the period, saying, "I locked myself in my office" and started chanting, "you can make it . . . you can and must make it." Johnson tried to get some bank-financed working capital but was refused. He cynically said, "It was twenty years before I got a loan from a bank. And I was in business forty years before I got what I consider a white man's loan—a loan based on my signature alone." The experience proved worthwhile as once he survived the debacle he never again allowed the firm to become cash poor due to out-of-control growth.

Once Johnson overcame his early bout with bankruptcy he took aim at the large advertisers like Zenith, Ford, MGM, and Capitol Records. He personally concentrated on educating the mass consumer industrial giants about the large consuming public that read his magazines and was an untapped market for their products. Johnson told them that 12 percent of the population was black and that 12 percent of their advertising dollars should be so directed. Gradually, one by one, they started to place ads in *Ebony* and then *Jet,* a new publication he launched in 1951. *Jet* was what Johnson called a "fast black magazine," which was to mimic its double entendre name—quick like a jet plane and velvet dark black for its readership. Jet was a weekly news magazine in the likeness of the *Reader's Digest* and became affectionately known as the "Negro's Bible," causing Maya Angelou to say, "If it wasn't in *Jet* it didn't happen." After four decades *Jet* still sells approximately one million copies weekly.

Johnson launched two other magazines, *Tan Confessions* and *Copper Romance,* in 1950 in response to the true confessions craze. In 1951 he matched *Look*'s entry called *Quick* with a black version called *Hue*—a pocket-sized feature magazine. By 1965 *Ebony* was selling 900,000 copies a month while its three sister magazines, *Jet, Tan,* and *Negro Digest,* were selling 2.3 million copies per month.

By 1951 Johnson's influence became noted nationally and he became one of the young men selected as the U.S. Junior Chamber of Commerce's Ten Most Outstanding Young Men. By 1973 Johnson had diversified into a line of black cosmetics, which he named Fashion Fair Cosmetics in honor of his highly successful Ebony Fashion Show, established in 1958. Here was a man who not only learned to deal with change but was one who delighted in the dynamics of new ventures and market opportunities. Johnson has always contended that his business success was based on his ability to deal with change. He wrote, "Never being satisfied with the #1 rating I got last year" was the basis of his great success. Such thinking became instrumental in Johnson Publishing becoming a conglomerate by the late sixties.

Johnson perpetually looked for new opportunities to leverage his energies and growing expertise as an entrepreneur or to make his current publications bigger and better. His creative bent had philosophical overtones, which can be seen by the

Newly sworn-in President Clinton reaches out to hug poet Maya Angelou after she delivered her inaugural poem on the west steps of the Capitol during 1993 inauguration ceremonies in Washington. (AP/Wide World Photos)

Shirley Chisholm, the first black woman to run for president, addresses students at North Carolina State University, February 7, 1972. (AP/Wide World Photos)

Thurgood Marshall stands in front of the Supreme Court Building on September 1, 1967, following his swearing-in as Justice of the Supreme Court. (AP/Wide World Photos)

Colin Powell waves from the podium as he practices his speech, August 11, 1996, at the San Diego Convention Center. Powell was the final speaker of the Republican National Convention's opening night. (AP/Wide World Photos)

Paul Robeson (*right*) leaves the federal courthouse with defense attorney George W. Crockett, Jr., on September 20, 1949. Robeson had appeared as a defense witness at the Communist Conspiracy trial. (AP Wide World Photos)

Superstar Michael Jackson leaves the stage of the Monte Carlo Sporting Club after receiving five Music Awards during the ceremony of the World Music Awards, May 8, 1996. (AP/Wide World Photos)

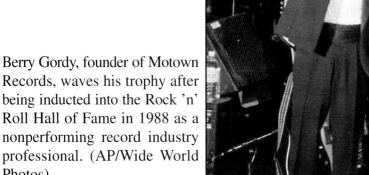

Berry Gordy, founder of Motown Records, waves his trophy after being inducted into the Rock 'n' Roll Hall of Fame in 1988 as a nonperforming record industry professional. (AP/Wide World Photos)

Michael Jordan poses with the 1993 NBA Finals Most Valuable Player trophy on June 23, 1993, in Chicago. (AP/Wide World Photos)

Oprah Winfrey is shown in this May 1996 photo, at the same time her fitness book topped the *Wall Street Journal* nonfiction bestseller list. (AP/Wide World Photos)

Reginald Lewis, chairman and CEO of TLC Beatrice International Holdings. (AP/Wide World Photos)

John H. Johnson, chairman and CEO of Johnson Publishing Co., poses with his daughter Linda Johnson Rice at the company's headquarters in Chicago. (AP/Wide World Photos)

Nelson Mandela acknowledges the vast Trafalgar Square crowd from the balcony of South Africa House in London, July 12, 1996, during his four-day state visit to Britain. (AP/Wide World Photos)

President Clinton looks on as Bill Cosby speaks at the White House on July 29, 1996, during a conference to discuss children's television. (AP/Wide World Photos)

incisive names he gave to his various publications and enterprises. He chose the name *Ebony* because it means "fine black African wood," which is symbolic of himself and his beautiful pictorial magazine. This history-making publication has enjoyed the largest circulation of any black magazine for over fifty years and grossed in excess of $200 million in 1995 with nine million readers per issue.

When his former employer, Harry Pace of Supreme Life, fell upon hard times, Johnson's ex-boss asked him to make an investment. Johnson was given a board seat and when the firm continued to experience financial difficulty he invested more and more into the company. By 1974 the firm was in serious financial trouble and the now supersuccessful Johnson invested a final $1 million to become the controlling shareholder with an investment of $2.5 million. This story has a Horatio Alger type ending, with the former office boy becoming the dominant stockholder, CEO, and chairman of the board. The boy with Mississippi mud on his shoes had made it to the big time. He had gone from the welfare rolls to a Rolls Royce within two decades.

Johnson always relied on a business ideology with philosophical implications. His admonitions to his employees and any others who would listen were:

- I believe the greater the handicap the greater the triumph.
- I believe that the only failure is failing to try.
- I believe in the silent power of the possible.
- I believe in the power of persuasion.
- Never burn your bridges.
- Going first class is the best revenge.

What Makes John Johnson Tick?

John Johnson is a classic entrepreneur who is by anyone's definition the consummate risk-taker who enjoys living on the edge. He confirms this need to take big risks for big opportunities in his autobiography, saying, "I believe in risk and daring . . . living on the edge is the summit of life." Johnson has a Promethean type temperament (intuitive-thinking), one in which the person is looked on as an "architect of change." These types prefer to seek out the opportunities and possibilities in life rather than be on the dole and are visionaries who work on their ideas with ingenuity and logic. They never allow life's quantitative realities to dissuade them from its qualitative possibilities.

John Johnson achieved great success through great drive, tenacity, and vision with the ability to take risk the most instrumental in the creation of his publishing empire. Johnson is an introvert who relishes his privacy and a visionary who relies more on his heart than his head to make decisions. Always the manic workaholic, Johnson lived and died by the admonition, "Set goals and work night and day to achieve them." Johnson was a very faithful and dedicated family man who always treated his employees like family. Once a part of the Johnson team, employees virtually never left. Johnson became their mentor and charismatic leader and treated them all like one big family. Johnson is the consummate salesman who believes in the art of persuasion to be successful in business.

MYTHOLOGICAL HERO MENTORS

During his teens Johnson became a fan of Dale Carnegie's *How to Win Friends and Influence People,* Napoleon Hill's *Think and Grow Rich,* Horatio Alger stories, and Booker T. Washington's *Up from Slavery.* These and countless other inspirational books became his fictional escape from the realities of the Depression and he fantasized about these larger-than-life heroes until the fantasy and reality became clouded in his mind. Johnson envisioned himself as one of the characters in the Horatio Alger books he loved. The mythological hero mentors became his solace when the future looked dim and inspired him to work even harder to achieve his goals. By identifying with these mythical mentors Johnson was able to envision himself with few limits and that imagery helped in the creation of the Johnson Publishing empire.

Once in school a white teacher by the name of Mary Herrick became a real-life mentor to him. She let him know that he was special and could achieve and her belief in him helped his ascent to the pinnacles of power. When she suggested he change his name from Johnny to John he did so. Harry Pace turned out to be another real-life business mentor and was followed by a Democratic Chicago politician named Earl Dickerson. These individuals played an important early role in the formation of the John Johnson mystique. But throughout his life Johnson's mother, Gertrude, was to be his true inspiration. She was his hero and role model and he would turn to her when things were bleakest. Once when he was facing certain disaster she asked him, "Are you trying real hard?" When he responded yes, she told him, "Whenever you're trying hard, you're never failing. The only failure is failing to try." He was emotionally committed to his mother like few other men, writing, "For fifty-nine years . . . I called her at least once a day."

INSECURITY BREEDS GREATNESS

Johnson wrote in his autobiography, "Failure is a word that I don't accept." He admitted "I'm too insecure . . . to have people around me who believe that failure is a possibility." Like most other great people, Johnson is afraid to fail and that very emotion has contributed enormously to his success. Such people are driven more by the fear of failure than they are by the gratification of the win. But drive is what ultimately contributes to their success. Johnson once fired a person who said he couldn't make it, saying, "I've got to fire you. I'm not sure I can make it myself. The last thing I need is someone telling me that I can't make it." Johnson confirmed his basic feelings of insecurity when he wrote, "I used to lock myself up in my office and say the word *success* over out loud over and over, like a Buddhist monk chanting his mantra."

In *Succeeding Against the Odds,* Johnson gave some insight into his success as a function of his insecurity, writing, "On November 1, 1942, I was poor, ambitious, and scared to death. On November 1, 1987, I'm rich, ambitious, and scared to death." Then, when he was being awarded the Entrepreneur of the Decade Award in 1987, he told the Black Enterprise audience, "I run scared every day."

LIFE CRISES AND TRAUMAS

Seldom is there found such an inspirational example of success resulting from trauma. Johnson's emotional description of his and his mother's desperate flight for their lives is a story befitting a Hollywood script. The family physically ran to a Mississippi levee in a desperate attempt to beat the raging waters of the Mississippi, which were headed their way and ultimately washed away their home and all their personal possessions. This nine-year-old boy became imbued with a "survival imprint" that never left him. John Johnson the adult was never so psychologically eloquent as when he said, "The boy on the levee was the father of the man and the publisher." This near-tragic experience was highly instrumental in Johnson's later struggles to form and then save his publishing company.

The levee incident would not be the last crisis Johnson would face. Later he worked like a madman to avoid bankruptcy when *Ebony* took off and he couldn't keep up with the runaway train. He was actually insolvent during the *Ebony* cash crisis of 1946–47 and surviving that crisis instilled in him many important values necessary for his later success. That experience became a catalyst and showed Johnson that "PMA"—a positive mental attitude—was the crux of success.

Charisma

One of Johnson's favorite aphorisms is, "I believe in the art of persuasion," which indicates just how steeped he was in the art of leading others through the power of communication. Johnson's employees speak of the hypnotic impact he has on people. Former employees talk of his charismatic charm. They often turned down other jobs with more money or a better job in order to remain with Johnson. Those employees I spoke to idolized him and saw him as the messiah of black publishing. Most would have followed him anywhere.

Competitiveness

Johnson was an aggressive competitor. Whenever a new potential business opportunity presented itself, like the true confessions craze in the fifties, he jumped on it and if it didn't work out got out just as quickly. As a true entrepreneurial visionary he thrived on the competition of someone attempting to take his market. He said, "Whenever I found a white magazine with strong black readership, I brought out a black counterpart, using names which tried to capture the color black." During this period he launched *Tan Confessions* (1950), *Copper Romance* (1950), *Hue* (1951), and *Jet* (1951). *Jet* became an instant success as a "fast black magazine" and has survived for three decades.

Confidence

John Johnson believes. His optimism is so pervasive that he is convinced that problems are only harbingers of success. He wrote in his autobiography, "I believe there is an advantage in every disadvantage, and a gift in every problem." Another of Johnson's favorite aphorisms is "I believed in the plastic power of the possible"—a result of a youth spent fantasizing about the positive admonitions of Dale Carnegie and Napoleon Hill. After he had become quite successful Johnson met the famous positive thinking guru W. Clement Stone and told him, "I've been practicing PMA—positive mental attitude—since I started my first business. I didn't know what to call it, and I didn't know how to define it, but I was doing it—and it helped me survive."

Passion and Drive

Johnson acquired his enormous drive from a deprived youth and watching his tenacious mother fight off adversity. Of the time his mother made him repeat the eighth grade he wrote, "People laughed at us." But her tenacity and indomitable drive to achieve her objective was forever imprinted on his subconscious and left him forever in her debt. Johnson wrote fifty years later, "They told my mother that she was crazy," but it was this experience which changed his life and from that day forward he would not be denied. He was an intensely driven man, becoming the top student in Chicago's DuSable High School and then a student of success. A highly introspective man, Johnson saw this in himself and wrote, "Success is my hobby." This passionate attitude for success has contributed to his becoming one of America's most successful black entrepreneurs.

Hypomania

Johnson describes himself as a "workaholic" with "restless energy," a trait he says started very early in life. He wrote in his memoirs, "I was a working child. I learned how to work before I learned how to play. When most children were experimenting with their first toys, I was hard at work, helping my mother and stepfather." John Johnson then grew into a Type A workaholic adult whose self-worth was always inextricably tied to his success. He never had time for a vacation and when he was off work he was thinking about it. Like most Type A personalities, he was always in a hurry to accomplish more and more and set higher and higher goals to meet. He was an indefatigable overachiever who lived by his self-imposed motto: "I set goals and worked night and day to achieve them. . . . Work is my vacation." Johnson's standard workweek was always eighty hours, but to him it was not work. It was a labor of love. In his sixties Johnson still was able to keep three secretaries busy hustling to keep up with his frenetic schedule and administer his affairs. At age seventy he was still working a schedule that would fatigue most younger man.

Independence

Always the rebel, Johnson never subscribed to the rules of the establishment. He created his own rules and expected others to abide by them. He spoke of his renegade spirit saying, "It's not satisfaction but dissatisfaction that drives people to the heights. I was goaded. I was driven to success by the whip of social disapproval." Johnson was an independent nonconformist who clearly understood that all great wins in life—personal and professional—are found where others fear to go. In other words, find out where the pack is and go elsewhere, and that was not only John Johnson's style but proved to be the basis of his great success.

Perfectionist

John Johnson was so imbued with being perfect that he admonished underlings who did not comply with his rules of excellence in all things. He told them, "Failure is a word I don't accept." Johnson's uncompromising demand for quality and superior effort helped make *Ebony* and *Jet* better than the competition, but also made him a feared boss. Those employees incapable of meeting his high standards of excellence left him after a short time. Those who adhered to his rigid style and demands for excellence stayed long and prospered. Former employees described him as "a control freak" who had to be involved in every facet of the business, the true definition of the perfectionist.

Temerity

Taking high risk for the chance at a big win is synonymous with the entrepreneurial personality. In fact, most textbooks define entrepreneurship as the art of taking risk. John Johnson probably owes much of his enormous success to his ability to live on the edge in all business ventures. Risk taking is his forte. His maxim on business success is: "Victory is certain if we have the courage to run our own race." He likes to use metaphors to make his point and one of his favorites for the aspiring entrepreneur is "in order to get lion's cubs, you have to go into the lion's lair." He often said,

"It was the dare, the gamble, that captivated me." Living and selling dangerously were fundamental in Johnson's companies.

Tenacity

Johnson said, "Persistence pays off," and believed it, since he would not have survived without perseverance. In 1943 he was struggling to survive with his first venture, *Negro Digest,* and in a desperate attempt at solidifying his circulation above the subsistence level he saw the opportunity to do so by contacting Eleanor Roosevelt to write an article called "If I Were a Negro." The First Lady politely replied that she just didn't have the time to do the article for *Negro Digest.* Most people would have given up after being turned down by the president's wife. Not John Johnson. He never accepted her refusal and kept after her to write this article. His persistence paid off when she finally capitulated and wrote the column for him. It appeared in the October 1943 issue of his magazine. True to Johnson's prediction, circulation doubled overnight and insured the success of his magazine.

Johnson's friends told him he was just lucky in enticing Eleanor Roosevelt to write an article for him. He responded, "Luck is a word we use for an order that is not understood. I made some of my luck. I made it by working hard and trusting the logic of events . . . it was as usual the wages of a persistence that refuses to take no for an answer."

Testimony to Johnson's tenacity is his $3 million investment in *Ebony South Africa* in 1996 at age seventy-eight. At an age when most people are enjoying the fruits of their success, Johnson personally put this deal together and took responsibility for the editorial functions of the magazine.

Vision

"You have to change images before you can change acts and institutions," according to this intuitive visionary. Johnson clearly understood that great success first occurs in the mind and then in reality. Johnson is one of those utopian thinkers who always operated with a right-brain vision and saw the big picture and long-term potential in any opportunity. He was able to follow his sense of what "could be" instead of what "wasn't possible" and never listened to the so-called experts who continually told him he would fail. He said, "At every critical turning point in my life, people, black and white, always told me no at first. And I almost always turned the no's into yes'es."

Will to Power

John Johnson, like all great entrepreneurs and creative geniuses, has a powerful sense of self that borders on egomania. He believes in himself to such a degree that he appears to have a "Superman-like" persona, which enabled him to overcome much adversity in his life. His internalized belief system proved to be the genesis of his acquisition of power in business and personal communications. Johnson utilized this power in "willing" the *Negro Digest* into being. In his words, "I'd produced this miracle by smoke and mirrors." The amazing thing is that his miracle was created but a few years after he had been a welfare recipient who was relegating to sleeping on a cot in South Chicago. Johnson resorted to willpower to overcome the reality of his existence and admitted, "I was willing to go anywhere . . . to do anything in order to not go back to that miserable existence." In a moment of emotional expression in his memoirs he wrote, "I had decided once and for all. I was going to make it or die."

Summary

Despite John Johnson's incredible success he is still beleaguered by people who judge him by his color. He says he is still often treated like the chauffeur "when I get out of one of my Rolls-Royces," which he admits "comes with the territory." A few years ago he was invited to Washington for a party welcoming Prince Charles to the United States. He and other dignitaries showed up and Johnson and his wife Eunice were humiliated by the parking lot attendant who "automatically assumed that I was the chauffeur, like every other black he'd seen that night." The attendant walked up and told him, "Park the car over there, boy." Johnson responded with some inflamed rhetoric that he says was more suited to Eddie Murphy and Richard Pryor, but he was incensed by the racial epithet. Johnson told the attendant, "I'm no boy. I'm a guest," causing the attendant to say, "Yeah, and I'm the president." Such are the travails of an eminently successful black who is still not accepted for what he is.

Johnson's huge success has led him to associate with some very esteemed company from all walks of life. He is seen as "the spokesman" by many of his fellow blacks, who have relied on him to communicate black messages through his magazines. This control over millions of monthly magazines has elevated Johnson into a position of power felt from Congress to the White House. Jesse Jackson refers to him as "The Godfather" and when Martin Luther King, Jr., was alive they were on a first-name basis. Johnson has dined with seven presidents, many times at the White House, and traveled with ambassadors. He has socialized with the likes of Sammy Davis, Jr., Mikhail Gorbachev, Nelson Rockefeller, and former New York City Mayor Robert Wagner.

This entrepreneurial genius was the recipient of the coveted Spingarn Award in 1966, the Horatio Alger Award in 1965, was named Magazine Publisher of the Year in 1972, and inducted into the Black Press Hall of Fame in 1987. *Forbes* in the mid-eighties listed him as one of America's four hundred wealthiest individuals, with an estimated net worth of $200 million. Johnson has enjoyed his success by driving the finest automobiles and living on a Palm Springs mountaintop next to Bob Hope. He admits that he sees "going first class as the best revenge." He started the second largest firm in America owned and operated by a black man (Reginald Lewis's TLC Beatrice is number one) and is arguably the greatest black entrepreneur in American history. Lewis didn't buy companies with the panache of Lewis or develop products with the flair of Gordy, but what he created was entirely from the sweat of his own brow and with his own money. He did not leverage other people's money like Lewis or earn monies by exploiting the talents of others like Gordy. He is one of America's quintessential entrepreneurs of any race, creed, or religion. John Johnson dared go where others feared to tread and his great temerity and tenacity makes him a creative genius who has changed the world dramatically.

JOHNNY (JOHN) H. JOHNSON
Promethean Temperament (NT)
America's Most Successful Black Businessman
born January 19, 1918, Arkansas City, Arkansas

Dominant traits: Risk-taker, strong work ethic, persistence and drive; private and visionary; rational and structured

Motto: "Never burn your bridges"; "Going first class is the best revenge"; "Positive mental attitude"

Religion: Fundamentalist Christian

Philosophy: "Failure is a word I don't accept"; "I believe in the silent power of the possible"; "I believe the greater the handicap the greater the triumph"

Politics: Democrat and black social activism in print—supported Martin Luther King, Jr., and Jesse Jackson

Nickname: John (real name Johnny); "The Godfather" (Jesse Jackson)

Creation/innovation: *Negro Digest* created at age 24 with $500 borrowed on mother's furniture

Successes: *Ebony* launched 1945, the #1 black entertainment magazine for fifty years; *Jet* (launched 1951) top black gossip magazine

Vices/hobbies: Voracious reader of self-help publications; "Success is my hobby"

Romantic liaisons: Married Eunice Walker with two adopted children, John Jr. (deceased) and Linda Johnson Rice

Self-description: "The food and drink of my life is trying to succeed . . . the timing was right and I worked hard"

Birth order: Firstborn of Gertrude Jenkins and Leroy Johnson; half-sister, Beulah, 14 years older

Parental influence: Mother a dominating influence due to tenacity, temerity, and work ethic

Early transience: Followed levee camps as child; at age 9 home washed away; age 12 to Vicksburg; age 15 to Chicago

Parents' occupations: Mother a domestic and father an itinerant sawmill laborer; stepfather laborer

Role models: Mother, businessman Harry Pace, politician Earl Dickerson

Hero mentors: Mary Herrick, white civics teacher, "most unforgettable person I've known"; Dale Carnegie self-help

Formal education: Arkansas City colored school (1932); DuSable High School Chicago 1936 with honors

Life crises: At age 8 father killed in accident; at age 9 Mississippi levee broke and "we were running for our lives"

Metamorphoses: "The boy on the levee was the father of the man and the publisher"; 1947 insolvency

Charismatic: Has disciples who never leave him; "I believe in the power of persuasion"

Competitive: "It was the dare, it was the gamble, it was the deal that captivated me"

Hypomanic: A frenetic "rushing sickness" lifestyle demands three secretaries in his 70s

Independent rebel: "I was driven to succeed by the whip of social disapproval"

Indomitable "will": Of *Negro Digest:* "I had decided . . . I was going to make it or die"; super willpower

Intuitive vision: "You have to change images before you can change acts and institutions"

Drive: "The reason I've been #1 for so long is that I've never been satisfied with last year's #1 rating"

Risk-taker: "I believe in risk and daring"; "living on the edge . . . is the summit of life"

Self-confident: A "Positive Mental Attitude helped me survive."; "I believed in the plastic power of the possible"

Tenacious: "Survival is in my blood"; "Persistence pays off . . . refuse to take 'no' for an answer"

Workaholic: "I set goals and work night and day to achieve it"; "Work is my vacation"

Honors: Many including: Horatio Alger Award, 1965; *Forbes* 400 Richest Americans; 1987 Entrepreneur of the Decade

12

Michael Jeffrey Jordan—Competitor

World's Preeminent Athlete—All Universe

"If you're not going to compete, I'm going to dominate you."

The sculpture immortalizing "His Airness" outside the Chicago United Center gives credence to Michael Jordan's skill as the quintessential basketball player— a true kinesthetic genius. It bears the inscription, "The best there ever was. The best there ever will be." Few people ever attain the degree of competence or adulation of the fans as has Michael Jordan. Not many superstars ever become so revered and idolized during their lifetime and certainly not during their playing days. They must retire or die to become an icon like Jordan. He is one of those unusual sports heroes who has been deified while still playing the game. Only Babe Ruth and Pele ever reached icon status while still donning their athletic gear. After Jordan led the Bulls to the 1996 NBA championship, university sports psychologist Steve Lerch said, "Fans worship Michael Jordan with much the same intensity as they worship religious figures." Jack Chirst, professor of pop culture at Ripon College, says, "Jordan is a pop icon. I think he is comparable to the Beatles and Elvis. Only Babe Ruth in sports ever achieved the state of idolatry of His Airness. His "Q" rating for TV transcends entertainers.

The great Martin Luther King, Jr., had to die to become immortal. Michael Jordan just had to announce, "I'm back!" Who else could have come out of retirement and made the headlines of the national news media with just two words: "I'm back"? No one, with the possible exception of Babe Ruth in sports, or rock stars like Elvis or Michael Jackson in entertainment. The world has never seen such a media explosion like the one that accompanied Jordan's return to the Chicago Bulls in the spring of 1995. Few celebrities ever ascend to the ethereal levels of Jordan. *Maclean's* in 1993 called him "Baryshnikov with a jump shot."

Negotiating his new contract in 1996, His Airness gave Chicago Bulls owner Jerry Reinsdorf an ultimatum, saying, "I would like to be the highest paid in the game." Reinsdorf was left no choice when journalists like Bryan Burwell of *USA Today* wrote, "Pay Jordan what he wants—end of discussion. He is more than the greatest basketball player to play the game. His Airness is Ruth, Joe Dimaggio, Santa Claus, and King Midas rolled into one. Icon. Athletic marvel. Walking marketing phenomenon." Reinsdorf capitulated and made Jordan the highest-paid player in the history of team sports with a one-year deal for over $30 million. With endorsements it pushed Jordan above his $60 million earnings for 1996 with projections upward of $100 million in 1997.

Michael Jordan is in this book because, like the others, he is self-made and not a product of his genes. Most people think of Air Jordan as a naturally gifted athlete who became great because of some genetic gift that allowed him to jump out of the gym. Not so! His dad, the late James Jordan, told Al Thomy of the *Sporting News* in 1984, "His leaping just didn't happen. He worked at it." Mitchell Krugel went even further in suggesting even Jordan's height was a by-product of his obsession with becoming a great basketball star. In describing Jordan's manic need to succeed after being cut from his high school basketball team, he said, "He was so dedicated to making the team that he spent much of that summer hanging on monkey bars to try to grow or at least stretch a few extra inches. With nobody in his family taller than 5 feet 7 inches, perhaps this helps to explain how Michael grew a foot beyond any other Jordan."

A MANIC SUCCESS SYNDROME

Michael Jordan is the classic case of a person using competitive drive and a mania to win to reach the pinnacle of success in life. Michael Jordan has had an internalized need to be number one since he was a small boy in North Carolina. The drive was in evidence when he won the MVP award as a Little League pitcher when nine and became more ingrained in his unconscious after sinking the winning shot to beat Georgetown for the NCAA championship as a college freshman. This "success imprint" then led to other feats such as winning College Player of the Year twice while at North Carolina followed by Rookie of the Year honors in the NBA. Jordan then drove himself to such an extent that he won the NBA scoring title seven consecutive years, which contributed to the Chicago Bulls winning the NBA crown for three successive years in the early nineties.

Four times Jordan was named the NBA League MVP (1988, 1991, 1992, and 1996) and four times he was the MVP of the NBA Finals (1991, 1992, 1993, and 1996). Jordan's scoring records are too numerous to detail, but he holds the most scoring titles—nine—in the history of the NBA, breaking Wilt Chamberlain's mark of eight in 1996. As this is being written he leads the league in scoring for 1997 with above 30 points per game, which will break Chamberlain's record. Jordan holds the all-time scoring average for a season at 32 and also the all-time scoring title for playoffs. He has been voted to the All-Star team every year he has been in the league.

Jordan's unbelievable competitiveness and ability to self-motivate was never more apparent than one night in Boston Garden on March 28, 1990, when Larry Bird pulled his competitive chain. Jordan says, "Larry Bird is the greatest trash talker and mind-game player of all time. He taught me everything I know about getting into folks' heads." Bird told Jordan that night, "I'm about to bust your tail." Bird had made a mistake and His Airness went out and scored 63 points, an all-time high in playoff history, that night.

Jordan's greatest scoring feat was against Cleveland, when he scored 69 points and grabbed 18 rebounds. He was the Defensive Player of the Year in 1988 in addition to winning the scoring title, a dual accomplishment that may never be broken. Jordan was named to the league's All-Defensive team from 1988 to 1993 and then again in 1996. Other awards include two Olympic gold medals. His competitive drive can be summarized in his June 5, 1996, quote in *USA Today* when Gary Payton was touted as the man who would stop Jordan since he was younger and quicker. Payton made the fatal mistake of saying, "I can play this game as well as he can." Jordan told a reporter, "You can play on my level, huh? Well, I'm going to show you exactly what level that is, OK? . . . You think you can come in and dominate me? On my floor?" That is the mental power of Michael Jordan, who is driven to be the very best. That drive manifests itself in a manic behavior second to none.

THE PERSONIFICATION OF SUPERMAN

Jordan is the consummate athlete. He plays golf to a seven handicap and was a promising professional baseball player with the Chicago White Sox farm team until the 1994 strike ended his career prematurely. When he quit basketball in 1993, teammate Scottie Pippen said, "He's leaving the game as the greatest player in the world." Bulls owner Jerry Reinsdorf gave Jordan the ultimate tribute, saying, "I used to think that Michael Jordan was the Babe Ruth of basketball. I have now come to believe that Babe Ruth was the Michael Jordan of baseball." Larry Bird said, "No one was ever better than him." After Jordan scored 63 points in a 1986 playoff game against the Celtics, Bird described Jordan as "God disguised as Michael Jordan." Bob Cousy said on his retirement, "As far as I'm concerned Michael was Nureyev against a bunch of Hulk Hogans. His talent is that far above anyone else's." Coach Larry Brown gave him the supreme compliment, saying, "Michael's the only guy I would pay to see practice." Teammate John Paxson said, "Many years from now I'll be able to tell my grandkids about the time I played with the greatest player in the world. . . . He is the best basketball player I have ever seen." After the Bulls made the fastest start in the history of the NBA in 1996, winning an unprecedented 90 percent of their games, with His Airness once again leading the league in scoring, announcer and former basketball All-Star Danny Ainge told *USA Today,* "Michael's the most famous pro athlete and maybe the most famous person in the world today. He's Elvis."

Innovative Contributions

The "reverse slam dunk" is Air Jordan's legacy. For those readers not conversant in the nuances of basketball that means dribbling to the basket and jumping in the air, turning 180 degrees while in the air, and stuffing the ball successfully through the basket. Not a simple maneuver by any means, but when done with grace and rhythm it is a majestic move that few athletes can imagine, let alone accomplish. His second innovative contribution was made during the All-Star slam-dunk contest when he took off from the foul line (ten feet from the basket) and remained airborne until reaching the basket and majestically stuffing the ball. His "Be Like Mike" Gatorade commercial caught on and elevated him above the pack.

When Jordan announced his return to basketball, the most amazing impact was seen in the stock market. On March 14, 1995, the stocks of those firms whose products he endorsed rose by $2 billion in one day. McDonald's rose $1 billion, General Mills, $500 million, and Nike, $200 million.

Personal History

Despite the fact that Jordan refers to himself in the media as a "a country boy"—due to having been raised in Wilmington, North Carolina—he was really born in Brooklyn, New York, as the fourth of five children of Delores and James Jordan. He was born on February 17, 1963, and shortly afterward the family moved to Wilmington. Jordan's father, James, was in the military when Michael was born but left when he was offered a supervisory job at the General Electric plant in Wilmington. His mother worked in customer service at a local bank. Jordan has two older brothers, James Jr. and Larry, and one older sister, Deloris. His younger sister is Roslyn. The amazing thing about this extensive family is that not one member is taller than 5 foot 7 inches. Both parents were of average height, as are all his siblings. Only Michael grew to 6 foot 6 inches. And none of the family members was athletic, with the exception of Larry, who at 5 foot 7 inches was never tall enough to make it in college athletics. Jordan's trademark habit of sticking his tongue out when making a big play on the basketball court was learned by watching his dad fix cars. When frustrated he would stick out his tongue.

The Jordans are a closeknit family. The parents encouraged their children to work hard and proceeded to teach them by example. Striving for excellence was standard fare in the Jordan household. Jordan told reporter Bob Greene, "My heroes are and were my parents" when asked where he had acquired his drive and work ethic. James Jordan confirmed this, saying, "In our family . . . we try to make something happen rather than waiting around for it to happen." Jordan's mother especially influenced him through actions, not words. He said, "By watching her I learned that you have to be serious about what you want out of life." On the topic of drugs and crime Jordan says his family warned him of the dangers of such vices. The children were warned against "the traps . . . the drugs and drink, the street that could catch you if you got careless."

Baseball, not basketball was Michael's favorite sport as a child. He was a standout on the sandlots of North Carolina and playing sports kept him out of the trouble that afflicts so many other latchkey children. He pitched for the local Little League team and threw two no-hitters, an achievement which he still prizes to this day. By the ninth grade he was quarterback on the football team, pitched on the baseball team, and played guard on the basketball team, since he was still well under six feet. His nickname was "Rabbit." Jordan's father was highly competitive and infuriated him as a kid by never allowing him to win at pool. Jordan's older brother Larry did the same in one-on-one basketball and dominated him as a kid. Jordan got his revenge as a teenager when he vowed never to lose to him again. Jordan always wore the number 45 while he was in middle school, but in high school his brother Larry had that number so he cut it in half and selected 23, a number that he has since made famous.

TRAUMA

As a sophomore Jordan was cut from the Laney High School basketball team, which proved so traumatic it transformed him from a mere aspiring athlete to a manically driven superstar. He said, "I went to my room and I closed the door and cried. For awhile I couldn't stop. . . . I cried so hard. It was all I wanted—to play on that team." He later said, "I knew I never wanted to have that experience again" and has worked hard enough to ensure he was never faced again with sitting on the sidelines. Crisis for Jordan proved to be the mother of his creative success. From that day forward Jordan got up at 6:00 A.M. and drove to the gym with coach Clifton Herring and practiced for hours to ensure he would not only make the team but become the greatest player he could become. Practicing the fundamentals of shooting, passing, and dribbling, and more importantly jumping, jumping, jumping, were at the forefront of his motivations. Jordan practiced and practiced until he couldn't play anymore—it paid off. Those days of hard work as a fifteen-year-old transformed Jordan into a unique athlete—a heretofore unheard of 6 foot 6 shooting guard.

HIGH SCHOOL PHENOM

Between his junior and senior years in high school Rabbit's skills were further honed at the Five Star Basketball Summer Camp in Pittsburgh. At this camp Jordan said he finally felt that he was special. He described the feeling as being "tapped on the shoulder with a magic wand." He returned home from that summer camp to become the star of Laney High School, averaging 27.8 points per game in 1981 and graduating with excellent grades so that he could attend the college of his choice. More importantly, Jordan realized an even greater dream by growing to a height of 6 foot 5 inches. Dean Smith, the esteemed coach at North Carolina

University, offered him a grant-in-aid scholarship to play for the Wolfpack. He enrolled in the fall of 1981.

UNIVERSITY OF NORTH CAROLINA

Coach Dean Smith said when he first recruited Jordan he saw a difference between him and the other athletes. He said, "What impressed me most about Michael was his love for his parents and family." That first season at North Carolina was not fun for Jordan, since he had worked diligently to hone his personal skills and the Wolfpack's style was based on Dean Smith's team-oriented approach. Michael flirted with leaving school during that first season but was talked into staying by assistant coach Kevin Loughry. Jordan averaged only 13.5 points per game during the 1981–82 season, but became immortal in the annals of North Carolina basketball by sinking the winning shot in the NCCA final against Georgetown. This was the first NCAA championship for Coach Smith, and the Wolfpack fans and students started calling him "Superman" along with other superlatives although Superman is probably the most apt of them all.

Jordan came into his own as a sophomore and led the Atlantic Coast Conference in scoring with 20 points per game. He was voted a unanimous All-American for 1983. Jordan then won back-to-back Player of the Year honors as the best college player in the country and was selected to play for the Olympic team to be coached by the infamous Bob Knight. Knight was so impressed with him that he gave a tribute to Jordan, saying, "Michael is probably the best athlete playing college basketball." After his junior year Jordan became the third selection by the Chicago Bulls in the draft that year behind Hakeem Olajuwon and Sam Bowie. Sam who? The Bulls offered Jordan a seven-figure, five-year contract to lead them to the promised land and Jordan became their messiah. Jordan began his pro career in the fall of 1984 but continued taking classes at North Carolina, finally earning his bachelor's degree on December 31, 1986.

Professional History

In 1984–85 Jordan led the NBA in scoring with 2,313 points, was named Rookie of the Year and starting All-Star guard, and won the Seagram Award as the best NBA player. In this his rookie year Jordan averaged 28.2 points per game with 5.9 assists and 2.4 steals and, most remarkable for a guard, he led the Bulls in rebounds with 6.5. The most gratifying statistic for the Bulls was the drawing power of this emerging superstar. Attendance rose by 87 percent over the previous year but rebounded with Jordan on board. In his second year, 1985–86, a foot injury sidelined Jordan for all but eighteen games. Without Air Jordan in the lineup, the Bulls lost forty-three of sixty-four games. When Jordan returned the team was revitalized and made the playoffs the last week of the season. This proved providential, as His Airness made playoff history on April 20, 1986, in a loss to the Boston Celtics by scoring an unprecedented 63 points. The Celtics fans were captivated by Jordan's gravity-defying moves and the media began taking notice of a man who acted as if he had a giant "S" emblazoned on his chest.

John Paxson joined the Bulls as Jordan's running mate in 1986 and their tandem leadership took the team to another level. Paxson was just as amazed by his teammate's skills as the fans and told a reporter, "Wherever he goes, people want to touch him. . . . He is one of God's special children." At the All-Star game during the 1986–87 season, Hang Time, as Jordan was now known, won the slam-dunk contest. His heroics that afternoon enthralled the crowd. He dribbled the ball the length of the floor and with tongue hanging out in classic Jordan fashion took off from the foul line, leveled off in midair, then appeared to rise again to make a dramatic dunk to the adulation of the crowd. During this memorable season Jordan crossed another milestone by becoming only the second man in NBA history, after Wilt Chamberlain, to score over 3,000 points in a season, averaging 37.1 points per game. And the Bulls set an all-time season attendance record for the year. If Jordan had any political ambitions like his friend Charles Barkley, he could have won the mayoral or governor's election.

In 1988 Jordan won what he considers his most valuable award, since it was earned through sweat, tears, and agony. Through very hard work he was named the Defensive Player of the Year. He also won the MVP award at the annual All-Star game and once again led the league in scoring with a 35-point game average. In 1988–89 His Airness won his third consecutive scoring title, with a 32.5-per-game average and won again a year later with a 33.6-point average. By 1990–91 the Bulls had attracted a better supporting cast for Jordan's incomparable talents and the team not only won the division title riding Jordan's 31.5 scoring average, but went on to win the NBA championship over Magic Johnson's Los Angeles Lakers.

REPEAT AND THREE-PEAT

The next year Jordan averaged 30.1 points per game and led the team to the championship against the Portland Trail Blazers. "Three-Peat" became the rallying call for the team when they opened the 1992–93 season, and Jordan once again led the way with a 32.6 point scoring average to match Wilt Chamberlain's feat of seven straight scoring titles. The Bulls then beat the Phoenix Suns and Jordan's golfing buddy Charles Barkley in the finals with His Airness scoring a record-setting 41 points a game during the series.

PITCHMAN EXTRAORDINAIRE

McDonald's recognized Jordan's special flare by sponsoring him and Larry Bird in a game of mythical horse that became McDonald's most popular ad campaign. The company was so impressed with the results that they launched the McJordan Special sandwich. Jordan earned $35 million in endorsements in 1993, $30 million in 1994 (even after he had retired), and $40 million in 1995, which put him on top of *Forbes* listings of the highest-paid athletes for four consecutive years. Jordan had become the darling of Madison Avenue, with the highest possible "Q" rating for television endorsements.

EUPHORIA AND TRAGEDY

The summer of 1993 proved to be the most euphoric and traumatic period in Jordan's young life. He worked feverishly to three-peat and the win over Phoenix didn't come until mid-June. Then the Michael Jordan Sports Bar Restaurant opened in downtown Chicago. He had not had a break the previous year due to the 1992 Summer Olympic Games, which were held in Barcelona, Spain. He and his Dream Team mates won the gold medal. By the finals of the 1993 NBA playoffs, his father turned up missing in rural North Carolina. When his father turned up murdered, the stress of all this took its toll on Jordan and without notice he announced his retirement from basketball on October 6, 1993. The sports world went into shock and almost pleaded that he reconsider. Many things had contributed to his rash decision, not the least of which were fatigue from a year of nonstop competition, his father's murder, and the media hype over his alleged gambling problems in Atlantic City and on the golf links. All of these together were more than he cared to deal with. Jordan was rich enough to quit and did.

GOLF AND BASEBALL

The media hype over Jordan's gambling on the golf course came to a head during the same period when he was grieving over his father's death. Jordan had a reputation for gambling on anything from a half-court shot after practice to cards on the bus with teammates, to his most famous losses on the golf links. The disclosures by a nefarious California golf hustler who was attempting to benefit from the media hype brought to light the fact that Jordan had lost the princely sum of $500,000 to him. Now to most people that is a lot of money, but it only represents less than 1 percent of Michael's annual income, or less than a week's wages.

Jordan married Juanita Vanoy in a Las Vegas chapel in 1989 and by 1993 they had three children and, always a family-oriented man, he decided to spend more time at home rather than field stupid questions over his gambling on the golf course, which was no one's business, including the media.

By spring 1994 Michael was once again in the headlines after announcing he would try out for the Chicago White Sox farm team and would attend spring training. He immediately became a hit with the media, causing such a stir that spring training came close to a media circus. The Birmingham Barons was his new home. Jordan never became proficient at hitting the curve ball and finished the strike-shortened season batting .202 with only two home runs.

"I'M BACK!"

Rested and finally recovered from his father's murder, Air Jordan announced his return to basketball on March 18, 1995, to a media blitz that was second only to a declaration of war. The media were clamoring for stories and instead received from him a succinct "I'm back!" Jordan would later add, "I tried to stay away as long as I could, but it's hard when you love something for so long. You miss the game." Jordan demonstrated flashes of his old brilliance but was rusty from the layoff and averaged just 26.7 points per game for the balance of the 1995 season. But one memorable night at Madison Square Garden he lit it up like the old Air Jordan, scoring 55 points against the tenacious defense of his nemesis the New York Knicks. The Bulls eliminated the Knicks from the playoffs but were themselves eliminated by the emerging Orlando Magic, led by the heir apparent to Michael's position as Mr. Basketball, Shaquille O'Neal.

In the 1995–96 season Jordan was on a mission to quiet those critics who questioned his position as the world's greatest basketball player. He not only quieted them, he dumbfounded them by winning an unprecedented eighth scoring title, averaging over 30 points a game, eclipsing Wilt Chamberlain's seven titles and winning his fourth Most Valuable Player award. Further evidence of his consummate skills was a *USA Today* survey of 301 NBA players, coaches, trainers, and general managers who ranked Jordan as the "Best Player" with 132 points, followed by Hakeem Olajuwon of Houston, who received but 25. The coup de grace was the Bulls breaking the record for regular season wins, going 72-10 for the season. The previous mark, held by the 1971–72 Los Angeles Lakers, was 69 wins. By season's end not even Jordan's worst media critics denied that Jordan was back and still the king of the NBA.

What Makes His Airness Tick?

In this book Jordan is the subject who most exemplifies a competitive personality who will go to virtually any length to win. He is an introverted visionary with a rational approach to problem resolution. Air Jordan is driven, aggressive to a fault, and cherishes his privacy. He exhibits most of the behavioral characteristics of the world's creative geniuses. He is what Jungian psychologists label a Promethean temperament (intuitive-thinking). Such people seek the opportunities and possibilities in life and have long-term vision. They see the big picture in all things and prefer to operate on that vision rationally and logically. His 1996 film debut in *Space Jam* is testimony to his need for self-actualization. Jordan Cologne gives further credence to his driven nature.

One Chicago Bulls executive warns new players, "Don't play cards with Michael." Pippen and Grant never listened to this sage advice and paid the price in financial losses. When *Sports Illustrated* did a story in 1993 on Jordan's propensity for gambling, they asked a teammate about his competitive nature and the teammate told them: "This guy is a killer. He's the most viciously competitive player I've ever seen." Jordan's competitive nature urges him to bet on his abilities as an athlete whether it be shooting half-court shots after practice or making a putt on the golf course. The magazine labeled Jordan "an extremely competitive personality."

Jordan values his privacy and demands quality time with his family. When playing on the road he often spends Thanksgiving Day or Christmas Day alone and eats in his room with security guards guarding his hotel room door. He will not leave his room and face the hassle of fanatic fans who refuse to give him any space. Getting to the top includes never being able to attend a movie or walk into a restaurant without complete pandemonium breaking out. Such is the price of superstardom. Consequently this superstar lives within himself—both emotionally and mentally.

This visionary is introspective and convinced that intuition plays a large role in his athletic prowess. He told a writer that winning the 1987 All Star slam-dunk contest originated out of "instinct and intuition." Jordan is a control freak and master self-motivator. Wearing a new pair of Nikes for each game is one of the techniques he uses to "psyche up" for a game. He described it as "making me feel good every game."

MYTHOLOGICAL HERO MENTORS

Jordan is a grounded person whose first heroes were his parents. Then, during his high school years, David Thompson became his basketball hero and role model. It was Thompson who inspired him to become a great leaper. For those not familiar with David Thompson, he became famous at the University of North Carolina for being a guard who could sky above taller backcourt players and dunk the ball in dramatic fashion, causing the crowd to go into a frenzy. Jordan decided early in life to emulate Thompson's electrifying moves on the basketball court and ended up refining the art of his role model.

A "success imprint" occurred when Jordan made that buzzer shot to defeat Georgetown for the NCAA championship. He says, "My career really started when I made that shot. I was fearless after that." At crunch time he now demands the ball due to that "success imprint."

INSECURITY BREEDS GREATNESS

A fear of losing is what motivates Jordan to greatness. He told a reporter, "When I was first in the league, and everyone was talking about Bird and Magic, my main drive then was that I was afraid. . . . Afraid I was going to be overlooked, and everything I did was toward that end." The fear of losing drove Jordan like nothing else in his life, whether it was cards, golf, or basketball. He said, "I never want anyone else to win when I'm playing." Every game is the biggest. He lives by the philosophy: "Every time I step onto the court, if you're against me you're trying to take something from me." Fear is always lurking in the back of his brain, which should give some insight to the rest of us, who are not nearly so successful in our professions.

Strange as it may seem, one of the world's greatest athletes cannot swim. He is petrified of the water and attributes this failing to having almost drowned as a child. Young Michael and a friend were swimming in the Atlantic when the friend was caught in an undertow and drowned. Jordan was just seven at the time and the experience left its mark on his psyche. Then at age twelve he had another close brush with death. He was in a pool with friends at King's Mountain amusement park and suddenly went under water. He wrote in *I'm Back,* "I just kept going down. I went down once, twice, and the third time, one of my teammates grabbed my hand and put me on the side of the pool. I wouldn't have made it otherwise."

LIFE CRISES AND TRAUMAS

Being cut from the Laney High School team devastated Jordan. He has lived in dread of that personal failure ever since. Jordan is what he is today because of that rejection, which has motivated him to become an overachieving superstar. He told himself he never wanted to feel like that ever again in his life and has worked to ensure he didn't. The "success imprint" took and has led him toward a life of driven passion for excellence.

Charisma

Henry Schafer of Marketing Evaluations, who compiles the Q ratings for television said, "Jordan's charisma, character, and aura rival those of Bill Cosby, Robin Williams, and Magic Johnson." Bulls teammate Elston Turner observed, "He is the first athlete I've ever seen whom the fans treat like Michael Jackson. He needs a police escort to hotels; girls cry when they see him." The *New York Times* wrote in 1983, "He can excite a crowd like a Sunday morning preacher," and Mike Douchant of the *Sporting News* wrote in 1984, "Jordan is a showman under control. Sometimes Jordan spontaneously performs an electrifying high-wire act." Donald Dell, the head of ProServ who functions as Jordan's agent, says, "Jordan has a charisma that transcends his sport." Jordan can captivate a crowd like no other athlete. Biographer Bob Greene in *Hang Time* compares the public's attitude to Jordan to the idolatry of Elvis in 1956–57, Babe Ruth in 1927, Joe Louis in 1937, and Michael Jackson in 1985. They all had a godlike persona that transcended the norm.

Theirs is the power to move mountains. One such example occurred when an eighteen-year-old girl who was unable to get Jordan's autograph laid down in front of his car outside Bulls Stadium and told him, "I'm not getting up until you give me your autograph. I wouldn't mind being run over by Michael Jordan." She got her autograph. Just another day in the life of a charismatic superstar.

Competitiveness

If nothing else, Michael Jordan is a competitor. The Bulls' coaches warn new players, "Never challenge Mike." After practice His Airness enjoys shooting baskets for money, often for $100 a shot. His father told *Newsweek*, "Michael has a competition problem," causing Jordan to tell *Ebony* after his father's untimely death, "I don't believe I've ever heard of Competitors Anonymous." Charles Barkley gave further evidence of his friend's competitive nature by saying, "Michael Jordan is the only person in this entire world that I've ever met who is as competitive as I am." Jordan told *Ebony*, "I love to compete and it isn't the money. I just love competition. I like the challenge. . . . If I'm going to play then I'm going to play to win. That's enjoyable to me. That's fun." Without doubt competitiveness is the driving force behind Michael Jordan's success.

CONFIDENCE

Autograph seekers have always been a wonder to Jordan, who sees their needs as a lack of self-esteem. Jordan could not understand their motivations, since he was never so starstruck. He explains, "I've always had so much self-confidence that a name on a piece of paper is not motivational." An example of Jordan's gigantic optimism occurred at the end of a season in a game of no import against the struggling Charlotte Hornets. Jordan bet one of his teammates he could make a free throw with his eyes closed, then went out and swished the ball. The incident was kept quiet but later spawned a McDonald's TV commercial on the McJordan Special, where Jordan performs the deed in an ad.

Jordan believes in himself and that belief arms him against the various controversies that surrounds the life of an athlete. When asked about the "boo-birds" in hostile arenas, Jordan replied, "If they hate me, that only energizes me. I look forward to them booing me. It makes me better." That is the confidence of a champion who is not deterred by adversaries but spurred on to greatness by their taunts.

Hypomania

A teammate told *Sports Illustrated* that Jordan often drives his sports car like he is on the Indy Race track, reaching 125 miles per hour on the Chicago Eisenhower Expressway on his way from home to practice. Teammates described him as having "extremely high energy" and "rarely sleeps." Former coach Collins agrees, admitting on television, "Michael is always hyper." Experts say that one of the variables found in powerful and successful people is the ability to get by on little sleep. Sources confirm that he sleeps sparingly and one magazine reporter wrote, "He only limits himself to 18 holes of golf a day if a typhoon is approaching."

Jordan acquired his work ethic from his father, who told a reporter, "Work was the biggest similarity between Michael and me." He told the *Sporting News* in 1984, "If you have dreams you have to work hard." All of Air Jordan's coaches through high school, college, and the pros have consistently agreed that Jordan works harder than any other player. His success is highly tied to his manic work ethic. Former Bulls coach Doug Collins said, "Every day he had this need to show he was the best. . . . Throw away all the talent. The way he practiced put him on a level above everybody else." If he were a businessman he would be classified a Type A. His success on the court is tied closely to his feelings of self-worth, which is manifested in competitiveness.

Independence

Michael Jordan is a quiet, unassuming person who does not appear to be your typical renegade. But like most people who excel in life he is prone to violate traditional mores and established policies. A strange confirmation of Jordan's rebellious nature comes from biographer Bob Greene who discovered that Jordan never listened to the advice of any of his coaches at any time in his storied career. He said, "I never follow along. I'm never paying attention" to what they are telling the team. When the coaches are diagramming plays on the board, Jordan said he was preoccupied elsewhere. He told Green he purposely ignores their advice. He said, "I don't think the coaches are aware I'm not listening. I'm looking at them and sitting there, but my mind is totally somewhere else." When questioned about this defiant approach to team athletics, he responded, "I know what to do! There are only a certain number of ways you can do a certain play." When coaches attempt to give him direction, he says: "I don't want to hear it. I want to go out and play. Just go play the game. That's when it's time for me to pay attention." This is surprising dialogue from the ever-congenial Michael Jordan, but typical of the findings on eminent people.

Passion and Drive

Michael Jordan is energy incarnate. He is so "obsessed with winning" he is able to block out all else while on the court. His mad passion for winning has made him extremely competitive. He told *Ebony* in 1993, "As long as I have energy. And I almost always have energy, I have to be doing something. Most of the time I prefer anything with competition involved. I don't care what it is—ping pong, golf, cards, shooting pool, or playing basketball." He told biographer Greene, "I never want anyone else to win when I'm playing," which is the mark of a man with an abnormally high amount of testosterone. Another mark of psychically driven individuals is their reading habits. Type A personalities virtually never read fiction and Jordan confirms his own predilection for books as "I never read fiction at all. Fiction doesn't appeal to me." Intensity is one of the trademarks of the driven person, and former coach Doug Collins confirms Jordan's highly charged nature, saying, "Michael is the most driven and intense player I ever coached."

What is the derivation of Michael's great drive? It appears that psychosexual or libidinal energy played a large part. According to authorities on the subject— Napoleon Hill, Frank Farley, and Charles Garfield—most eminent people have an inordinantly high sex drive at the seat of their success. His Airness offered insight into his internal motivations when he told biographer Bob Greene, "It all began with girls." Jordan described taking up sports because it attracted girls. They were his inspiration for becoming a star. He told a reporter, "When I was a teen I was never very successful romantically. . . . They always wanted me to be their friend, not their boyfriend. They always wanted the athletes." He told sportswriter Bob Greene, "Why do you think I took up sports? So girls would like me."

Perfectionist

Excellence is the god of His Airness. He told Larry King, "I'm a perfectionist." He is driven to be the very best he can be. Perfection pervades his very being. This can be discerned from his attire. He dresses like someone out of *GQ* and his shirts are stiffly starched, pants pressed, and shirttail neatly tucked inside his pants. The grunge look so popular in the early nineties never found its way into Jordan's wardrobe or psyche. He not only demands perfection from himself but also from the other players on the Bulls. Notice on TV what he does when someone drops a pass or makes a mental error. He is all over them, just as he is on himself when he makes the mistakes of a mere mortal.

Temerity

"Risk" and "Air Jordan" are synonymous terms. He uses the analogy that in baseball he was never a singles-type guy but "I was always the type of guy that went for the home run." Jordan finds comfort in speed and going for it all and has lived his life with that axiom. His father admonished him as a kid who preferred the euphoria accompanying high-risk wins to the mediocrity of low-risk ventures. Jordan would tell his father: "Why go for the base hit when you can for all four bases?" He added, "That was my logic. And that's how I played."

Jordan made the headlines for his enormous losses to a golf hustler in the early nineties when a nefarious gambler named Eddie Dow was indicted in North Carolina. A $108,000 check was found that led to the $1.2 million he lost to Richard Esquinas, the California golf hustler. Jordan loves to bet on anything he does as a method of self-motivation. This competitive spirit is testimony to his level of testosterone, which has been highly correlated to risk taking, competitiveness, sex drive, and creativity. It isn't winning but the euphoria of competing and thrill seeking which is the key driving force in Michael Jordan's success.

Tenacity

Jordan's motto is: "I cannot accept not trying," which is synonymous with tenacity. He continues to shoot the basketball even if it is not going in the basket. He perseveres even when he is not on top of his game. This happened in his first game back after retirement, when he made only seven of twenty-eight shots. But Jordan knew it was just a matter of time, while mere mortals would have thought the worst and would have possibly quit in disgust. He persisted and through hard work came back to average 27 points a game for the balance of the 1995 season and capped off his comeback with a 55-point performance against the hated New York Knicks in the playoffs. Even more indicative of Jordan's tenacity is the ridicule he lived through attempting to hit the curve ball while playing left field for the Birmingham Barons in 1994. Regardless of the adversity, he never gives up, which is why he is a superstar.

Vision

His Airness credits much of his success on the basketball court to an internalized vision that endows him with the confidence to perform at the highest level. He is able to envision success prior to achieving it. This is a special intuitive insight found in innovative people. Jordan told Jerry Sullivan of *Newsday* in 1987 that it was just "instinct and intuition" that allowed him to win the slam-dunk contest. In his 1995 *I'm Back* Jordan wrote, "The first time you've hit a jump shot with no time on the clock, you can always go back to that moment. You have the confidence because you've done it before. I wasn't afraid to take a big shot in the professional ranks because I had made one when I was a snotty-nosed kid in 1982 to beat Georgetown."

A testimony to the intuitive vision of His Airness came in a late-season game in Charlotte. After retiring, Jordan admitted to going to the foul line and attempting to make shots with his eyes closed. He bet a teammate, and with one watching, sank two free throws. Such is the confidence and intuitive talent of a megastar.

Will to Power

Michael Jordan is a man in control, or, in business terms, he is a "control freak." He admitted to sportswriter Bob Greene, "I need to be in control all the time." Jordan despises being told what to do, which is further evidence of his indomitable willpower. After he made the shot that won the NCAA championship against Georgetown, Jordan was nicknamed "Superman" by both the media and school student body. These people never knew how close they were to the truth since

Michael Jordan is the personification of the Nietzschean "Superman" ("Overman") persona who is in total control of his destiny. Those who assume power in the Nietzschean scheme of things gain power and one only has to watch His Airness on the basketball floor to discern who has the power. Every time the game is on the line no one has the ball but Jordan and he insists on having it. Jordan's last-minute heroics are legend, especially in Cleveland and Los Angeles, where he has repeatedly made shots with no time remaining to drive the nail in the coffins of those cities' two teams. If anyone ever had an unconscious "Superman" psyche it is Michael Jordan.

Summary

When Michael Jordan was ready to announce his retirement, Bulls Coach Phil Jackson, a highly respected and erudite coach, made an emotional attempt to alter his decision. He told Jordan that he had a special quality that should not lay dormant. He said, "Mike, you are a genius, like Picasso or Shakespeare, and by retiring are depriving others of seeing, and being inspired by, your gift." Jordan was moved but not enough to change his mind. But it was the first time someone of Jackson's intellectual bent had referred to his talents as genius. After Jordan had led the Bulls to yet another championship in 1996, Jackson said, "Coaching is like coaching Michelangelo. He's a genius at work."

Jordan's genius is not that of an Einstein, a rational intelligence for solving abstractions, but a kinesthetic-type genius as defined by Harvard's Howard Gardner. Gardner has defined genius as falling into seven different categories or intelligences. One of those he defines is a "bodily" or kinesthetic-type genius, such as was possessed by Martha Graham in dance and which His Airness certainly has in abundance. Anyone who has watched Jordan float through the air with such majesty and grace would have to agree that he is a creative genius by Gardner's definition.

Regardless of what His Airness does in the future, he is already an established hero of gargantuan proportions. He will always be looked upon as the twentieth century's quintessential athlete in much the same way as Babe Ruth and Joe Louis are. His mystique transcends the basketball court. Harvard clinical professor of psychiatry Alvin F. Poussaint describes Jordan's mystique saying, "Michael Jordan is viewed as a phenomenon, someone who has an aura of being superhuman. His athletic prowess is enhanced by his personality. . . . Jordan has this wholesome, nice-guy image that children and adults love." And Poussaint could have included, that they want to emulate. Michael Jordan is unquestionably a man who has used his own inner drives and personality to become the very best in his profession and that is what makes him an unqualified creative genius.

MICHAEL JORDAN
Promethean Temperament (intuitive-thinker)
World's Preeminent Athlete
born February 17, 1963, Brooklyn, New York

Dominant trait: Competitive to a fault; introvert with intuitive-thinking approach to life; driven
Motto: "If you're not going to compete, I'm going to dominate you"; "I love to compete"
Religion: Southern Baptist
Philosophy: "Heart is probably the biggest key to success" and "I go for the home run"
Nickname: Rabbit (as a kid); M.J.; His Airness; Air Jordan; Hang Time
Creation/innovation: Reverse slam dunk; family-man image in profession dominated by drugs and tough guys
Successes: Highest TV "Q" rating; income of $40 million a year; All-State; All-American; All-NBA; 4 NBA MVPs; All-Universe; NBA Rookie of Year; 3 NBA titles; most NBA scoring titles (8); 2 Olympic gold medals
Vices/hobbies: Golf, baseball, gambling, sports cars
Romantic liaisons: Married Juanita Vanoy, 4 years his senior after first child; family man with three kids
Self-description: "I've tried so hard to be a respectable person"

Birth order: Fourth of five children (James, Deloris, Larry, Mike, Roslyn) of James and Deloris
Parental influence: Father: competitiveness; mother: "Be serious about life"
Early transience: Brooklyn, New York, to Wilmington, North Carolina, as a small child
Parents' occupations: Father in Air Force and G.E. supervisor; mother bank employee
Role models: "My parents"
Hero mentors: "My heroes are and were my parents"; David Thompson in basketball
Formal education: Laney High (1981); U. North Carolina (1986); left school as junior to enter NBA draft
Life crises: Almost drowned at ages 7 and 12; trauma after cut from high school team as sophomore; father's murder
Metamorphoses: After cut said, "I didn't want to have that feeling ever again" and worked to insure he didn't; NCAA shot to win championship over Georgetown, "My career started . . . I was fearless after that"

Charismatic: *N.Y. Times*: "He can excite a crowd like no other"; ProServ: "a charisma that transcends his sport"
Competitive: "Never challenge Mike"; "If I'm going to play then I'm going to play to win"
Hypomanic: "I almost always have energy"; Coach Collins: "Michael is always hyper"; sleeps sparingly
Independent rebel: "I never listened to the coach. . . . My whole life I never did . . . my mind is totally somewhere else"
Indomitable "will": "I create stuff as motivation"; "If they hate me that energizes me"
Intuitive vision: "Basketball is like meditation to me"; Bulls trainer Orth: "He has spectacular vision"
Libidinal drive: "I started to play sports . . . so girls would like me. . . . Absolutely!"
Perfectionist: Told *Sporting News* in 1984, you must "strive for excellence"
Risk-taker: "I was always the type of guy who went for the home run"; drives very fast sports cars
Self-confident: "I've always had so much self-confidence"
Tenacious: Very persistent and perseveres in the face of tragedy: "I can't accept not trying"
Workaholic: Practices harder than anyone on team; "If you have dreams you have to work hard"
Honors: Countless, including Michael Jordan Freeway in North Carolina plus every possible basketball honor

13

Reginald F. Lewis—Hypomanic

Corporate Takeover Mogul Extraordinaire

"No skill or vocation is a white man's exclusive province."

Reginald Lewis became the world's preeminent takeover specialist by outmaneuvering and outdealing the Wall Street experts. He left this world prematurely but his heritage is one that will not soon be forgotten or matched. This man was a driven Type A personality who made himself into one of the greatest deal makers this country has ever seen. This kid from the inner city of Baltimore rose to become Wall Street's consummate leveraged buyout deal maker—a power broker of enormous integrity and influence. Lewis was a strange combination of class and manic temerity that would not be denied. No one of any race or creed was his equal when it came to making a financial deal, despite the fact that math and accounting were not his strengths. What Lewis had was an inner sense of what was "behind the numbers," which others looked at as sacrosanct. Lewis was conversant with numbers far beyond his academic skills and that ability helped make him rich and powerful beyond his wildest dreams. He made so much money that he became a philanthropist in middle age, spending the last five years of his life giving away enormous amounts of money.

This man who was infamous for chasing money demonstrated that money was only a way to keep score of his successes and failures and had little or nothing to do with personal motivation. When he had more than he needed, Lewis began giving it away with complete disdain. The story of Reginald Lewis makes Horatio Alger stories pale in comparison. Lewis was able to take a very average résumé of academic achievement and parlay it into a Harvard Law School education. He was the first man ever admitted to Harvard Law School without so much as filling out an entrance application. He not only accomplished this unprecedented feat, he then talked the school into financing his education plus room and board. Maybe Harvard knew what others did not as they got their money back with huge dividends in July 1992 when that famous alumnus donated $3 million to build a new International Law Center on the Harvard campus. It was the largest single grant in Harvard's 175-year history and the first time a building at Harvard had been named for a black person.

Lewis became a certified business mogul after he pulled off one of the largest leveraged buyout (LBO) takeovers—and the first ever for a black man—when he closed the deal for McCall Pattern Company in the mid-eighties. How did he pull off such a deal? With expertise and dedication to detail! This perfectionist demanded the very best of himself and his associates, a hypomanic driven to win at almost any cost. He had dedicated himself as an attorney to becoming "the industry expert" on Minority Small Business Investment Companies and parlayed that knowledge into history-making deals. McCall was such a deal and it is what made Lewis rich and famous since it opened up many important doors that otherwise would have remained closed. What is surprising is that this man made his mark in the world of high finance despite the fact that he had failed math twice at Virginia State. This clearly demonstrates that something else was at work here.

Even financial whizkid Michael Milken looked up to this black man who had parlayed a $1 million investment into a $90 million profit in just three years—an unheard of multiple on any investment. Lewis made $90 million in profits for his investors and $50 million for himself. This deal then armed him with the confidence and moxie to pull off the biggest buyout deal in America and he went for it despite enormous odds. At the end of the decade Lewis closed what would become the largest LBO transaction in American history when he successfully took over international food conglomerate Beatrice Foods. He pulled off this deal within months by utilizing the windfall profits, expertise, and contacts acquired during the McCall deal. He leveraged the McCall resources into an LBO acquisition of Beatrice for a $950 million coup that shook the investment world, causing Michael Milken to say, "Lewis knew more about the company than the people who ran it."

At the time Lewis closed the TLC Beatrice deal in 1989 he instantly became the richest black person in America. At age eighteen Lewis had confided to a white school buddy from Baltimore named Ellis Goodman, "I'd like to be the richest man in America." It took him thirty years but he was on the way. *Forbes* in its 1992 magazine with the four hundred richest Americans listed Lewis with a $400 million net worth, far and away the highest of any black person and greater than all but a few other Americans of any race. The TLC Beatrice acquisition also elevated Lewis into the top executive position of a billion-dollar company with an annual salary of $22 million. Not bad for a ghetto kid who preferred to play quarterback than study math.

The Beatrice LBO was a major coup for this Baltimore street kid as Beatrice controlled sixty-four different companies located in thirty-one countries on three continents. It was by far the largest company ever to be operated by a black man. In 1988 TLC Beatrice became the only black-owned company to break the magical $1 billion revenue barrier. By any barometer Reginald Lewis had become the quintessential LBO specialist and the most-noted black business tycoon ever. And he had accomplished all this in less than ten years. At age thirty-five he had still been a struggling New York City attorney, but by age forty-five he was earning a $22 million salary and was living in Paris managing a major international enterprise. By 1990 Lewis had began work as a serious philanthropist and he was still not fifty.

Innovative Contributions

Reginald Lewis had a unique macrovision that enabled him to mastermind huge deals that were beyond the comprehension of mere mortals. His genius was a unique ability to "get behind the numbers" and manipulate them to fit his own needs. He lived by the admonition that you "managed the numbers or they managed you," a lesson learned from many heartrending failures during his early years attempting to become a takeover specialist. Lewis learned from his mistakes and never repeated them.

One example of Lewis's innovative ability came to the fore after he had taken over McCall Pattern. He was an impatient and intolerant overachiever who pushed all of his employees beyond any human standard. He suddenly became obsessed with optimizing the bottom line and that demanded maximum utilization of all plant assets. Return on capital became Lewis's God and to achieve optimum return on McCall's assets he was faced with maximum utilization of the plant equipment. When he discovered that the firm's presses were underutilized, he told his executives to solve the problem. When they gave up, he solved it himself through the innovative move of starting a greeting card production operation during the downtime on the presses. His solution would become an important new product for the company, which became a producer of greeting cards. This new profit center solved an asset utilization problem and dramatically improved profits and enhanced the company value.

Personal History

Reginald Francis Lewis was the only child of Carolyn Cooper and Clinton Lewis. He was born in Baltimore on December 7, 1942, a day of infamy for the American military, but a day of fame and fortune for the Lewis clan. Carolyn was just seventeen when Lewis was born and would ultimately become the major influence in his life. Lewis was sent to live with Carolyn's parents, the Coopers, shortly after his birth. Some of the Cooper children, who were his aunts and uncles, were not much older than Reginald and saw him as a gifted child: they pampered him and doted on him as a "wonder child." Lewis's mother remained his true love. Lewis was the recipient of the love of an extended family and his grandfather became his substitute father, and the reason "I never had a fear of white people," since Sam Cooper had "little tolerance for racism." This environment allowed Lewis to play with older children, a habit he would never lose. Lewis attended St. Francis Xavier

Elementary School in East Baltimore, where he was further indoctrinated in structure and Catholic dogma.

Lewis's father was a proprietor of numerous small businesses and successful at none. Lewis wrote, "My mother left my father when I was 5." Carolyn worked as a waitress and as a night clerk in a department store, always holding two jobs, which would become the operating style of her overachieving son. She often told him, "Through thick and thin, it's the two of us. You can depend on the Lord, yourself, and me." Then Lewis's life changed dramatically: when he was nine his mother remarried and Lewis finally moved out of his grandparents' home to West Baltimore. Jean Fugett would become his stepfather, and like his mother was a positive influence, since he also worked two jobs in addition to attending college at night to finish his degree.

DOTING CREATED A SUPERSTAR

During his formative years Lewis found himself surrounded by doting relatives, mostly his mother, grandmother, aunts, half-sisters, and even uncles. For many years as a child he was king of the roost, which instilled in him a feeling of power, imprinting in him a super self-esteem. Lewis was treated as the "center of the universe" and later in life expected similar adulation from his business associates. Such early nurturing often molds a person into an overachieving powerhouse and just as often into an arrogant know-it-all. Reggie Lewis had both traits in abundance, which helped him become the richest black man in America. This financial mogul was a very private person and preferred to regress into his own world to ferret out his problems, but he was considered abnormally self-confident, arrogant, and egocentric by his peers and associates.

When Lewis was ten his mother had a son named Jean Jr., soon followed by Anthony, twins Joseph and Rosalyn, and finally Sharon. Jean Jr. would become his protégé later in life, and after playing football in the National Football League would mimic his older brother by getting a law degree and ultimately working for Lewis. Lewis was learning that hard work was the way to get ahead in life and was the road to success. Following in the footsteps of his mother and stepfather he got his first job selling the local black newspaper. He built his route from ten customers to over a hundred in a short period. Carolyn taught him not to argue with delinquent customers over money, turning that distasteful task over to her. She also gave him a lesson he would never forget.

MORAL: SET YOUR TERMS UP FRONT!

When summer came Lewis signed up for summer camp and left the newspaper route to his mother. She delivered it and collected the money. When the young entrepreneur returned from camp expecting a windfall from his paper route and asked his mother, "When are we going to settle up?" she told him there wasn't anything to settle up—she had delivered the papers and therefore the money was hers.

She was teaching him a lesson in business finance he wouldn't ever forget. Lewis became enraged and told his mother, "I'm gonna get me a lawyer. I'm gonna sue you!" She explained, "Set your terms up front" and went over the logic and ethics of her decision, explaining to him that the person who performs always gets the rewards. Lewis was devastated and the experience went a long way to his eventual decision to become a lawyer so that he would never again be taken advantage of in any business venture.

WORK EQUALS SUCCESS

Lewis was always interested in the finer things in life, including sports cars, art, and fine clothes. He was always willing to work hard in order to feed his needs for fastidious fashion and the best the world had to offer. It wasn't the money that was so important to Lewis but what the money could buy. He worked two jobs throughout his high school years while lettering in three sports—a tough act for anyone, even an overachiever like Lewis. His tenacious work ethic and drive separated him from the pack during high school.

Lewis attended parochial schools in grammar school but did not have high enough test scores to get in the Catholic high school. He decided to attend a high school where he could showcase his athletic prowess. Dunbar High was such a school and is where many national sports heroes had gone before him. It was at Dunbar that he became known as "Bullet" Lewis. Lewis excelled in football, basketball, and baseball. He became the star quarterback, man about campus, and manic overachiever. Always more mature than the other kids, he was like a man among boys. An uncle said of this period, "He always saw himself a little man . . . not a high school kid." William Smith, a member of Lewis's class, said, "He was a really mature fellow. . . . Reggie knew how to read a stock market sheet. I didn't even know what a stock market sheet was." Lewis was very independent and bought his own British sports car to drive to school. The little adult was already steeped in the important qualities of the power broker and superstar, causing a half-brother to reflect, "He was always focusing on the future. The next accomplishment. The next objective."

Lewis was an overachieving "C" student who accomplished miracles through sheer charisma and hard work—a universal finding in supersuccessful people. His drive was superhuman, working two different jobs while attending school full-time and attending sports practice after school. He worked full-time on weekends and often had dates interspersed in his frenetic schedule. Lewis wrote in his autobiography, "I would get about four hours of sleep, maybe an hour of study, a quick look at the sports and business pages and then I'd make a mad dash for school, which was across town." At one of his jobs an employer at a Jewish country club asked him, "What are you trying to do, conquer the world?" A four-sport star in high school, Lewis won an athletic scholarship for football to Virginia State in 1961 even though he had graduated 118th out of 196 students from Dunbar High.

JOCK-TURNED-SCHOLAR

A shoulder injury at Virginia State ended his athletic career when Lewis was a junior. He had continued working through this period, operating a sales route through three states to the amazement of his schoolmates, who were barely able to cope with school and sports, let alone a business venture on the side. That was always Lewis's style and the reason for his great success in life. Once he had no athletic future Lewis started dedicating his enormous energies to his education and future as a businessman. He decided to become a lawyer but continued his frenetic work schedule, perpetual dating, and dedicated study.

Lewis graduated from Virginia State in 1965 and pulled off the most remarkable sales coup of his young life by getting himself invited to a Rockefeller Foundation summer session at Harvard. His timing was impeccable, since it was the era of the 1964 Civil Rights Act, where Martin Luther King, Jr., was at the height of his influence, and Harvard was attempting to give deserving young blacks a look at an Ivy League environment prior to their attendance at some other school. Harvard's agenda, however, was not Lewis's agenda, and when he told his roommate at Virginia State, Alan Colon, about his summer program, Colon told him, "Reg, this is just for the summer. Don't set yourself up for a major disappointment." In typical confidence, bordering on arrogance, Reg responded, "Alan, just watch—I'm going to Harvard."

HARVARD

The Harvard summer program was a dedicated effort to acquaint deserving black students with a prestigious law school so they would be motivated when attending a law school in some other part of the country. Harvard's plans did not deter Lewis, who went to Harvard with only one thought in mind—to get in no matter what he had to do. On leaving Virginia State he told Colon, "Come September I will be in the incoming class at Harvard Law." The odds of him accomplishing this were overwhelming if not impossible. But the irrepressible Lewis came in like a lion on a mission and blew away the staid professors who were running the session. Professor Sander was one who reflected on Lewis's attendance, saying he had "self-assurance and argumentative skills," adding, "He's got real drive and energy and fight and insight. He stood out among those students."

Biographer Blair Walker wrote of this entrepreneur's indomitable will to win, "He had an unswerving, total commitment to the product he was selling—Reginald Lewis." Once Harvard capitulated and offered him a place in its fall law school program, it finally occurred to Lewis that he was incapable of paying the tuition. He had spent enormous energies and work to get into a school that he couldn't afford. But Harvard shocked Lewis when it offered him a full scholarship, including room and board since school officials knew of his background and inability to pay. Lewis became the first student in history to be accepted at Harvard without so much as filling out an admissions request.

Lewis repaid Harvard manyfold by becoming a model minority student and overachiever who not only gave the school much notoriety due to his enormous successes in life but then magnified those social benefits by pledging $3 million to the school in 1992. Lewis graduated in 1968 and was offered a job at a prestigious New York law firm—Paul Weiss, Rifkin, Wharton and Garrison. He used this position as a learning experience before pursuing his own personal goals of heading his own law firm. As with most self-sufficient entrepreneurs, Lewis was not one to work for others. He was his own man and after two years learning the securities and venture capital businesses struck out on his own. At age twenty-six he met and married Loida Nicolas, a woman of Philippine extraction who also had a law degree, from the University of the Philippines. With a new wife and a new law practice, Lewis was on his way to conquering the world of business and high finance.

Professional History

In 1973 Lewis opened his own law firm, Lewis and Clarkson, in order to "do the deals myself." He worked feverishly learning all of the nuances of the venture capital and leveraged buyout businesses. He became arguably the most knowledgeable individual on Wall Street on MESBICs—the minority investment vehicles used to get government funding for new ventures. Most people view Lewis's tremendous achievements as an overnight success. Lewis disagrees with that assessment, saying, "It took twenty-five years of hard work to get to where I am." He was referring to the myriad companies he attempted to buy, the deals that fell through and those that just blew up in his face, the years of diligent negotiating that groomed him for the big one. In 1983 Lewis had created the TLC Group, which was an acronym for "The Lewis Company," for the express purpose of having a vehicle for buying and selling companies, his great dream in life.

Lewis's first takeover target for TLC was Parks Sausage, which was headquartered in his native Baltimore. He worked diligently to close this deal and followed all of the prescribed formulas learned at Harvard and in law practice. He was sure he had the deal. When he lost it and reflected on the reasons why, he concluded that it was not because of anything he did or did not do, but because of the credibility gap caused by the color of his skin. He had a million-dollar check in his briefcase to close the deal but never had the chance to pull it out because the company decision-makers were sure he "couldn't back it up" and accepted a cheaper offer. But this was not to be Lewis's first lesson in high finance. He had an even more crushing episode with a California firm by the name of Almet. The company produced aluminum furniture and fit his buyout formula quite well. He worked diligently to make sure he didn't make the same mistakes as before. Lewis was convinced this acquisition was a "sure thing" and once again at the eleventh hour the chairman of the board backed out of the agreement without one hint of why. They had agreed on all the important financial details of the transaction and this heartbreaking loss almost destroyed Lewis. He was convinced he was snakebit and couldn't understand why he couldn't make a business deal the same way he could throw a touchdown pass. Lewis was learning the hard way that big business is not always played on a level playing field.

This proved to be the great crisis of his life. Lewis wrote in his memoirs, "I came close to a breakdown." Always a driven man, control freak, and perfectionist, he became introspective and concluded, "I was not ready." His failures had conditioned him to take the steps that would ultimately make him a superstar of the LBO. Had he not been so crushed by his first failures it is questionable whether he would have been so successful with McCall and Beatrice Foods. He sat down and in a period of great introspection told himself, "If you are not ready, all right: Then get ready, get ready." And did he get ready. Lewis embarked on a self-education program in which he tore apart every major LBO deal ever done. He studied every nuance of every deal he could find and analyzed the key players necessary to make the deal. If the experts could make these deals then so could he, and Lewis decided to mimic the experts in what psychologists call "neuro-linguistic-programming." He modeled himself after the masters, moved his firm to 99 Wall Street, and began emulating the moves necessary to make the big deal. Lewis concluded that "image was everything" and started surrounding himself with the people with image who could help him. Michael Milken was one of these and the two became good friends.

SUCCESS BEGETS SUCCESS

Lewis's first real deal was the acquisition of a defunct St. Thomas, Virgin Islands, FM radio station in July 1992. It was not a big deal, but he had put it together and closed it. It turned out to be less than successful financially but it demonstrated to the financial community that he could put a deal together and operate it just like any white financier. This acquisition also offered Lewis an opportunity to visit the islands with his family, where he installed his half-brother Jean Fugett as CEO for maximum control. Lewis had mortgaged everything he had to put this deal together but he saw it as the price necessary to get in the game of high finance. He was right and by 1983 it gave him the necessary credibility to acquire McCall Pattern Company from Norton Simon via a levered buyout.

McCall Pattern was an old-line firm that had been in a steady decline for many years and Lewis's purchase of it was viewed as questionable at best and stupid at worst. His strategy was to buy the company, improve its return on assets, and sell it at a higher multiple while proving to the world that he could operate a major company. Lewis was intent on establishing himself as a turnaround guru and the challenge whetted his massive appetite for turning lemons into lemonade. McCall Pattern was a 118-year-old firm generating $52 million in annual revenues with a very unexciting technology, according to the Wall Street experts. It had declining revenues and profits for some years and most New York investment bankers were not interested, which opened the doors for a neophyte risk-taker like Lewis. He admitted to a strategy of "buying it at a cheap price, lighting a fire under management, reducing expenses, and increasing profitability." While attempting to close the deal, his race once again became an issue, which was always an irritation to this man who demanded to be treated equally and was willing to fight for his right to be treated so. One of the key people in the negotiations was a man named Peter Ackerman, who raised the issue. Lewis told him emphatically, "I don't talk about your Jewishness, so don't you talk about my ethnicity. It's not relevant to anything that we're doing."

Lewis closed the deal for McCall Pattern on January 29, 1984, for $22.5 million after a horrific eight months of putting out so many fires that a normal person would have long since given up on the deal. Lewis had masterfully played puppeteer to groups of bankers, financiers, investors, and lawyers. Norton Simon had erroneously assumed all along that there was a white backer and Lewis was just a front man for this bigger operator. They were so convinced that he was a go-between they never really took him seriously other than as an attorney representing a white client. They were never convinced that he was the man until after the deal was closed and were shocked when he came in to take over the reins as owner/operator with 100 percent control of the company.

Lewis had leveraged and borrowed on everything he owned to raise the $1 million loan necessary to close the deal. In fact, he had not invested one cent of his own but had resorted to leverage by getting short-term loans for the million by pledging all his personal assets including his home. Leverage is a two-edged sword that has the ability to make its owner mega-returns or mega-losses depending on the success of the venture. Money expands or contracts in direct proportion to the leverage (debt). In this case Lewis benefited by expansion. He ensured the company performed well by improving the revenues while cutting costs, which dramatically improved profits. All of these measures dramatically improved the return on assets and reduced debt service. As chairman and CEO Lewis implemented four years of cost-cutting measures and used innovative financial maneuvers to increase the return on assets. He was eminently successful in turning around the operations and this "loser" suddenly became a "winner" and a valuable company to investors, bankers, and potential suitors. When Lewis took over sales were at $51.9 million and profits at $6 million. Within three years he raised revenues to $63 million and doubled profits to $14 million. He then sold the firm to a British firm for three times what he had paid for it, netting $50 million for himself in the process. He had pulled off the impossible, parlaying a $1 million note into a $50 million windfall in just three years, which earned him a reputation as someone to be reckoned with on Wall Street.

TLC BEATRICE

Before the ink was dry on the McCall deal Lewis was busily working on a deal that would dwarf it. Empowered by his recent success, he tendered an offer to acquire Beatrice Foods. Beatrice Foods was a highly successful international food conglomerate that no longer fit in the long-range investment strategies of Kohlberg, Kravis, and Roberts of R. J. Reynolds fame. The firm had operations spread throughout the world with sixty-four companies operating in thirty-one countries. This was a billion-dollar LBO opportunity that whetted the appetite of a man who just demonstrated he could operate a multimillion-dollar firm and was anxious to try his hand at operating a billion-dollar operation. Putting this deal together demanded the patience and dedication of a master chess player. It took nine months of wheeling and dealing on three continents. Lewis slept only four hours a night for over nine months of constant negotiations with individuals of various nationalities and persuasions. This was Lewis's kind of deal, which fit his manic style and multifaceted need for excitement.

After months of grueling negotiations and infighting he finally closed the Beatrice deal in October 1987 for $985 million. It proved to be the largest international LBO transaction in history. Drexel and the various investment bankers had agreed to all debt in closing the transaction with a proviso that Lewis sell off various assets to reduce the debt. Beatrice Foods was acquired from Kohlberg, Kravis, and Roberts and Lewis immediately embarked on a ten-month program of selling off satellite operating divisions to reduce the unmanageable level of debt. Lewis became a raging storm, flying from country to country making deals. He successfully sold off $867 million in assets by 1989. This miraculous undertaking made Lewis both rich and famous. He not only sold off enough of the firm's assets to pay off the purchase price but in the same time had somehow managed to increase sales on those remaining divisions to more than the original whole. In other words, Lewis had bought a huge firm, sold off many of its parts for the total cost of the acquisition price, and then managed to increase sales of what remained by 1990 to the original numbers. By 1990 the remainder of the firm was exceeding the revenues of the original. The financial genius of Reginald Lewis was poignantly apparent to the most jaundiced Wall Street banker.

Lewis became chairman of the reorganized company he had named TLC Beatrice and had an ownership position of over 50 percent of a firm with a billion dollar in assets, $1.5 billion in revenues, and $94.3 million in profits. This time Lewis had masterminded a brilliant financial buyout of a complexity that would have been lost on most Wall Street bankers and in the process he had realized a personal windfall of $300 million. His annual salary of $22 million was a mere pittance to the now superrich Lewis.

What Made Reginald Lewis Tick?

Lewis was a classic Type A personality who was a workaholic and a manic overachiever. One of his associates in his law practice characterized his bombastic style as, "I want the best you can give me only I want it as fast as you're capable of doing it." During the TLC Beatrice closing months, a typical day for him included thirteen to fifteen hours on a plane with as many as fifteen takeoffs and landings between three continents with critically important meetings held at each stop. During Lewis's days at McCall, biographer Walker said, "He worked as though possessed. He acted as though every decision carried life and death ramifications."

Lewis had what psychologists call a Promethean personality. He, like the mythological Prometheus, defied the gods in order to bring sense and science to man. He never considered the consequences of his moves, only the potential opportunities that they offered. He perpetually sought knowledge for its own sake and made decisions in an intuitive-thinking manner by rational analysis of his macrovision.

Lewis's success was inextricably tied up in his driven personality. He had a volcanic temper, demonic work ethic, indomitable will, huge ambition, and psychic energy. Through the sheer power of will he overcame all adversity.

MYTHOLOGICAL HERO MENTORS

Lewis was a voracious reader as a child. He was intrigued with fairy tales and identified with comic book heroes like Batman and Superman. He identified with the larger-than-life success of such protagonists and decided very early in life to become the greatest he could be so he could escape from the degradation of Baltimore's inner city. At first he thought his vehicle would be sports, but once he became injured his visions of success turned to law and business ownership as the route out of the ghetto. Lewis used imaginary heroes to remove all limitations to his greatness and was convinced that hard work and dedication were the secrets of all success in life.

INSECURITY BREEDS GREATNESS

Reginald Lewis always blamed himself for any failure, even though he often screamed at his associates when they didn't meet his high standards for excellence. He intuitively knew that the vehicle to success was internal, not external, consequently he never blamed others for any of his failures. He looked inside himself and this insight proved effective. His morbid fear of failure drove him and is what ultimately made him so extraordinarily successful in life. He always insisted on asking himself what else he could do and became a self-motivated man frightened of failing to such a degree that he drove himself demonically to ensure that he wouldn't fail. Experiencing early failures in his quest to become an LBO specialist drove him into what he labeled a "numbing depression" and "stinging self-doubt." And those feelings motivated him to a supereffort that guaranteed him success.

LIFE CRISES AND TRAUMAS

When Lewis was six he overheard his grandparents speaking about racial prejudice and the unfairness of blacks having to live and survive in the inner city of Baltimore. They looked at Lewis and said, "Well maybe it will be different for him." The ever-audacious Lewis looked at his grandparents and told them, "Yeah, cause why should white guys have all the fun?" This conversation obviously left a lasting impression on this young boy since he remembered the conversation some forty-five years later and was conditioned enough to title his autobiography *Why Should White Guys Have All the Fun?* He grew up to become a black overachiever who never allowed white men—or anyone for that matter—to intimidate him.

Another validation of this moral took place when Lewis was seventeen. He was working as a waiter in a local country club and was overachieving like always. When he worked extra hard one night and a woman left him a pittance of a tip he was dismayed. The white lady pulled him aside and told him, "Reggie, you know your skin is dark, so you have to work harder. One day I'm sure you'll earn a good living." He found her tone patronizing and her demeanor downright rude when she gave him a $2 tip for hours of arduous effort far beyond the call of duty. He was emotionally incensed by this woman, writing, "Almost immediately I felt sort of an athletic surge go through my body, but remained controlled and thought to myself, 'You poor soul, you don't know who stands before you. A good living! I plan to, and I will have more money than you will ever have.' "

Charisma

Even as a student, Reginald Lewis's friends said he "dressed more for the board-room than the classroom." Lewis had a dashing persona about him that made everyone stand up and take notice. He never asked for power but in pure Niet-zschean style took it. One illustration of this took place when his half-brother Jean Fugett was playing tight end for the Dallas Cowboys and his stepfather came to Shea Stadium to watch the game with Lewis. They found themselves in a freezing stadium where the wind-chill factor was below zero. The ever-charismatic Lewis told his stepfather, "Follow me and act like you know where you're going." He marched up the steps and into the press box, sat down, and watched the rest of the game in warmth with the press corps. His imperious boldness made the press think he was the guest of the club owner or a reporter. They did not question his right to be there. He had the charisma of a cult leader.

R. Lowenstein, a Harvard law school classmate, characterized Lewis as a person who "just felt that he could do pretty much whatever he wanted to or felt like." Much of his style and charisma were enhanced by his dapper attire. Lewis dressed apart from the crowd. He looked the part of one who is in command and then assumed control of the situation which was often given to him just out of sheer submission to his will. Lewis was a strong speaker and leader, which made it difficult for others to refuse him. His strong sense of self would not be denied. His flamboyant lifestyle began in high school when he bought a British sports car and later graduated to Cristal Champagne, Bentleys, Cuban cigars, stylish clothes, the Harvard club, and fine art. His presence and style were that of one who demanded—and got—the best.

Competitiveness

Lewis was an intensely competitive human being. His law partner Clarkson said, "It was warfare all the time with Reg." A high school teammate said, "Reg was a tremendous competitor. He was a take charge type guy" and as quarterback "You couldn't joke in the huddle. He would say, 'Shut up!' " As a lawyer and businessman Lewis was so competitive that he would intimidate his legal associates. But he always had a knack for handling customers with kid gloves. Competitive spirit was highly instrumental in his success as a takeover specialist and the only way he was able to survive the dog-eat-dog world of Wall Street.

Confidence

Reginald Lewis's confidence bordered on egocentrism. In high school, he said, "I never doubted my ability" and was thought of by his athletic coaches as the kid who "came to play." His junior varsity baseball coach said Lewis exuded optimism and self-confidence. He once said, "I am the best. I am the greatest," and told his coaches, "I play to win."

Optimistic to a fault, Lewis was sure he would get accepted to Harvard when any other person would have given up without trying. Lewis's college roommate at Virginia State said of him, "He never waited for doors to open. He kicked them open." Lewis's legal partners and associates characterized him as a person who "radiated self-confidence." He once made a point with his office staff: "I am the franchise around here."

Passion and Drive

School chum Melvin Smith speaks of Lewis's driven nature as a teenager, "He always had a purpose. . . . He had a master plan. . . . When other guys were reading comics, he was reading the *Wall Street Journal*." Blair Walker, reporter for *USA Today* and collaborator on the Lewis autobiography, characterized Lewis as having "unrelenting drive and confidence, making him a natural leader." A high school coach told Walker that Lewis's supersuccess in school and in business were due to his "obsessive drive." Lewis's passions were obvious even to his competitors. A black lawyer, Orlan Johnson, a competitor and a man Lewis had once interviewed, observed: "I've never seen a black guy that was so driven to be successful. He was hot-tempered and he wanted to get things done. He didn't like mistakes."

Hypomania

Lewis got his first job on a paper route at age ten and continued working through his school years despite the fact that he played sports and was an overachieving student. Only at Harvard did Lewis concentrate on school solely. At every other time in his life he juggled a number of balls in the air simultaneously and appeared to thrive on pushing himself beyond the abilities of mere mortals. Lewis always had more on his plate than was physically possible to finish, which is a classic trait of the Type A personality.

Lewis slept an average of four hours a night all through high school and college, a typical finding in most Type A personalities. He lived for work and took on far more projects than were possible to complete without a herculean effort. Walker described him as having a "demon work ethic" which could not be quenched. He was a workaholic and fully expected his associates to match his enormous energy and work ethic. His "megawatt intensity" caused his high school football coach to reflect, "Sometimes, Reggie was so intense you'd think he was going to explode." Tom Lamia, a legal associate who accompanied him on his whirlwind due-diligence trip through Europe, said he was unable to keep up with the manic Lewis. After one marathon trip to visit the Beatrice Food subsidiaries located in many countries, Lamia described himself as being near collapse while Lewis remained composed and energized. Lamia observed: "One of the things that made Lewis so successful was his incredible stamina. . . . It was like I had been run over by a truck. Reg seemed fine. He looked great and had on this new Italian suit." Lewis was always impatient and in a hurry to complete a deal. His need for speed paid big dividends, but his life in the fast lane may have contributed to his premature death. Biographer Walker concluded, "Practically everything Lewis achieved was extracted through hard work and titanic struggle."

Independence

As an only child, Lewis learned self-sufficiency early in life. His mother remarried when he was nine and had five children in quick succession, but this only served to give him even more autonomy. This early freedom taught him to cope on his own. He became his own man, insisting on making up his own mind on the nature of the world. Biographer Walker described him as a "fiercely independent" person who never allowed the establishment to deter him from pursuit of his dreams. Lewis always marched to his own tune, often to the consternation of his legal associates. Kevin Wright described him as a "very private person" who "did not like people touching him."

Lewis was a renegade who was not afraid to be different, an iconoclast who schoolmates said "was always thinking ahead of everybody else." According to Blair Walker, race was never a factor in his life and though he was different in color from whites, he saw himself as their equal and felt he was just as different from blacks as whites. He adamantly "refused to view race as an impediment or handicap to achievement" and never asked for any privileged treatment because of his race. Lewis saw his marriage to a Filipina as intercultural not interracial, which is how most progressive diversity experts now view such marriages. Race is a transitory factor and only affects those who have some kind of racial hangup. He demanded to be treated equally by all people and insisted that race be left out of any negotiation.

Perfectionist

Lewis was a fastidious neat-freak. Everything he wore had to be just perfect and every bit of work that anyone did for him had to meet the highest standards. Excellence was his barometer for any performance—his or others—and anything less bore his wrath. He was notorious for his perfectionism, which prompted his flight crew to show Lewis their ultimate respect by making sure his plane was impeccably clean for its final flight to Baltimore for his funeral. Perfection was the one Lewis quality about which everyone agreed. Blair Walker described him as obsessive, saying, "Lewis would even rate novels or magazine pieces he was reading. . . . It didn't matter that perfection was usually unattainable—the quest for perfection was its own reward."

Temerity

When Lewis made the deal to buy a St. Croix FM station, which turned out to be a loser, he was unable to raise the capital from financial institutions and pledged his home and family-owned property to make the deal. Risk is the god of all great entrepreneurs. They worship at the altar of risk and the higher the better since no great wins occur without great risk. Although most scrupulously manage the risk so it does not bury them, Lewis was always willing to live on the edge to make a deal just as he did on the FM station acquisition in St. Croix. Lewis would negotiate tirelessly about pennies while betting millions on the deal.

Both of Lewis's LBO successes—McCall Pattern and Beatrice Foods—were highly leveraged, a word synonymous with risk. Each of these ventures would have fallen apart had Lewis not been willing to pledge the assets of the entities and debt to close the deals. That meant that servicing the debt was critical to survival. Had he not been able to maintain high cash flow from the beginning of the takeovers, the firms would have failed, but that was the area that Lewis carefully monitored and is what turned out to be his genius.

Tenacity

If nothing else, Lewis was tenacious. He became preoccupied when on a deal and could not be dissuaded from giving it 100 percent of his attention until it was finalized. Once he decided to buy the St. Croix FM radio station he pursued the head of Broadcast Capital, John Oxendine, like a man possessed. Oxendine described Lewis's tenacious pursuit of him as "very, very aggressive." He recalled sitting in a New Orleans convention hotel and eating breakfast during the time of the negotiations and looking up to see Lewis walking toward him. Lewis had flown from New York on the chance of meeting Oxendine. Lewis smiled and asked him what else would be needed to consummate the deal. Oxendine was amazed at such zeal and described Lewis as a "very articulate, very persistent, and very tenacious" man who would not be denied.

Vision

Reginald Lewis was a right-brain-driven visionary who was far more interested in the possibilities of a big deal than the security of the status quo. One indication of his macrovision was teaching himself to speak French so that he could better communicate and motivate his Paris executives at TLC Beatrice. Lewis's half-brother Jean Fugett gave insight into this visionary when he said Lewis "was more interested in future opportunities than present successes." Fugett described him as "always focusing on the future."

Based on the findings in this study, Reggie Lewis was a classic Promethean personality who was far more interested in building new castles in the sky than occupying them. Had he lived he would have ultimately spun off many of the operations of Beatrice or resold the operation after he had made it into a profitable enterprise. Lewis's true talent was seeing the big picture while analyzing the numbers in any new business deal. He not only got into the numbers but, in his words, "got behind them" and never allowed the numbers to cloud his vision of the overall opportunity. This was the foundation of his particular genius, which set him apart from the pack.

Will to Power

Legal associate and friend Tom Lamia described Reggie as a "powerful person even before he became rich." Lamia said, "He could be bullying at times, he could be charming at times, and he could be bullying and charming in the same conversation. Reg could intimidate people rather easily." That is the description of a man who has a handle on his own inner powers of persuasion and control. James McPherson, his Harvard roommate, said, "Whatever he had it was powerful. . . . It was some kind of magnetism or power."

Control was always important to this driven entrepreneur. In fact, he was a control freak both professionally and personally. He had to have control and the power that control manifested in making a deal. When he didn't have control over his destiny he figured out how to get it. His butler, Lucien Scott, described Lewis as having to control every facet of the evening meal to such a degree that he had an electronic buzzer installed under his chair in order to signal the kitchen of his every need. Scott also described his obsession on the tennis court as something out of a James Bond movie. He demanded each meticulous detail be in place when he showed up to play a match. According to Scott: "His Prince tennis racket resting against the back of the courtside chair. Two cans of Penn tennis balls had to be beside the racket, with the seals on the cans unbroken. An opened can was an indication that the balls inside might not be fresh, an unacceptable condition for Lewis. The umbrella for the courtside table needed to be in place and opened. Underneath the table was always a cooler containing water, ginger ale, and Lewis's beloved Diet Coke. Across the back of each chair would be one white towel for each of the combatants. Only then would Lewis be ready for war."

Summary

When Reginald Lewis's mother kept his paper route money at age ten it taught him an invaluable lesson that you must always "make your deal in the beginning." He never forgot that valuable lesson, which contributed to his becoming America's leveraged buyout guru. Reggie was a brilliant but hard-nosed deal maker who had a penchant for privacy and a need for philanthropy. The greatest honor was granted him in the late eighties when he was invited to become a member of the board of the prestigious Business Roundtable where the elite heads of Fortune 500 companies discussed the state of American business. Near the end of his life Lewis became enamored of giving away monies he had worked so desperately to earn. He gave $3 million to Harvard, $1 million to Howard University, hundreds of thousands to Virginia State, plus countless other smaller amounts to family members and charities. He argued over pennies in closing his multimillion-dollar deals and then generously gave away millions to prove money was only a means of keeping score on your successes.

Lewis was a control freak who used a Harvard Law School degree to open the doors to the white power elite and once inside he overwhelmed them with his insight and knowledge of deal making. He had the unique talent to see the big picture (macrovision) while operating with an acute awareness of detail (microvision). Not often does one find this combination of highly honed skills in the same individual. In 1994 *Black Enterprise* called him "the most prominent black entrepreneur of his generation." Howard University President Franklyn Jenifer said, "Reginald Lewis represented the best of all we talk and dream about."

After being diagnosed with terminal brain cancer, this power broker demonstrated his awesome optimistic view of life saying, "I know I'll beat this thing."

It was the one thing he would not be able to control and he died one month after a medical checkup made the tragic discovery in December 1993. Lewis died in January 1994 and the family received a note from President Bill Clinton that said, "Reginald Lewis's commitment to excellence, his life of achievement, and his deep concern for his fellow man were an inspiration to me and to all who knew him." Bill Cosby summed up his creative genius. He wrote, "Reggie Lewis is to me, not was, is to me what Joe Louis is to me. What Jackie Robinson is to me. Regardless of race, color, or creed, we are all dealt a hand to play in this game of life. And believe me, Reg Lewis played the hell out of his hand."

Reginald Lewis's favorite motto was "Living well is the best revenge." And did he have some revenge! He acquired a specially built private jet—a Canadair Challenger 607-RL—and lived in three palatial abodes, including a $4-million Gatsby-style estate named Broadview in East Hampton, a Paris apartment, and a Manhattan condo, each decorated with a multimillion-dollar art collection. Most of Lewis's art was displayed at Broadview, which was a twenty-five-room Georgian estate that also housed his 550SL Mercedes convertible. In Paris Lewis lived in an opulent, eighteenth-century Left-Bank Louis XIV apartment in the historic Place du Paois Bourbon. Lewis always ate at the prestigious Harvard Club in Manhattan or in Maxim's while in Paris. He wore custom-tailored Italian suits costing $2,000 each and smoked only imported Cuban cigars. He expected the best and lived out his greatest fantasies once he was able to afford his exquisite tastes. He had worked very hard to become the wealthiest black man in history. This innovative visionary decided early in life that he wanted to be the very best he could be and he became the protagonist of his greatest dreams.

REGINALD FRANCIS LEWIS
Promethean Temperament (NT)
Business Tycoon, Corporate Takeover Guru, and Philanthropist
born December 7, 1942, Baltimore, Maryland; died January 19, 1993, Manhattan, New York

Dominant trait: Introvert with volcanic temper, indomitable will, huge ambition, and energy incarnate

Motto: "Success is the best revenge"; "No skill or vocation is a white man's exclusive province"

Religion: Catholic upbringing—lost in struggle for success

Philosophy: "Act like you know where you're going"; "Mean what you say, say what you mean"

Politics: Apolitical but seriously considered running for U.S. Senate from New York as a Democrat

Nickname: Bullet Lewis (as high school quarterback); "Reg" to business associates

Creation/innovation: McCall Pattern acquisition from Norton Simon; utilized latent press time to print greeting cards

Successes: Wealthiest black man in history; $1 million investment in McCall became $90 million in 3 years; Beatrice Foods worth $950 million

Vices/hobbies: Reading, tennis, Cuban cigars, Harvard Club, corporate jet, British sports cars, art

Romantic liaisons: Ladies man while single; married Filipina Loida Nicolas at age 26

Self-description: "I came to play"; "I never doubted my ability"; "I am the greatest"

Birth order: Only child of Carolyn Cooper and Clinton Lewis, with five step-siblings by mother and Jean Fugett

Parental influence: Grandparents Cooper raised him; doted on by many females: "center of universe" for four aunts

Early transience: Moved four times as child in latchkey environment, creating total independence

Parents' occupations: Father unsuccessful entrepreneur radio shop/restaurant; mother a waitress—a major influence

Role models: Stepfather Jean Fugett worked his way through college at night; mother who kept paper route money

Hero mentors: Fairy tales of superheroes; his mother instilled in him a need to be great

Formal education: Parochial school; Dunbar H.S., 1961; Virginia State, 1965; Harvard Law, 1968—overachieving C student

Life crises: Baltimore ghetto; parents divorced when age 5; losing two deals in 1970s spurred him on to greatness

Metamorphoses: Loner: self-sufficient; Harvard paper *Defenses to Takeover Bids* created takeover interest

---

Charismatic: Friend: "He just had an air about him"; Lamia: "Reg was powerful even before he became rich"

Competitive: Walker: "Intensely competitive"; Clarkson: "It was warfare all the time with Reg"

Hypomanic: "Megawatt intensity. . . . He acted as though every decision carried life and death ramifications"

Independent rebel: Loner as child, self-sufficient; "His" rules were the only important ones

Indomitable "will": Got into Harvard by sheer bravado and willpower; narcissistic belief in infallibility

Intuitive vision: Clarkson: "Reg was a real dreamer"; following instincts at McCall made him rich and famous

Libidinal drive: A "ladies man" reputation throughout school years until his passion was sublimated into demonic work ethic

Risk-taker: High leverage his operating style: St. Thomas FM station, McCall Pattern, and Beatrice Foods

Self-confident: "He had an air of confidence"; strong sense of self which would not be denied

Tenacious: Walker: "Pit bull tenacity"; College roommate Hart: "He had tenacity that made him special"

Workaholic: Walker: "Practically everything Lewis achieved was extracted through hard work and titanic struggle"

Honors: *Forbes* America's richest black man in 1993; on the board of the Business Roundtable

14

Nelson Mandela—Tenacious

Social Activist and
First Black President of South Africa

"Struggle is my life."

Few men have overcome as much adversity to reach the pinnacle of power as Nelson Mandela. This tenacious wunderkind is truly inspirational. How many men would sacrifice their entire adult life for a cause? Or spend twenty-seven years in prison in pursuit of a dream? Not many! Nelson Mandela was attracted to the cause of black equality early in life and then spent the rest of his life chasing that dream.

Mandela's given Xhosa name was Rohihlahla, which translates literally to "troublemaker"—a fitting name for a man who dedicated his life in open rebellion against the white-supremacist government of South Africa. At one point, in the early sixties, Mandela left his family and went underground for seventeen months, where his daring exploits earned him the name the Black Pimpernel. It would appear "troublemaker" was an image he had internalized, and he lived to perpetuate that internal image.

This tenacious idealist thought his mission in life was to lead black South Africans to freedom and equality in their homeland. Once old enough he understood that his homeland of South Africa had been taken over by immigrants and then dominated by them to the extent that his people were not even allowed to vote or own land where they wished. So Nelson Mandela became an impassioned social activist. The more he studied, the more incensed he became. The more he fought for equality, the more stringent were the laws limiting his people in their own country. The original Dutch immigrants were known as Afrikaners. They landed in South Africa three hundred years ago and had lived in mortal fear of a black insurrection ever since their solution was total subjugation, which ultimately led to the despicable laws known collectively as apartheid.

Nelson Mandela became committed to the destruction of apartheid as a very young man and spent the rest of his life pursuing resistance aimed at enacting change. His goal was the destruction of apartheid and few men, including him, thought it possible during his lifetime. Mandela could not have foreseen that his years in prison would prove to be the catalyst for such a change that he, and most political strategists, thought could only be enacted through violent revolution. Because of the role played by Mandela, the changes he could only dream of as a young man occurred fast and completely through an evolutionary set of complex events. His martyrdom prevented the devastation that a revolution would have caused. In part by sacrificing his life in prison, international pressures forced the changes which otherwise could only have happened through force.

As Joseph Campbell would have said, "From Mandela's sacrifice came bliss." He had followed his bliss, which had led him to the promised land. He succeeded not because he had convinced the opposition that he was right, but because he had tenaciously demonstrated to the world the abominable system that was in place. World economic pressures and financial sanctions were the guns and bullets that finally took their toll on those in power; they capitulated to money, boycotts, and public opinion and not bullets, bombs, and guns. Nelson Mandela won the war because he had been willing to lose the battle for his personal freedom—a very dear price that gained the empathy of men everywhere. Had Mandela not been a willing participant in this titanic struggle it is quite probable that South Africa would still be toiling under the jackboot of racial subjugation.

Mandela's release from prison at age seventy-two and the destruction of apartheid were synonymous events, not a Jungian synchronicity but a cause-and-effect event of great international import. He had martyred himself in the eyes of the world and South Africa benefited from that martyrdom and repaid Mandela in kind when at the age of seventy-five its citizens elected him president. Mandela's price was great but, as in all great risks, his win was also beyond anything he could ever have imagined while growing up in an African village under the tutelage of a Zulu chief.

When Mandela was released from prison in 1994 he had been greeted by a fanatical group of fifty thousand black and white sympathizers who listened intently to his impassioned speech, which ended with a repeat of the prophetic words he had recited twenty-seven years earlier at the 1964 trial that ended with his incarceration: "I have fought against white domination, and I have fought against black domination. I have cherished the idea of a democratic and free society in which all persons live together in harmony and with equal opportunities. It is an ideal which I hope to live for and to achieve. But if need be, it is an ideal for which I am prepared to die."

The shock of Mandela's unbelievable accomplishments is not that he survived to become the president of South Africa at the advanced age of seventy-five, but that he became the hero of many white as well as blacks, Indian, and colored South Africans. When this charismatic man donned the green-and-white soccer jersey of the mostly white South African Springboks in June 1995, the 63,000 mostly white fans began crying passionately "Nelson! Nelson!" This proved to be the most overwhelming display of white acclaim that any black had ever received in South

Africa. Apartheid had died a violent death on his release from prison and many of those who had been brainwashed into seeing Mandela as a demented devil were now eulogizing him. A South African poll in the spring of 1995 showed Mandela to be over twice as popular as the governing party he leads, an astounding achievement for a man who had been depicted as a Satan for nearly three decades.

Bishop Desmond Tutu gave credence to the tremendous power of this visionary when he said, "Nelson Mandela is the power that he is because he is a great man. He is quite simply a giant of a man with an enormous intellect." This was further confirmed in October 1993 when Mandela traveled to Sweden to accept a joint Nobel Peace Prize with President F. W. de Klerk. After his 1994 election to the presidency, he traveled to the United States to accept an honorary doctorate from Howard University. At a White House dinner in his honor, President Clinton gave Mandela a warm welcome and spoke of the admiration for his tenacity, saying: "You have been a genuine inspiration to the American people and to freedom-loving people around the world—people still marvel at the price you paid for your conviction." After Mandela's first year in office, Chris Erasmus of *USA Today* wrote that, "It's generally agreed that Nelson Mandela gets an A+."

The most glowing tribute to Nelson Mandela came from the camp of his fiercest rivals. Johan Grobelaar, formerly of the Afrikaner Resistance Movement, said of him: "A year ago, if someone shot Mandela, I and a lot of other Afrikaners would have been celebrating." However, "The more I see of him, the more I think he is really a Godsend—he's the one person who can bring South Africans together . . . black and white, Afrikaners, Zulus, and Xhosas." What a tribute to a man of seventy-seven who spent the majority of his adult life either underground, banned (without freedom of speech or movement), or in prison.

Innovative Contribution

Just one of the many firsts for this dedicated freedom fighter came when he and law partner Oliver Tambo formed the very first black law practice in Johannesburg in 1952. Later Mandela joined with political mentor Walter Sisulu and law partner Tambo to found the African National Congress Youth League. This occurred on Easter Sunday 1944 and six years later Mandela was elected president of the Youth League. Within two years his energies contributed to the founding of the Defiance Campaign, designed to organize peaceful protests. These political moves all contributed to a fast-spreading reputation as a man who was an enemy of apartheid and the white-supremacist government. Mandela was imprisoned for nine months in 1952 to slow him down.

Mandela spent his life immersed in what he called "the struggle" against the unjust laws of white supremacy. But even more inspirational to him personally was being told by Dutch immigrants where he could live, work, and travel, and, even worse, being denied the right to vote for who would represent him in government. The South African whites had controlled the laws and economic system in South

Africa for over three hundred years. This enterprising minority of white Europeans were determined to stay in power just as Mandela was determined to gain some semblance of freedom and equality for the South African black majority. Like most of the Western world, Mandela could not understand how two million whites could dictate the laws of the nation whose native blacks numbered eight million. The original inhabitants of this nation not only couldn't vote, they were not allowed to own property outside their native villages or even to travel without a pass. The Afrikaner government had passed apartheid laws pegging the land available for black ownership at 12.7 percent and whites at 87 percent, even though blacks represented 80 percent of the population and whites 20 percent.

After this unfair distribution Mandela pledged his life to changing what he saw as an abominable inequity to his people. At first he thought he could change the unfair laws through legal means and studied law in order to understand the existing system of discriminatory laws he wanted changed. Mandela dedicated his life to this challenge but finally realized that more serious resistance would have to be used in order to effect the necessary changes.

Personal History

Mandela was born Rohihlahla Mandela in 1918 in a tribal village in Umtata, which is located in the Transkei territory of the Eastern Cape of South Africa. His father, Henry Gadla Mandela, was chief of the Xhosa-speaking Thembu tribe, but lost much of his power and wealth just after Nelson's birth due to political infighting. This forced his mother to move to Qunu village when Nelson was just one year old. His mother, Nonquaphi, was one of four wives of Henry and they saw him just once a month when he made a conjugal visit. By age five Mandela had become a "herd boy," spending much of his time roaming freely through the fields and valleys of the Transkei. In his autobiography he wrote of that early freedom, saying, "As boys we were mostly left to our own devices."

The name Nelson was given him by the Methodist Mission School he attended as a young child. This is also where he learned English and became conversant with the Christian Bible. Nelson grew up in a multilingual educational environment where the teachers spoke both English and Xhosa. In school Nelson was baptized Methodist but was regaled with Xhosa tales of great warriors by his mother, who was a native African who had not been influenced by the European immigration. He said, "My mother would enchant us with Xhosa legends and fables which stimulated my childhood imagination." This environment molded him into a product of the forest. He wore only a blanket until he started school, when his father cut off his trousers to create the first Western clothes he would own.

When Mandela was nine his father became ill and arranged for the young boy to become a ward of the Thembu chief, Jongintaba. The Great Chief became his substitute father after his own father died and Mandela was sent to live at the palace in the village of Mqhekezweni. Here he met his new foster brother, Justice, who was the heir apparent to the chiefdom. Justice became Mandela's closest friend and confidant. He was four years older than Mandela and soon was a role model and teenage idol. At age sixteen both boys were sent away to the Clarkebury School, which was some distance from the village and would be Mandela's first experience with Western conveniences such as running water, flush toilets, and toothpaste. It was at this time that Mandela was circumcised in a tribal ritual, given the name Dalibunga, and made the proud owner of his first boots and Western clothes. Mandela moved on to Wesleyan College at Fort Beaufort at age nineteen and then matriculated at University College in Fort Hare at age twenty-one. He was elected to the Student Representative Council at Fort Hare and in a fight similar to those fought in American universities in the sixties was caught up in a student administrative rebellion.

In Mandela's senior year the students voted to boycott the elections unless the school authorities accepted their demands. Rather than become embroiled in this controversy, Mandela resigned. The headmaster told him he would be expelled if he resigned. He wrote, "I knew it was foolhardy for me to leave Fort Hare, but at the moment I needed to compromise (my values), I simply could not do so." He felt strongly that he had every right to resign and became incensed over the loss of his rights. The young maverick left school and was summarily expelled for his actions. He was offered a reprieve by the college president, but defiantly refused, which would become a consistent behavior pattern for this strong-willed renegade.

The "Troublemaker's" foster father, the regent, was furious and arranged a marriage for both him and his foster-brother Justice on the premise that if they weren't students they were men and should be married and start a family. Both boys were renegade spirits and concocted a plot to escape. They ran away to Johannesburg rather than accept an arranged marriage to someone they had never met. Their escape was pure Hollywood and the chief spent the next few years attempting to find them, which kept the two in an underground status in the metropolis of Johannesburg. Mandela had decided to become an attorney while sitting at the side of the Great Chief, as he thoroughly enjoyed the life of negotiator and arbitrator. It would be 1942 before Mandela was able to pass his final examination for his bachelor's degree and enroll in classes for the law. This early exposure to the underground proved to be a great training ground for his later life.

Johannesburg was a thriving metropolis, which appealed to Mandela's nature. It was here Mandela met his political mentor, Walter Sisulu. Sisulu not only encouraged Mandela to study law but helped him enroll at Witwatersrand University and arranged for his first job as a policeman at the Transvaal mines. While working as a policeman the chief's henchmen located him, but the wily fugitive was able to flee to a suburb called Alexandra. This refusal to be dominated or to capitulate to the will of others would become a consistent pattern in Mandela's life. It was at this time he met and married his first wife, Edith Ntoko. She worked as a nurse to support him while he continued his law education. Edith was the cousin of Walter Sisulu and their marriage was one of constant conflict. The couple were married in 1944 and proceeded to have three children: Thembekile (1947), Makgatho (1950), and Makaziwe (1954).

It was not until 1944 that Mandela became a social activist. Before he had been sensitive to the issues but was distracted by family and education. His mentor, Walter Sisulu, was very involved in the movement, as was a man named Oliver Tambo, who would ultimately become Mandela's law partner. These three were the nucleus of a group that formed the Youth League of the African National Congress. The Marxist theories of dialectical materialism were in vogue at the time and Communist ideology became closely linked with the Youth League. Over the next ten years the league would be responsible for many nonviolent general strikes and boycotts against the white supremacist government. Mandela and his group were well established when the government passed the abominable apartheid laws in 1950. The laws only served as further inspiration for these passionate youths in their pursuit of black freedom.

Professional History

Nelson Mandela's political career was officially launched when he was elected president of the Youth League in 1944. Upon election he immediately implemented a creed of "passive resistance" as the league's primary mission to enact change. He became a student of Gandhian passive resistance measures and was constantly fighting those black dissidents who preferred a cause of violence and revolution. At this juncture of Mandela's life he was a towering man who dominated most peers of either race. He was a striking man intellectually and proved physically intimidating to most people, especially whites. He was a mesmerizing speaker who dressed meticulously and became a role model for African black men, who tended to listen and follow him. White government officials hated Mandela but also feared him since he was their equal in presence and intelligence and had a huge following of native blacks. His power conjured up fear in the government officials, who began resorting to more and more sanctions and forceful actions to maintain power and control.

Mandela made a grand appearance on the streets of South Africa, where blacks were normally invisible to whites during the forties and fifties. An illustration of the magnetic power of this man came from a white man who was witness to Mandela's imposing persona in Cape Town: "I noticed people turning and staring at the opposite pavement and I saw this magnificent figure of a man, immaculately dressed. Not just blacks, but whites, including white women, were turning to admire him."

By 1950 Mandela had become recognized as a major leader of the black civil rights movement. He was elected president of the African National Congress (ANC) and called for a strike on Republican Day. This memorable action proved even more successful than originally planned but resulted in the deaths of eighteen Africans and thirty injuries. The black passive resistance incited the police to resort to force and brutality far beyond what was needed or expected by Mandela. It prompted Mandela to write years later, "That day was a turning point in my life."

Mandela and his social activist friend Oliver Tambo opened up their law firm in 1952. It was the first black law firm in Johannesburg and took on mostly civil rights actions in which both men were passionately interested. Mandela was becoming increasingly more active in the cause of equality and freedom for his people and organized the Defiance Against Unjust Laws campaign in 1953. By September 1953 he had been "banned"—restricted legally from attending public gatherings—for two years and confined to Johannesburg by the Afrikaner government. This was the beginning of the end of normalcy in his life. He also received a nine-month suspended sentence for political activism. By 1954 Mandela's political activism was getting the attention of the white leaders of South Africa. The Transvaal Law Society petitioned the Supreme Court to have him removed from the rolls of practicing attorneys for having been convicted as a leader of the Defiance Campaign. In defiant response Mandela said: "I found myself treated as a criminal—an unconvicted criminal. I was not allowed to pick my company, to frequent the company of others, to participate in their political activities, to join their organizations. . . . I was made, by the law, a criminal, not because of what I had done, but because of what I stood for, because of what I thought, because of my conscience."

Now restricted in the role he could play as a "banned" citizen, Mandela began writing a series of truculent articles for the ANC journal *Liberation*. He continued working on ways to overthrow the unfair apartheid laws and by December 5, 1956, his efforts became intolerable to the government leaders, who filed charges of high treason against him and his cohorts. He, Sisulu, and Tambo, plus many others, were arrested for their obstructive tactics and subversive leadership campaign which marked the beginning of many years of tortuous court battles, fighting, fleeing, and finally imprisonment.

DIVORCE AND MARRIAGE

Political activism contributed in the dissolution of Mandela's first marriage. When he returned from a court hearing one day his wife and children were gone, tired of the endless fighting and turmoil. Ntoko filed for divorce, which was granted just as Mandela was preparing to defend himself for high treason. It was at this time that he met and fell in love with a woman eighteen years his junior—Nomzamo Winnie Madikileza. The two freedom fighters were married in June 1958, just two months prior to the opening of his famous treason trial. Their romantic time together as a couple was destined to be short-lived, as Mandela was constantly in court or on the road for the cause. He seldom came home and when there was accompanied by his renegade friends. Winnie described him in her 1984 book *Part of My Soul Went with Him* as a "health fanatic" who was an "economic disaster at home." She said they hardly got to know each other before he went underground: "It was the most inspiring time of his life—he was totally with them, totally part of the people he has sacrificed his life for. . . . Nelson came home with Duma Nokwe and other leaders of the outlawed ANC and simply said, 'Oh darling, just pack a few things for me in a suitcase.' . . . I packed his bag, but by the time I took it out he wasn't there. He was gone. That was the last I saw my husband as a family man." Winnie said she saw him frequently when he was underground but never knew when that knock on the window would occur. The man now known as David had sacrificed his family life for his professional cause in both marriages. He never thought twice about the price he was paying not because he didn't want to be married or be with his children but because of his desperate need to "follow his bliss," as Joseph Campbell would say.

TREASON TRIAL

As a defense attorney Mandela was brilliant. He was not only eloquent in his arguments but became a nationally known hero to the native blacks and to all international freedom fighters because of his eloquent diatribes in the courtroom. The famous treason trial lasted four and a half years, during which time Mandela was free on bail so that he could act as his own counsel. During the trial a massacre in Sharpeville, in March 1960, ignited a wave of angry protests. The passive resistance started taking on more characteristics of sabotage and put Mandela at ever more risk from the authorities. He finally won release for himself and his cohorts but the years of freedom-oriented rhetoric had taken its psychological toll on him. When the trial was over, instead of going off for a rest he was reenergized for the larger battle to destroy apartheid. He had not only convinced the judge but had indoctrinated himself—the destruction of apartheid was no longer a judicial case but a philosophical mission he unable to control. Mandela had become a passionate social activist no longer capable of a normal life. He went home from the trial and told Winnie to pack his bag and proceeded to go underground for the next year and a half. This marked the end of life as a father and husband and marked the beginning of his life as a James Bond–type freedom fighter, underground fugitive, and international conspirator.

THE BLACK PIMPERNEL

Mandela became a nocturnal animal or "a creature of the night," as he writes in his autobiography. For the next seventeen months he was the most wanted man in South Africa, with warrants out for his immediate capture for having violated his "bans" and "black restrictions." The newspapers cast him as a romantic hero. His narrow escapes, daring escapades, and bold pronouncements to the media were depicted with such dashing intrigue that he became known as the Black Pimpernel. The name was well earned. He was in constant disguise, used the name David as an alias, and slept wherever he could find a safe haven. He would taunt officials by calling the media to announce his last caper and defiant act against the established government. He became "invisible" for a year and a half—a tough act for a six-foot-three giant of a man with enormous presence and a nationally known reputation.

Mandela successfully eluded the police for seventeen months before being captured disguised as a chauffeur in the province of Natal on August 5, 1962. The police had been informed of his whereabouts and Mandela was immediately brought to trial and sentenced to five years in prison. He was in the prime of his life at age forty-three. While in jail the police raided the ANC underground headquarters on June 11, 1963, and used the confiscated information to retry Mandela on counts of treason, sabotage, and conspiracy to overthrow the government. The trial began in October 1963 and ended in June 1964. Mandela was found guilty and sentenced to life imprisonment. He was sent to the maximum security prison on Robben Island, seven miles off Cape Town. He would not be a free man for another twenty-seven years.

LEADERSHIP

For the first fifteen years in prison Nelson Mandela was considered a nonperson and given few amenities. By 1980 international pressures came to bear and began to offer him some relief from the despicable conditions of prison life. He was then transferred to Pollsmoor Prison and allowed to mingle, read books, and write. In January 1980 three black nationalists armed with rifles took twenty-five hostages in a Pretoria bank and bargained for Mandela's release. The attempt failed but triggered worldwide support for his cause. By the mid-eighties international favor for the anti-apartheid cause began building, and began to peak after Winnie Mandela published *Part of My Soul Went with Him*. Soon after, South African President P. W. Botha bowed to international pressure, boycotts, and economic sanctions by offering to release Mandela from prison. The 1985 offer was made on the condition Mandela never again fight against apartheid—a condition Mandela was not about to accept. The resilient sixty-eight-year-old declined Botha's offer and delivered his renunciation in a passionate speech delivered by his daughter Zindzi: "I cannot sell my birthright nor am I prepared to sell the birthright of the people to be free. . . . What freedom am I being offered when my own South African citizenship is not respected? Only free men can negotiate. . . . I cannot and will not give any undertaking at a time when I and you, the people, are not free. Your freedom and mine cannot be separated. I will return."

One year after this courageous act the Commonwealth Eminent Persons Group was touring South Africa and visited Mandela and "found him an isolated and lonely figure." On his seventieth birthday in July 1988, the cry erupted from around the world "Free Mandela!" His martyrdom had not been in vain, and on October 29, 1989 his friend and one-time mentor, Walter Sisulu, was freed after twenty-five years in prison. Then, on February 2, 1990, President F. W. de Klerk shocked the world while making his traditional opening speech to Congress by lifting the bans on the ANC and the Pan-Africanist Congress and officially beginning the disbanding of apartheid.

On February 9, 1990, de Klerk informed Mandela that he would be released the following day. In typical Mandela fashion he said, "No, I need a week." The two agreed on a February 11 release date, which is when Mandela walked out of prison a free man after twenty-seven years of incarceration. A wild throng of fifty thousand watched him raise a defiant fist and say "Amandla!" meaning "power." The emotional throng responded "Ngawethu!" or "Power to the people." Mandela's freedom speech was broadcast around the world. No longer a young man but one who had just witnessed the fulfillment of his lifelong mission, he told a screaming mob of supporters, "I stand here before you not as a prophet but as your humble servant."

PRESIDENT

Mandela was elected president of the Africa National Conference in July 1991, replacing his one-time law partner, Oliver Tambo. In October 1993 he and de Klerk were awarded the Nobel Peace Prize. Just six months later Mandela's ANC received 67 percent of the popular vote in the first free election in the nation's history and Nelson Mandela acceded to the head of the South African government. He had moved from the Big House to the penthouse in two years. A compassionate man, Mandela placed two opposition leaders, de Klerk and Mangosuthu Buthelezi, in his cabinet. He even appointed Winnie to his cabinet even though they had officially separated a year earlier. The "troublemaker" was sworn in as president on May 9, 1994, to a jubilant multitude of black supporters in his home country and to international acclaim.

Burying the horrors of apartheid, however, did not come without a price. Mandela has been hailed as a savior and the country has prospered economically as well as socially. He successfully avoided a "racial bloodbath" by winning the election and appointing the opposition politicians to help with the transitional government. In late 1995 murder and crime was rampant in the country, in part due to the destruction of law and order during years of apartheid. Family values were destroyed and the very fabric of life suffered from the inhumanity that persisted during those awful years. There is a natural transformation period taking place which is exorcising past social sins. During this period Mandela was forced to fire his rebellious and divisive ex-wife, Winnie, due to her refusal to comply with the government's platform of conservative economic policies. Mandela has told reporters he plans to serve his nation until age eighty, at which time he will retire to the Transkei plains of his youth, where he has since built a new home.

What Makes Mandela Tick?

Mandela's friend Archbishop Desmond Tutu wrote, "You might have much of the world's riches, and you might hold a portion of authority, but if you have no *ubuntu,* you do not amount to much." The Nguni word means "the quality of being human as manifested in human acts socially, politically, and economically." In Xhosa it means honoring a trusting, interdependent, reciprocal relationship, which an individual needs for autonomy and self-expression. This one word epitomizes Nelson Mandela.

He was tenacity incarnate and his renegade nature allowed him to rebel against an unfair system. Who else would suffer the degradation of jail for so long merely to prove a system of government wrong? This renegade visionary didn't mind being alone, and utilized the solitude to grow stronger internally. An introverted personality allowed him this luxury, which would probably have destroyed anyone energized externally.

Mandela was never once in fear of his life. He liked to say, "The struggle is my life," and he was sincere in saying it. He was able to use his charismatic charm to move mountains. His dream of a free Africa took precedence over all else, including family and personal amenities. Family was relegated to second place, as were personal desires. Winnie wrote in her memoirs, "Nelson was busy twenty-four hours a day, you just couldn't tear him from the people, from the struggle. The nation came first. Everything else came second. His commitment was total."

PROMETHEAN TEMPERAMENT

Mandela exuded the classic traits of the Promethean personality, where the search for truth is of primary importance and dealing with life is accomplished with ingenuity and logic through an intuitive-thinking style of behavior. These types tend to become the architects of change and seek knowledge and truth above all else. Mandela certainly personifies those characteristics and views life as a quest for the "qualitative" not the "quantitative." He was a true visionary who sought opportunity instead of the status quo.

MYTHOLOGICAL HERO MENTORS

Mandela lived his life fulfilling the internal self-image of himself formed on the plains of the Transkei. Whether he realized it or not, he was unconsciously imprinted with the Xhosa heritage and the name Rohihlahla—"troublemaker." His mother contributed to his internal imagery by reciting stories of the mythical tribal heroes during his impressionable years. She was continually "enchanting him with legends and fables," which, he wrote, "stimulated my childhood imagination." He admitted in his memoirs, "My imagination was fired by these African warriors" and "I was moved by the broad sweep of African history, and the deeds of all African heroes regardless of tribe." While in school, this early inspiration was reinforced when Mqhayi—a mystical Xhosa African poet—"electrified" him. This man "instilled pride in my heritage" and he concluded, "I felt like one of the chosen people" after this man left.

Later, Mandela would become intellectually inspired by the philosophical writings of the world's great revolutionaries: Marx and Engels, Mao Tse Tung, Che Guevara. Mahatma Gandhi was one social/political role model and for a while he adopted Gandhi's passive resistance methodology for effecting change. Walter Sisulu was his first political activist mentor in Johannesburg and was instrumental in Mandela's completing his law degree. All of his heroes were larger-than-life iconoclasts who defied the establishment to make their mark in the world. Their mental images were so imprinted on his psyche that they helped remove all limits to his own achievement.

INSECURITY BREEDS GREATNESS

Mandela's law partner, Oliver Tambo, gave some indication of his motivations, saying, "His wit and confidence helped to dissipate his fear." Even though Mandela was often scared of the outcomes of his many ventures he used that fear as a motivator. He never allowed fear or insecurity to interfere with his fight against the white power elite. He said the distractions of "the struggle freed me from any lingering sense of doubt or inferiority I might still have felt; it liberated me from the feeling of being overwhelmed by the power and seemingly invincibility of the white man and his institutions." After he became president he said, "I felt fear more times than I can remember, but I hid it behind a map of boldness. The brave man is not he who does not feel afraid, but he who conquers that fear."

LIFE CRISES AND TRAUMAS—SUCCESS IMPRINTS

When Mandela's father died he was just nine. He was sent to a faraway village to live with a powerful chief and the trauma of this transformed him into a resilient and strong individual. Mandela was now being groomed as a counselor and leader of men, which caused him to reflect in his memoirs, "I felt a sense of awe mixed with bewilderment. Until then I had no thought of anything but my own pleasures—to become a champion stick-fighter. . . . I had no thought of money, or class, or fame, or power. Suddenly a new world opened before me. . . . In that instant, I saw that life might hold more for me than being a champion stick-fighter."

Mandela wrote of his metamorphosis, "I watched and learned from the tribal meetings" and was "profoundly influenced by observing the regent and his court." Nelson discovered his "destiny" as becoming "a counselor to the Thembu king" and at sixteen started "dreaming of being a lawyer." The "success imprint" of negotiating life-changing conflicts led him to pursue a law career and the larger import of his work led him to the presidency of South Africa.

Charisma

Bishop Tutu described Mandela as a man with a "shadow—substance, presence. He was regal. He is quite simply a giant of a man." Friend and biographer Mary

Benson describes him as "electrifying, a passionate man with a great zest for life." Mandela himself wrote, "As an attorney, I could be rather flamboyant in court. I did not act like a black man in a white man's court. When trying a case I often made sweeping gestures and used high-flown language. . . . I sometimes used unorthodox tactics with witnesses." A six-foot-three man with magnetic charm and allure, Mandela was able to move mountains.

During the time spent underground as David, Mandela was pursued as the nation's most wanted man. His flamboyance was without parallel, earning him the image of a dashing modern Robin Hood, defying authority for the rights of all men. This image ultimately grew until Mandela became an icon. The long years in prison turned him into a messiah. One of Mandela's many strengths was his ability to attract a wide diversity of people to his cause—Indians, whites, coloreds, and blacks. Another skill was his ability to communicate with various ethnic groups in their native languages. Mandela speaks fluent English, Xhosa, Afrikaans, Sisulu, Zulu, and Nokwe French, endearing him to the people of those nations.

Competitiveness

Mandela is fiercely competitive, as only one can be who takes up boxing as a form of exercise and entertainment. He worked out in the gym every evening for many years until he was forced underground. The competitiveness of boxing provided a release for Mandela's stored-up aggressions against the white supremacists he encountered daily. It provided a respite from the daily routine. He said, "Boxing is egalitarian. In the ring, rank, age, color, and wealth are irrelevant."

He gave insight into his competitive nature during his thirties, writing, "I had come of age as a freedom *fighter,*" with special emphasis on the word *fight* because it was so inextricably ingrained in his persona. Mandela's competitive spirit had been nurtured during his youth, when he competed in soccer and cross country running where, he said, "training counted more than intrinsic ability." Mandela was careful to admit that he had always "compensated for a lack of natural aptitude with diligence and discipline." Legal advocate Harold Wolpe gave further testimony to Mandela's competitive nature, describing his court behavior as "friendly but distant . . . and cuttingly aggressive."

Confidence

Mandela has the unique ability to face impossible situations with consummate optimism. One example was when he walked into his high treason trial smiling, with resolute confidence and appearing in full control. He was convinced that he would win despite the advantage held by his adversaries. Truth and right were on his side and that is what drove him even though he was fighting with an adversary who not only controlled the judicial system but who made the laws he refused to accept.

Mandela maintained a positive attitude in spite of his lifelong battles with a governing body that thought of him as inferior.

Hypomania

Mandela said of himself, "I led a life where I'd hardly enough time even to think." A typical Type A workaholic, he always placed work ahead of family, causing Winnie to comment, "Nelson was busy twenty-four hours a day." Winnie had long since given up any hope for a normal relationship with him, saying, "He was almost impossible to live with. . . . He belongs to them. . . . Everything else was second. His commitment was total." Mandela was so immersed in his work his eldest child at age five once asked her mother, "Where does daddy live?"

Biographer Mary Benson described him as a man with "tormented energy." He described himself as "relentless" with what he termed a "soul force."

Independence

Nelson Mandela was a renegade. His life as an iconoclast began when he joined a student strike in college rather than capitulate to the power of the authorities. This defiant act cost him his degree, since he was expelled and then forced to run away when his father reacted by insisting on an arranged marriage. It appears Mandela was preordained to live out his heritage as a "troublemaker," although he saw his actions and behavior as freedom of choice. When offered a compromise by the head of the university he refused and willingly accepted the consequences of his bold decision. He had given up his education, home, family, and friends to respect his beliefs—a continually recurring theme in the life of Nelson Mandela.

Nelson Mandela admitted, "In those days [during the Defiance Campaign] I was something of a rabble-rousing speaker. I liked to incite a white audience. . . . We were always defiant." Mandela felt he had acquired his defiant nature from his father, who he described as "proudly rebellious," adding, "It is a trait I recognize in myself."

Passion and Drive

Mandela was a passionately driven man who was inspired to fight by the nihilism of the apartheid system of government. He said, "This insane policy is diametrically opposed to every concept of human rights." He was willing to sacrifice his own freedom for the cause of justice and freedom and told the people not to give up the cause when he went underground, assuring them, "I will not leave South Africa, nor will I surrender." He was steeped in the belief that "trying counted more than intrinsic ability" and he spent his life overachieving due to that fundamental principle. In his memoirs Mandela wrote, "I maintain that nurture, not nature, is the primary molder of personality." He drove himself and others because of that belief. It also cause him to do everything in excess. He was a health fanatic, a boxing fanatic, a freedom fanatic, and a people fanatic. Passion defined Mandela's very being, and that passion was the reason he won the 1994 election to the presidency of South Africa.

Perfectionist

Excellence defined Mandela. When making a speech he demanded that every word be meticulously scrutinized to assure the correct meaning. It was the one quality that separated him from many other potential leaders in his country. He was a well-oiled machine who was fastidious in his appearance as well as his delivery. One of the reasons Mandela insisted on delaying his release from prison in 1994 was that he was not prepared with the speech he knew was very important to the cause of his people. Therefore he told de Klerk to delay his release by a week so he could prepare what he knew would be picked up by the international news media. President de Klerk delayed it by only a couple of days, which forced the perfectionist to work fast.

Temerity

Mandela was convinced that "nonviolent action often took more courage and determination than overtly aggressive action." Great risk and courage of his convictions were the secret of Mandela's power. Using this he soon became a role model for his followers and never allowed any form of intimidation to divert his actions. He sacrificed his family, his law practice, and his freedom for his values and risked his very life for the cause of freedom. Many times he flirted with death during his turbulent life underground, but was never deterred by the inherent risk in his role as leader of the ANC. He blatantly defied his adversaries, taunting them with phone calls, and openly flaunted his presence. Risk never deterred him personally or professionally.

Tenacity

This tenacious man never quit. Mandela started out in a native village but persevered to learn the ways of the Western world by the time he reached adulthood. It took him to age thirty-four to obtain his law degree; patience he had. He was a multifaceted man who worked in a law office, fought for equality, and went to school while raising a family. He never even got his first driver's license until age forty. This man was willing to pay virtually any price to achieve his goals and the ultimate win in that battle of wills was his election as president of South Africa in 1994 at age seventy-six. That success came with heavy baggage. He had endured twenty-seven years in prison and could have been released many times had he been willing to accept deportation or other political sanctions acceptable by the Afrikaner government. But his personal freedom was never as important as his commitment to the struggle.

Vision

Psychologists would describe Mandela as a macrovisionary—a right-brain-driven man who aspires to the possibilities and opportunities in life rather than accepts the status quo. An opportune future is always more exciting to the Mandelas of the world than a certain present. He is a classic Promethean personality who has an intuitive sense for the possibilities in life. The big picture was his god, causing him to set long-term goals. Mandela was never deterred by the many detours along the way to his chosen objective. He always took the long-term view in any great controversy and that unique ability made him victorious in battles begun decades earlier. Mandela was the type to mortgage the present for the future, not the reverse, which is the classic operating style of the bureaucratic mentality he was fighting.

Will to Power

Mandela relished raising his fist in the air and exclaiming "Amandla!" Fikile Bam described Mandela's powerful influence when he said, "Once you've put a man in prison for life there's nothing else you can do to him—except kill him." Bam added, "He becomes a power in his own self." A resilient will to power is intrinsic to the movements and acts of Mandela. He personifies the aphorism that "power accedes to he who takes it." Mandela assumed the power of his people while in prison and they willingly gave it to him. Even while incarcerated he wielded far more power than his oppressors—they just didn't know it until it was too late. His willpower spawned his charismatic power, which in turn resulted in "titular power," none of which was gained by violence or money. Mandela is a testament to one gaining power through right and truth and Gandhian *satyagraha*—soul force. That is the ultimate power and Mandela had it like few others in the world.

Summary

F. W. de Klerk and Nelson Mandela were awarded the Nobel Peace Prize in October 1993 for their joint effort in the destruction of apartheid. Mandela said in accepting the prize that it wasn't his efforts but those of the thousands of freedom fighters who lost their lives in the struggle for equality and peace. In his acceptance speech he gave de Klerk great credit for recognizing the inequities in South Africa and having the temerity to correct them. When asked how he could make peace with his mortal enemy, he said, "To make peace with an enemy one must work with that enemy, and that enemy becomes one's partner." This was a great tribute from a great man. And Mandela proved his magnanimity and great political insight by offering his chief adversaries and political enemies key positions in the new government.

Associated Press reporter John Daniszewski, commemorating Mandela's seventy-seventh birthday in 1995, called Mandela "a venerated liberator of blacks and also the hero of many white South Africans." He characterized Mandela as a "legend" and the "most celebrated politician of any race this polarized country has ever seen." The media has described Mandela as a "magic man" in his leadership abilities. His ability to lead forty million African subjects from three hundred years of servitude is an indication of the force of his great power. He accomplished what no one thought possible, even himself, during those despicable days languishing in prison.

Most experts fully expected a civil war in South Africa. As recently as 1993 most Africans and international political authorities saw no way out of a divisive conflict in order to make South Africa a country where peaceful coexistence was possible. Nelson Mandela is probably the only man on earth who could have kept that from happening and no adulation is great enough to acknowledge his contribution. The Middle East, Bosnia, and other India/Pakistani conflicts pale in what could have happened. His long walk to freedom was a horrendous price to pay but his release and assumption of power had paid enormous dividends to his people including whites. Those in the world who worship peaceful coexistence owe this man an enormous debt of gratitude.

Mandela describes his political strategy as metaphorical to cattle tending: "You stand at the back with a stick. Then a few of the more energetic cattle move to the front and the rest of the cattle follow. You are really guiding them from behind." Smiling, he concludes, "That is how a leader should do his work." His consensus-style leadership forced him to oust his disruptive ex-wife, Winnie, from her government seat since she was opposed to his economic moves, which were long-range. She had been fighting too long in the trenches to compromise her ideals.

Mandela's strength as a leader has been his grassroots simplicity and high integrity. When in public he often meets a young African boy who is impressed with his position. The boy will say, "Ah, you're a big man, man!" Nelson looks at the boy and replies smiling, "And what did you have for breakfast today?" the implication being that they are equal except for title. True leaders understand the need to be respected as a leader but identified with as one of the pack. The secret is having both qualities. Mandela has always had that unique ability, which makes him the consummate creative political genius. Mandela lived his life by the principle, "If you never give up, you cannot lose."

In his twilight years a romance has blossomed between Mandela and Graco

Machel of Mozambique. Reporters have said that he appears like a "lovestruck teenager." Machel is twenty-seven years his junior but mesmerized by this symbol of hope for South Africa.

ROHIHLAHLA (NELSON) MANDELA
Promethean Temperament (NT)
Social Activist and First Black President of South Africa
born July 18, 1918, Umtata, Transkei Territory, South Africa

Dominant trait: Tenacity personified; introverted intuitive renegade and workaholic

Motto: "Struggle is my life"; "Power to the people"; "I will not leave South Africa, nor will I surrender"

Religion: Methodist, Wesleyan Church; educated in missionary schools

Philosophy: "We are not antiwhite, we are against white supremacy"; a Gandhian-like dialectical materialism

Politics: African National Congress (ANC)—democratic socialism

Nickname: English teachers: Nelson; the Black Pimpernel and David while underground

Creation/innovation: Cofounder, ANC Youth League; persevered for African black equality; 1st black law practice

Successes: President, ANC Youth League, 1950; President ANC, 1991; Nobel Peace Prize, 1993; President of South Africa, 1994

Vices/hobbies: *Communist Manifesto* by Marx; Mao Tse Tung's ideology; boxing and soccer

Romantic liaisons: Married nurse Evelyn Ntoko (four children); 2nd marriage to Winnie Madikizela (two daughters)

Self-description: "I try not to be a rabble rouser"; "I cherish a free society . . . an ideal for which I am prepared to die"

Birth order: Firstborn son of Henry Gadla Mandela and Nonqaphi; foster brother Justice kindred spirit

Parental influence: Mother nurtured, father visited monthly; after father died raised by Chief Jongintaba from age 9

Early transience: Moved at age 1 to Qunu, at 9 to Mqhekezweni, at 16 to Clarkebury, at 19 to Healdtown, at 21 to Fort Hare

Parents' occupations: Father chief counselor to Jongintaba, chief of Themba tribe, who became substitute father

Role models: Chief of Themba tribe and son Justice; Marcus Garvey; Haile Selassie; Walter Sisulu; Oliver Tambo

Hero mentors: Xhosa legends and heroes of battle; poet Mqhayi Xhosa; Mao Tse Tung; Che Guevara; W. E. B. Du Bois

Formal education: Mission schools; Clarkebury School; Wesleyan College; University College; Witwatersrand Law School

Life crises: Father died when 9; runaway to escape arranged marriage at 21; treason trial and 27-year imprisonment

Metamorphoses: Dreamed of becoming Thembu counselor/arbitrator/lawyer after watching regent at age 16

Charismatic: "Electrifying speaker"; Bishop Tutu: "Shadow presence, regal, and zest for life"

Competitive: Boxing—an outlet for aggressive energy; enjoyed athletic competition

Hypomanic: Excessive tormented energy; always sacrificed personal life for professional causes

Independent rebel: Name means "troublemaker"; led Defiance Campaign to overthrow white rule in South Africa

Indomitable "will": Bishop Tutu: "Mandela is the power . . . because he is a great man . . . a giant of enormous intellect"

Intuitive vision: Envisioned the needs of his people; foresaw the inevitable end of white supremacy

Passion: "I compensated for a lack of natural aptitude with diligence and discipline"

Risk-taker: Always lived life on the edge; refused P. W. Botha's offer of freedom to win it all

Self-confident: An optimist who believed in victory long before anyone else thought it possible

Tenacious: Success due to "doggedness" not "cleverness"; waited 27 years in prison for redemption

Workaholic: "I led a life where I'd hardly enough time even to think"; classic workaholic

Honors: Nobel Peace Prize, 1993

15

Thurgood Marshall—Confident

Mr. Civil Rights—The Social Conscience of the Civil Rights Era

"Ours is a government of men—not laws."

Thoroughgood Marshall was his original name, but it proved far too time-consuming to write, spell, or explain to friends, so this renegade changed it to Thurgood while still in grammar school. The name Thoroughgood had been adopted by his paternal grandfather in order to pacify Civil War army officials who demanded that he have two names. Nevertheless our protagonist became psychologically imprinted with the inherent values of the name as he was patiently "thorough" in all he did and pursued the "good" in his chosen field of judicial activism. Marshall confirms my belief that we all live our lives fulfilling internal self-images of ourselves, even when these images, names, or labels are arcane or weird. The self-actualizing Thoroughgood Marshall epitomizes the concept better than most.

On Marshall's death in 1993, *People* wrote, "With the law as his weapon, Thurgood Marshall was determined to change the world—and he did." Many people regard Marshall as the most important American litigator of the twentieth century. President Lyndon Johnson believed this to such a degree that he defied his Southern constituency by appointing Marshall to the Supreme Court in 1967. He would hold the post for the next twenty-four years. In 1961 President Kennedy had been impressed enough to appoint him to the U.S. Court of Appeals, which led to his post as solicitor general in 1965. Marshall was the first black ever to hold these two top-level positions in our criminal justice system. Marshall earned these appointments through his diligent years of service as legal counsel of the National Association for the Advancement of Colored People (NAACP), where he spent twenty-three years fighting the legal wars of his people in county, state, and federal courts throughout the nation. Marshall spent most of his life working inordinately long hours for subsistence wages while taking enormous personal risks. During those years as the legal counsel for the NAACP he won twenty-nine of thirty-two cases adjudicated before the Supreme Court. Some of those wins will go down in history as the greatest legal battles ever won in any nation or in any court of justice.

His legacy can be summed up in these words: "I did the best I could with what I had." Marshall's voice was the "voice of authority," the "voice of reason," a "voice with an unwavering message." Marshall was cynical, persuasive, and through much skill and great courage changed America more than even the great Martin Luther King, Jr. Marshall often made his points with an irreverence often lost on ignorant whites. An example occurred when New Orleans political boss Leander Perez called him a "buzz-headed nigger from New York," causing Marshall to respond, "Hell! I'm not buzz-headed." Marshall loved to regale his listeners with stories that were steeped in metaphorical anecdotes meant to shock them into a sympathetic understanding of what it meant to live and work in Jim Crow America. One story spoke of when he soiled his pants because the Baltimore City restrooms were off-limits to blacks and he failed to make it all the way home in time via streetcar. Here was a young attorney who owned his own business and was denied the right to use a city convenience. He liked to tell the story so his lawyer-trained associates in Congress could better empathize with the antiquated system he was attempting to change. He liked to describe himself as a child of the South, saying, "You could get your ass killed just trying to go see a Tarzan movie."

Harvard law professor Randall Kennedy says, "I can't think of another lawyer who has done as much for racial equality." Former NAACP Executive Director Benjamin Hooks felt, "Without Thurgood Marshall, we would still be riding in the back of the bus, going to separate schools and drinking 'colored' water." According to Yale law professor Drew Days, "He has been a conscience. In the law he remains our supreme conscience." Sandra Day O'Connor reflected on her interactions with Marshall after he retired, calling him "a man who immerses himself in human suffering and then translates that suffering in a way that others can bear and understand. He is a man who sees the world exactly as it is and pushes on to make it what it can become. No one could avoid being touched by his soul." John J. Curtin, Jr., president of the American Bar Association, gave credence to this, saying, "His eloquence as a lawyer gave a voice to those who had no voice." Marshall's friend and biographer, Carl Rowan, gave this incisive description of the man: "Marshall never pretended to be other than what he was: driven, sometimes compassionate, but often ornery; hardworking, hard-cussing, and sometimes hard-drinking; hard-to-get-along-with under pressure, self-effacing and graceful in triumph."

This son of a Pullman car porter rose to the most powerful judicial post in the United States. He did it his way and without the benefit of money, social status, or exceptional brilliance. Marshall worked diligently to get to the top and once there refused to put on airs or function any differently than before his arrival. With Marshall you got what you saw and that was his genius. Thurgood Marshall, arguably, changed the United States social system more than any man in history. For that he is the consummate creative genius of social justice and will be so recognized by history.

Innovative Contribution

Thurgood Marshall earned his nicknames, Mr. Civil Rights and Mr. Desegregation, by riding the rails to Southern cities in the days when blacks were not only held in disrespect but were ridiculed. This daily grind of case after case for the NAACP with numerous life-threatening experiences molded him into a feisty competitor who was not afraid of any fight, physical or mental. As so often is the case, Marshall was looked on as an overnight success in 1954, after he won the famous *Brown* v. *Board of Education* case before the Supreme Court. But this precedent-setting victory was the result of many years of sweat and heartache.

Mr. Desegregation had been fighting for this decision in county, state, and federal courts for twenty years. His first case was the 1935 University of Maryland student discrimination appeal, where he successfully got the first black ever, Don Murray, admitted to Maryland's law school. But with the *Brown* ruling Marshall made litigation history. Alan Dershowitz, high-profile Harvard law professor, gives an incisive description of the man who could have earned millions chasing high-profile law suits and corporate clients but who elected to pursue a labor of love: "The Marshall era was characterized by a vindication of the rights of the downtrodden, the underdog, the minority, and the unpopular. It was personified by the only justice in American history whose entire distinguished career at the bar was in the service of the poor, the disenfranchised, and the victims of discrimination."

Judge Irving Kaufman said Marshall always "stressed the human side" of a case and "because of him we are all more free."

Personal History

Thurgood Marshall was born the second son of William Canfield Marshall, a Pullman car porter, and Norma Williams, a primary school teacher, on July 2, 1908, in Baltimore, Maryland. One great-grandfather had been an immigrant from the Congo as a slave and according to Marshall's memoirs became the toughest of the lot. Both sides of the family were racially mixed, which in later years would give rise to his nickname as the "Mulatto Lawyer."

Like many of the subjects in this book, a major influence in Thurgood's early life was his paternal grandmother, who told him, "If you have the guts you can beat city hall." Marshall remembered this admonition but also learned much from both sets of grandparents, who had an entrepreneurial bent as shop owners in Maryland. Marshall's uncle Fearless was an iconoclast; he was the source of much of Marshall's cynicism.

Discrimination faced Marshall at every crossroad along the way. He said, "My father was castrated mentally and emotionally by the bigots who controlled employment." Marshall contended his father was the most instrumental person in his life, telling *U.S. News and World Report,* "He never told me to become a lawyer, but he turned me into one. He did it by teaching me to argue, challenged my logic on every point, by making me prove every statement I made."

The Marshalls relocated to Harlem when Thurgood was a baby and lived there for five years. Marshall described life in Harlem as a devastating experience for the family, and they moved back to Baltimore when he was five. It was here that he learned life in the big city by trailing along after his father to the Chesapeake Bay Club and on Diamond Jim Brady's railway car. The boy began working at age seven. His first job was at Hale's Grocery store in Baltimore. He would not quit working until age eighty-three, when he retired as Supreme Court justice.

Mr. Civil Rights was an incorrigible youth, a gang leader and roustabout who was forever getting into trouble. He refused to study in school, causing one assistant principal to challenge his flippant attitude over study and education in general. This man soon became the target of the young reprobate's madcap behavior and perverse style of retribution. This miscreant arranged for three girls from his gang to meet with the assistant principal in his office. Then, staging his moves with the precision of a choreographer, he had five of their friends burst into the office just as one of the girls jumped on the astonished educator's lap, catching him in apparent *flagrante delicto*. Marshall delighted in telling this bizarre story of delinquency in action, which he described as "working marvelously." Another such escapade earned the young rogue the wrath of Principal Lee, who banished him to the furnace room to memorize the U.S. Constitution. Marshall relates this as a "terrible experience," but in retrospect it left a lasting impression on the wayward youth. He never forgot the lines of this great document that proved so important in his future. In a few years Marshall would become an expert on the Constitution and would often use it to his advantage.

Despite Marshall's wayward youth, he was a voracious reader and graduated with honors from Baltimore's Douglas High School in 1925. He enrolled in what was then known as the "Black Princeton"—Lincoln University in Oxford, Pennsylvania. Marshall gained a reputation at Lincoln as an unsavory and recalcitrant prankster and womanizer. The school repeatedly threatened him with expulsion for his rowdy and drunken behavior. Twice he was thrown out of school for fraternity pranks and he admitted to having six fraternity pins out at one time. He was engaged nine times during the first two years at Lincoln. He would later admit to spending his college days "chasing women and drinking booze."

The fun-loving Marshall was a premed student with expectations of fulfilling his mother's dream of becoming a respected dentist. Marshall's renegade behavior kept him from it. A white professor, H. F. Grimm, flunked him out of anthropology for defying him and casting aspersions on his sex life. Marshall totally disagreed with Grimm's philosophy on sexual intercourse, but did not object until Professor Grimm started preaching to the class that sexual intercourse was strictly forbidden except for the purpose of propagation of the race. Marshall now believed he had gone too far and asked Grimm in class if he had had sex only three times since he had just three children. The professor was not pleased with this cynical bit of logic and flunked him unceremoniously. Marshall was unable to get into dental school without passing anthropology, so he resigned himself to a life of law instead.

While at Lincoln Marshall fell passionately in love with Vivean Buster Burey. He brought his fiancée and her family home to meet his family, but was almost blindsided by his cynical Uncle Fearless, who told Vivean and her family, "I've seen that you are a fine young lady. You ought to be beware of Thurgood. He *always* was a bum, he *is* a bum, and he always *will be* a bum!" Vivean ignored this sage advice and married Marshall despite his horrible reputation, which evidently was rampant even within the Marshall family. Marshall settled down after marriage and graduated from Lincoln with honors in 1930. He would never again be profligate, but would continue his passion for poker and pinochle for the rest of his life. Marshall settled for a life as a litigator and applied for admission to the University of Maryland Law School.

Applying to the segregated University of Maryland proved to be the catalyst for change in his life. He would never quite recover from the despicable actions of Law School President R. A. Pearson, a zealous segregationist, bigot, and racist who ignored Marshall's request for admittance to the school. In Marshall's words, Pearson said "to drop dead." He never recovered from this overt rejection but decided to enter the all-black Howard University in nearby Washington, D.C. Marshall did not have the money to pay for a private law school education, but his doting mother once again came to his rescue and pawned her engagement ring to pay his tuition.

Marshall would never forget the University of Maryland's rejection and when he graduated from Howard magna cum laude in 1933 turned down a Harvard fellowship in order to enter practice and file a lawsuit against the school. At Howard Marshall met the man who would become a lifetime mentor and would instill in him the attributes and vision that would make him great. Dr. Charles Houston was the head of the law school at Howard and became Marshall's teacher, mentor, boss, and guardian angel for the next ten years. Marshall later wrote, "Charlie Houston was one of the greatest lawyers I've ever been privileged to know. He was a perfectionist of the first order. I have seen him writing a brief and spending the whole day looking for one word—just the right word." When Marshall graduated from Howard he refused the Harvard fellowship and implemented his plan to quench the fire burning in his belly over the University of Maryland rejection. This fire had to be put out before Marshall could do anything else and he set out to rectify the abominable segregation at his home state's law school. Marshall hung out his shingle in Baltimore and immediately started in motion a program with his mentor at his side to rectify the wrong done him by President Pearson.

Professional History

Marshall set up his new law practice with a lot of energy but no money. He quickly found a student by the name of Don Murray who wanted to go to the University of Maryland Law School and filed his first lawsuit against the school with the assistance of Houston. They prevailed and Murray enrolled as the first black law school student anywhere south of the Mason-Dixon line. Pearson resigned and Marshall was ecstatic. Unfortunately, he was also dead broke.

The young lawyer struggled in his law practice because he was always more interested in pursuing truth and justice than representing wealthy clients and making money. Marshall admitted to changing phone numbers every few months to fend off creditors and surviving by threatening to sue the phone company if it disconnected his phone. He often took on new clients just for the experience and charged them no fees. This was not conducive to solvency. Marshall bought stationery but couldn't pay for it and struggled to survive as an independent professional until he volunteered his services to the local chapter of the NAACP in 1934. Marshall's timing was exquisite; within two years his former mentor and teacher Charles Houston was appointed legal counsel for the NAACP headquarters in New York and in 1936 Houston brought Marshall into New York as his assistant. Until this time Marshall and his wife were struggling and were forced to live with his parents. In New York they finally had their own home.

MR. CIVIL RIGHTS

Houston retired from his position at the NAACP in 1938 and Marshall replaced him as the head counsel for the NAACP on a subsistence salary of $2,400 a year. His work at the NAACP would encompass the next twenty-three years and earned him the moniker of Mr. Civil Rights, the Mulatto Lawyer, Mr. Desegregation, and less complimentary epithets by his adversaries. He worked endless hours at terrible risk to his life for the next two decades and never earned more than $15,000 annually.

As the NAACP's counsel Marshall became a vagabond traveling the United States constantly in a passionate attempt to assault the Jim Crow "separate but equal" laws in particular and segregation in general. He took on innumerable local cases that were invariably defeated in the lower courts with the understanding that the fight would end up in appeal at the Supreme Court. It was these cases that took most of Marshall's time. He personally adjudicated all appeals at the regional or national level while functioning as an advisor to the local attorneys in the local court actions. His first NAACP case took place in 1939 and by 1958 he had argued thirty-two cases before the Supreme Court, winning twenty-nine.

LANDMARK VICTORY

Marshall's most important victory occurred on May 17, 1954, when the Warren Court ruled unanimously in *Brown* v. *Board of Education* that "separate educational facilities are inherently unequal." The decision overturned the result of an 1896 case known as *Plessy* v. *Ferguson.* According to political analyst and Marshall biographer Carl Rowan, this unanimous ruling was instigated by inside political maneuvering that altered history. In researching this important episode in

American politics, Rowan uncovered some interesting ramifications of the decision. The chief justice of the Supreme Court at the time was a Southerner, Fred Vinson, a Kentucky native who was the mortal enemy of desegregation. Marshall said, "You know we Negroes have a sixth sense for detecting which white person is for us or against us? My sixth sense told me that Vinson in mind and heart was my enemy." A few months before the case was to be heard he said, "I have to keep believing," because anything can happen. A few months before the decision Vinson suddenly died of a heart attack.

Vinson's timely death proved to be the catalyst that proved providential to Marshall and his cause. President Eisenhower appointed California liberal Earl Warren to replace Vinson and then proceeded to attempt to sway Warren in the *Brown* case in a clumsy way that backfired. Eisenhower succumbed to Southern pressure and invited new Supreme Court Justice Earl Warren to the White House for a private dinner on the pretext of meeting some new friends and valued associates. He very carefully seated Warren on his right according to social protocol, but violated all tradition by seating the chief counsel for the South in the *Brown* case, John Davis, next to Warren. And, adding insult to injury, he attempted to apply pressure on Warren by blatantly suggesting that "Southerners are not bad people" and that they really didn't want to see their "sweet little girls required to sit in school alongside some big, overgrown Negroes."

This flagrant and inappropriate attempt to sway a resilient, self-made liberal like Warren proved counterproductive. Warren not only was not impressed with the president's unsubtle maneuver, he used his powers to demonstrate forever that he could never be swayed by such tactics, doing all he could to make sure the final verdict was unanimous. Marshall was blown away when the unanimous ruling came in and in his jubilance announced, "We hit the jackpot." He said, "I would have bet all the tea in China that it wouldn't be unanimous." He called Warren "the greatest leader I've ever run across in my life." Eisenhower had unintentionally become Marshall's ally. No other case would ever have the import of this one and Marshall without knowing it was on his way to greater things because of the notoriety and adulation from this great victory.

On September 23, 1961, President Kennedy appointed Marshall to the United States Court of Appeals for New York, Vermont, and Connecticut. It took over a year for his confirmation due to strong opposition from Strom Thurmond and other Southerners intent on seeing him rejected. After two years as a circuit judge, a Southern president, Lyndon Johnson, who was intent on showing he was not prejudiced, appointed Marshall to the third-highest post in the justice department—solicitor general. He was the first black ever to serve as solicitor general of the United States. In this position Marshall argued nineteen cases before the Supreme Court and won fourteen. Then, just two years later, Johnson appointed this grandson of a slave to replace Tom Clark, the grandson of a Confederate soldier, to the highest court in the land. Marshall became a member of the Supreme Court on October 2, 1967, and served as the liberal conscience of America for the next twenty-four years.

THE GREAT DISSENTER

Marshall served long and well, fully intending to defend those legal battles of equality and justice he had spent a lifetime cultivating. When asked if he was finally satisfied with the state of social justice, he responded with typical Marshall bombast, "I'll be dead before I'll be satisfied." Marshall was a staunch opponent of capital punishment and an advocate of women's rights, abortion rights, and First Amendment rights. His philosophy was to wipe out all the trappings of white supremacy. His objective was always aimed at "humanizing the criminal justice system" even when it was not necessarily favoring one of his own. When Muhammad Ali refused to register for the draft, he personally enforced the ruling to imprison Ali.

RENEGADE LITIGATOR

When a clerk told Marshall, "You have to come down on this side of this case," the irascible curmudgeon screeched, "Say what? Step closer so I can be sure you're hearing me. I don't have to do a damned thing except to stay black and die." Marshall was always in favor of every individual's right to privacy. He said, "Keep Big Brother out of the bedroom," adding, "If anybody had tried to come in my father's house without a warrant he'd kill him." Mr. Civil Rights never abided by the "good ole boy" rules of the Court, which said that justices see no evil, hear no evil, and surely speak no evil. One of his more controversial statements came in a speech in Hawaii, his second wife's birthplace, where he said the Constitution was not meant to be "fixed" and wasn't necessarily "profound," but was "defective from the start." He told the audience "the Constitution required several amendments, a civil war, and momentous social transformation to attain the system of constitutional government" that we have today.

Ill and aging in 1991, Marshall finally retired at age eighty-three. His departure from the court proved as controversial as when President Bush nominated Clarence Thomas to succeed him. The irony is that these two black men espoused totally different ideologies. Some saw Marshall's liberalism as left of Karl Marx and Thomas's conservatism as right of Attila the Hun. Understandably, Marshall vigorously opposed the Thomas confirmation.

What Made Marshall Tick?

This was a man who lived his life in constant controversy and high risk. He proved unflappable in the face of the gravest dangers. When young he decided not to take life too seriously, saying, "I intend to wear life as a very loose garment and never worry about nothin'." This attitude allowed him to face the fiercest battles with aplomb and risk with disdain. It armed him with a laissez-faire philosophy that served him well, even after he had reached the pinnacle of power in the highest court in the land. He liked to say that the real heroes were the strong blacks who stayed and fought the local battles day after day while he jumped on the fastest train out of town. Marshall was a fearless competitor who changed the world by daring to be different and adopting an attitude of self-confidence that would not be denied. Biographer Rowan described his awesome confidence as "overoptimism."

On the Myers-Briggs personality profile Marshall is classified a Dionysian temperament (sensing-perceiving), which is one who works via "action" and "cleverness." He was a negotiator who loved freedom and lived his life by the motto "Eat, drink, and be merry." The Dionysian temperament is the "artisan" who is superb at handling crisis, troubleshooting, firefighting, and negotiating. They are good at problem resolution and demand their freedom. They are pragmatists who value spontaneity. Marshall fits this model perfectly.

The tenacious visionary was self-confident and irreverent but never gave up. He was a simple man who voted his conscience despite the consequences or even the implications of racial controversy. During the period of the turbulent sixties when Stokely Carmichael was crying "Black Power," Marshall became incensed over what he perceived as this revolutionary approach to resolving racial injustice and wrote, "Anarchy is anarchy, and it makes no difference who practices it. It is bad, it is punishable, and it ought to be punished." He insisted the ballot would deliver more "Black Power" than any cries of "Burn, baby, burn." Marshall was even cynical about Martin Luther King's marches, saying, "All that walking for nothing. They might as well have waited for the Court decision."

An intransigent, Marshall was always his own man and everyone knew it. He often resorted to off-the-wall comments in response to bias and prejudicial remarks. James Polling of *Colliers* wrote of Marshall in 1952, "If he is paradoxical it might almost be said to be deliberate. He has consciously chosen to follow a hedonistic, non-worrying philosophy."

MYTHOLOGICAL HERO MENTORS

As a student Marshall identified with the mythological heroes from his African ancestry. He loved to regale guests with stories of his heritage that were not only interesting but bizarre testimony of his belief in the power and strength of his origins. He told biographer Rowan:

> A big game-hunting family had picked up my great-grandfather on one of their safaris into the Congo and brought him back to the Eastern Shore of Maryland—only to find this black man who didn't cotton to the idea of slavery. He expressed his objections so rebelliously that one day the slavemaster said to him: Look, I brought you here, so I guess I can shoot you, which is what you deserve. I can't in good conscience sell you to another slaveholder. So I'm gonna set you free on one condition. You get the hell out of this county and never set foot here again.

Marshall's father inherited this fighting spirit and certainly instilled it in young Thurgood. He told him, "Son, if anyone ever calls you a nigger, you not only got my permission to fight him—you got my orders to fight him." While in college Marshall became the protégé of law professor Charles Houston, who became a real-life role model. Houston taught Marshall how to wage war using the law instead of guns. Biographer Rowan says that Marshall's grooming demanded the "intervention of an outside force more disciplined and dominant than his family." Houston was the person who filled that role and "Marshall was transported from 'bum' to national hero." Marshall confirms the huge influence of his mentor saying, "I saw this man's dedication, vision, his willingness to sacrifice, and I told myself, 'You either shape up or ship out.' " He shaped up.

INSECURITY BREEDS GREATNESS

Marshall lived his life, as most blacks do, suffering the grossest abuses, rejections, insecurities, and lack of civility, all facets of social decency that whites take for granted. No matter the degree of achievement or amount of financial security, if a black person finds himself or herself in the wrong part of town at the wrong time of night, ridicule, abuse, arrest, or worse can result. Marshall's most earthshaking rejection occurred when the University of Maryland refused to admit him or even consider him for admission to its law school for no other reason than his color. He never got over that abject rejection and that "imprint" motivated him to alter his career to the fight for social justice. That one act changed his life, launching him in the pursuit of a mythological god called civil rights.

LIFE CRISES AND TRAUMAS

Marshall lived his early life as most blacks of his era did—traumatized by discrimination and rejection. He often told of how his older brother, William Aubrey, was "killed" by a physical infirmity due to his "constant rejection due to racial discrimination." His brother Aubrey was a medical doctor who was passed over, gave up, and then died as a result of his overt rejection.

One time when he found himself in Mississippi attempting to change trains for the trip north, Marshall ran into "a big feller with no uniform on, but a noticeably long pistol on his side" who said, "Nigger, what are you doing here?" When Marshall explained he was just changing trains, the man told him with an animosity that can be nurtured only in the Jim Crow South, "Well, there's only one more train coming through here today and that's at four o'clock, and you damn sight better get on it, cause the sun is never going down on a live nigger in this town." Such was the degradation and persecution that was the motivation for his great drive, which led to his later success. To his credit Marshall never resorted to the use of force in his battles but always employed the law to exact his revenge.

Marshall came precariously close to death when a lynch mob attempted to hang him in Columbia, Tennessee, in 1946. He had just won acquittal for twenty-four blacks and a limited sentence for another, which infuriated the local police and Klu Klux Klan. Marshall wrote of driving back to Nashville in order to catch a train back north when "the mob followed me out across the Duck River. . . . It was composed equally of state troopers and city police." The police were a part of the plot and stopped his car. The inflamed crowd picked him up and were carrying him to the river for a lynching when suddenly a car full of blacks drove up with guns to stave off this inhuman act. The police feared a shootout and massacre with national media exposure, which caused the Klan leader to yell, "The niggers have guns." This created a panic and the Klan members fled. A shootout would have resulted in many deaths but the undeterred Marshall saw it as just one more instance to fight for litigation to change the system. He had already expected to die this night and had little to say to the media afterwards. Later he commented, "I don't deserve the credit. The people who dared to stand up, to file lawsuits, were beaten and sometimes murdered after I spoke my piece and took the fastest goddamn train I could find out of the area." Such traumas gave Marshall the inner drive required for his herculean fight for equality and freedom.

Charisma

Milton Murray of Tennessee witnessed the Columbia lynch mob scene and said, "I would lay down my life today for that man because he gave me a renewal of life. He made it possible for me to be a man. . . . I owe a debt to the bravest, proudest man this country ever produced—Thurgood Marshall." Such was the effect of this man, whose allure was by action as well as by dialogue. No matter the venue Mr. Civil Rights was a charismatic figure. His booming voice could always be heard above the crowd and his disciples would have followed him anywhere. He could move crowds and influence leaders with his streetwise metaphors and stories of the tragedy of bigotry. Marshall's homespun parables were classic because they were true-to-life scenarios of the overt discrimination that existed at the time.

Competitiveness

The Great Dissenter envisioned himself as a prizefighter disguised as a lawyer. He often reminisced of his days in Harlem partying with Joe Louis. As a Supreme Court justice he liked to say, "I enjoy the fight. . . . I love peace, but I adore a riot. You've got to be angry to write a dissent." A law clerk wrote, "Marshall's combative spirit is evident in the tone and strength of his dissents." Never afraid to confront the opposition head-on, he could be bombastic, a style guaranteed to get the attention of his adversaries. He told a reporter, "I love a dissent. You have to get real mad to write a good dissent. I love a war. When young lawyers apply to clerk in my office, the first thing I ask is, Do you like writing dissents? If you don't, baby, this is not the office for you. Yep, get my juices jiggling and I'll write a helluva dissent."

Confidence

Marshall was a confidence freak. During the battle of *Brown* v. *Board of Education,* young reporter Carl Rowan wrote, "I left Marshall that fall day of 1953 thinking that he believed in himself and his cause so much that it was impossible for me and others not to believe in him." Even many of Marshall's most loyal supporters thought he was overly optimistic about most cases. He was never deterred in the face of the direst adversity, always believing he could win. This positive mentality is what made him great. No peer, adversary, or constituent ever accused him of humility. He believed in his destiny and fulfilled it because of a tenacious belief in the possible.

Hypomania

Marshall took his first job at age seven and never quit working until he was nearly on his deathbed. Marshall was always a megalomaniac on a mission and refused to quit until the mission was over. When he first started traveling for the NAACP he was never home, slept little, and spent interminable time on trains to remote problem sites. A "killer" schedule caused him, at age thirty, to confide in his tolerant wife, "Shit, I'm sure I can make it till I'm forty." He said, "She didn't think that was much of a damn joke." Rowan wrote of Marshall's killer schedule saying, "Houston was working himself to death at age fifty-four. Marshall was on a mission of perhaps earlier self-destruction." Historian John Hope Franklin wrote, "I have never seen a man work so long and so hard and I never worked for a harder taskmaster."

At the Supreme Court Marshall gained the reputation as a delegator. What the critics fail to understand is that Management 101 decrees that every executive should delegate anything possible since there are so many important strategic matters that are not delegatable and it is incumbent on the boss to differentiate between the two. The higher up the ladder, the more delegation is necessary, and at this time he stood on the highest ladder of all. The almost thirty years he spent traveling in the boondocks proved highly productive to his overall experience of delegating. He would say, "When it comes to productivity, there's no substitute for being young, hungry, and angry." He was all of these much longer than most.

Independence

This renegade spirit was the classic iconoclast who never listened to any expert or followed tradition. He only listened to his own voice of ethical justice. He was an irreverent and irascible maverick who violated societal norms and even went so far as to denigrate the Constitution as a document meant to be changed. This caused an enormous flap in Washington but Marshall refused to capitulate to the will of his peers and told them: "Ours is a government of men, not laws." He was a staunch believer that laws are only created to meet the needs of men, not vice versa. One admirer said that, "He used the Constitution the way Moses used the Ten Commandments."

During the trying period when attempting to win the *Brown* v. *Board of Education* case, Dr. Charles Johnson, head of Fisk University, found a precedent for use in securing the victory. Marshall was asked who would be responsible for writing the argument. He replied without hesitation, "The head nigger's gonna write this up!" in an irreverent reference to himself. He often used this self-deprecating term, which he would have found unacceptable if used by others. Shock and impiety were often the instruments he used to gain the attention of his adversaries.

Marshall's metaphorical stories were not only incisive but an effective way to let the world know that bigotry and discrimination existed around every corner. Marshall liked to tell the story of the time he was invited to a White House luncheon while serving on the Supreme Court. He found himself seated next to a born-again Christian woman who insisted on talking about what he referred to as this "born-again stuff." He said, "Madam, please, I can't be born again." When she asked why, he responded, "My mother's dead," which only infuriated this religious zealot. It is never easy espousing merely emotional rhetoric to a renegade spirit.

Passion and Drive

Marshall was a driven man. During the *Brown* v. *Board of Education* litigation he said he was continually caught up in thinking of his adversary, Chief Justice Vinson, saying, "I thought of him every day and every night." Passion was the lifeblood of Thurgood Marshall, as it is with most eminent power brokers. Marshall drank hard, worked hard, played cards hard, and pursued his beliefs with the passion of a man possessed. His immersion in each case caused him to become impervious to time, current events, people, or even the day of the week. Such intensity took its toll, as it always does. Just as Michael Jackson repeatedly collapses from the fervent passion of his efforts, so do driven executive types like Thurgood Marshall. Most people see such emotional collapses as normal but do not expect high-profile lawyers to be so inclined. Consistent with this, Marshall worked feverishly and then often collapsed. He had nervous breakdowns in 1943, 1946, 1948, and 1954 all just after some great emotional battle. A heart attack in 1976 was also attributed to his passionate drive.

Perfectionist

Marshall was an exacting person who demanded excellence from himself and his associates. His exacting nature and need for excellence led to his graduating number one in his law school class at Howard University. This success imprint stayed with him for the rest of his life and made him successful in each of the jobs he took. His professional mentor, Charles Houston, was one of the causes of his need for excellence, since Houston was an inveterate perfectionist. Houston molded his student with this trait and it proved to be a key element in both men's rise to fame and notoriety.

Temerity

Marshall never feared the unknown and spent the better part of his life living on the edge. Threats on his life, contracts for his head, or race-crazed lynch mobs never deterred Marshall from continuing his struggle for freedom and equality for his people. He was a gambling spirit who loved a challenge in cards or life. He approached everything head-on, believing that democracy could not flourish amid fear. He adamantly believed, "We must go against the prevailing wind. We must dissent from the indifference. We must dissent from the apathy. We must dissent from the fear. Take a chance, won't you? Knock down the fences that divide. Tear apart the walls that imprison. Reach out; freedom lies just on the other side." Marshall was the consummate risk-taking success story. He dared to gamble with life and won the lottery of equality due to his great temerity.

Tenacity

Evidence of Marshall's perseverance is his statement, "I'll be dead before I'll be satisfied." He often told his constituency, "I have to keep believing, because I know our cause is right." Complacency often accompanies success, but the super-successful power brokers never stop chasing their dream until it is complete. Marshall persevered despite all adversity. Despite the numerous roadblocks he encountered he never gave up his fight and went to his grave driven by the need to see equality prevail through the criminal justice system.

Vision

When Marshall was appointed to the Supreme Court, *Newsweek* magazine gave credence to his intuitive powers, saying, "He always looked at the big picture. He never wanted to win a battle if it would lose him the war." The magazine's analysis was right on target, as Marshall relied heavily on his "gut" and "right-brain" intuitive sense of what was the right approach to win. He told biographer Rowan, "You know we Negroes have a sixth sense for detecting which white person is for us or against us." Marshall's long-term macrovision gave him an edge over his adversaries and often gave him a special insight into the right course to take on some major issue.

He instinctively knew that he had to have the press on his side in order to get the attention of the masses and to open important doors to equality. His assessment was, "No matter what the judges said in the short term," public sentiment was the most critical element in achieving his objectives. To this end he courted the media even more than the judges, until they finally began writing positive stories on his cause. The *New York Times, Time,* and the *New York Herald Tribune* wrote articles on his litigation. His sense for the importance of the "qualitative approach" in contrast to the Cartesian mentality where man is machine was never more pointed than when he told Rowan, "Everything now has your serial number. I mean, you even got your Social Security number on your driver's license now." Mr. Desegregation understood well that the world is qualitative not quantitative, and true success goes to those who understand the essence of this important concept. Rowan wrote, "He possessed an instinct for the critical fact, the *gut* issue, born of exquisite sense of the practical."

Will to Power

Thurgood Marshall was a pragmatist who was the master of his own will. As a youth he learned to control his strong will, perceptively recognizing that he was the only one in charge of his destiny. Rowan wrote, "He could be just as prim, proper, and scholarly as needed . . . or as rambunctious, irreverent, outrageous, as needed." He was a man who could alter his behavior to fit the situation. His style emanated from within, as with all powerful people. This superman "had nerves of steel" according to Rowan. He just didn't care who he embarrassed or who had to coerce to win an argument or important case. Internalized energy was his strength and the power that catapulted him to the very pinnacle of American criminal justice.

Summary

On Marshall's death in 1993 *People* wrote an article eulogizing his impact on America, saying, "With the law as his weapon, Thurgood Marshall was determined to change the world—and he did." At his appointment to the Supreme Court *Newsweek* gave him the ultimate tribute when they wrote, "In three decades he has probably done more to transform the life of his people as any Negro alive today, including Nobel laureate Martin Luther King." Georgetown professor of constitutional law Thomas Kratenmaker wrote, "When I think of great American lawyers, I think of Thurgood Marshall, Abe Lincoln, and Daniel Webster. . . . He is certainly the most important lawyer of the twentieth century." Senator Orin Hatch paid him the ultimate compliment, saying, "I don't know of anyone on the bench who has had a more profound effect on American jurisprudence."

After a few drinks Marshall loved to expound on his rejection by the University of Maryland Law School and would pontificate: "The sonafabitches turned away the guy who finished number one at a better law school—Howard." It was the University of Maryland's snub that inspired Marshall and he never stopped attempting to rectify the damage done by an abominable system that insisted on white supremacy at any cost. Marshall's need for revenge against the white bastions of power transformed him from a kid chasing a law degree into a caped crusader fighting ignorance and bigotry in every community of the nation he so dearly loved.

It is a strange coincidence that the two Baltimore subjects in this book were buried within five days of each other in January 1993. Marshall and Reginald Lewis, two extraordinary sons of Baltimore, were laid to rest the same week. A throng of eighteen thousand mourners attended Marshall's funeral and they viewed this man appropriately lying in state atop a bier in the Supreme Court where he had made such an impact. This was the same setting in which Abraham Lincoln had lain in state just over a century earlier. Fittingly, a sympathetic mourner placed a copy of the Supreme Court's *Brown* v. *Board of Education* decision on his coffin as a tribute to Mr. Desegregation. At the bottom of the first page of this history-making opinion, the anonymous admirer wrote, "You shall always be remembered."

Thurgood Marshall was a towering figure in the evolution of the American way of life and influenced the U.S. judicial system as much as any man who ever lived. He was a man who never stood on procedure or decorum but demanded freedom and justice for all people. He spent his life ensuring that this dream became a reality.

THURGOOD MARSHALL
Dionysian Temperament (SP)
First Black Solicitor General and Supreme Court Justice
born July 2, 1908, Baltimore, Maryland; died January 24, 1993, Bethesda, Maryland

Dominant trait: A confident extrovert who was persuasive, brash, irreverent, and a cynical fighter for equality

Motto: "I love peace, but I adore a riot"; "Equal justice under the law"

Religion: Episcopalian and 33rd degree Mason

Philosophy: "To wipe out all the trappings of white supremacy"; "Ours is a government of men, not laws"

Politics: Democratic, but backed whatever party supported the causes of black equality

Nickname: "Mr. Civil Rights"; "Mulatto Lawyer"; "The Great Dissenter"; "Mr. Desegregation"; friends:"Turkey"

Creation/innovation: Ended Jim Crow separate-but-equal school segregation with 1954 *Brown v. Board of Education*

Successes: Won 29 of 32 cases argued before Supreme Court; 1st black Supreme Court Justice, 1967

Vices/hobbies: Poker, pinochle, cigarettes, bourbon; a teenage hellion: wine, women, and gambling

Romantic liaisons: Engaged 9 times in college; married Vivean Burey in 1929; Two sons by 2nd wife, Cecelia Suyat

Self-description: "Head Nigger in Charge"; "I intend to wear life as a very loose garment and never worry about nothin' "

Birth order: 2nd son of William Canfield Marshall and Norma Williams, both mulattoes of 3rd-generation Africans

Parental influence: "My father turned me into a lawyer without ever telling me what he wanted me to be"

Early transience: Baltimore to Harlem as child for 5 years then back to Baltimore

Parents' occupations: Father Pullman car waiter; mother elementary school teacher; both grandparents shop owners

Role models: Paul Robeson, W. E. B. Du Bois, Dr. Charles Houston, William Hastie

Hero mentors: W. E. B. Du Bois book; Howard law professor Charles Houston, his mentor/boss at NAACP

Formal education: Bachelor's in premed/humanities Lincoln, 1925; law degree, Howard University, 1933, cum laude

Life crises: Early rejection due to racism; Columbia, Tennessee, KKK mob tried to lynch him, 1946

Metamorphoses: Denied entrance to Maryland Law School—"never forgot," "vowed to get even"

Charismatic: Mesmerizing leader and speaker; Milton: "I would lay down my life for that man"

Competitive: "I enjoy a fight"; "His combative spirit is evident in the tone and strength of his dissents"

Hypomanic: Rowan: "maddening activity," "Driven to write the most convincing brief possible"

Independent rebel: "Irreverent" and "irascible" violator of norms

Indomitable "will": "Thurgood had nerves of steel. He just didn't give a damn how many whites he embarrassed"

Intuitive vision: *Newsweek*: "He always looked at the big picture. He never wanted to win a battle if it would lose him the war"; used his "sixth sense" to anticipate enemies; "Exquisite sense of the practical"

Drive: Rowan: "A driven man"

Risk-taker: Race-crazed lynch mobs never deterred him; "Democracy cannot flourish amid fear"

Self-confident: "Overly optimistic" in face of direst adversity; "Humility not one of his strengths"

Tenacious: "I'll be dead before I'll be satisfied"; "I have to keep believing, because I know our cause is right"

Workaholic: A megalomaniac on a mission; first job at age 7 and didn't retire until age 83

Honors: Harvard law professor Randall Kennedy: "No one has done as much for racial equality"

16

Colin L. Powell—Strong Work Ethic

First Black Chairman of the Joint Chiefs of Staff

"Perpetual optimism is a force multiplier."

Colin Powell is a self-made man who rose to become the chairman of the Joint Chiefs of Staff through little else but hard work, tenacity, and a passion for family values and the structure he found in the military. His success is a clear demonstration of the fundamental tenets of the American dream, where finding a comfortable niche and working diligently to achieve will lead to the very top, with wealth and fame not far behind. Powell is the personification of the rags-to-riches story where the boy dreams of heroism while living in a ghetto and wakes up forty years later to find that he is the living reality of that childhood dream.

Powell represents all that is good about a system that allows an inner-city youth to rise from nothing to something while overcoming great adversity. What allowed a kid to avoid the drugs, crime, and degradation of Fort Apache in the South Bronx, to not only rise to the top of his chosen profession, but be pursued by the nation's power brokers to take residence at 1600 Pennsylvania Avenue? It was character, tenacity, and hard work coupled with some luck and great timing. Powell's luck was being born of parents who instilled values and threatened his life if he ever touched drugs. It also helped being black at a time when there were few blacks in the military with Powell's extreme dedication and character. Powell was also fortunate to have reached the pinnacle of power in concert with a Gulf War that needed his brand of nationalism and strength of character and conviction.

Much of Powell's success was due to being a workaholic who attacked whatever task he was given with the greatest vigor and without complaint. He was able to do this because he had "followed his bliss," in the words of Joseph Campbell, and saw his job as fun not work. Powell biographer Howard Means wrote in 1991, "Powell is a rare combination—a soldier with a diplomat's touch and the training of a White House insider." Powell's willpower and timing were never better than when he led Operation Desert Storm in the 1991 war against Iraq's Saddam Hussein. When the ambitious dictator invaded Kuwait and defied the West to stop him, there were few men in the world better suited to do so than Colin Powell. Powell organized the joint NATO forces behind him and clearly demonstrated to Hussein and the world that he could not and would not be intimidated. Powell's passionate words to a national television audience gave the world a taste of that strength and resolve when he said with conviction and little emotion of Hussein's army, "We are going to cut it off and then we are going to kill it." That demonstration of confidence and determination instilled confidence in the American people and forever shaped Powell's image as a strong and resourceful leader. Means would later give further credence to Powell's power, saying, "If [military commander Norman] Schwarzkopf hadn't had Powell, he would have self-destructed."

According to *USA Today,* in the fall of 1995, "Powell attained the highest success rating of any other person in the United States." This occurred during his book tour and had been enhanced by the rumors of his presidential candidacy. It is nothing short of amazing that this uncomplicated and simple man could rise to such heights through little else but hard work, strong character, and tenacity. Powell's appeal were those old-fashioned qualities more famous in another age. His "character," " integrity," and "family values" were the key attractions for the media and what the polls found to be his strongest traits. Powell is surely not erudite, nor driven like most ambitious politicians, nor a visionary in the innovative sense. But he was honest, forthright, and worked very hard to succeed at whatever task he is given. It appears that there is a place at the top for people espousing such qualities.

Powell's power came from traditional values like objectivity and introspection, which played a major role in his success. He was always quite honest with himself about his own strengths and weaknesses. He never deluded himself into believing he was brilliant like Henry Kissinger, a charismatic leader like John F. Kennedy, or a military genius like Douglas MacArthur. Because of this candid outlook Powell very adroitly avoided his weaknesses and pursued his strengths, both personally and professionally. Few people have that insight or self-control. He selected the military as the professional venue in which to satisfy his own personal needs for structure and esprit de corps, since he was steeped in the need for family. The military provided a practical and establishment-driven professional life where "tradition," "control," "structure," and a "sense of duty" are required. These traits are good fits to his Epithemean (sensing-judging) personality.

"Colinmania" became rampant during the fall of 1995, when Powell spent two months promoting his book, *My American Journey.* During this tour Powell's popularity skyrocketed, until he decided not to pursue the presidential nomination because of its impact on his family life and due to the "depression" suffered by his wife. This rock of stability had become the political frontrunner for a three-month period without even throwing his hat into the ring. His power was based on integrity. *Time* characterized him as "The Desert Storm Demigod." Syndicated columnist Bill Maxwell referred to him as a "compelling human being" who espouses "sensible centrism." *Vanity Fair* labeled him "The Great Black Hope," while *Newsweek* called him "the most respected—and most intriguing—man in public life," going on to say, "Right now his personal-approval level is somewhere close to Mother Teresa." *USA Today* labeled Powell a "national icon," while Eisenhower biographer Stephen Ambrose said, "Colin Powell is a combination of king and prime minister and father figure." The constant notoriety led Barbara Walters to name Powell the number-one most fascinating person for 1995 on her December television special.

Colin rejected those kingmakers who wanted him to run. The *Wall Street Journal* said, "There is no question that General Powell's exemplary character could have positive cultural consequences . . . he would be far more effective than any white politician at delivering a message of traditional values to the black community." The retired general was the clear frontrunner in all the polls, which predicted he would easily defeat incumbent Bill Clinton, whose integrity paled in comparison to Powell's. Powell finally went on national television on November 8, 1995, to reject a candidacy for president to the chagrin of many supporters. He said, "My family is uppermost in my mind. . . . The sacrifice and changes are too great and the presidential race demands a passion and commitment that I do not now have."

Innovative Contribution

Powell's greatest innovation was inextricably wrapped up in his ability to rise from Fort Apache to the highest position in the military, which is virtually never given to a nonwhite or non–West Point graduate. After reaching the pinnacle of power in the Pentagon, this son of poor immigrants from the South Bronx became the favorite son of the conservative Republican party. In virtually every poll Powell was the favorite of white voters, with black voters far behind—an unbelievable accomplishment in twentieth-century America. In a *U.S. News and World Report* poll Powell was a favorite son of 73 percent of whites compared to only 57 percent of blacks. A *Time* poll had him attracting 47 percent of the vote if he teamed with Senator Robert Dole. That would have won the election for him. Powell had accomplished the impossible. He had broken through the imaginary black ceiling of race and became a potential candidate viewed as colorless by the white majority. His "rags-to-repute" image had removed race as an issue, causing the *USA Today* to say, "General Colin Powell is a marketer's dream: He has nearly 100 percent brand recognition and no history of product defects." This immensely popular man had transcended race and political muckraking. He was one of the few men in history who appeared capable of lighting the fires of the politicians just on the potential of running as a presidential candidate. That in itself qualifies him as a creative genius.

Personal History

Our superhero was born Colin Luther Powell on April 5, 1937, in Harlem, the first son and second child of Jamaican immigrants Luther and Maud McKoy Powell. His bloodlines were mixed, which is not unusual for Jamaican families. Both parents had African, English, Irish, Scottish, and Arawak Indian ancestry. Powell's father even had a trace of Jewish blood, which may have contributed to Colin's early interest in the Yiddish language. Powell's sister, Marilyn, was six years his senior and not a major influence in his life due to the age difference, since she was away at college by the time he was eleven.

The Powell family moved twice by the time Colin was four. He was nurtured during those early years by his maternal grandmother, Gram Alice McKoy, since both his father and mother worked long hours in the garment industry. Powell's father was the major influence in his life. He wrote, "Pop was an eternal optimist" and "my mother was the perennial worrier." Powell latched on to his father's optimism and used it to his benefit in rising through the military, where negative comments are verboten. Powell wrote in his memoirs, "Pop was the most formative figure in my life," adding, "I had been shaped, not by preaching, but by example, by moral osmosis." The family moved again when Powell was six and this time it was into the Hunts Point area of the South Bronx. As Powell relates in his memoirs, "We kept our doors and windows locked . . . burglaries were common. Drug use was on the rise. Street fights and knifings occurred" and it was not impossible for Powell to stumble over a dead body in the hallway.

Powell grew up without the negativity of racism or discrimination. Where he lived everyone was ethnic and it is only where the majority are the same that those who are different find themselves discriminated against. Powell's street was known as "Banana Kelly" and there he learned to play stickball with friends of many nationalities and colors. All his street friends spoke different languages or had a unique dialect, and English was often the second language heard on the streets. Yiddish, Italian, Greek, and Spanish were heard more often than English. Powell wrote, "Everybody was a Jew, an Italian, a Pole, a Greek, a Puerto Rican," or black. Life revolved around the streets, where stickball, stoopball, punchball, sluggo, and hot beans and butter dominated his early life.

MILITARY HERO WORSHIP

Powell's early memories revolve around the screaming newspaper headlines, news reports, and movie marquees eulogizing the fierce World War II battles and their heroes. Pearl Harbor, Corrigidor, Bataan, the Battle of Britain, and the Battle of the Bulge were imprinted in his unconscious as heroic battles won by courageous men. These early memories were affixed to his psyche along with feelings of strength and power, where military heroism was the ultimate determinant of victory. This young boy with few amenities or outside interests became caught up in dreams of war heroes where the battles were romantic adventures with Powell as protagonist.

Colin Kelly was a hero during those early days of the war. His death had an enormous psychological impact on Powell. Kelly was killed in an air battle with the Japanese battleship *Haruna* two days after Pearl Harbor and won the Distinguished Service Cross for bravery. Colin Kelly's name was in every headline at the time and was on the lips of all the kids in Powell's neighborhood. Soon they were all pronouncing Powell's name "Coh-lin" instead of "Cah-lin." From that point on he became known as "Coh-lin" in memory of the dead war hero. Powell ended up memorializing that name by dedicating his life to the military. Powell's cousin Vic came home from the war one day with a captured Nazi helmet and gave it to young Colin as a present. Powell was so mesmerized by this war memento that he carried it with him for the next forty years through every stop in his vagabond life in the military.

Jamaican parents are famous for their insistence on the very best education for their children and the Powells were no exception. They saw education as the door-opener for achievement in life and always insisted that their son attend the finest schools, which was not necessarily in the best interest of Powell, who was at best a very average student. Powell's parents got him accepted in the prestigious Stuyvesant High School, but the guidance counselor, who had tested Powell, "advised against it" because he would be set up to fail in competing with the more talented students. He attended Morris High instead and immediately went to work after school, as was the Jamaican style. The Jamaicans had a reputation in New York as "black Jews" for their dedicated work ethic, and Powell fell into that same style with a job at a local toy store named Sicker's. The store was in a highly ethnic neighborhood. He worked there for six years and there he learned Jewish mannerisms and a smattering of Yiddish. During summers he worked at the local Pepsi bottling plant mopping floors and then working his way up to deputy shift leader. At Pepsi Powell said he learned a very valuable lesson: "All work is honorable." Powell figured if you mop the floors better than anyone you will get ahead. He did and learned a perfectionism of the mundane. He would remember this lesson for the rest of his life and it became the foundation for much of his success. Powell graduated a semester early from Morris High; he was only sixteen when he received his diploma. It was diligence, not brilliance, that made him successful—a consistent saga in Powell's life.

ROTC

The future general's parents once again interceded in his education by demanding he study engineering in college. They insisted he enroll in the City College of New York (CCNY) in an engineering major that proved beyond his intellectual capability. Powell soon learned this when a professor asked him to envision a cone in space being intersected by a plane. The introspective youth knew immediately he was over his head and changed majors since such intuitive vision was beyond his comprehension. He switched to geology in his second semester rather than flunk engineering. Uninspired as a sophomore, he stumbled on the Reserve Officer Training Corps (ROTC) program and became inspired—it venerated everything he personally held dear. This became an instant love affair of the mind and body. Powell signed on with the elite Pershing Rifles and started making a mark for himself as a motivated student of military strategy and structure. He wrote, "It was the discipline, the structure, the camaraderie, the sense of belonging . . . what I craved." The military was simply an extension of family and both endorsed those values he holds dear, both professionally and personally.

Powell graduated from CCNY on June 10, 1955, with a degree in geology. Far more important than gaining his sheepskin was the fact that he had been accepted as a full-time army officer and was assigned to duty in Fort Benning, Georgia. Powell signed up for a three-year hitch, which his family saw as a temporary reprieve before he got a real job. But Powell was a military man emotionally, physically, and mentally and would never leave the structure he revered. In the army, he learned to follow orders. One of the first tests of his temerity came during basic training, when he was forced to take the "Slide for Life"—sliding at high speed down a rope suspended high above a body of water. He said of the experience in his autobiography, "It was one of the most frightening experiences of my life." During this same period he was told he would jump out of an airplane, another military order he faithfully followed but with grave reservations. After basic training the young lieutenant was assigned to a two-year tour in Germany, after which he was sent to Fort Devens in Boston.

During his Boston appointment Powell met Alma Johnson on a blind date. Alma was a southern aristocratic black woman from a sophisticated Alabama family that initially felt Powell was an unfit mate for their talented daughter. Johnson had graduated from Fisk University at age nineteen and was in Boston studying audiology at Emerson College. On their first date Powell was captivated by her intellect and physical presence and pursued her vigorously. Just two months later he received his orders to go to Vietnam. Johnson informed him she was not about to wait around for a vagabond army man who might or might not make it back from that hellhole. She told him she wouldn't ever write him, which prompted an immediate proposal from a man in love. The couple were married in Birmingham, Alabama, in August 1962, just days before Powell would leave for his first tour in Vietnam.

Professional History

Powell arrived in Saigon an inexperienced and naive junior officer on Christmas Day 1962. He made captain while in Vietnam and found the truth of jungle warfare, saying, "We had been out for nearly two months. I had seen men hurt. I had seen men die. But I had yet to see the enemy." Powell's son Michael was born while he was in the jungle, and it was some time before he learned of the birth. In

Vietnam Powell was first labeled a soldier who "walks on water" or "fast burner," someone officers predict is a "comer." Powell was wounded on a patrol near the border of Laos when he stepped into a booby trap. He was awarded the Purple Heart. One of Powell's superiors described him at that time as "gung ho," adding, "he stuck out in that group. He came across as a number one, a very intelligent individual, very articulate. He had charisma. . . . He'd say 'Trust me' . . . and I believed him."

In August 1964 Powell was transferred back to Fort Benning, where he spent the next three and a half years. It was there that he was selected from an elite group of young officers to attend Fort Leavenworth's Command and General Staff College, which proved to be the first of many timely and brilliant career moves that set him apart from the pack. Powell's timing was exquisite, as the Civil Rights Act had been just passed by Congress and Powell had all the earmarks of one who deserved to be helped. He deserved everything he got, but timing was sure on his side.

Powell graduated second out of 1,244 army officers attending staff college in June 1968, which earmarked him for a second tour in Vietnam. He arrived in Vietnam on July 27, 1968, and caught the attention of General Charles Gettys, who had been summarily impressed with his graduating second at Leavenworth and requested Powell as his "plans officer." This decision, according to Powell, "enormously influenced my career." Once again hard work to get into Leavenworth and even more hard work in the school program paid huge dividends, a fact not lost on this highly reflective and goal-oriented individual.

His burgeoning career was once again enhanced when he, Jack Treadwell, and General Gettys were involved in a helicopter crash in the jungles of Vietnam. Powell, bleeding and with a broken ankle, managed to drag Gettys out of the burning copter and then returned to pull Treadwell from the wreckage. This won Powell the admiration of his superiors and he was awarded the Soldiers Medal and Legion of Merit for his valor. Two months later Powell was able to persuade the brass to allow him to enroll in the military's MBA program at George Washington University. Powell was accepted and began work on the degree in September 1969. He graduated with honors in 1971, made lieutenant colonel, and was assigned to an office job in the Pentagon. This proved to be another move with providential timing. The visibility and valuable connections with the "right people" helped him land an appointment as a White House fellow. Once again his race didn't hurt him, but to Powell's credit he was always able to excel in each assignment, which kept him on a fast track.

The feminist movement was at its peak when Powell became a White House fellow. He and the other fellows were asked to meet with Gloria Steinem, the feminist leader of the time, who had just launched *Ms.* magazine, in order to better understand and deal with female issues. A key to Powell's ultimate success and candid introspection of his own talents can be seen in this experience. He later confided with a fellow military officer, who described Powell's insight into who he should do battle with and who he should submissively acknowledge as a superior.

According to the officer, "Powell kept his mouth shut because she was smarter than he was. He could tell if he opened his mouth, he was going to get eaten up." Powell said of the experience, "I knew when I was overmatched," which is a tribute to his self-knowledge and long survival in a bureaucratic world.

Now a colonel, Powell returned to the world of soldiering when he was transferred to Korea in 1973. After two years in that assignment he returned to attend the War College in Washington, where he was trained in the finer nuances of warfare. He graduated in 1976. He was then assigned to Fort Campbell, Kentucky, as a brigadier general in charge of the Second Brigade of the 101st Airborne Division. In 1979 he moved to the Department of Energy, where he made valuable political contacts, Caspar Weinberger and Frank Carlucci. These men had first come in contact with Powell when he was a White House fellow and then again at the Pentagon. Howard Means wrote in 1991 that Carlucci was "Powell's godfather of godfathers."

By 1981 Powell had decided to get back into the field and left Washington to become assistant division commander of the Fourth Infantry Division in Fort Carson, Colorado. Carlucci said, "We put him in Fort Carson to get him another star." At age forty-six Powell was promoted to major general and appointed special assistant to Weinberger, who was then secretary of defense. Working in this high-level political environment Powell became familiar with the machinations of Washington and political warfare. He was able to clearly demonstrate his strengths of leadership and to "chair a meeting." Assistant Secretary of State Elliott Abrams said Powell has "the ability to end a meeting with some kind of decision. . . . That's a rare talent and a real talent." Powell was gaining a reputation as a man of action with a bent for administration—abilities seldom found in the same person.

CHAIRMAN

During the mid-eighties Powell once again opted for a field assignment in Germany but within less than a year was asked personally by President Reagan to return to the United States as his national security advisor. The general had been in his new post for but three months when in February 1988 General Manuel Noriega toppled the Panamanian government. Powell was not involved in this political skirmish but would be later. After eighteen months as national security advisor President Bush appointed Powell to the highest position any military man could ever aspire. He was made the chairman of the Joint Chiefs of Staff on October 1, 1989, leaping over many more experienced men and many West Point graduates who normally gain this lofty position as head of all military operations. This was the most prestigious and sought-after post and it was held by a poor ethnic boy who had survived the rigors of the inner city and made it to the very pinnacle of power. Hard work and tenacity had paid off.

Some would say Powell's race was a major factor in his quick rise in the military during a period of overt affirmative action. Not so, say most of his superiors and peers in the military. The army was a perfect fit for Powell's personality characteristics. He loved order and structure and the military brought out his greatest strengths. He demanded a familial organization within which to operate and where else is the camaraderie more family-like than in the military? Powell excelled and probably moved a little faster than his contemporaries because of his race. He admitted in his memoirs, "I had an intuitive sense that this was a career that was beginning to open up for blacks." Retired Colonel Ben Willis says, "Powell would have made it to the top if he was purple."

In mid-December 1989 the bottom fell out of the Panamanian problem, with Noriega threatening to close the Panama Canal. This proved to be Powell's first military crisis and he handled it with the decisive precision for which he has now become famous. With the methodical meticulousness of a surgeon, General Powell implemented Operation Just Cause, which saw eighteen hundred soldiers drop out of the sky into Panama on December 20. Within four days Noriega had been captured and the Panamanian problem had been resolved with Noriega safely ensconced in a Miami prison. There were twenty-three American deaths and 324 wounded, while Noriega's forces had suffered 500 casualties.

OPERATION DESERT STORM

Just one year later a far more critical crisis would surface. The Persian Gulf War broke out on January 17, 1991, due to the aggression of Saddam Hussein, who had laid siege to Kuwait. This war would make Colin Powell not only a hero, but one of America's most visible men. During this conflagration Powell was highly sensitive to the philosophical nature of the American people and offered his insight to the *Washingtonian*: "You simply have to have buried deep in your psyche the fact that the American people are not that patient. They like rather quick results whenever possible." Faithfully following this understanding, Powell gave the people what they wanted—a fast and decisive resolution to the conflict.

Along with his many advisors and in concert with field leader General Norman Schwarzkopf, Powell masterminded Operation Desert Storm, which was employed to stop Saddam Hussein in his tracks and clearly demonstrate to him the power and might that he would face if he was to persist. The allied military operation expelled the Iraqi army from Kuwait in just forty-five days. The Allies lost 244 troops, including 146 Americans. *Newsweek* estimated that 100,000 Iraqis were killed in the conflict. Powell's memorable words on CNN reverberate in the minds of most people years later. He told the American people, "Our strategy for going after this army is very, very simple. First we are going to cut it off, and then we are going to kill it." Four years later Powell was taking blame for not killing it, since the invasion of Baghdad never took place and Saddam Hussein remains in power. Powell's critics say he should have destroyed Hussein at whatever the cost, but Powell maintains the cost of lives was not worth one man's hide. Powell continues to maintain that the mission was complete and further killing unwarranted. Biographer Means reports that, "Powell was probably the best thing that ever happened to Schwarzkopf . . . there never was a moment of doubt who was in charge. . . . If Schwarzkopf hadn't had Powell, he would have self-destructed."

Colin Powell had made it to the very top and proved his mettle by excelling in every crisis with which he was confronted. He retired from his position as chairman of the Joint Chiefs of Staff on September 30, 1993, in order to spend more time with his family and to begin writing his memoirs. Powell's book, *My American Journey,* which was finally released in September 1995, and his $6 million advance for it, went a long way toward repaying him for the years of work for his country. Powell became the darling of the speaking circuit in 1995 and his pay was the princely sum of $60,000 per speech, which enabled him to earn $1 million from lecturing alone. Not bad for an inner-city youth born of immigrants who was just an average student. Powell told a Chicago audience at the 1995 National Booksellers Convention, "Only in America can someone as ordinary as I achieve such great heights."

What Makes Powell Tick?

Colin Powell became rich and famous by taking a different tack than the others in this book. His personality type is the exact opposite of the others studied and is unique in the sixty-odd creative geniuses studied in my other books. Powell is not the intuitive visionary—Promethean temperament—so common among the other subjects. He is detail-oriented to a fault and prefers dealing in facts, not possibilities. New York Times News Service writer Michiko Kakutani describes Powell as a "problem solver" and "not a visionary," characterizing him as a "hardworking bureaucrat."

On the Myers-Briggs scale of personality preferences Powell is classified a sensor-judger, an extrovert and "thinker" who prefers the "rational" to the "emotional" in decision making. Such a profile makes Powell a classic "traditionalist" or "guardian," which is the perfect fit for a bureaucratic position. In psychological jargon, Powell is classified an "Epithemean temperament." Such personality types are appropriately known as guardians who value duty. They are highly dependable, on time, and value order and structure. Powell is also highly industrious and practical, which would make him a superb leader in any structured organization. By contrast, these qualities would make him a terrible entrepreneur or architect. Powell was introspective enough to see this and carefully avoided jobs requiring great vision.

MYTHOLOGICAL HERO MENTORS

As mentioned earlier Powell was inspired by military heroes as a young boy. He grew up with a mythical image of military men as "saviors" and "supermen." Being associated with World War II flying hero Colin Kelly was just the start. The archetypes of Jung and Campbell all wore uniforms in the unconscious of Colin

Powell. In Joseph Campbell's words, "powerful myths were the manifestations of his character—the spontaneous productions of his psyche." Powell gives some evidence of this in his memoirs when he says, "I still have vivid memories of the war years." Further confirmation comes from his statement, "*Back to Bataan, Thirty Seconds Over Tokyo, Guadalcanal Diary,* and *The Bridges at Toko-Ri . . .* were burned into my consciousness during my most impressionable years."

Real-life role models and mentors also bombarded Powell's early life. When he became infatuated with the Pershing Rifles in college, he befriended an overachiever who became his hero/mentor in the ROTC. Ronald Brooks was his cadet leader, his first mentor, and idol. Powell said of Brooks, "I had found a model and a mentor. I set out to remake myself in the Ronnie Brooks mold." He mimicked Brooks's every move. It worked, as he succeeded Brooks as the cadet colonel for the entire CCNY regiment. The old "hero imprints" were further reinforced during this period when Powell won a competitive drill award and was named "Best Cadet." He carried the award—a commemorative desk set—with him for the next thirty-five years, and it sat prominently displayed on his desk at the Pentagon when he was the chairman of the Joint Chiefs of Staff.

INSECURITY BREEDS GREATNESS

Colin Powell was quite candid in his memoirs about his fear of going down the "Slide for Life" at Fort Benning, which he called "the most frightening experience of my life." He also had the same aversion for jumping out of airplanes. Like other great people, his insecurities motivated him to overcome them. He never denied his fears but performed with valor in spite of them. An example is his making it all the way to Airborne Ranger and Pathfinder—top of the line in the military—despite his fears in those fields of action. Powell said, "In the Army you face fear and death with blind obedience" and followed his own advice. He told *Newsweek* (September 11, 1995), "War is a deadly game" and not a pleasant experience, but, just like most great leaders, when the Gulf War became a reality he went all out to win it with little or no compassion. His fears became the driving force for his achievements.

LIFE CRISES AND TRAUMAS

Powell experienced two traumas during his formative years that transformed his character and molded him into a better person. When he was fifteen Father Weeden of St. Margaret's Episcopal Church selected him as part of a group of deserving youngsters to attend a church camp near Peekskill, New York. During the session Powell fell into bad company who coerced him to sneak out and buy beer. They were caught with their stash by Father Weeden, who confronted the whole group with the evidence and asked for the culprits to confess to their indiscretion. No one stepped forward and the whole group was about to be punished. After some hesitation Powell gathered up the courage and stepped forward admitting, "I did it."

He was sent home from camp and expected the worst from his parents, who were irate. He was in the middle of being castigated by his mortified parents when Father Weeden called to tell them of the incident. He advised them of the transgression and added, "But your Colin stood up and took responsibility. And his example spurred the other boys to admit their guilt." Recounting the experience some forty years later, Powell wrote, "My parents beamed. From juvenile delinquent, I had been catapulted to hero. Something from that boyhood experience, the rewards of honesty, hit home and stayed." Another "success imprint" had been recorded on his subconscious mind. A negative experience had turned into a positive, character-molding event.

A second such occurrence was the ROTC character-saving experience Powell encountered as a sophomore in 1954. He was quite certain by this time that he was not cut out for an academic life. The City College of New York was at this time a hotbed of liberalism and the ROTC was just years from being phased out as persona non grata in academia. Such organizations were detested by the intelligentsia as programs of the hated warmongering establishment and the curse of academic freedom. Powell was not deterred by this sentiment, since the ROTC represented everything he held dear in life. Being accepted proved to be the turning point in his life. "All I ever looked forward to was ROTC," said Powell of the time, recalling, "I was much affected by forms and symbols." He said, "The drill hall became the center of my universe," and, "I had found something that I did well. I could lead." The metamorphosis also enhanced Powell's schooling, since he pulled straight A's in ROTC, which allowed him to graduate with a C average.

Charisma

"Colin," says retired Colonel James Garvey, "stuck out. He came across as, number one, a very intelligent individual, very articulate. He had a charisma about him. When I say charisma, he didn't have to speak loud for people to listen. He's a very handsome guy—his stature alone attracts attention." Henry Lowder, an officer in Vietnam, was one of those who labeled Powell a "water walker." After Powell pulled General Gettys out of a burning helicopter, Lowder commented on his image, saying, "You didn't know how far he was going to go, but he was clearly an outstanding officer." Biographer Means spoke of his charismatic appeal, writing, "When Colin walks into a room all the eyes turn towards him." One aspect of such presence is the stride, the confidence, the ability to make people believe you *know* the way. Colin is a highly believable individual which attracts others to him and this is why he rose so fast in the military.

Competitiveness

This assertive leader was highly competitive and combative when it came to winning military challenges. He would spend whatever energy it took to win. He learned this in the ROTC when he was named the best cadet after working very hard to be the very best. That "success imprint" remained with him and he worked diligently to win any contest. While serving in Korea under "Gunfighter" Emerson, Powell's competitive nature was revealed. Emerson insisted his troops become the physical elite of the army and implemented a competition that included a four-mile run before breakfast each morning plus a calisthenics program that was physically draining. Emerson gave Powell an order to lead the First Battalion of the Thirty-second Infantry to victory over the hated Armored Division. Powell recalled that event in his memoirs and said, "I was determined. . . . I was not going to let a bunch of soldiers who rode around all day in mobile pillboxes beat infantrymen in a foot race." He said in typical Powell fashion, "I went flat out," and handily won the competition.

When asked by Howard Means about racism, Powell admitted that he resorted to aggressiveness throughout his military career. He let it be known to those who tried to discriminate or who attempted to use racism as a weapon: "I'm going to beat you. I don't care what you think of me; I don't care what you think about my background or whether I'm black, I'm white, I'm yellow. You're going to have to beat me, as they say in basketball, in my face." James Bostic, a White House fellow who served with Powell, said, "I think he's a competitor . . . intensely involved . . . he's competitive in wanting to do it very well, in fact better than it's ever been done before." Further testimony to a highly competitive spirit is Powell's love of the game racquetball, which is arguably the most personally combative sport next to boxing. He played racquetball daily and while in Germany had a court built in his residence to play with anyone who could keep up with him. Colin Powell used a highly competitive nature to overcome adversity and it proved important to his ultimate success in life.

Confidence

Two "rules for success" that adorn Powell's Washington office are indicative of his positive attitude and optimistic persona: "It can be done!" and "Perpetual optimism is a force multiplier."

Powell's biographers have described him as a man with "much self-confidence" that contributed greatly to his success. His military training was "can do" and "don't ask, just execute," which instilled in him the positive belief system so necessary to superachievement. Much of Powell's enormous success is due to a strong self-esteem. He acquired this optimistic persona from parents who decided early to arm him with a strong self-image in order to survive life in Fort Apache and to cope with the racism he would face as an adult. It worked.

Hypomania

Colin Powell could be the model for an obsessive work ethic. In his memoirs he places work as the second most valuable lesson in life, just after multiculturalism. In other words, after the race issue, Powell views work as the most critical trait for high achievement. He certainly followed his own advice in this area and worked diligently to master whatever he undertook both personally or professionally. His number-three lesson for success is "family" and not surprisingly it was in the home where he acquired his work ethic. Powell's Jamaican parents instilled in him the values of hard work. They truly believed that people could outwork their problems.

Powell started work while in middle school, first in a Jewish retail toy store in the Bronx and later during summer vacation at a nearby Pepsi plant. At Pepsi he was soon recognized as a "worker" even though he mopped the floors. Powell learned a great lesson in this menial position. He said, "I decided to be the best mop wielder there ever was" and was soon promoted to bottle loader. By the next summer Powell had been promoted again to deputy foreman. A "success imprint" was left with him that work does lead to just rewards, just as his parents had said.

Further testimony to Powell's strong work ethic was his graduating a semester early in high school despite having little academic aptitude. Powell was in a mad dash to finish whatever he started and never allowed others to deter him from his goals. Hard work was endemic to his family. Charles Duncan, one of his former associates from the Department of Energy, wrote, "He has stamina—he simply outworks the opposition. . . . There's no limitation to hours or energy." Twelve-hour workdays were average for Powell—an unheard-of trait in the military or any other bureaucracy.

Independence

Powell was not a rebel but he was always his own man. He played within the rules but was nonetheless strong-willed. Howard Means said of him, "He's not a hawk; he's not a dove; he's an owl." While on a national book promotion tour during the fall of 1995, Powell was castigated by the Republican right for his prochoice views. This took some guts, since he was considering running for the nomination of the Republican party, whose platform had been prolife for some years. Powell eloquently defended his stance, saying, "Abortion is a matter between a woman, her family and her conscience and God"—a position diametrically opposed to the right-wing Republican party platform in 1996. Powell took a similar unpopular stance on the affirmative action controversy in 1995 after a referendum was placed on the California ballot against all instances of giving favor to minorities. Powell had been helped dramatically by affirmative action in the military and felt strongly about totally eliminating it: "We're all going to be equal, and if anybody needs a little bit more help to be equal, we're going to give him that help." Colin Powell spent his life making sure that he didn't rock the bureaucratic boat, but has shown that he has the guts to support his own personal values and beliefs on highly flammable issues.

Passion and Drive

On September 19, 1995, General Powell told Larry King on CNN, "You do the very best at any level and success will follow." That is the drive and determination of a man who was passionately driven to be the best soldier he could be. He was a man ardently driven to overcome his own personal frailties and deficiencies. He knew being black was a hurdle he would have to overcome and one of the weapons he chose to use to do battle was an obsession with details and military knowledge. Powell was driven to know more about his chosen field than any other soldier. It was this resolve that led him to the very top.

Perfectionist

Powell is a demanding taskmaster, an admirable trait for anyone in the military, where allegiance, execution, and excellence are expected of everyone. A system that punishes a person for a spot on a belt buckle is the right profession for an "adaptor"-type personality (see Kirton's styles in chapter 5). Adaptors are those managers who prefer "doing things excellently" as opposed to "doing things differently." Powell is the personification of this type personality. He demands excellence from himself and his people and anything less is unacceptable. These qualities were first instilled in him at home, then in college at ROTC, followed by basic training, where no fault was acceptable. One button not polished, one spot on the uniform, or one hair out of place results in severe punishment. In the military anything less than excellence can prove disastrous to person, unit, or country, especially in combat. Years of dedication to this principle indoctrinated Powell to such a degree that he became a perfectionist.

Temerity

Risk and the *military* are synonymous terms. A life in the military is not for meek or gentle souls and Powell fit in quite well, since he had grown up in an area where guns and violence were not the exception but the rule. The only time he was less than thrilled with risk was during Ranger training, when he was forced to parachute. He said, "If I never have to parachute again, that will be fine with me, yet there was never any doubt in my mind that I would do what had to be done." Powell waxed philosophical about the experience, saying, "Physical danger that people face and master together bonds them in some mystical way. And conquering one's deepest fears is exhilarating." Powell practiced what he preached when it came to exhilaration. One of his favorite pastimes while stationed in Germany was revving up his BMW to 105 mph on the autobahn, where there are no speed limits. Fast cars and speed tend to be a key element in the lives of powerful people and Colin Powell is no exception. They tend to view risk as an obstacle to overcome and use it as a self-motivator. Two tours in Vietnam were evidence of Powell's ability to face risk and defeat it.

Tenacity

Captain Wilford Morse wrote a personnel review on Powell in 1959 in which he said, "Powell is tenacious, firm yet polished." That assessment proved accurate and it left a lasting impression on Powell. He worked diligently to improve himself and was persistent in the pursuit of all his goals. Evidence of this important trait lies in Powell's enrolling in every military higher education school made available to him, even though he was not considered an academic and was actually less qualified intellectually than most of those in attendance at these schools of higher learning. After joining the army, Powell attended the U.S. Army Command and General Staff College at Fort Leavenworth and George Washington University in the military's MBA program, became a White House fellow, and capped everything off with the National War College. Not bad for a mediocre student who admittedly was not an academic. Such perseverance led him through all the key chairs to the top one as chairman of the Joint Chiefs of Staff.

Vision

Powell is not what psychologists would label an intuitive person, but he had what General Grant Green labeled "a shit detector." He added that Powell was "absolutely incredible" at getting to the point and able to "cut through the crap to get to a decision." Handling the details in a intuitive way is one of Powell's strengths even though he is the first to admit that he is not a visionary in the classic definition of the word. Seeing the big picture is critical to the strategic planning functions demanded of all leaders and innovators. It is also imperative for top military leaders, who must envision the whole field of operations in order to implement the best tactical plans of attack. Strategic thinking is one of Powell's strengths and it was clearly demonstrated in the actions in both Panama and Kuwait. One of those rules to live by that are prominently displayed on his desk is "Have a vision." Powell strives to abide by that rule but recognizes that in most things he is more interested in the details and facts than the possibilities and opportunities.

Will to Power

Biographer Howard Means gave insight into Powell's inner persona when he wrote, "Powell understands in his genes the power game." This was Means's way of saying that Powell was capable of controlling his own destiny despite the machinations of Washington politicians and other bureaucratic bumpkins. If nothing else, Powell is a strong-willed human being who is driven by some internal energy that is not easily extinguished. He has demonstrated an ability to repress his ego when it is apparent that others are more knowledgeable. He is introspective enough to understand that operating on moxie alone is a recipe for failure and would rather rely on inner feelings when not conversant with all the facts. He says, "Never let your ego get so close to your position that when your position goes under, your ego goes with it." This is the statement of a man in control of his own destiny.

Summary

Colin Powell is an extremely well-grounded human being who has a grasp of his strengths and weaknesses to such an extent that he was willing to sacrifice immediate honors for future opportunities. This philosophy was behind his refusal to run for the presidency as either a Republican or an independent at a time when all the polls had him beating President Bill Clinton. How many people could have suppressed their ego enough to have made that decision? Not many!

Powell is a "guardian type" personality who values family and structure over power and image. He is a stabilizer, consolidator, and traditionalist who has risen to great power and success by abiding by the fundamental tenets of hard work and high integrity. These are hardly the traits found in politicians and Powell apparently saw this dichotomy when he made his earthshaking decision in the fall of 1995 to not pursue the presidency.

Colin Powell was dealt a very mediocre hand of cards when it came to socioeconomic status, money, and IQ. He played his hand as well as it could be played and consequently ended up with a full house that led him to the penthouse of power in the military. Few men of any race have ever achieved so much with so little, and virtually no blacks, especially those electing to work in a bureaucratic organization. Such organizations are almost always dominated by white power brokers, leaving little opportunity for black men out of the South Bronx.

COLIN L. POWELL
Epithemean Temperament (SJ)
Military Leader and Chairman, Joint Chiefs of Staff
born April 5, 1937, New York City, New York

Dominant trait: Extroverted pragmatist with strong work ethic, high integrity, and "guardian" temperament

Motto: "If you want to make it you have to be better than white people. You have to be the best"

Religion: Episcopalian

Politics: Democratic ideology; registered Republican (voted for Reagan and Bush)

Philosophy: "It ain't as bad as you think"; "Get mad, then get over it"; "Perpetual optimism is a force multiplier"

Nickname: "Black Jew"; "Water Walker"; "Cap the Knife" (Pentagonese for control mentality)

Successes: 1st black to be chairman, Joint Chiefs of Staff, 1989

Vices/hobbies: Racquetball; running; repairing old Volvos

Romantic liaisons: Married Alma Vivian Johnson; father of Michael, Linda, Annemarie

Self-description: "Only in America can someone as *ordinary* as I achieve great heights"

Birth order: Only male; older sister, Marilyn; of Jamaican immigrant parents Luther and Maud Powell

Parental influence: Raised in Fort Apache, S. Bronx; grandmother's influence until 10; surrounded by diversity

Early transience: Born in Harlem and moved three times, settling in S. Bronx; a latchkey environment: working parents

Parents' occupations: Father shipping department manager, active in church; mother garment district seamstress

Role models: General Charles Gettys; Frank Carlucci; Caspar Weinberger; Fred Malek; John Whickam

Hero mentors: WW II hero Capt. Colin Kelly; "My first memories were of war"; George Marshall; Dwight Eisenhower

Formal education: Morris High School, 1954; CCNY, BS in geology, 1958; National War College, 1970; George Washington U., MBA, 1971; White House fellow, 1972–73

Life crises: Fort Apache in South Bronx was survival training for life; Vietnam booby trap: punji stick through foot

Metamorphoses: ROTC saved him from mediocre college career

Charismatic: "When he walks into a room all the eyes turn towards him"; "He is believable"

Competitive: "He's a competitor . . . wanting to do it better than it's ever been done before"

Hypomanic: Graduated high school a semester early; "There's no limitation to his hours or energy"

Independent rebel: "He's not a hawk; not a dove; he's an owl, in between"

Indomitable "will": "Powell understands in his genes the power game"

Intuitive vision: "Have a vision"—one of fundamental rules for operating in life

Drive: A Puritan ethic with passionate energy and need for excellence

Perfectionist: "Colin Powell is rare combination of soldier with diplomatic touch and the training of White House insider"

Risk-taker: Fearless in combat; "You're going to have to beat me" mentality

Self-confident: "He had so much self-confidence in early 20s—destined to succeed despite odds"

Tenacious: Told "Keep your ass clean for 20 years and we'll make you a Lt. Colonel. . . . It was my goal"

Workaholic: "I decided to be the best"; associate: "He has stamina, he simply outworks the opposition"

Honors: Legion of Merit Vietnam; Purple Heart; Bronze Star; Soldiers Medal for Valor

17

Paul Robeson—Rebel

All-American, Shakespearean Actor, Social Rights Activist

"I've never accepted any inferior role because of my race or color. And by God, I never will."

Paul Robeson was a Renaissance man who was ahead of his time. He began exploring his African heritage thirty years before Alex Haley's *Roots* and was preaching "black is beautiful" long before it was in vogue in the sixties. His pathmaking included playing Shakespearean parts onstage and in the movies at a time when black parts were limited to Amos and Andy stereotypes. This strong-willed man refused to bow to the pressures of economics, prejudice, or political correctness, spreading the gospel of freedom for everyone in total defiance of the establishment. Robeson was an erudite spokesman for black equality—a true Promethean spirit who sought truth, equality, and freedom wherever he could find it.

Robeson had the temerity to defy the masses and saw through the despicable Joe McCarthy when he was being touted as the country's right-wing savior. Robeson was a man of total principle and unparalleled integrity who could not be duped by political crackpots like McCarthy or be intimidated by congressmen. He was brighter than most and saw through their political machinations like few others could. When he encountered McCarthy's brand of anticommunism, he wrote in a paper titled "The Big Truth": "Any kind of general war will destroy the peoples of the world." He called the political dogma of the right-wingers the "Big Lie," which he described as the "destruction of constitutional rights of free speech, press, and religion."

In his 1958 book, *Here I Stand,* he attacked America's involvement in foreign conflagrations, and was once again way ahead of his time when he wrote, "Shall Negro sharecroppers from Mississippi be sent to shoot down brown-skinned peasants in Vietnam?"

This pathbreaking man excelled in so many areas it is frightening to think what he might have achieved in a nonprejudiced society. Robeson was simply awesome in everything he attempted and is arguably the greatest black talent who ever graced this planet. In college he excelled as a baseball catcher, basketball center, javelin thrower, and the first All-American football player in the history of Rutgers University. He graduated as a Phi Beta Kappa in prelaw while finding time to work his way through school. In fact, Robeson worked his way through high school, college, and law school, while winning every debate entered on the debating team and starring in school plays. He played pro football to subsidize his education at Columbia Law School, where he also graduated with honors. After such an esteemed educational career, Robeson was offered a fellowship to Harvard,which he turned down in order to pursue his dream of becoming a New York City lawyer. When overt discrimination denied Robeson his dream of a law profession, he became frustrated and succumbed to offers to go on the Broadway stage for Eugene O'Neill.

Robeson then demonstrated his true genius to the world by becoming America's most renowned Shakespearean actor. Incredibly, he was able to accomplish this unbelievable feat without ever taking a singing or acting lesson. What a remarkable human being! Robeson physically, mentally, and emotionally dwarfed the mere mortals who came in contact with him. He was a man among boys and many whites were clearly unable to accept such a gigantic intellect as their superior. Further testimony to Robeson's eminence is when he decided to play Othello in Russia and so taught himself to speak and write Russian. When he performed in China he did the same with the Chinese language. Then again with Japanese and Arabic. This demonstration of erudition continued on and on until Robeson was able to perform Othello in twenty-seven different languages. Words cannot describe the multifaceted talents of this oft misunderstood and maligned Renaissance man.

There was little that Robeson was incapable of conquering. Writer Ossie Davis said of him, "Paul was a man and a half, and we have no category, even now, to hold the size of him." One example of his herculean powers was demonstrated to a sophisticated audience at the refined Swarthmore College in 1955. Robeson decided to illustrate the importance of the arts as a catalyst for international peace and sang sixteen songs in English, German, Yiddish, Chinese, Russian, and one dialect of African of which he knew many. The audience was unable to always understand him but was blown away by this remarkable display of intellectual precocity. Experiencing such a spectacle of grandiosity by a black man was a mesmerizing experience for those in the audience.

No one who ever saw Paul Robeson perform forgot him. Jerome Kern dedicated the classic song "Ol Man River" to Robeson when he wrote it for the Broadway hit *Show Boat*. Every time Robeson sang it for the next thirty years audiences were reduced to tears. When he first performed *Emperor Jones,* the New York *World Telegram* critic wrote that the audience was delirious with "passionate response" to him as actor due to his great "emotional strength." John Johnson, the founder of *Ebony* magazine, met Robeson at a cocktail party in the fifties and wrote of the experience: "I don't think I've ever seen a more impressive man." Elizabeth Shepley Sergeant wrote in the *New Republic,* "He is not merely an actor and a singer of Negro spirituals but a symbol. A sort of sublimation of what the Negro may be in the Golden Age." C. L. R. James, author of *The Black Jacobins,* wrote of Robeson, "I've met a lot of people in my parts of the world and he remains . . . the most distinguished and remarkable of them all." Jim Brown, a man not known for giving credit to anyone let alone a fellow football star, told a 1995 College Football Hall of Fame audience where he and Robeson were being inducted, "Robeson was the most talented individual who ever lived." Announcers at the event referred to him as a "veritable superman."

Shortly before his death *Ebony* in 1972 selected Robeson as one of the ten most important black men in history. Earlier he had been awarded the Spingarn Medal for high achievement by the NAACP. Both Germany and Russia bestowed "Peace" awards on him. Unfortunately his political activism and refusal to capitulate to political correctness kept Robeson from being acknowledged for his great contributions to the stage and entertainment. His one wish was granted to him forty-eight years late when the College Football Hall of Fame elected him to their elite group of athletes in 1995. Surprisingly, there was still political pressure to keep him out of this esteemed group due to his reputation as a rebellious political activist. Posterity will show that Paul Robeson was a giant among mere mortals and a black who never achieved his rightful place in society. One reason for his lack of recognition is that he so intimidated the white males of his era that many of them went to great lengths to pull him down to their level.

Innovative Contribution

Robeson spent the better part of his productive life in the passionate pursuit of equality and freedom instead of in creative endeavors. He used his enormous talents in a valiant but doomed effort to change societal views on race while sacrificing valuable time in productive contributions to entertainment. He would say, "My song is my weapon" in a metaphorical expression of his approach to effecting social change. He used that weapon throughout his turbulent life to break new ground and to defy American Jim Crow laws. Robeson's great talent allowed him to open doors that were not open to lesser beings and once they were open he attempted to level the playing field for himself and his people.

This Renaissance man was way ahead of his time. His work as a social activist came close to destroying him but it ultimately led to him becoming a superb role model for many emerging young black entertainers during the thirties, forties, and fifties. He was frustrated by the lack of support from his own people and once proclaimed, "Sometimes I think I am the only Negro living who would not prefer to be white." Despite this, Robeson personally helped many of his people break through the proverbial black ceiling and his trailblazing efforts allowed them to reach the top. Lena Horne, Harry Belafonte, and Sidney Poitier were but a few of the stars who looked up to Paul Robeson as the one who paved the way for their acceptance into mainline America. Poitier knew the magnitude of Robeson's influence on blacks in the entertainment industry. He once told a reporter, "Before him no black man or woman had been portrayed in American movies as anything but a racist stereotype." When a London reporter asked Harry Belafonte how he could have humor in his act while Robeson was always so serious, Belafonte responded, "It is because of the price Mr. Robeson paid that I can afford to have a sense of humor."

This superstar willingly sacrificed money and fame to support his ethical values. He gave up making motion pictures at the very height of his professional career in order to send Hollywood a message about their insistence on portraying blacks in stereotypical roles. He told the movie executives, "I thought I could do something for the Negro race in films. . . . The industry is not prepared to permit me to portray the lie or express the living interests, hopes, and aspirations of the struggling people from whom I come."

TRAILBLAZING SOCIAL ACTIVIST

Paul Robeson believed art was beyond the scope of racial injustice and that it truly should stand on its own. He wrote in his memoirs, "Art is one form against which such barriers do not stand." It must be remembered that in this era Robeson was unable to eat in a decent restaurant from 10th Street to 125th Street in Manhattan. When Robeson's high school senior class went to Washington, D.C., he was forced to remain home because he was unable to stay in the same hotel in our nation's capital as his white classmates. One of the more ludicrous instances of racial inequality occurred in Manhattan. Robeson happened to be the honored guest at a prominent Manhattan restaurant when the management relegated him and his party to the basement for the award ceremony. During the festivities Robeson began singing; ironically, everyone in the restaurant moved to the basement to hear him sing, leaving the upstairs empty.

Biographer Philip Foner wrote, "Paul Robeson was a forerunner of what is now called detente . . . and also a forerunner in the campaign to educate the American people concerning the truth about Africa." Robeson was one of the early exponents of "Black Power," which he expressed in *Here I Stand*: "I am going to think and feel as an African—not as a white man." He was emotionally and intellectually dedicated to the preservation of black culture, saying, "Africa has a distinctive culture which is ancient but not barbarous. . . . They produced great talkers, orators and where writing was unknown, folktales. . . . I am the same. . . . I hear my way through the world. In my music, my plays, my films, I want to carry always this central idea; to be African." Robeson was convinced that his African heritage was instrumental in his almost psychic sense for sound, music, language, and social interaction. He was one of the first to say that blacks had special gifts but his vision extended far beyond just racial issues. He was one of the few people who saw through Hitler's bombastic rhetoric and predicted his demise in Russia when such a prediction was totally unfounded based on the facts. Robeson proved near-clairvoyant in his vociferous opposition to the Spanish Civil War, the Korean War, and the Vietnam War. Pacifism was one of the ideologies that Robeson supported, but when it came to race he was willing to use force. Robeson constantly harangued his people to use the power of numbers to exact some equality. They were deaf to his philosophical rebukes. Robeson attempted to lead them to the promised land but they were not interested in being led. One of his 1950 diatribes was based on using the power of numbers:

> If 15 million Negroes say, and mean it, no more anti-Semitism, then there shall be no more anti-Semitism! If 15 million Negroes . . . demand an end to the persecution of the foreign-born, then the persecution of the foreign-born will end! If 15 million Negroes say there shall be no more Jim Crow in America, then there will be no more Jim Crow! If 15 million Negroes are for peace, then there will be peace!

Paul Robeson's intuitive insight was lost on a subjugated people who were not as willing to fight for equality as he was. Robeson was certainly a precursor of Martin Luther King, Jr., Malcolm X, and Stokely Carmichael for change in racial matters, but proved just as prescient in the political arena. Biographer Lloyd Brown said in 1971, "Just imagine how much loss of life, how much devastation would have been averted had his countrymen heeded Robeson then, at the very first sign of U.S. intervention in Vietnam." Political writer Mary Sparling McAuliffe also confirms his great insight, saying, "Paul Robeson was in many ways the most important authentic voice of America in the era of the Cold War."

Personal History

On April 9, 1898, Paul Robeson became the eighth child born to William Drew Robeson, an ex-slave-turned-minister, and Anna Bustill, a schoolteacher. He was born in Princeton, New Jersey, where his father was the pastor of the St. Thomas African Methodist Episcopal Zion Church. As with all slaves, Robeson's father was named with his slaveholder's surname, in this case, Roberson, but when he escaped at age fifteen he dropped the "r" and began calling himself Robeson. William Drew Robeson was a self-made man in all that term connotes. He fled north and joined the Union Army in 1861 and then worked his way through Lincoln University with the aim of becoming a Protestant minister. After many births Anna was in ill health and almost blind when Robeson was born. Consequently, young Paul was essentially reared as an only child since his older brothers and sisters had left home to pursue their education or find work. This contributed to much doting by siblings, aunts, uncles, neighbors, and his father.

Robeson's father was of African ancestry and his mother was of African, English, and Indian ancestry. The two had met at Lincoln and were both in their mid-forties when their most famous child was born. Robeson's father was fired from his ministry at the Princeton Presbyterian Church when Paul was one. The family barely survived this tragedy because the ever-resilient William would never accept defeat. He was a survivor and became a super role model for his youngest son. He bought a wagon and started hauling ashes for the affluent Princeton families. A terrible crisis befell the family when Robeson's nearly blind mother didn't see some hot coals and they ignited her dress, burning her to death in a horrific accident in their home. Robeson was five at the time of this tragedy and he and his despondent father became inseparable soulmates.

Robeson's father, siblings, and relatives felt terrible about the child's plight of having no mother and doted on him to an extreme. After his mother's tragedy Robeson's many relatives nurtured and "mothered" him. His father was very indulgent but told him, "Stand firm son, stand firm to your principles!" After his father's admonition he said, "You bet I will Pop, as long as there's a breath in my body." Robeson recalled the time in his memoirs, "The people claimed to see something special about me. They felt I was fated for great things . . . and because of that belief they added an extra measure. You got something boy, something deep down inside, that will take you to the top." Robeson would later give credence to his early training and grooming in Princeton, saying, "My career as an artist in America and abroad, my participation in public life, the views which I hold today—all have their roots in the early years."

When Robeson was nine his father was still attempting to better himself and took a job in a grocery in nearby Westfield, New Jersey. The two inseparable survivors moved to that city and lived above the storeroom. The boy attended a racially mixed grammar school and his father, who was now sixty-two, soon became the town's preacher. Three years later, when Paul was twelve, his father once again returned to his avocation as a minister, and the two moved to Somerville, New Jersey. In Somerville Robeson began to impress people, graduating from middle school at the head of his class. He then enrolled at Somerville High School, where he would begin to get the attention of classmates and teachers as a special person. Transience and crisis had made their mark, molding a self-sufficient, driven, resilient, creative genius.

Robeson was encouraged to recite poetry, study the classics, and read the Bible as a very young child. His father read Virgil and Homer with him to illustrate the importance of the classics in his intellectual and cultural development. Robeson visited his father's church and participated in many of the activities with much older people. His father constantly taught him far beyond his years and instilled in him the traits that would someday make him great. Robeson's father encouraged him to "aim high" in school. When Robeson once brought home four As and one B on his report card, his father admonished him for not being the best. The boy was shocked, and told his father, "Nobody gets 100 percent." His father responded, "Well, what's 100 percent for?" The comment instilled in Robeson a passion for perfection that would haunt him until his grave. From that day on his father would ask him, "Are you at 100 percent?" and his overachieving son, never wanting to disappoint his soulmate, made sure the answer was "Yes!" Robeson never lost his father's obsession with perfection and lived the balance of his life making sure he never finished any task at 90 percent.

Robeson's nurturing father was the greatest influence on his life and achievement. Their closeness contributed to a bond that drove Robeson throughout his life. He wrote in his autobiography *Here I Stand,* "I loved my Pop like no one in the world. I adored him, looked up to him, would have given my life for him in a flash." It was his father who instilled in him the "bedrock integrity" that so defined his character. Integrity was his father's "ruling passion," which was closely followed by a demand for setting "high goals" in life. His father instilled in him the moral that "money or other personal gratification" were only by-products of living an exemplary life. What should really be eulogized was the "highest development of one's own potential."

Robeson learned independence through early transience, where he learned to cope with the unknown, tragedy, where he learned to deal with mortality, and discrimination, where he decided being different wasn't necessarily bad. Even the excessive doting and parental indulgence Robeson received as a child contributed to his iconoclasm, since it instilled in him an egoism that culminated in arrogance and defiance. Robeson confirmed this when he wrote in his memoirs, "Somewhere in my childhood these feelings [of rebellion] were planted." An example of this grooming occurred in Princeton when he was quite young. His older brother was knocked down on the sidewalk by a bigoted white. Embarrassed that his young brother had witnessed such degrading behavior, his brother told him, "Listen kid, don't you ever take it, as long as you live." Robeson responded, "I never will!" and went on to write in his autobiography, "That explains my life. I'm looking for freedom, full freedom, not an inferior brand." At Somerville High School, Robeson began to be noticed as someone special, which infuriated the racist principal named Ackerman. The principal hated Robeson's superiority and success and did everything he could to beat him down. Robeson would later write, "He hated me for my color," and, "The better I did the worse his scorn." Despite such opposition Robeson excelled in the glee club, baseball, track, football, and debating, and many white teachers took him under their wing and encouraged him to overachieve.

In 1915 Robeson graduated from Somerville High School with honors but Principal Ackerman prevented him from knowing about a competition for a Rutgers University scholarship. Once he found out about the competition he was distraught, but decided to go for it anyway even though he would have to cram four years of testing into one exam instead of the four that the other students had taken, since they were apprised of the scholarship months earlier. Robeson worked day and night, studying with a passion born of discrimination. He wanted to score well more than anything in the world. His diligent work paid off when he got the highest score on the exam, to the chagrin of the bigoted principal. This would not be the last time Robeson would disappoint a racist through the sheer power of his will and overachieving beyond the realm of the norm.

Robeson entered Rutgers on a scholastic grant-in-aid in the fall of 1915 and when he decided to try out for the football team was met by a storm of protest by the white players, who were opposed to him being the first black to ever compete for Rutgers. No black had ever played on any Rutgers sports team and the football players plotted together to make sure that Robeson was not the first. They decided to put him in the hospital so he could not play, and even if he recovered they fully expected him to quit rather than deal with such rejection. During his first day of football practice he was attacked ferociously on every play from scrimmage. Every player hit him hoping for a mortal injury, attempting to break some bone or draw blood. After that first disastrous day of practice Robeson had incurred a broken nose and a dislocated shoulder, and he was bleeding from numerous lacerations. Robeson spent days in the infirmary. He was broken emotionally and physically and had decided to quit when his father and brother visited him. They told him, "Robesons don't quit."

After this superman was released from the doctor's care he returned immediately to the football field intent on retribution. His description of that day was pure Horatio Alger. According to the *New York Times,* Robeson said, "On the first play from scrimmage I made a tackle and was on the ground . . . when a boy came over and stepped hard on my hand. He meant to break the bones. The bones held, but his cleats took every single one of the fingernails off my right hand. That's when I knew rage!" Paul suddenly decided to "kill" a player named Kelly who was the instigator of this organized mayhem. Robeson was just a freshman but he was a mountain of a man for the time. He was 6 foot 3 inches and 230 pounds of pure muscle and vented his rage on those in his path. This man, who was normally a gentle giant, became an enraged, unstoppable bull. On the next play he saw the whole team running at him and with his adrenaline out of control he extended an enormous arm and dropped the first three men in his path. Robeson reached the ball carrier, Kelly, and picked him up high over his head. He was about to destroy him by driving his head into the ground but was stopped by a coach afraid for the life of his star player. "I got Kelly in my two hands and I got him up over my head. . . . I was going to smash him so hard to the ground that I would break him right into two, and I could have done it. But just then the coach yelled the first things came to his mind, 'Robey, you're on the varsity!' " Robeson would ultimately become friends with the white players, since he had earned their respect as a man who was not to be dealt with lightly, and that this was a man they wanted on their team.

Robeson was named to the Walter Camp All-American football team in both his junior and senior years. This was the first such honor for any Rutgers athlete, white or black. Most sportswriters of the time acknowledged Robeson as the greatest defensive end to have ever played the game. Shockingly, the overachieving Robeson also found time to win a total of fifteen letters at Rutgers in basketball, baseball, football, and track. While excelling in athletics Robeson was still able to achieve the 100 percent that his father always demanded by being inducted into the Phi Beta Kappa Society for scholastic achievement while earning admission into Rutgers's exclusive Cap and Skull Honor Society. If this wasn't enough, Robeson was a member of the Debating Club and he won every oratory event he entered. The school paper, *Class Prophecy,* got caught up in the potential of this superstar and predicted he would become the governor of New Jersey. The epitome of respect for Paul Robeson came when the Rutgers school paper summarized his outstanding college career with this succinct appraisal of his future: "He has dimmed the fame of Booker T. Washington and is the leader of the colored race in America." On graduation in 1919 Robeson was asked to address the class and selected the topic that would set the stage for his later political activism. His topic was "The New Idealism." As always, he was mesmerizing.

Robeson decided to study law and was accepted at both Harvard and Columbia law schools. He chose Columbia because it was in New York City and he could be near his home and live in Harlem, which was the black Mecca. Robeson's beloved father had died while he was at Rutgers and the emerging star was now on his own and forced to support his law school education. He worked for a short time as the assistant football coach at Lincoln College, sang at the Harlem Cotton Club, waited tables at the exclusive Newport Country Club, and played professional football for the Akron Indians and Milwaukee Badgers. During one summer Robeson was paid handsomely to act in a London play named *Voodoo*. He spent the summer in England, which began his long love affair with Europe.

While at Columbia Robeson married a student he met there by the name of Eslanda Cardozo Goode. Essie, as he called her, was a chemistry graduate student. They were a brilliant and attractive couple who married in August 1921. Essie encouraged Robeson to pursue an acting and singing career although he had little interest in entertainment as a profession. Robeson admitted that his work in London was purely a lark to visit Europe and be paid handsomely for his efforts. Essie proved instrumental in his show business career and finally convinced him to play the role of Jim in *Taboo,* which ran briefly on Broadway in 1922. Robeson was adamant about finishing his law degree and practicing law as a profession, but capitulated to his wife's desire that he go onstage even if it was temporary. Robeson was a perfectionist at everything he ever attempted and was unsure of himself in a career in which he had no training. He wrote of his early attitude to singing and acting, "I had never had a lesson in singing in my life! . . . I knew nothing of either art." Robeson was psychologically committed to a life of law and professionalism, but it was not ready for him.

Professional History

Robeson graduated from Columbia in 1923 with such esteemed work that Harvard offered him a fellowship. By this time he was fed up with schooling and decided to begin his chosen profession as a New York City lawyer. He passed the New York bar exam and set out to find work in the city. He was rejected by firm after firm, mostly due to race. After months of being rejected he finally decided that no law firm was prepared to employ a giant Negro. He was ready to give in to his wife's constant badgering to pursue a career in show business when he finally found a part-time position writing briefs at a prestigious law firm. Then a white secretary adamantly refused to take dictation from Robeson, which destroyed his confidence and instilled in him a bitterness that would fester over the years. Robeson wrote of the experience, "I put on my hat, walked out, and never returned."

Eugene O'Neill had heard Robeson sing at the Cotton Club and was so impressed he decided that Robeson was the only person to play the key role in his new play *Emperor Jones.* O'Neill pursued Robeson until he finally accepted the paltry sum of $75 a week for the role. Robeson was still depressed over his rejection in law and accepted to placate his wife. Suddenly Robeson found himself immersed in a show business career, one he had not sought or valued. Rejection, however, followed him to the theater. The New York media and theater-going public were outraged that a black man would be appearing onstage as the star. The media hype caused such a sensation that a lynch-mob undercurrent was present when Robeson was finally about to make his Broadway debut in *Emperor Jones.* Robeson created a sensation in New York with his portrayal of the Caribbean dictator Jones. He received rave reviews by the critics who described his performance with such adjectives as "brilliant" and "magnificent."

When O'Neill signed Robeson to play opposite the white actress Mary Blair in *All God's Chillun Got Wings,* the head of the Georgia Ku Klux Klan telegrammed O'Neill threatening his son's life if the play opened as scheduled. O'Neill returned the telegram with a note scribbled at the bottom—"Go fuck yourself." He and Robeson proceeded despite the furor and the overachieving Robeson was committed to giving his traditional 100 percent effort to the new venture. The controversy reached its zenith when the New York press fueled the debate and the president of the Prevention of Crime wrote "It was a damnable thing" for Paul to play opposite a white woman. The press predicted a riot on opening night. O'Neill, fearing a race riot, took precautions by hiring an underworld thug to protect his stars. He retained a steelworker named Slim Nugent to protect Paul. Nugent was placed outside Paul's dressing room. When Robeson showed up, Nugent took one look at this gentle giant and said with all seriousness: "Is that the big ape I'm supposed to guard? Well, listen, if anything starts, just get out of his way and pile up the ones he knocks down." The predicted riot never materialized and Robeson went on to rave reviews for his performance.

Robeson's first Broadway role commenced in 1924 and lasted for a year. He was now on a roll and in great demand. He made his Hollywood debut in a silent movie titled *Body and Soul* in 1925 and met Lawrence Brown, who convinced him to go on tour singing gospel and spirituals. Singing proved to be Robeson's first love, making use of his innate talent for expressing his soul in black gospel music and spirituals. Brown began a concert tour that would last for some years. Robeson's renown was growing geometrically. He accepted a contract to open in London playing once again O'Neill's *Emperor Jones.* During this period Robeson cut his first records of spirituals and gospel music on the Victor label.

Robeson's wife had become his business manager and agent. She toured Europe with him, which began a long love affair with the continent for these two intellectual blacks who despised the Jim Crow laws so prevalent in America. In Europe they never thought about where they could stay or eat. They were able to freely go where they wished and enjoy their friends without fear of retribution or racial prejudice. Hotels in Europe had no policies of racial discrimination and this alone made the Robesons feel like they were free. No longer did they worry over being embarrassed or rejected as they would certainly be in almost any city in America. Essie became pregnant while they were in Europe and returned to New York to give birth to their only son, Paul Jr., who was born on November 2, 1927. Essie had always been sickly and she nearly died in childbirth. Robeson stayed by her side, but the childbirth began the end of their loving relationship.

Jerome Kern had heard Robeson sing Negro spirituals and was so impressed he had written the classic *Show Boat* in 1928 with him in mind. Robeson played the part of Joe and sang the song "Ol' Man River," for which he would become internationally famous. His performance led to sensational reviews and he was acclaimed by the media, who wrote of him in glowing terms like "glorious," "superb," and "marvelous." The *New Yorker* magazine referred to him as the "promise of his race" and nicknamed him "King of Harlem." In 1929 Robeson made his debut at Carnegie Hall to a packed house, resulting in more rave reviews. Robeson soon found himself elevated to superstar status in both America and Europe, straddling many diverse entertainment media.

Robeson succumbed to the problems of many successful people. His adulation was pervasive and since most of his fans were white, not black, he found himself working and partying with more whites than blacks. White women were unable to resist his magnetic allure and he was incapable of resisting their romantic entreaties. He became very promiscuous and engaged in numerous notorious affairs with white society women in both America and Europe. Essie chose to ignore his indiscretions but had the temerity to write a biography—*Paul Robeson, Negro*—in 1928 in which she disclosed his flagrant affairs. Robeson was furious with her for writing of his transgressions and in 1930 he filed for divorce, triggering a two-year separation.

During this period Robeson lived and traveled alone and spent much of his time mastering the languages of the various nations he visited. He was intent on singing and performing in the native languages of the country in which he was engaged. He learned to sing spirituals and perform *Othello* in the various cultures in which he found himself and over the next fifteen years he would record over three hundred songs in two dozen languages. He also began research into his African heritage, which would evolve into a lifelong study of African languages and cultures. By 1934 Robeson had mastered twenty-seven languages including Russian, Arabic, Chinese, and numerous African dialects.

Robeson's greatest critical acclaim would come from playing the lead role in *Othello,* which he first introduced at London's Savoy Theatre in May 1930. After the first performance he was forced to take twenty curtain calls and the theater critics wrote that he "was born to play Othello." In May 1933 he made a movie version of *Emperor Jones*. He was now spending the majority of his time in Europe. When he returned to America he made the movie *Sanders and the River* and without his knowledge the producers added scenes praising British imperialism and depicting blacks in stereotypical roles. This infuriated Robeson and led him ever closer to a total break with Hollywood and American political ideology.

Robeson started spending more and more time in London and now began an earnest study of dialectical materialism by Karl Marx. His interminable search for truth and knowledge had few limitations. He was becoming more and more erudite, to the chagrin of his adversaries—white supremacists and master race advocates were endorsing the fascist dictatorships of Hitler and Mussolini to counter the mounting threat of communism. True to his Promethean temperament Robeson pursued the opposing ideological beliefs of the masses, as did many intellectuals in the mid-thirties.

Robeson turned to the ideology that opposed fascism. He made the first of many trips to Moscow in 1934 to discuss the movie *Black Majesty* (it was never produced). While traveling through Germany he was accosted by storm troopers, which left an indelible impression on him, pushing him ever further to the left. Once in Moscow Robeson was profoundly impressed that Russian children were educated against racism, a stark contrast to the master race theories of Nazism and the Jim Crow laws of America. Robeson was so impressed with the desegregated society in Russia that he sent his nine-year-old son, Paul Jr., there to be educated starting in 1936 "to insure he was not exposed to the prejudices of the Western world."

Robeson finally returned to America to make the movie *Show Boat* and once again was met by rave reviews for his rendition of the song "Ol' Man River." He followed that movie with another titled *King Solomon's Mines*. During this period he started becoming more vocal about America's imperialism. His first overt act of social activism took place in June 1937 at a benefit in London supporting the Basque refugees and backing Republican Spain in its civil war. During this conference he took sides, proclaiming, "The artist must elect to fight for freedom or slavery. I have made my choice." He would write some years later, "I went to Spain in 1938 and that was a major turning point in my life. There I saw . . . the upper class—the landed gentry, the bankers and industrialists—who had unleashed the fascist beast against their own people." This trip marked the beginning of many years of controversy in which Robeson backed many unpopular causes. These ethical stances on highly controversial social issues would cost him the most productive years of his life. He paid a terrible price for his political philosophy, which he did not totally comprehend until years later. In the 1950s he told the House Un-American Activities Committee, "I have sacrificed literally hundreds of thousands, if not millions, of dollars for what I believe in."

The American debut of *Othello* with Robeson in the lead role opened at the Schubert Theater in New York on October 19, 1943, to great critical acclaim. The critics said Robeson gave the most realistic and passionate portrayal of the tragic Moor that had ever been witnessed by an American audience. Its run of 296 performances exceeded that of any Shakespearean drama on Broadway. A coast-to-coast tour resulted and Robeson was hailed as "magnificent" by critics in the South, Midwest, and West who were fortunate enough to witness this great Shakespearean actor. During the thirties and forties Robeson played the role of protagonist in a total of thirteen movies and twenty Broadway musicals. His charismatic presence, magnificent baritone, and electrifying energy were enough to carry any play or movie. Every time he played the role of Joe in *Show Boat* and sang "Ol Man River" it virtually stopped the show. In the words of one critic, "He caused a mild riot when he finished singing. The show stopped. He sang it again. The show stopped. They called him back again and again."

Despite his sullied reputation Robeson was never a Communist and believed passionately in what he called "scientific socialism." He always justified his renegade actions and his avid support of the Soviet Union on the ground that they were for racial freedom. Robeson wrote, "In Soviet Russia, I breathe freely for the first time in my life. . . . When these people look at me they were just happy and interested. There were no double looks, no venom, no superiority." He told the politicians who insisted on labeling him a traitor instead of a freedom fighter, "I am a radical and I am going to stay one until my people get free to walk the earth." Robeson's great mistake was attempting to use logic on an emotional issue. He attempted to appeal intellectually to irrational people. He assumed that logic would prevail, but it was not truth or knowledge that the masses understood in midcentury America but the status quo of a white-supremacist lifestyle. When Robeson used the argument that "my brother graduated from the University of Pennsylvania and is now working as a railway porter," the politicians or bigoted masses were not moved, since that was his brother's problem, not theirs.

Robeson's biggest mistake was attempting to intersperse the professional with the personal. He tried to resort to the use of his "professional strengths" (singing) to achieve "personal goals" (equality). The public misconstrues such attempts and always make you pay economically. In other words, by touting the benefits of communism Robeson so infuriated the nonintellectuals who bought his records or attended his movies that they refused to pay for his performances and in the case of the politicians enacted their own revenge by taking away his freedom to travel. Robeson's personal views virtually destroyed him professionally. What a terrible price he had paid for his naivete in believing he could "use his song as his weapon." What occurred was his weapon was taken from him by his adversaries. What is tragic is that it was his timing that was his enemy. Had he been espousing his philosophies two decades later (like Martin Luther King, Jr., and Malcolm X) he would have been labeled a savior and great social-activist. Unfortunately, all Robeson received for his efforts were loss of income, freedom, and persecution as a Communist sympathizer. Nelson Mandela was closer to being a Communist than Robeson and he will be revered by history.

Paul Robeson preached a far-left ideology when the world was far-right. In twenty years he would have been eulogized as a god and savior but during his era he was spit upon and despised as a traitor. Most people became convinced he was a card-carrying Communist even though he had testified under oath in California that he had never been a member of the Communist party. His greatest problems began after his speech at a 1949 World Peace Conference in Paris, where he urged all American Negroes to stop fighting for a country that suppressed their basic freedoms. This caused such a furor in the United Stated press that Robeson was soon depicted as a Red menace and dangerous ex-patriot. The media dissent was then perpetuated by the era of McCarthy madness, motivating the State Department to take away Robeson's passport. One of the most talented men in history was forced into unemployment and a welfare status. He was unemployable in America and unable to gain employment in any other nation, including Canada, since he had no passport.

In *Here I Stand* Robeson wrote, "The truth is I am not, and never have been involved in any international conspiracy, or any other kind, and do not know anyone who is." Robeson was convinced the "struggle for Negro rights was an inseparable part of the antifascist struggle." His true belief was in "scientific socialism," but his attempt to explain this to Congress and the media fell on deaf ears. The FBI and State Department initiated a plan to destroy Robeson and they succeeded. He hit the very bottom in 1950 and never really recovered. By 1953 he was forced to sell his Connecticut home and move into a Harlem apartment. This terrible crisis occurred during the height of his fabulous career and he never recovered. First, the State Department illegally took away his passport in 1950 and did not return it until 1958, therefore making Robeson destitute at the height of his career. The Supreme Court found the government's action unconstitutional in 1958, but it was too late by then. Robeson was then sixty years old and his spirit was broken. Even the blacks deserted him when Jackie Robinson snubbed him in public, concert halls refused to book him, his records mysteriously disappeared from record stores, his name was removed from books of famous people, and the FBI shadowed his every move. Robeson became a captive in his own country with no way to earn a living.

When Robeson finally regained his passport he bid farewell to America with a performance at Carnegie Hall in 1958, his first in eleven years. That engagement was followed by a West Coast tour and a one-recording session prior to his leaving the United States for good. Robeson would not return for the next five years but was forced to briefly when he suffered a debilitating nervous breakdown while on tour in the Soviet Union. He was never able to fully recover, as he was a broken man. Robeson signed on to do a concert tour in Australia and New Zealand in 1960 and played *Othello* in London and Moscow before returning to the United States to officially retire in December 1963. Robeson had an illustrious career that mesmerized everyone who ever witnessed his passionate performances. It is truly unfortunate that for a decade in the prime of his life Robeson was made impotent by the establishment. War and government intervention had destroyed him. He certainly must bear some of the blame for his naive approach to political activism, but the bureaucratic neanderthals certainly must take most of the blame for destroying the professional life of a creative genius.

What Made Paul Robeson Tick?

Paul Robeson had the classic Promethean temperament with an intuitive-thinking preference for dealing with the world. In other words, he was a visionary with a preference for rational behavior which made him great and helped destroy him. The visionary (intuitive) part of his personality demanded that he pursue the possibilities for his race and the opportunities in entertainment. The rational (thinking) part of his personality demanded an impersonal response to the establishment, which was determined to make him conform. Like most Prometheans, Robeson was a man who analyzed new ideas with logic and ingenuity. He was more interested in the qualitative—freedom and equality—than the quantitative—his personal income and success. He sought knowledge for its own sake and was truly an architect of change and a man ahead of his time.

MYTHOLOGICAL HERO MENTORS

Robeson immersed himself in the classics as a youth and was encouraged to recite poetry and sing black spirituals. He often escaped into the fictional characters in his books and songs. In Princeton Robeson acquired his interest in his African heritage and wrote, "As a boy in Princeton . . . I dreamed and dreamed of the land of my forefathers and mothers. . . . I early learned to orate, to develop my speaking voice. I sang the songs of my people." He wrote, "Folk songs are in fact a poetic expression of a people's innermost nature. This is utterly and completely true for the song culture of my people." In church he escaped into gospel music, which left its mark on a young black man being raised in a white-dominated society.

Insecurity is in each subject. It cannot be eliminated. Reminiscing about his days as a Rutgers football star, Robeson said, "I don't think I ever went into a football game without being nervous and scared to death." Onstage he was extremely self-conscious, which he attributed to awkward size and inexperience. He was always contrite and insecure about his lack of entertainment experience and wrote, "I had never had a lesson in singing in my life. . . . I knew nothing of either art, acting, or singing." Insecurity is present in many of his statements like "I am not free so long as any of my people are enslaved," which kept Robeson in a constant state of "becoming." In other words, he always tried harder because of an innate fear of failure. Despite the towering success he had achieved onstage he lived in mortal fear of being replaced in his parts by a white actor with a charcoaled face. He saw actors like Al Jolson as waiting in the wings to replace him, which drove him to seek perfection.

LIFE CRISES AND TRAUMAS

Robeson's life began with a series of traumas. When he was one year old his father lost his job as minister of the Princeton Presbyterian Church. At age five his mother was burned to death. Then his father had to move to keep food on the table and keep Robeson in school. These events were then magnified by the discrimination he faced on the streets of upper-class Princeton and when Principal Ackerman attempted to keep him from becoming a successful student at Somerville High School. In the end his father's loss of employment instilled in him the "success imprint" of the survival instinct. The Ackerman experience instilled in him the "success imprint" of superiority in the face of those who would deny him equality. This left such an impression on Robeson that he wrote forty years later, "Deep in my heart, from that day on, was a conviction, which none of the Ackermans of America would ever be able to shake. Equality might be denied, but I *knew* I was not inferior."

Charisma

Paul Robeson was a powerful force, both physically and intellectually. He was capable of intimidating the most macho males or eliciting passionate emotions from the most insensitive theater audiences. Robeson could bring audiences to tears. The head of his Rutgers debating class said, "He could make the audience weep." Critic Julian Mayfield wrote of Robeson, "When he laughed he made the room shake." Those people who met him came away spellbound by the awesome presence of this physical and intellectual giant. "When he shakes your hand a transfusion takes place," wrote Hy Kraft, a scriptwriter who had worked with Robeson in the forties.

Competitiveness

Robeson was combative in life, on the stage, and in his relationships. An indication of this is his aphorism, "My song is my weapon." Another indication of his competitiveness occurred while working his way through college as a professional football player. Playing professional football alone is testimony to a competitive nature, but Robeson, as in most things, was exceptional in whatever he pursued. After a game where his Milwaukee team trounced a Chicago team led by Olympic hero Jim Thorpe, the Chicago players decided to foist their revenge on Robeson so that a black could not cherish this victory. They devised a plan to gang up on him and beat him into submission. Sensing possible problems, Robeson's teammates suddenly disappeared, leaving Robeson to defend himself alone. Two fight promoters were in the stands and witnessed the attack by a whole team on one lone combatant. They were so impressed with Robeson's competitive fighting spirit that they offered to train him to fight the legendary Jack Dempsey, the reigning heavyweight boxing champion of the world. Robeson was a competitor who spent his life fighting for his beliefs until it cost him his home, his health, and his profession. He wrote, "I fight for the right of the Negro people and the other oppressed."

Confidence

Robeson wrote that he had gained confidence from standing in front of many people in the pulpit in his father's church at the age of nine. If this instilled in him his great self-esteem it was then honed by constant successes in every venue he attempted. Think of winning every extemporaneous speech while on the Rutgers Debating Team while earning Phi Beta Kappa and All-American in football. Such success begets success. One starts believing oneself to be infallible. Robeson once conceded, "I haven't ever been nervous of the public or frightened of appearing before a lot of people."

Hypomania

Robeson had a mania for excellence and achievement. He was the classic Type A personality who confused success with self-worth and this helped him achieve enormous success beyond the norm. Robeson's father had instilled in him the work ethic that he would use to achieve great success in life, although his wife continually accused him of being lazy. What she never understood was that his procrastination was due to his need for perfection. Robeson wanted it right whereas she saw his delays as being wanton neglect. True to form for the Type A personality, Robeson never limited himself to just one activity. He was multifaceted and always kept many balls in the air, more than most men could comprehend. When not working on the stage, making a movie, or recording, Robeson was making a political speech on social activism or learning a new language by which to perform his songs or plays.

Independence

This renegade defied the establishment at every turn in his life. He said, "I am a radical and I am going to stay one." No roadblock was too great for him to go around or through. Robeson had the temerity to say, "I have the greatest contempt for the Democratic press," and then wrote, "I challenge this vicious system to the death. . . . I've never accepted any inferior role because of my race or color. And by God I never will." He loved to change the lyrics of his most famous song, "Ol' Man River," from "I'm tired of livin' and feared of dyin' " to the more rebellious "I must keep fightin' until I'm dyin'." Robeson was never more defiant than when the United States Congress took away his passport and attempted to prove that he was a Communist sympathizer. He adamantly refused to acknowledge their authority over him and pled immunity under the Fifth Amendment rather than allow them to intimidate him or treat him like a pawn. Much of Robeson's success was due to his rebellious spirit, but it also led to much of his turmoil.

Passion and Drive

Robeson's father instilled in him the need to perform at 100 percent no matter what it took. He never forgot his father's admonition and drove himself to be the very best he could be. This is why Robeson was never arrogant or conceited about his adulation. He always felt he could do better. Jim Light, Robeson's director in *Emperor Jones,* called Robeson's great drive "imposing," and said that, "He had a deeper feeling about his race than the theater could satisfy." Robeson's portrayal of Othello onstage was awe-inspiring. One critic said, "His emotional power was terrifying. In the jealousy scenes he literally foamed at the mouth."

This megastar was driven by some mystical internalized power he described as "emotional energy." He was not steeped in Freudian psychology but what he was describing was the "psychic energy" Freud felt was instrumental to all achievement. Robeson often spoke of the time at Rutgers when the whole team decided to hospitalize him and his experience of "rage" so great it scared him. Robeson told one reporter, "One time I went out of my head in a rage and night after night out there on the stage I remember it." Libidinal drive, power, and success are highly correlated and Paul Robeson's life confirms that axiom. He was possessed of very high psychosexual energy and spent much of his early life in liaisons with various women. White women especially were drawn to him and he was never one to deny them. He participated in numerous blatant affairs in virtually every foreign country in which he performed. During his early days in London a friend spoke of his high libidinal drive, saying, "I think women occupied second place, but they were . . . always there."

Perfectionist

Robeson is the model of this distinguished group for perfectionism. He was a perfectionist who never liked to finish anything for fear it was not sufficiently exacting. He insisted on perfection in everything he did either personally or professionally and it drove other people crazy, including his wife. Essie actually accused Robeson in her biography of being lazy, which only demonstrated that she didn't understand him well. Robeson's procrastination was akin to an engineer not releasing a product for fear it isn't perfect. Robeson operated on the same premise in entertainment. Excellence was the motto by which he lived his life and it had been instilled by a father who pushed him to be the very best.

Temerity

Anyone capable of taking on a football team after they had put him in the hospital was well steeped in temerity and risk taking. Never afraid of any confrontation, Robeson told a reporter in 1949, "I've overcome my fear of death," thereby letting the establishment know that he could not be coerced or frightened into conformity. When Congress attempted to intimidate him during the fifties anti-Communist hearings, he told reporters, "They can't scare me and they can't run me out of this country." Robeson lived on the edge in his concerts, in acting roles, and especially in carrying out his social activism. Paul Robeson's ability to look fear in the face is one of the main things that made him great.

Tenacity

No matter how bad things got, Paul Robeson never quit. He persevered in spite of being blackballed by the entertainment industry and the perpetual harassment by the FBI, the State Department, the U.S. Congress, and even the black community. Robeson persevered against the racial discrimination he experienced as a high school student, then again as a freshman at Rutgers, and then when forced to change careers when racial prejudice prevented him from pursing a law career. None of these events defeated him but only sufficed to instill in him a defiance that could not be altered later in life when the political bureaucrats attempted to destroy him. Despite all, he persisted to become one of the world's great artists. During the attempt by the U.S. government to defeat him, he told reporters, "I am determined to defeat those who would imprison my voice."

Vision

Robeson was convinced that as a black man he had inherited a special vision. His wife wrote that he had "a sort of sixth sense which successfully steers him past nearly all the wrong turnings straight on to his goal." Robeson was certainly highly intuitive in respect to his understanding of global change. His "inner logic" or right-brain vision on stage made him special. He wrote, "I, as an African, feel things rather than comprehend them. . . . I think my natural gift for language has brought this more clearly home to me than anything else." In describing his African roots he was in fact describing his Promethean temperament of intuitive-thinking. Robeson said, "I have a need for creative equilibrium between the spiritual and the material, between a life of intuition and feeling, and that of logical analysis." He further confirmed this when speaking of his approach to acting: "All I do is feel the part—I make myself believe I am Othello and I act as he would act." He correctly predicted Hitler's demise and the freedom of the African states. Such was his intuitive vision.

Will to Power

This visionary was able to reach down deep to his "inner-will," or what he referred to as his "core," which "stopped me from being shattered during difficult times." He was driven from some internal mystical power to overcome all obstacles in his path and once said, "I want to lead the Negro out of this new Egypt into a new promised land." He was convinced that he was powerful enough to succeed in such an awesome undertaking. Such power conviction is what Nietzsche labeled "will to power" where a protagonist as "superman" like Robeson would change the world left adrift by God. Robeson was prepared for such a task and took on the whole United States government in a valiant attempt to obtain equality and freedom for his people. Seldom has anyone exhibited such strength of character or internal power as Paul Robeson during the decade between 1946 and 1955.

Summary

On April 15, 1973, a seventy-fifth birthday salute to Paul Robeson was held at Carnegie Hall by those who knew and loved him. Sidney Poitier, Harry Belafonte, Coretta Scott King, and Zero Mostel were just a few of those who came to sing his praises and revel in his power. Unfortunately, Paul Robeson was in Philadelphia and too ill to attend this professional farewell. He wrote a letter to be read on stage by his son that ended with this cryptic line: "Though ill health has compelled my retirement, you can be sure that in my heart I go on singing:

> But I keeps laughing
> Instead of crying
> I must keep fighting
> Until I'm dying,
> And Ol Man River
> He just keeps rolling along!

This was a great legacy from a man who changed the world by daring to challenge the establishment. Robeson never blamed anyone for his own inadequacies and only asked that he be treated equally and evaluated on talent, not color. He never lived to see that happen but his activism opened many doors for his race, who were able to walk through comparatively unobstructed. In the late fifties W. E. B. Du Bois gave a lasting tribute to Robeson, saying, "Paul Robeson is without doubt today . . . the best-known American on earth—Europe, Asia, Africa, West Indies, South America. Only in his native land is he without honor and rights." Sadly, that is still so as he has never received his rightful due as a consummate creative genius.

PAUL ROBESON
Promethean (NT)
Athlete, Singer, Actor, Civil Rights Activist
born April 9, 1898, Princeton, New Jersey; died January 23, 1976, Philadelphia, Pennsylvania

Dominant trait: Charismatic rebel and iconoclast; extroverted intuitive thinker; competitive visionary and high integrity

Motto: "All men are brothers"; "My song is my weapon"; "I am a radical and I'm going to stay one"

Religion: African Methodist Episcopal Zion Church

Philosophy: "The struggle for Negro rights is an inescapable part of the antifascist struggle"

Politics: Democrat with socialist and Communist leftist leanings; believed in "scientific socialism"

Nicknames: "Robey"; "King of Harlem"; "American Othello"

Creation/innovation: Forerunner of Black Power movement, detente, African independence, and anti-imperialism

Successes: All-American; Phi Beta Kappa scholar; lawyer; internationally renowned actor/singer; and activist

Vices/hobbies: Sports; women; foreign languages

Romantic liaisons: Married Essie Cordoza Goode in 1921 and soon after began many scandalous sexual liaisons

Self-description: "I'm an artist. I don't understand politics"; "I'm going to think and feel African—not as a white man"

Birth order: Last born of 8 children of father William, an ex-slave-turned-minister, and schoolteacher Anna Bustill

Parental influence: "Mothered" by siblings, aunts, uncles; "I love my Pop like no one in the world. I adored him"

Early transience: At 9 moved from Princeton to Westfield, New Jersey; at 12 to Somerville; and at 17 to New Brunswick

Parents' occupations: Father preacher who ran trucking firm; mother schoolteacher of African, English, Indian ancestry

Role models: W. E. B. Du Bois; father, who escaped slavery at age 15 and was a self-made man

Hero mentors: Eugene O'Neill; Spirituals "are in fact a poetic expression of a people's innermost nature"

Formal education: Somerville H.S., 1915; BA, Rutgers, 1919; LLB law degree, Columbia, 1923

Life crises: At age 5 mother died tragically; as a freshman teammates at Rutgers broke his nose and dislocated his shoulder

Metamorphoses: Overcame discrimination by high school principal, which instilled an "inner resolve for life"

Charismatic: Magnificent man physically, intellectually, and verbally; he "made audiences weep" with his "vitality"

Competitive: Wrote "Song is my weapon" for fighting establishment; once took on a whole pro football team

Hypomanic: "Emotional power was terrifying"; in *Othello* jealousy scenes "he literally foamed at the mouth"

Independent rebel: "I have the greatest contempt for the Democratic press"; "I challenge this vicious system"; "I am a radical and I am going to stay one until my people get free to walk the earth"

Indomitable "will": Challenged the FBI, State Department—"I am determined to defeat those who would imprison my voice"

Intuitive vision: Wife: "Guiding instinct and sixth sense"; on stage utilized "gut" and "spiritual" instinct

Drive: Father inspired him to 100 percent achievement in all things; enormous libidinal drive

Risk-taker: Said of congressmen, "They can't scare me and they can't run me out of this country"

Self-confident: "I haven't ever been nervous of the public or frightened"; apprenticed on father's pulpit at age nine

Tenacious: Refused to quit after Rutgers team tried to injure him; returned with vengeance that couldn't be denied

Workaholic: Years of political isolation and frenetic schedule led to exhaustion and nervous breakdown in 1961

Honors: Stalin and German Peace Prizes; 3 honorary Ph.D.s; Spingarn NAACP Award; Football Hall of Fame

18

Oprah Winfrey—Charismatic

Talk-Show Hostess Extraordinaire, Actress, and Television Producer

"My legacy is not quantitative, but qualitative."

Oprah Winfrey is an alluring personality who has a sixth sense for anticipating the inner thoughts of her guests and her audience. She intuitively knows just the right questions to ask and almost appears precognitive in anticipating her viewing audience's thought processes. All of this adds up to a woman with the charm of a magician plus an intellect's wizardry who has earned her reputation as America's "Everywoman." Oprah Winfrey has achieved what few entertainers have ever attempted in appealing to a wide cross section of America including millions from every race, religion, and creed.

Winfrey still owns the daytime television ratings, even after they fell precipitously when she decided to forego any more shows on sensationalism and sleaze during the 1994–95 season. This decision caused a falling-out with her long-term producer and friend Debbie DiMaio. She changed the show's philosophical message and content and defended her decision saying, "I cannot listen to other people blaming their mothers for another year. We're not gonna book a show where someone is talking about their victimization." Winfrey then terminated DiMaio and changed the format of the show to one that better fit her own keen sense of family values. In a spring 1995 interview on CNN Winfrey told Larry King, "I intend to use my life, and show, for the good."

Money is never a major factor in any of Winfrey's business decisions. But since she changed the format of "The Oprah Winfrey Show" she has earned in the neighborhood of $75 million a year, prompting some sources to predict that she would soon become America's first black billionaire. Winfrey is a woman who follows her conscience and idealism and that winning combination, if well executed, results in fame and fortune every time.

By the mid-nineties, "The Oprah Winfrey Show" was broadcast into 99 percent of America's homes where fifteen million viewers each day are glued to her therapeutic approach to talk-show entertainment. The show is broadcast to sixty-five countries and is the highest-rated syndicated show in history, grossing a staggering $180 million annually. "The Oprah Winfrey Show" has consistently drawn 55 percent more viewers than "Donahue," which was her closest competition before he retired his show in 1996. Winfrey is only the third woman, behind Mary Pickford and Lucille Ball, and the first African American to own her own studio—a $20 million, 100,000-square-foot television and production facility operated under the name Harpo (Oprah spelled backward).

The Queen of Daytime TV has won every television broadcasting award for talk shows. In 1995 she was the recipient of the Emmy for "Best Talk Show Host"—the fifth straight year she won that award. In 1988 she was voted the International Radio and Television Society's "Broadcaster of the Year," the first black to have earned that honor and the youngest ever to have been so honored. She was named *Good Housekeeping*'s 1992 Most Admired Woman and followed that with the Horatio Alger Award in 1993. In 1994 Winfrey was named the Entertainer of the Year.

Having accumulated a net worth of $250 million before age forty gives testimony to this woman's business genius. And she is not one to hide her money under the proverbial mattress. She entertains lavishly, owns three palatial estates worth many millions, spends money on clothes in the image of Jackie Onassis, and travels extensively. Winfrey has materially changed daytime television forever. She is an empathetic interviewer who has her finger on the pulse of her guests. She has a remarkable ability to communicate without monotony, titillate without offending, motivate without moralizing, and educate without preaching. The *Washington Times* summed up Winfrey's mystique by writing, "This phenomenon can't be reduced simply to terms like *charisma* or *star quality*. Something much more profound is going on!" I agree and believe that her charismatic persona makes Winfrey's a creative genius without parallel.

Innovative Contribution

The media has described Winfrey as the "conscience of our times." She gave a lot of credence to that title in 1995 by insisting that her guests take responsibility for their lives. She decided to operate professionally in context with her personal philosophy and told Larry King, "We are responsible for our victories and our defeats" and "I'm tired of people blaming others for their own ineptitudes." She told him, "Television is the most powerful vehicle of communications on earth" and that she intended to use it "to lift people up." Winfrey went on to say that everyone has a calling in life and "I'm convinced mine is TV where I can leave a legacy that is qualitative, not just quantitative."

Using "The Oprah Winfrey Show" to assist her viewers in learning how to deal with adversity has proven to be an admirable goal, and although a questionable medium for an entertainment show. Winfrey has decided to become innovative and creative, which always pushes the envelope of acceptability. More importantly, it will hopefully demonstrate to other purveyors of culture that the media is far more than just an entertainment vehicle, but one that can effectively educate, motivate, and communicate important messages to the masses. Her decision to forgo ratings, the Bible of the entertainment industry (and basis of attracting new sponsors), is magnanimous indeed. She has promised to communicate without muckraking, to titillate without trashing, and to educate without monotony. These are not easy objectives to achieve. Rick Kogan of the *Chicago Tribune* wrote, "Oprah knows it could take years to see if this kind of 'high road' approach will pay off. But she wanted to do it and she can afford it." What price intuitive vision?

Personal History

Oprah Winfrey was born on January 26, 1954, the only child of Vernita Lee and Vernon Winfrey in Kosciusko, Mississippi. In her irreverent words she was conceived under an oak tree for her parents one and only relationship. Vernon was in the army and left to go back to camp after Winfrey's birth. Vernita, who was just eighteen at the time, deposited her new daughter with her mother, Hattie, for rearing while she took off to Milwaukee to work as a domestic. Vernita had two more illegitimate children in Milwaukee while Winfrey was being raised by her grandmother in Mississippi. Her unusual first name came about due to a mixup. Meaning to name her Orpah, for Ruth's sister-in-law in the Bible, the midwife transposed the second two letters on the birth certificate and thereby created one of the world's most original names.

Winfrey's authoritarian grandmother was her female role model and became her substitute mother for the first five years of her life. The family lived and toiled on a Mississippi farm that had no indoor plumbing. Winfrey's grandfather was a tyrant and negative influence, but her grandmother instilled in her the moral integrity which is Winfrey's trademark on daytime television. As a child Winfrey was more comfortable without shoes and dresses than with them. She coped by creating her own entertainment and befriended the animals for company. After her grandmother had taught her to read the Bible at age three books became Winfrey's escape and their fictional heroes her emotional companions. In 1993 she told a book show audience, "I owe everything I have to books." She told biographer Nellie Bly: "I am what I am today because of my grandmother, my strength, my sense of reasoning, everything, all of that, was set by the time I was six years old. I basically am no different now from what I was when I was six years old."

A precocious child, Winfrey made her first speech at age two when she addressed the Baptist congregation in Kosciusko, Mississippi at Easter. The parishioners were in awe of this precocious little girl who had the temerity to stand up in front of the congregation and speak the words of the Lord. They praised her as a "special" and "gifted" child who was fast becoming known in the town as "the little speaker." Winfrey was given a rousing ovation after one speech and the acclaim made such a lasting impression on her that she announced to her grandmother, "I will work by talking." Winfrey has certainly fulfilled that prophecy!

Winfrey has said, "I grew up loving books." They became her outlet for her inner frustrations. In her words, "It was a way to escape to another person's life." The books led her to aspirations of becoming a missionary and then a preacher. Once her grandmother enrolled her in kindergarten, the precocious Oprah promptly wrote a note to the teacher insisting that she belonged in the first grade. The astonished teacher promoted her. When it came time to go to second grade Winfrey's mother had become established in Milwaukee with her two other children and sent for Oprah. In Milwaukee Winfrey once again demonstrated her strength: "I didn't think it was necessary to go to the second grade, so I told my teacher and was moved into third grade."

As a child the Queen of Daytime TV had dreamed of becoming a fourth-grade teacher. Her first real-life role model was her fourth-grade teacher, Mrs. Denvor. Winfrey recalled years later, "She believed in me. Made me believe I could be anything by introducing me to books and reading." Winfrey now proudly says, "I am now a teacher. I have millions of students. I consider my TV job as teacher and facilitator to my viewers."

After visiting her father in Nashville one summer Winfrey decided to stay, which began a vagabond life between Milwaukee and Nashville. Winfrey moved between these cities five different times while attending a dozen different schools prior to high school. During one of her sojourns in Milwaukee she was molested, which took its toll on her emotionally to such an extent that she came close to delinquency. A nineteen-year-old cousin raped her at age nine and for the next five years she was repeatedly abused by various adults. Afraid of speaking out, she suppressed the abuses and years later told a reporter, "I sold my silence for an ice cream cone and a trip to the zoo." The torment of her sexual abuse drove the confused teen more deeply into the fantasyland of books. Winfrey's stepsisters made fun of her and she responded by retreating further into her fantasyland of books. "I would hide in the closet and read by flashlight." In Winfrey's words, her halfsisters "made fun of me thinking I was trying to be 'somebody.' I was."

Her father had remarried and Winfrey's life in Nashville was far more grounded than her life in Milwaukee, but her mother kept insisting she live with her. During one term at age twelve in Nashville, the articulate girl was once again asked to speak before a church congregation. She was paid $500 for the engagement and was so exhilarated by the experience that she came off the dais and told her father, "I plan to be famous." She started keeping a diary to record her journey.

Winfrey became an independent spirit due to the terrible feelings of remorse and guilt over her continual molestations. She rebelled in order to escape the unpleasant reality of life by becoming a holy terror and teenage delinquent. On several occasions she destroyed family possessions and faked a burglary in order to get a new, more fashionable pair of glasses. She ran away from home twice and at fourteen became totally incorrigible. During one escapade she stole money from her mother and ran away. While living by her wits on the streets she spotted recording star Aretha Franklin getting out of a limousine and convinced Aretha that she was abandoned and needed money. Franklin gave her enough money to rent a hotel room and live the life of an affluent adult for a few days. When the funds ran out she returned home to the wrath of a furious mother. Vernita Lee was convinced her wayward daughter was totally incorrigible and decided to have her interred in a juvenile detention hall. Fortunately for Winfrey there was no room and Vernita was forced to call Vernon and send her back to Nashville. That was the beginning of Winfrey's metamorphosis. She would not see her mother again for many years.

When the wild child landed back in Nashville she was pregnant. The baby was born prematurely and died shortly after birth. Winfrey told Randy Banner of the *New York Daily News* in 1986, "My father saved my life." Vernon was a barber and owned a confectionery shop where he put his daughter to work. She said later, "It's because of him . . . I am where I am today." He made her go to the library every two weeks and select five books and then write a book report on each. She became a well-adjusted A student and went on to win the Elks Club oratorical contest, which guaranteed her a scholarship to Tennessee State. She was then invited to the White House as an Outstanding Teenager from Nashville's East High. On a roll, Winfrey was crowned Miss Black Nashville and Miss Tennessee while a freshman at Tennessee State, where she was majoring in drama.

In 1971 the blossoming teen was a contestant in the Miss Black America Pageant, which led to her being offered a part-time coanchor job with the CBS affiliate WTVF-TV in Nashville. She was just nineteen but finally in the profession that best utilized her talents. *Cosmopolitan* interviewed her in 1986 and asked if she wasn't just a token black at the Southern station. She responded, "Sure I was a token. But, honey, I was one happy token." The overachieving teen was petrified to be on a major network television program at age nineteen and was terrified of the thought of going on air live. She told herself, "I'll just pretend I'm Barbara Walters." The ploy worked. Despite these early successes her disciplinarian father kept a tight rein on his renegade daughter, causing her to say later, "I was the only news anchor in the country who had to be home by midnight."

As the news anchor Winfrey chased down stories in the Nashville suburbs. While on assignment in a redneck part of Nashville, she offered to shake hands with a white supremacist shopowner who told her, "We don't shake hands with niggers down here." The ever-articulate Winfrey shot back, "I'll bet the niggers are glad." Despite such racist experiences, Winfrey was well on her way to a television career. The television exposure in Nashville got her regional recognition and she was soon offered a job in Baltimore as coanchor of WJZ-TV doing the six o'clock news. By now she was a senior at Tennessee State and she wasn't sure if she should accept the offer. She went to a favored teacher at Tennessee State for advice and was told that she was only attending college to get an opportunity like she was just offered. To the chagrin of her father Winfrey accepted the Baltimore job.

Professional History

This visionary's professional career really began on April Fools' Day 1976 in Baltimore. Two years later she became coanchor of WJZ-TV's "People are Talking" morning show. She was the first female, black or white, to work as a news anchor in Baltimore TV. She soon became frustrated working in a job that had little compatibility with her unique talents. The anxieties of underachievement caused her to use food as solace. She ballooned to over two hundred pounds. Her personal life was a mess and the news job was not working out so she ate to overcome all the negativity in her life. The crisis turned out to be her catalyst to greatness, when she became introspective about her life.

The management at WJZ-TV was disenchanted with her news coverage expertise and demoted her. According to station management she was too emotional. They told her to "toughen up" or else. Toughness was never her strength and after nine months she was terminated and offered another position due to the long-term contractual commitment the station had made in hiring her. Winfrey's reassignment to a morning show proved providential. She began doing cut-ins for "Good Morning America" and her on-air charisma came across and overshadowed her incompetence at reporting. Winfrey was finally on the right track.

The station immediately recognized Winfrey's sensitivity, interpersonal skills, and empathetic interviewing talents. They assigned her to a cohost position with Richard Sher on "Baltimore Is Talking," a morning talk show akin to the "Regis and Kathie Lee Show." After the first show Winfrey said, "I came off the air and I knew that was what I was supposed to do. It just felt like breathing. It was the most natural process for me." She spent the next seven years with cohost Sher interviewing guests on topics ranging from divorce and child rearing to the Ku Klux Klan. The show was a huge success in the ratings game and garnered higher local ratings than Phil Donahue's nationally syndicated show.

But as her professional career was taking off, Winfrey's personal life declined to an all-time low—to the point where she considered suicide. It was during this low period in Baltimore, Winfrey later tearfully admitted, that she smoked cocaine in order to please her boyfriend Bubba Taylor who had refused to marry her and coerced her into a divergent lifestyle. Winfrey told a startled TV audience in 1995, "It is my great shame. . . . I was so in love with [him] I would have done anything." When an offer came in the fall of 1983 to host a WLS-TV Chicago morning talk show she immediately accepted in order to escape Baltimore and a less-than-successful relationship.

Winfrey's rating success in Baltimore led to her being picked up by Dennis Swanson to host "A.M. Chicago" with a four-year contract at $200,000 per year. The emerging superstar was not yet thirty but had made it to the big time. Within three months Winfrey had dethroned the man who had become known as Mr. Mom—Phil Donahue, an institution in daytime talk shows. Within a year Winfrey's show was renamed "The Oprah Winfrey Show" and Winfrey would soon become known as the Queen of Daytime TV.

Winfrey described her success formula as, "We go to the heart of the matter, we go for the absolute gut." Her brutal honesty and empathetic interviewing of a wide spectrum of guests proved to be the right ingredient for her consummate success in the talk-show business. Her guests ranged from the erudite to the arcane. Many came from the fringe element and included bizarre and shocking topics. Programs featured "penis size," "transvestites," and "unwed mothers." Winfrey told the media, "I don't try to change people. I try to expose them for what they are." Jesse Jackson told her, "I was more nervous when I met you than Mikhail Gorbachev. Because you're more unpredictable." He was referring to her on-air comments like, "Bring a big one home to Mama!" when she shocked her audience during a show on penis size. Winfrey's off-the-wall comments improved her ratings until she became "Everywoman" to American housewives. Friend Maya Angelou has characterized Winfrey as "America's most accessible and honest psychiatrist." In 1987 *People* magazine wrote, "Oprah has a mind as quick as any in television, yes Carson and Letterman included."

In 1985 Quincy Jones was in Chicago and caught the Winfrey show in his hotel room. He was immediately convinced she was the perfect person to star in his production of Alice Walker's award-winning book *The Color Purple*. He asked her to play Sophia, an older woman who was caught up in the degradation of the American South. Despite no acting experience she was superb playing this part and proved to be a multifaceted entertainer. Berry Gordy's admonition to the Hollywood moguls that "blacks have been acting all their life just to survive" seems to apply here—with relatively little experience Winfrey did a good job portraying Sophia. She totally identified with the character, causing movie critic Gene Siskel to report, "Oprah's performance was shockingly good." Siskel wrote, "She exudes basic honesty in her role of this desperate black woman." In line with the motivations of all creative geniuses Winfrey told her agent, who was hassling for a better deal, "Jeff, I'd do it for nothing—please don't ask for more money."

By 1988 Winfrey was fast becoming a business tycoon. She formed Harpo Productions to produce "The Oprah Winfrey Show," and invested $20 million in a 100,000-square-foot production studio in downtown Chicago. By 1993 revenues from her award-winning show had reached an unprecedented $100 million, with Winfrey's take a cool $50 million a year. Her program had become the highest-rated TV talk show in history. Winfrey's success improved further by 1995, when she struck a better deal with her syndicator and distributor, King World. The show's annual revenues increased in 1996 to $250 million, which resulted in $171 million in personal income for the years 1995 and 1996. This placed Winfrey at the top of the *Forbes* list of top entertainers for the second straight year.

Despite her enormous success Winfrey has remained a workaholic. She arrives at the studio every morning at 6:00 A.M. and doesn't leave until it is time for dinner. Her success is due to her operating like she is number five even though she is really number one. Her prodigious energy and desperate need to be the best ensures her of remaining number one in an industry that is notoriously fickle. This woman is the perfect example of moving from the proverbial outhouse into the penthouse through tenacity, hard work, and drive. A millionaire by age thirty-two she is now worth hundreds of millions and predicted by *Forbes* in 1995 to become the first black billionaire. Part of Winfrey's economic revenge is owning a Challenger 601-3A jet, four homes, including a 160-acre Indiana farm, an apartment in downtown Chicago valued at $1 million, an 85-acre ski ranch in Telluride, Colorado, plus a Santa Fe, New Mexico, estate. Such are the spoils for those who work hard and pursue the qualitative over the quantitative.

What Makes Winfrey Tick?

Winfrey is an extrovert with an intuitive bent probably enhanced by a right-brain orientation resulting from her left-handedness. She is a visionary woman that psychologists label an Apollonian temperament—an intuitive-feeling type on the Myers-Briggs Type Indicator scale. She is highly sensitive and makes most decisions based on how she "feels" in contrast to how she "thinks." Winfrey is a human dynamo who works very hard to be the best she can be even though she hardly needs the money at this stage of her career. She exudes a magnetic charm and an empathetic feel for her guests that contributes to her magic and mystique. She is an inspirational, cultlike figure to her daytime "ministry."

This charismatic woman is arguably the greatest saleswoman in the history of television. She has demonstrated an ability to get both male and female guests to do or say almost anything on air. This is a rare talent that sets Winfrey apart from the pack. If most people are only as sick as their deepest secrets, this woman is one of the best adjusted and sanest individuals on the planet. Baring her deepest and darkest secrets to her audiences has endeared her to her fans and created a bond that is fundamental to her success.

MYTHOLOGICAL HERO MENTORS

As a child Winfrey chose heroes from fairy tales and books to emulate. Cinderella and female protagonists helped her believe that she was special and the world her oyster. Books were her escape and the Bible and novels her fantasy vision of success. Winfrey told an audience at the Fountainbleau Hotel in Miami Beach in 1993, "Books were my way to escape to another person's life." She went on to say, "Reading helped me get my first job in radio" and she then described how books had become her solace and escape from an unhappy childhood.

Winfrey's real-life role model and mentor was her fourth-grade teacher, Mrs. Denvor. She "taught me to have a love of learning." Other real-life role models were her grandmother Hattie and her father, Vernon. It appears Winfrey's mother was a negative role model, which has influenced her decision to avoid marriage so as not to make a mistake. Winfrey's professional role models were Diana Ross and newscaster Barbara Walters. She emulated both of these women during those periods when she questioned her own ability. Her spiritual mentors are Maya Angelou and Marianne Williamson. Angelou calls Winfrey "one of America's Roadmakers" and the two have had an extremely close personal relationship, with Angelou functioning as her substitute mother. Winfrey told Larry King, "Maya Angelou has been the greatest influence on my life as an adult." Marianne Williamson is Winfrey's human consciousness and personal improvement guru. But Winfrey's most influential mentors were fictional mythological characters who instilled in her the concept that she had few limitations to her greatness. They gave her the permission to remove all limitations to personal growth and achievement.

INSECURITY BREEDS GREATNESS

Writing her life story, Winfrey came to grips with her insecurities. She said being forced to "stand and look at myself naked" enlightened her. At first she said it "stunned" her and then "freed" her. She finally came to the conclusion: "As I peeled away the layers of my life, I realized that all my craziness, all my pain and difficulties, stemmed from me not valuing myself. And what I know now is that every single bit of pain I have experienced in my life was a result of me worrying about what another person was going to think of me." In September 1991 Winfrey told *Good Housekeeping*, "It's all about fear, all my problems, even my weight. When I'm heavier I feel safer and more protected, although I don't know what I'm trying to protect anymore than I know what I'm so afraid of." She admitted to *McCall's* in 1993, "Everybody deals with their fear differently. Some become overachievers like me, and others become mothers who kill." Winfrey openly admits to being driven by fear, and that her past abuse is what now drives her. It has armed her with tremendous resolve to "overcome and be the best I can be."

LIFE CRISES AND TRAUMAS

Winfrey's traumas began at birth and lasted through her mid-teens. She was an illegitimate child who bounced back and forth between her mother in Milwaukee and her father in Nashville for many years. Between the ages of nine and fourteen she was repeatedly molested and abused by various adults and relatives. Much of Winfrey's rebellious teenage delinquency was the direct result of her abuse, which she had repressed to avoid the awful truth. When she arrived at her father's home in Nashville in 1968 she bore an illegitimate child which didn't live. She told Barbara Walters, "I probably would not, without my past sexual abuse included, be able to handle what is happening to me as well as I think I am."

Charisma

This quintessential genius of daytime talk shows is the personification of the charismatic personality. She is a charismatic woman with an irresistible charm for millions of American housewives who faithfully tune in to "The Oprah Winfrey Show" as therapy for their personal conflicts. The *Washington Times* described her power of persuasion, saying, "This phenomenon can't be reduced simply into terms like *charisma* or *star quality*. Something much more profound is going on!" *Charisma* is the most operative word, however, since it is the defining difference between Winfrey and the rest of the talk-show pack. It is what has made Winfrey one of the most influential and wealthy women in America.

Competitiveness

Winfrey told Larry King that her marathon running demonstrated to her that, "I am far more competitive than I ever thought I was." She told *Redbook* in 1995 that when her physical fitness trainer Bob Greene needs to motivate her he uses her competitive spirit by saying, "See that woman in the pink suit? You can take her." She added, "And I'll kill myself to run past her. I love to be underestimated." It is this need to be number one that has made her so competitive. As in most female success stories, Winfrey is capable of tapping into her male qualities of aggression and drive. A unique assertiveness guides her.

Confidence

Any woman who said "I have always known that I was born for greatness" has a strong self-image in her subconscious. That is manifested in Winfrey's philosophy of "Uplift, encourage, empower!" These exhortations are all positive comments with optimistic messages resulting from high self-esteem. Ann Gerver, Chicago society editor, wrote in mid-1995, "Ever since she lost the weight, Oprah's become more confident and much more social. . . . The butterfly is emerging from the cocoon, slim, trim, and in control."

Winfrey wrote in her diary as a teenager, "I will be famous." Her half-sister Patricia says that Winfrey repeatedly told her she was destined for the top. When Winfrey returned from a trip to Hollywood at age fifteen she told her father, "One day, I'm going to put my star among those other stars" on Hollywood's Walk of Fame. Janet Burch, a Nashville psychologist, gives some insight into this part of her behavior. As a chaperone to the Miss Black America Pageant she said, "I have never seen anybody who wanted to do well as much as Oprah did. She used to talk about things, like how one day she was going to be very, very, very wealthy. . . . She believed it. People say, 'I'd like to be wealthy.' Oprah said, " 'I'm going to be wealthy.' " That is the positive demeanor necessary for one to become the richest female in show business.

Passion and Drive

When CNN talk-show maven Larry King asked Winfrey, "What drives you?" she responded, "To reach somebody. And effectiveness in raising people up to a new level." She added "You know, Larry, I never did it for money. I'm convinced my television show was my calling in life. Everybody has a calling and mine is TV." Half-sister Patricia said of Winfrey: "She always had big dreams, even when Oprah was little. . . . She told me many times, 'I'm going to be a star.' " Patricia told biographer Nellie Bly, "She just knew she was going to succeed. She always had drive and ambition. She was always head and shoulders above everybody else when it came to brainpower." Patricia also described Winfrey as "a wild child," saying she was very promiscuous during her teens, which gives further evidence of her high level of psychosexual energy.

Hypomania

Winfrey is a classic workaholic who finds solace in performing a task well and never allows time to become a factor in accomplishing her goals. She once told a reporter, "This is all I do, and I do it till I drop." Winfrey is a typical Type A personality who works more hours than the norm to ensure success. Associates say Winfrey sleeps but five hours a night and uses her weekend retreat on an Indiana farm to recover her energy for the next week. But even on the farm Winfrey reviews new scripts and projects and reads mostly nonfiction to enhance her knowledge of life. Rushing sickness is one of the descriptions that would accurately characterize the life of this creative wunderkind.

Independence

Winfrey's renegade spirit is found throughout her aptly named restaurant, Eccentric, located in downtown Chicago. It is adorned with avant-garde art, nude sculptures, and features a menu with such entrees as catfish, gravy and biscuits, and other holdovers from her life as a child in the South. On her show as in her restaurant Winfrey has operated like all great visionaries. She insists on violating tradition and refuses to be seduced by policy and procedures. She has never followed the traditional formats for talk shows. Her 1995 decision to scrap the scandal and sensationalism issues has once again showed her independent nature by killing off an extremely successful formula. She has never been afraid of defying the establishment on her show or in her personal life. She has purposely pursued a rebellious format for her shows and that willingness to defy the authorities has proved endearing to her adoring public. Being a maverick and attempting the new and different has set Winfrey apart from the pack and has kept her on top for over ten years.

Perfectionist

America's number-one talk-show hostess didn't get there by accepting the mediocre. She is a demanding taskmaster who insists on perfection for herself and her employees. Winfrey is a hands-on executive who is willing to roll up her sleeves and get in the trenches relative to the programming material on her show. She is the only person who can finally accept or reject any change of format for "The Oprah Winfrey Show." She is in many respects a control freak in the image of most great artists. Excellence pervades her very being and is at the seat of her demands for weight loss and meeting her own standards of behavior and physical looks. Her motto is "to strive for excellence."

Temerity

Like all great innovators, Winfrey finds comfort in ambiguity. She actually enjoys living on the edge both professionally and personally, a sure sign of a Promethean temperament. Winfrey enjoys risk far more than the norm and delights when she is able to tackle the unknown and successfully resolve the issues. New opportunities and possibilities are a positive force in her life, rather than a negative, as for most people, who are not so far out on the risk-reward curve. One indication of Winfrey's pioneering spirit is the fact that she selects sports that are not for the meek. She enjoys Alpine skiing and marathon running, an indication of her ability to tap into those inner male qualities.

With no formal business training Winfrey is the chief executive of her production empire employing over one hundred people in the running of a multimillion-dollar conglomerate named Harpo, Inc. She can well afford to hire staffs of experts to run her business but prefers to operate it herself. She is the board of directors, chairman, CEO, creative director, and star. She even writes her own checks. *Working Woman* wrote, "Control, both physical and fiscal, is the mantra at Harpo." Her friend and spiritual mentor Maya Angelou describes her as a woman who dares "go where the fearful will not tread. . . . She is one of our Roadmakers."

Tenacity

Oprah Winfrey prides herself on being a survivor. Winning the Horatio Alger Award in 1993 gives testimony to her perseverance. It is the award given to people who best personify the "rags-to-riches" road to success. Winfrey is such a person. She dragged herself up from the bottom to reach the top. She says, "I am the perfect example of someone who came from zip. I mean zippola, Mrs. Outhouse herself here." When she was fired as news anchor in Baltimore she could easily have given up and gone home to Nashville. She persisted doing her thing as a sensitive but stimulating interviewer. She merely changed her venue to fit her talents. Instead of reporting the news, which has little humanity involved, Winfrey gravitated to her forte—interviewing average people for the human-interest value. She persevered and it has paid off in huge dividends.

Vision

This visionary is highly intuitive. She has great empathy for her guests to the point that she sometimes seems clairvoyant and appears to know what her audiences want to hear and asks just the right question at the right time. She has the emotional feel of a psychiatrist and can probe into extremely sensitive subjects without alienating her guests. By selecting Whitney Houston's tune "I'm Everywoman" as her theme song she set the stage for her reputation as America's identity. A right-brain visionary, she sees the forest, not the trees and this talent allows her to adroitly pick her way through the emotional morass prevalent in her victim-oriented guests. She shoots from the hip and relies on her gut to guide her through the difficult sequences. Even the show's producer and audience are at a loss where Winfrey is headed, but her talent is following her soul into the uncharted lands of the downtrodden.

Will to Power

The Queen of Daytime TV knows where she is going and that is her ultimate power. She has negotiated much hard terrain during her trek to the top and now exhibits the strength of character and omnipotence that Nietzsche labeled the "Ubermenschen," "Overman" or "Superman" persona. Her power transcends cognitive awareness. It is not always discernable by the audience since it emanates from within her psyche. That is the genesis of Winfrey's real power. A highly spiritual woman, she often resorts to her unconscious in overcoming life's difficult moments. That is the nature of her creative success—a Nietzschean will to power that is driven by her internal need to self-actualize.

Winfrey's power of promotion is enormous, as many writers can attest. When Winfrey had her friend Marianne Williamson on the show to promote her book *Return to Love,* the publisher sold thirty-five thousand copies the first day. Within eight days over three hundred thousand had been sold, an awesome number considering that the average hardcover book in the United States sells approximately four thousand copies. Winfrey's diet book, *In the Kitchen with Rosie,* is another example of her ability to sell products. Written by her friend and cook, Rosie Daly, the book broke all records for an initial hardcover book and remained on the bestseller list for almost a year. Winfrey's name may be unusual but it is magic in the world of entertainment and commerce and her selling power is mindboggling.

Summary

Oprah Winfrey admits to being mystified by what she calls the "M" words—marriage and motherhood. She has lived for some years with her long-term beau and fiancé, Stedman Graham. She told *Redbook* in 1995 that she was still contemplating marriage with Stedman but wasn't in a big hurry. She admitted, "I would say I'm not going to have kids. What it takes to do it right, I don't have it. I think it would be immensely unfair to bring a child into the world and expect that child to fit into my lifestyle." She has sublimated her maternalism into a passion for work and has opted for the professional over the personal. This is a classic finding in both male and female creative geniuses. She told a reporter she "couldn't imagine putting him [Stedman]—or anyone—ahead of her career." Now in her early forties, Winfrey's biological time clock has just about run out.

Winfrey is one of the wealthiest and most powerful women in America, black or white. She is America's alter ego, loved, admired, and worshiped by a daily television audience on four continents. Contrary to her television persona, Winfrey is an accomplished CEO and is deserving of her $75 million annual earnings, since she did it the old-fashioned way—she earned it! Raised without indoor plumbing this creative genius can now afford to buy her own water company and she did it without leaving a lot of bodies in her wake which is so often the case with such enormous success. Winfrey is a compassionate and sensitive business mogul whose employees would kill for her. She is a creative genius who breaks new ground daily in making the world a better place.

OPRAH WINFREY
Apollonian Temperament (NF)
Talk-Show Host, Actress
born January 29, 1954, Kosciusko, Mississippi

Dominant trait: Charismatic with competitive drive; an extrovert with vision and spontaneity
Motto: "To strive for excellence. I want to be the best I can be"
Religion: Methodist
Philosophy: "Preparation is the basis of execution"; "Uplift, encourage, empower!"
Nickname: "Everywoman"; "Conscience of Our Times"; "Queen of Daytime"
Creation/innovation: # 1 talk-show hostess in the history of TV and creator of "The Oprah Winfrey Show"
Successes: Highest-paid entertainer in TV—$75 million annually during mid-nineties
Hobbies/vices: Books: "I owe everything in my life to books"; marathons; clothes; large estates
Romantic liaisons: Single with no children; lives with longtime boyfriend Stedman Graham
Self-description: "I intend to use my life for the good"; "My legacy is not quantitative but qualitative"

Birth order: Firstborn illegitimate daughter of Vernon and Vernita Lee; half-sister and brother
Parental influence: Latchkey child with free time to roam, read, and become self-sufficient; adores father
Early transience: Vagabond youth: Mississippi 6 years, Milwaukee 2, Nashville 2, travel
Father's occupation: Barber, grocery store owner, and church deacon
Role models: Mrs. Denvor, 4th-grade teacher; Barbara Walters; Diana Ross
Hero mentors: Father, Vernon; Barbara Walters; Maya Angelou; Marianne Williamson
Formal education: Grandmother taught her to read at 3, skipped second grade; Memphis high school; BS Tennessee State, 1987
Life crises: Raped at 9 by 19-year old cousin; abused and pregnant at 14; attempted suicide in 1981
Metamorphoses: Hit bottom in Baltimore, attempted suicide; then resolved "I will overcome" and did

Charismatic: America's conscience due to magnetic attraction and audience empathy
Competitive: "I am far more competitive than I ever thought I was"
Hypomanic: Sleeps but 5 hours; intense energy drives her to be the best she can be
Independent rebel: Never afraid to strike out on new venue despite expert opinion to contrary; "Eccentric" restaurant
Indomitable "will": Internally driven by indomitable willpower
Intuitive vision: A true right-brain driven visionary who sees the forest, not the trees
Libidinal energy: Passionate physically and emotionally—driven to excel from psychosexual energy
Perfectionist: Must be the best in all things; very intense
Risk-taker: Pioneering spirit in work and play: skier, marathoner, and entrepreneurial spirit in business
Self-confident: As a teen: "I plan to be famous"; "I have always known that I was born for greatness"
Tenacious: Persevered in spite of great adversity and made it to the top
Workaholic: A Type A personality; afraid to fail; works an inordinate number of hours to ensure success
Honors: 1993 Horatio Alger Award; 1988 Entertainer of Year Award, Most Admired Woman Award

19

Racial Differences of Overachievers

Right is of no sex, Truth is of no color
God is the father of us all, and all we are brethren.

Frederick Douglass

The children of darkness are frequently more determined and zealous than the children of light.

Martin Luther King, Jr.

It became quite apparent while researching these black wunderkinds that they were different from those featured in my three other studies, totaling forty-three non-blacks. They were also different from their less successful ethnic brothers. They even differed from the data found in other research on eminent and creative people such as the Institute for Personality Assessment and Research at Berkeley (1950–75), Howard Gardner's findings in *The Creating Minds* (1993), Dean Keith Simonton's work in *Greatness* (1994), and the largest body of pertinent data ever released (over 1,000 samples) in Arnold Ludwig's *The Price of Greatness* (1995).

It became obvious that these thirteen individuals differed relative to their social and family values and their primary motivations and methodology used to reach the top of their professions. The genesis of this chapter occurred because these differences were unexpected and varied from many of the findings in the research by other writers on the subject of eminent people. Some of the findings are also at odds with the stereotypical images projected by the mass media in the United States. Some of these differences were so dramatic that I decided to include this chapter after the book was effectively complete.

My previous research on innovative and powerful people in *Profiles of Genius* (1993), *Profiles of Female Genius* (1994), and *Profiles of Power and Success* (1996) featured nineteen Caucasian females, two Asian males, and twenty-two

Caucasian males. The similarity in behavioral patterns, early experiential factors, and childhood crisis were quite consistent across ethnic and racial lines. What proved different was the approach, methodologies, and motivations of these groups of subjects. The sixteen black power brokers in this book utilized many of the identical key success traits and behavioral characteristics found in the previous research, traits like drive, self-esteem, work ethic, tenacity, and vision. What differed was the supporting variables like social and family values, many of which the reader should find quite surprising. It is important to note that these differences are based on a small sample of sixteen individuals and should not be considered predictive of larger populations.

Diversity Breeds Greatness

I agree with educator Gareth Morgan, who says "creativity thrives on diversity." The wide diversity between ethnic groups as depicted in this chapter adds credibility to that statement and substantiates why America has been so dominant and competitive in world markets. The United States is the most culturally diverse nation on earth and despite the conflict and strife born of such diversity, without it we would have lost out on some incredible innovations and breakthrough concepts.

Socially Acceptable Renegades

These superstar blacks were socially acceptable renegades who lived on the very fringe of societal rules without falling over. What I found interesting was that many of the derogatory labels that have historically burdened a black attempting to innovate, create the new, or destroy existing dogma were the very elements that turn out to be the most critical to great achievement for anyone of any background. It is truly ironic that derisive tags worn by blacks like *aggressive, renegade, capricious, militant, arrogant, competitive,* and *whimsical* are the very factors that are fundamental to great success and necessary for high achievement.

These black subjects used nonconformity, competitiveness, aggressiveness, and thrill-seeking to break down the barriers in pursuing their creative ventures. Many could not have made it without an indomitable will and intransigent drive since they had to overcome the derisiveness rampant in a world not accepting of their color or ideas.

Linguistic Talents

Language is an auditory art not unlike the performing arts. Paul Robeson's ability to become fluent in twenty-seven languages, including Chinese, Russian, Arabic, and Yiddish was a direct function of an auditory learning style that appears to be more prevalent in blacks than nonblacks. Maya Angelou was fluent in seven languages while Nelson Mandela spoke English, Xhosa, Zulu, Sisulu, and Nokwe French. Shirley Chisholm, Reggie Lewis, and Colin Powell spoke two or more languages fluently, all of them without the benefit of formal training. These subjects had a kind of spiritual feel for the sound that apparently contributed to their success in the performing arts and entertainment professions. They were far superior to the nonblacks in linguistic ability.

Initiators of Cultural Change

As a white writing on black success it became eerily apparent to me that many of the fads, music, dress, entertainment, and fashions adopted by whites more often than not had their genesis in black culture. Many of the styles in clothes originate in the inner city prior to making their way to Madison Avenue. The same is true of colloquial expressions such as "talking trash" and "in your face." Music has proven to be one of the most glaring illustrations of this, with just one example being the renegade Duke Ellington, who became, arguably, the greatest jazz composer of all time by daring to improvise and violate all music tradition in his twelve hundred jazz compositions.

Sam Phillips, who discovered Elvis, had an insight into this black leadership role in cultural change. He exclaimed, "If I could find a white man who had the Negro sound and the Negro feeling, I could make a million dollars." When he discovered Elvis, who exactly fit his definition, he did very well indeed. Minstrel shows, ragtime, Dixieland swing, boogie-woogie, blues, and rock 'n' roll were all created by black musicians like Scott Joplin, Louis Armstrong, Duke Ellington, Billie Holiday, and Ella Fitzgerald. These musical genres were pioneered by blacks and later emulated by whites.

Berry Gordy was the first black to financially capitalize on black music. He did so by organizing the black artists under his label and vertically integrating the process with complete "artistic control" and distribution. Ironically, this great contribution to black music and success turned out to be one of Gordy's great problems. Many of the stars he created left him or filed lawsuits against him for having exploited them when they were too naive to understand contractual negotiations. Some of the stars who ultimately deserted him were Diana Ross, the Jackson Five, Gladys Knight, Stevie Wonder and Mary Wilson. People tend to have short memories once successful and they only saw him as a "control freak" and "mercenary" after they had learned their trade and no longer needed his services.

African-American Heritage

It is apparent that the African-American heritage has played a large role in what psychologists call "auditory learning." People with this propensity may "play the piano by ear" like Berry Gordy or learn to dance or sing like Maya Angelou. Gordy and Angelou relied on a unique emotional or internalized "feel" for music that is not often found in nonblacks to make their mark in the world. These thirteen subjects certainly had a far keener "sense of sound" than nonblack superachievers. They depended on an auditory feel to succeed in their professional and personal lives. Paul Robeson taught himself both to act and sing while Gordy taught himself to play the piano and Angelou took the few dance lessons she had and improvised it into her own style which she used to go on tour with *Porgy and Bess.* She wrote, "Music was my refuge. I could crawl into the spaces between the notes and curl my back to loneliness." In a similar way Michael Jackson learned by watching his older brothers, James Brown, and Jackie Wilson perform. Bill Cosby also learned stand-up comedy by mimicking others and innovating with no formal training in show business. Even Michael Jordan's ability to dunk a basketball appears to have its roots in Africa, not Europe, due to the elegance and grace of a Nureyev that is so critical to such an act.

Eugene O'Neill and Jerome Kern were quite visionary and were two of the first whites to spot the power of the black on Broadway. They saw in Paul Robeson a powerful force and wrote plays and music to fit his enormous talents. They produced plays and music for him like "Ol' Man River" which is a consummate example of capturing the sound and mood of the black spiritual. This song alone elevated *Show Boat* into a classic for both Broadway and Hollywood with Robeson as the star of both. Robeson's success is a classic example of this hypothesis, since he had never had a singing lesson and couldn't even read music but nevertheless became a great recording artist. His emotional feel for music was intertwined in his persona and rhythmic feel for the sound and the message of the song. He wrote in his memoirs that the spiritual was his musical heritage and he received this from attending his father's church services. He was convinced this is what had molded him into one of America's great black singers and a Shakespearean actor.

Spiritualism and Greatness

The spirituality of these wunderkinds bordered on the occult. They were passionate believers in their dreams and spent their lives pursuing those dreams despite all logical arguments to the contrary. Many of these fantasy dreams revolved around their mythological mentors. Their fictional role models instilled them with power and removed all limits to success which were critical in leading them to greatness.

All the subjects in this book were highly spiritual to the point of quoting Scripture. The Bible and its teachings were central to their lives. Furthermore, none of these subjects became enamored of unconventional religions or belief systems such as Buddhism, agnosticism, or atheism. In contrast, many of the nonblacks studied were intrigued by these unconventional belief systems, with people like Bill Gates, Steve Jobs, Ted Turner, Nolan Bushnell, Howard Head, Ayn Rand,

Isadora Duncan, Napoleon, the Marquise de Sade, and Picasso advocates of many of these nontraditional ways of thinking. Even the highly intellectual Robeson, who had bought into Marx and Engels's dialectical materialism, refused to buy into their atheistic ideology. Spiritualism was very important to these visionaries and pervaded their every move. It functioned as their support system during adversities and crises.

Ten Differences Found in Eminent Achievers

These eminent achievers exhibit differences that fall into ten social, political, familial, and metaphysical pedagogical categories. It is important to point out that more similarities than differences were found in these subjects and they probably were more like their successful nonblack counterparts than they were to the losers in their own race. It also appears their diversity was more a function of environmental and family influences than from any genetic heritage. It is also important to understand that these subjects are not necessarily representative of a whole population but only offer some insight into the operating styles of a small cross section of black overachievers. Although it is a very small sample—albeit a good sample of supersuccessful individuals from the latter twentieth century—it is not a large enough sample to prove that blacks as a group will always vary in the same way from other nonblacks.

If nothing else, the following list of ten differences offers some knowledge on the nature of the black superstar relative to those blacks aspiring to reach the top since many of the differences between these eminent blacks and their less achievement-oriented brothers are as great as between them and nonblacks. For more details on these differences, see figure 19.

1. Church-Religion-Spiritualism: Internal support system for blacks
2. Mothers-Grandmothers: Backbone of black family life
3. IQ and Formal Education: Far more critical to success for blacks (opening doors)
4. Insecurity as Key Motivator: Fear of failure and return to inner-city primary motivator
5. Less Dysfunctional Personality: Emotionally stable in contrast to nonblacks
6. Political and Social Activism: Blacks more politically active than whites
7. Science-Technology Aversion: A dearth of superstars in these professions
8. All Sensual But Few Promiscuous: Majority not as sexually flaky or lecherous as nonwhites
9. Racial Issues-Products-Services: Used as vehicle and catalyst to achievement
10. Personal-Professional Dichotomy: "We are family" mentality in business

Church-Religion-Spiritualism

All of these subjects were devoutly religious, which is far beyond the norm for any group and shockingly so from the research on eminent people. Arnold Ludwig studied over a thousand eminent people in 1995 and in *The Price of Greatness* disclosed that 40 percent were either atheists, agnostic, or believed in an unconventional religion like Zen. He found that only 28 percent attended an organized church regularly and that only 35 percent ascribed to a traditional religious dogma. In my previous studies on Asians and Caucasians, only 32 percent of the males and 56 percent of the females were found to be religious (believing in a super being and/or attending an organized church). Of those subjects, one-third were nonreligious—either agnostic or atheist, which is consistent with Ludwig's findings.

Overall, only 43 percent of the nonblacks previously studied were religious, a significant difference in what was found in these subjects. These thirteen visionaries were all deeply committed to the church and spent an inordinate amount of time and energy maintaining those ties. The only nondevout subject was Nelson Mandela. All of the others were able to quote from Scripture and knew the lyrics of church spirituals better than they knew the national anthem. Religion played a very important role in their lives, which cannot be said for most of the nonblacks studied. These subjects were not only well steeped in religious dogma but were quite spiritual in their views about life and their position in it. See figure 17 for further details on the beliefs of these subjects.

Nonblack Differences in Religiosity

The nonwhite visionaries used religion where needed but if it did not fit into their grand scheme of things they discarded it and pursued their own metaphysical ide-

FIGURE 17
RELIGIOUS AND POLITICAL PREFERENCES

Subject	Religious Preference	Political Preference
Maya Angelou	Fundamentalist Christian	Democrat
Shirley Chisholm	Methodist	Democratic
Bill Cosby	Religious pragmatic: Believes in a Supreme Being	Apolitical
Berry Gordy	Methodist	Apolitical
Michael Jackson	Jehovah's Witness dropout	Apolitical
John Johnson	Fundamentalist Christian	Democrat
Michael Jordan	Southern Baptist	Apolitical
Reginald Lewis	Roman Catholic	Democrat
Nelson Mandela	Religious pragmatist	African Nationalist Socialist
Thurgood Marshall	Episcopalian	Democrat
Colin Powell	Episcopalian	Republican
Paul Robeson	Episcopalian	Social Scientist
Oprah Winfrey	Methodist	Democrat

ology. Most, especially the males, did not believe in a supreme being or specific denominational dogma. Few of the males owned a Bible, let alone quoted from it, as these thirteen were wont to do. Many of the whites had a messianic complex and considered themselves the cornerstone of existence, particularly Napoleon, Hitler, Picasso, Howard Hughes, the Marquise de Sade, and Isadora Duncan. They were the incarnation of God in their minds and were not about to capitulate to another god. Others, like Ayn Rand, Nolan Bushnell, Nikola Tesla, Howard Head, and Bill Lear were either staunch atheists who believed in Nietzsche's statement that "God is dead," or found solace in some more esoteric metaphysical system.

Blacks Are Devoutly Religious

The blacks in this book were 100 percent Christian with the majority belonging to the Episcopalian or Methodist denomination (see figure 17). Reginald Lewis was the lone Roman Catholic and Michael Jackson the lone Jehovah's Witness. All were able to quote from Scripture and held the Bible and its teachings in high regard. They approached religion as if Christ was in their corner and would back them up in case of failure.

Mothers—Backbone of the Family

Black mothers and grandmothers were found to have had the most profound influence on their successful offspring to a far greater degree than among nonblack subjects. In nonblacks the mothers were the major influence but they did not dominate the family to the extent found in black families. White mothers doted on and nurtured their offspring in a valiant attempt to make them great, whereas the black mothers were more intent on arming their children with those qualities necessary to cope in a world of blatant prejudice. They molded these subjects into resilient overachievers and taught them to become self-sufficient. The mothers of these subjects were the dominating force both personally and professionally, within the household and without, financially and socially. This was a real contrast with families of nonblacks, where the mothers' influence was less overwhelming. This trend should not be exaggerated, however. Half of the subjects had fathers who played a significant role in their upbringing.

IQ and Formal Education

Black superstars tend to use education and their intelligence to make their way through the black ceiling. They use intelligence as a tool far more often than their white counterparts, who have a certain disdain for the conformity of formal education. Both groups were extremely knowledgeable in their given field of expertise but the blacks pursued formal education far more than their nonblack counterparts. This is consistent with other research. Arnold Ludwig in *The Price of Greatness* found that only 37 percent of his one thousand eminent people graduated from college or graduate school, with a full 45 percent lacking a high school diploma. Of the nonblacks I studied, just a third graduated from college (31 percent) and only 20 percent had graduate degrees, and 31 percent failed to finish high school. However, of the thirteen black subjects studied in this book, nine graduated from college and seven had graduate degrees, four of them in law. An amazing 69 percent of these eminent blacks graduated from college! And over half went on to attain graduate degrees, compared to only 9 percent of the nonblacks. This is truly remarkable. Only one black subject never made it through high school and that was Michael Jackson. This compares with almost one-third high school dropouts in nonblack superstars.

Seven of these thirteen had graduate degrees with four of these in law. It is telling that only Marshall used the advanced degree to achieve eminence in life. They all used education to open doors, but once open went on to gain success in other fields—Mandela in politics, Lewis in leveraged buyouts, Robeson in the theater, Chisholm in politics, Cosby in entertainment, and Powell in the military.

Precocious Children

These subjects were clearly more precocious than their peers while in school. Paul Robeson was a Phi Beta Kappa; Bill Cosby was tested as a "gifted" student; and Oprah Winfrey, John Johnson, Shirley Chisholm, and Thurgood Marshall all won college scholarships based on their academic credentials during high school. Winfrey skipped the second grade as did Johnson. Johnson also won a scholarship to the prestigious University of Chicago after graduating from high school but was never able to afford the luxury of taking advantage of it.

Language Acuity

The Caucasian subjects as a group were not nearly as proficient in foreign languages as these thirteen blacks. Maya Angelou, who never went to college, was fluent in seven languages, all of which she taught herself. Paul Robeson spoke, sang, and performed in twenty-seven languages, all of which were self-taught. Even hard-nosed businessman Reginald Lewis taught himself to speak French in order to communicate with his Parisian employees. Nelson Mandela speaks Xhosa, English, Zulu, Sisulu, Nokwe French, and other languages. Shirley Chisholm became fluent in three languages and Cosby in two. Colin Power speaks fluent Yiddish, Spanish, and English.

Insecurity as Key Motivator

Insecurity played a much stronger role in motivating these subjects than it did among the nonblack subjects. This difference was noted by Martin Luther King, Jr., "The children of darkness are frequently more determined and zealous than the children of light." Frederick Douglass was even more succinct, saying, "If there is not struggle, there is no progress." The fear of failure was obviously a driving force in the success of these greats. This is not surprising, given the overt discrimination most faced while growing up in Jim Crow America. The majority lived in mortal fear of waking up one day and finding themselves back in the inner-city projects. The fear of failure motivated them to stay on top so as to never be faced with the degradation of returning to their roots. Oprah Winfrey is a classic example of a woman who has made it to the pinnacle of success but continues to work as if she were the underdog. Bill Cosby once told an audience at Harlem's Apollo Club, "In show business you can be rich today and back in the projects tomorrow," which he attributed to the "black life-and-death struggle for real identity."

Malcolm X gave further confirmation to the basic insecurities of blacks as a motivating force when he told *Playboy* magazine in 1963, "The Negro from the big-city ghetto—when you get him, you've got the best kind. . . . Because he makes the most drastic change. He's the most fearless. He will stand the longest. He has nothing to lose, not even his life because he didn't have that in the first place."

Less Dysfunctional Personalities

Not one of these subjects exhibited the extreme sociopathic personality tendencies so common in the lives of my nonblack subjects, such as Bill Lear, Steve Jobs, Ted Turner, Edith Piaf, Maria Callas, Walt Disney, Madonna, Napoleon, Hitler, Howard Hughes, Nikola Tesla, and Picasso, all of whom exhibited manic-depressive tendencies and depended on mania for much of their creative energy. Arnold Ludwig's work *The Price of Greatness* found similar correlations between great success and abnormal behavior. Of his thousand eminent subjects, the majority suffered from some form of emotional dysfunction although he wasn't sure whether the mania caused the creativity or the creative pressure resulted in the dysfunction. I believe that abnormal success is dependent on abnormal behavior and drives.

Many of my nonblack subjects suffered numerous nervous breakdowns or became debilitated by severe anxiety or obsessive behaviors which caused many to attempt suicide. Only Paul Robeson of this group attempted suicide and based on the research only Thurgood Marshall and Michael Jackson were ever hospitalized for emotional problems. Over half (58 percent) of the nonblack male subjects exhibited symptoms of manic depression or hyperactivity. Just two of the blacks had symptoms of manic depression (Michael Jackson and Paul Robeson). The bottom line is that eminent blacks appear to be far more grounded than their white counterparts, even though most attained a similar degree of competence and success.

Political and Social Activism

Figure 17 illustrates the political affiliations of these visionaries. Most were quite active politically, especially in the area of civil rights. Four were clearly apolitical due to their overt distrust of politicians, whom they had learned to distrust early in life. After actively supporting Bobby Kennedy's run for the presidency in the late sixties, Bill Cosby became disenchanted with politics and has been quite vocal about his distrust of politicians ever since. Berry Gordy, Michael Jordan, and Michael Jackson are also highly apolitical and would just as soon not be involved in any of the controversy of political and social action. The rest of the subjects spent much of their lives involved in social and political activism. This is in direct contrast to the findings on nonblacks who avoided politics like the plague until the politicians began effecting one of their pet projects and then they got involved. Maya Angelou, Shirley Chisholm, John Johnson, Nelson Mandela, Thurgood Marshall, and Paul Robeson were passionate social activists. Colin Powell and Oprah Winfrey were sympathetic to the causes of justice, Powell quietly, Winfrey very vocally. Most of the whites were so immersed in their professional ventures that they had little interest in fighting for social reform and of course rarely faced the need to fight for their civil or personal rights or freedoms like these subjects.

Little Science Bent

Despite the obvious high intelligence of these thirteen wunderkinds, they and many other candidates reviewed showed little interest in technology or science. These individuals were certainly intellectually capable of becoming successful scientists, but for some reason, blacks have historically shown little interest in these professions. Robeson, Marshall, Lewis, Chisholm, Winfrey, Marshall, and Johnson were sufficiently capable of pursuing a career in the sciences but the thought never occurred to them. Of the thirteen subjects only Colin Powell enrolled as an engineering major in college at CCNY. But engineering was not his thing and he dropped out after one semester.

In contrast, Ted Turner, Nolan Bushnell, Steve Jobs, Bill Lear, Soichiro Honda, Bill Gates, Arthur Jones, Howard Hughes, Maria Montessori, Margaret

FIGURE 18	
RACE AS CATALYST TO SUPERSTARDOM	
Maya Angelou	Used innate feel for gospel and spiritual music to innovate in the theater which opened the doors to *Porgy and Bess* and *Roots* roles. Exorcised hidden ghosts of discrimination and bigotry with autobiographic *I Know Why the Caged Bird Sings,* which has become a model for biographical writing.
Shirley Chisholm	Followed Marcus Garvey's lead in black assertiveness and became social/political activist to enact justice and reform. Fought for gender and racial freedom and both led her to the pinnacle of political success.
Bill Cosby	Fought the "minstrel stereotype," which he labeled "Blaxploitation," and resorted to a positive approach to change it by creating Dr. Huxtable and his lawyer wife in "The Cosby Show" which dominated TV for a decade.
Berry Gordy	Married soul and black gospel music into pop and took it mainline for all races to enjoy.
Michael Jackson	Made black disco sound acceptable to masses. His work transcends race and this attitude has gained him a universal adulation from all parts of the world.
John Johnson	Filled a void in black-oriented news and entertainment with *Ebony* and *Jet* magazines, where the voice of black power and beauty reigned supreme.
Michael Jordan	Became a hero to millions of teenagers, white and black, by demonstrating the grace, power, and elegance of black movement on the field of sports.
Reginald Lewis	Became the acknowledged expert on minority enterprise small business investment companies as venture capital vehicles and used expertise to become the quintessential leveraged buyout guru.
Nelson Mandela	Successfully fought for freedom and equality in South Africa and defeat of apartheid.
Thurgood Marshall	Fought for freedom and equality as legal counsel for the NAACP and on the Supreme Court.
Colin Powell	Rode the wave of military integration and successful resolution of internal conflicts making him into a recognized "colorblind" leader.
Paul Robeson	*Othello* and *Emperor Jones* roles led the way in reducing the ubiquity of black stereotypes in the arts. Fought politically for racial equality, sacrificing millions in the process.
Oprah Winfrey	Used her TV bully pulpit to promote racial harmony and an understanding of other people's problems.

Mead, and Nikola Tesla were creative geniuses who chose to pursue a career in the sciences. Turner used satellites to create CNN, Bill Lear invented the Lear jet, Honda created an automobile empire, Nolan Bushnell invented video games, Bill Gates created Microsoft, Jones invented Nautilus equipment, Hughes started Hughes Aircraft, and Nikola Tesla invented the induction motor. Of these only Bushnell graduated from college and was last in his class at that.

Sensual But Not Promiscuous

Virtually all of these subjects had a highly sensual nature and appeared to have a strong libidinal drive but they showed relatively less propensity for promiscuity, multiple marriages, or extramarital affairs. This was quite different from the findings on the nonblack subjects. The high incidence of divorce and out-of-wedlock children in the black community was found to be a frequent case in the eminent nonblacks as well. These thirteen subjects were different, with the exception of Berry Gordy who had eight children by six different women only two of which he married. Paul Robeson was also sexually active outside his marriage with numerous scandalous affairs dotting his show business career, but no illegitimate children were found in his past. One might question the legitimacy of Michael Jackson's libidinal drive due to his perverse reputation and litigation surrounding his activities with teenage boys. In Michael's defense it appears he is far more asexual than hypersexual or homosexual, since he is desperately attempting to relive a lost childhood.

I found few instances of marital fidelity in nonblacks that I found in Colin Powell, Bill Cosby, Reginald Lewis, and Thurgood Marshall. All these men were sexually promiscuous prior to marriage but extremely chaste afterward in distinct contrast to Bill Lear, Ted Turner, Pablo Picasso, Soichiro Honda, and others. The nonblack women were even different in this area (see *Profiles of Female Genius*), namely Golda Meir, Madonna, Edith Piaf, and Isadora Duncan.

Racial Issues/Products

These thirteen subjects more often than not used racial inequities (Chisholm, Marshall, and Mandela), emerging markets and market voids for black products (Gordy, Johnson, Powell, and Lewis), or interest in black culture (Angelou, Cosby, Robeson, and Winfrey) to make their mark in the world. Angelou's first break was playing in *Porgy and Bess*. Johnson made it big by publishing a black entertainment pictorial magazine, *Ebony*. Berry Gordy hit the big time by taking black gospel music mainstream. Robeson became famous by singing black spirituals and playing Othello. Marshall got his start as legal representative to the NAACP. Lewis made it big by becoming "the" expert on minority enterprise small business investment companies. See figure 18 for detail on how all these individuals used ethnicity to make their mark in the world.

Even the tranquil Bill Cosby spent a great deal of his time and energy ensuring that television presented blacks as "normal" people and fought what he labeled the "minstrelization" or "blaxploitation" of blacks on TV. He first pioneered this when he portrayed a black hero in the controversial role of Alexander Scott on the NBC-TV show "I Spy" in the early sixties. Bill is fighting to ensure the integrity of blacks on TV but has adamantly refused to get caught up in Black Power or black militancy issues. The Black Power contingent labeled him an Uncle Tom for his refusal to become a spokesman for the virulent black militants during that turbulent period in the sixties and seventies.

Personal/Professional Dichotomy

Most of these subjects were guilty of marrying the professional and personal in virtually every endeavor. Most put their parent on the payroll; hired their children,
lovers (Berry Gordy did this repeatedly), and friends; and operated their business
enterprises as, so the lyric goes, "We are family." A few of the nonblacks showed
signs of nepotism but never totally confused their personal values with professional necessities as did these subjects. They maintained very close family ties and
nepotism ran rampant in their businesses. Their white and Asian counterparts utilized family members during the start-up stages, but once successful were careful
not to include family members or siblings in key positions within the company unless they were being groomed to run the company. This was clearly not the case
with these thirteen. Family was always first and foremost in their professional and
personal lives and there never was a clear demarcation between the two.

Family

The preponderance of these subjects was highly sensitive to the impact on their
families of their various business decisions and corporate moves. Not so with their
white counterparts, who relegated their families to second or third place in terms
of priorities. In fact, the Caucasians perpetually sacrificed their personal lives for
their professional goals and paid a very dear price in broken homes and multiple
marriages, a trend not found in these subjects. Some specific examples of these individuals' family orientation follows.

MAYA ANGELOU

Angelou adopted her name "Maya" from her beloved brother, Bailey, who said she
was "mya sister." Her mother, Vivian Johnson, was her role model, mentor, and
professional advisor, who instilled strength of character in her. Angelou once quit
the *Porgy and Bess* European tour to be with her son in California. All of her
writing and poetry elevate familial love and togetherness as next to godliness. She
wrote about having an illegitimate son at age sixteen "as the most important thing
that ever happened to me."

SHIRLEY CHISHOLM

Chisholm dedicated her life to pursuing her father's dream as delineated by
Marcus Garvey's philosophy. Chisholm lived at home until her mid-twenties and
never strayed far from the nest until her thirties. She treated her constituency as
family and involved her family in all her political races, with her husband acting
as campaign manager in her successful run for Congress. Chisholm's campaigning
involved eating chitlins and motza balls in the homes of her supporters.

BILL COSBY

He said after thirty years of marriage, "getting married was the best thing I ever did." This author never saw such a comment from any of the Caucasians studied. He reveres his family to such a degree that he created the sitcom "The Cosby Show" to eulogize the family as the most important element in society. All of Cosby's later work centered around parenting wayward teenagers and preventing their failure. Cosby once refused to keep one of his actors on "The Cosby Show" when the boy decided to drop out of high school.

BERRY GORDY

Gordy created Motown as a "family affair." A board meeting at Motown looked like a Gordy family reunion. He employed his mother and father and at one time or another all of his many brothers and sisters in the Motown organization. Many held key executive positions within the company. His parents remained on the Motown payroll until their deaths. Mistresses and lovers were hired at Motown as a standard operating procedure.

JOHN JOHNSON

Johnson so eulogized his mother he has not touched her office in the corporate headquarters of Johnson Publishing since her death and has left written instructions that it will not be disturbed as long as Johnson Publishing exists. He called her every day of his professional life, no matter where he was. Johnson once climbed a telephone pole in Haiti to tap into a line to place his daily call to his beloved mother. Johnson also employed his stepfather as head of maintenance of the Johnson buildings in downtown Chicago.

MICHAEL JACKSON

Through great pain Jackson has remained extremely close to his brothers and sisters despite a frenetic lifestyle as a rock-and-roll superstar. He built his mother a home in Los Angeles and when he wanted to break up the group and go single he agreed to keep the group together for his mother and did so for another six years.

MICHAEL JORDAN

Jordan told *USA Today,* "I always put family first, everything else is second." He employs his brother Larry as his business manager and his sister in other capacities. His Airness also employed his father as his press coordinator until his father's untimely death in 1993, which so devastated him that he announced his retirement two months later. Jordan's father and mother were his confidants, and when asked

FIGURE 19
DIFFERENT METHODOLOGIES OF EMINENT BLACKS AND NONBLACKS

The following are ten key social, political, familial, and motivational differences between eminent blacks and nonblacks. Both groups utilize similar traits and behavioral characteristics to achieve success but differ in their methodologies. These thirteen blacks differed from the forty-four nonblacks (nineteen females, two Asians, and twenty-two males) previously studied and from other research on eminent people.

1. **Church-Religion-Spiritualism—Fundamental support system for the black psyche.**
   All the black subjects had a close church affiliation and were highly religious, which was not found in the nonblack subjects, 33 percent of whom were nonreligious and less than half of whom were members of an organized church.

2. **Mothers-Grandmothers—Backbone of black family life.**
   The mother was the pillar of strength and solidarity for the family. They held the family together when fathers were absent. Family leadership and dominance differentiated black mothers from nonblack mothers.

3. **IQ and Formal Education—Critical for opening doors.**
   There was a huge disparity found in the formal educations of different ethnic groups. Nine of these thirteen blacks (69 percent) graduated from college and six had graduate degrees. Only one lacked a high school diploma, in contrast to 31 percent of nonblack college graduates and a total of 31 percent who failed to finish high school.

4. **Insecurity as Key Motivator—Drive instilled by fear of failure and return to the inner city.**
   Fear of failure and a potential return to the inner-city projects motivated these subjects more than in nonblacks and drove them to excel. Insecurity bred greatness.

5. **Less Dysfunctional Personalities—More emotionally stable.**
   Few incidences of dysfunctional behavior with possible exception of Paul Robeson and Michael Jackson in contrast to nonblacks where 58 percent were classified as manic-depressive and hypomania rampant.

6. **Political and Social Activism—Eminent blacks more politically conscious.**
   Whites seldom had time or inclination to get involved in politics. Blacks almost always did, although much of their support involved a fight for equality and freedom.

7. **Science/Technology Aversion—A dearth of superstars in these professions.**
   The black community lacks in superstars in science/technology in contrast to Caucasians, preferring arts, politics, and business. Technological innovation is apparently the province of whites.

8. **Sensual but Not Promiscuous—Majority not as sexually flaky or lecherous as whites.**
   Majority of blacks, contrary to popular belief, have higher ethical values than whites relative to marital fidelity and family values. Promiscuity not nearly as prevalent as in whites.

9. **Racial Issues-Products-Services—Vehicle for successful enterprise.**
   Blacks turned to ethnic-oriented products as vehicle to professional achievement. Nonblacks never adopted such a strategy.

10. **Personal/Professional Dichotomy—"We are family" mentality in business.**
    Blacks virtually never separated the personal from the professional and persisted in hiring family, friends, and lovers as employees, in contrast to Caucasians.

Sources: *Profiles of Genius* (1993), *Profiles of Female Genius* (1994), *Profiles of Power and Success* (1996), *Profiles of Black Success* (1997)

by a sports reporter about his heroes in life responded with characteristic humility, "My parents." He went on to say, "My heroes are and were my parents."

REGINALD LEWIS

Lewis's mother was his confidante, soul mate, and best friend even after he became a hard-nosed Wall Street lawyer and LBO buyout specialist. He kept his mother, Carolyn, involved in his life and she was instrumental in most of his major decisions. When he acquired Beatrice Foods for a billion dollars he installed his half-brother Jean Fugett as CEO. It was the third time he had offered Fugett a key position within one of his firms. Lewis took care of the family, bought them businesses, financed their educations, and then appointed Fugett his heir as chairman of Beatrice Foods just prior to his untimely death.

NELSON MANDELA

Mandela was groomed to become a tribal leader in the rural sections of southern Africa but rose instead to become president of South Africa. He so indoctrinated his wife Winnie in the destruction of apartheid that she became a renegade warrior to carry on his cause. She repeatedly went to jail in his behalf as one of his revolutionary civil activists. When he had to make a proclamation from prison he had his daughter read his statement. Even though Nelson and Winnie became bitter political enemies after his release from prison in 1990, and were later divorced, he insisted on keeping her on in Parliament—the ultimate in faithfulness to an embittered wife. Mandela looked upon his underground associates as family—they slept, ate, and fought together.

THURGOOD MARSHALL

Marshall lived at home with his parents and new wife even after graduating from Howard Law School. The couple continued living as a multifamily unit while he practiced law in Baltimore. He always revered family and felt his success was a family affair. Only when he was made Charles Houston's assistant at the NAACP in New York City did he finally move out of the family home and take up residence in Harlem with his wife. Thurgood considered all blacks family, especially the staff workers at the NAACP. When his wife died of cancer in mid-age he married a secretary at the NAACP headquarters who was of Asian ancestry because he envisioned her as family in respect to his lifelong cause of civil rights.

COLIN POWELL

Powell said he would refuse to run for president in the 1996 election without the prior consent of his wife, Alma. This sounded like lip service until he actually declined the opportunity to become a major candidate when his wife's depression took precedence over his professional life. A devoted father and husband, Powell sees the thorough institution of "family values" as the key to the resolution of America's problems. His parents nurtured him with these values and they have stayed with him.

PAUL ROBESON

Testimony to Robeson's family orientation is the fact that his wife, Eslanda, was his lifelong manager and stayed with him through many turbulent times and scandalous affairs. Despite Robeson's promiscuity, he never divorced his wife and remained at her side when she became terminally ill later in life. His family was of paramount importance to him. He revered his father. He treated all of his costars and associates just like family and was incapable of separating the personal from the professional, which ultimately destroyed him. Robeson defiantly sent his only son to Russia to be educated during the mid-thirties during the height of the Red hysteria period in world politics.

OPRAH WINFREY

Winfrey reveres her father but speaks little of her mother despite a sordid early life in which her mother played a key part. She is highly sensitive to childhood abuse since she experienced it firsthand. She has dedicated her show to the resolution of familial conflict. Family is high on her list of importance even though she has consciously elected not to have a family of her own. She recently flirted with the idea of adoption but feels it would not be fair to have a child or husband competing with her professional demands.

Summary

There is no question that diversity is a positive in any society and that the world is a melting pot that is inexorably erasing all ethnic differences. It is still some time before we all fit Washington's description of mulatto. But in the latter twentieth century it is apparent that blacks, whites, and Asians function differently in many ways. That does not make any group right or wrong—only unique. When it comes to the similar traits to achieve eminence and superstardom, blacks, Asians, and Caucasians are quite similar, although their methodologies and value systems appear to be quite different in many respects.

I am convinced "greatness is greatness" and color or ethnicity has nothing to do with the process. This book is about black success and genius but it should not have had to be written. Our society is homogenizing rapidly and diversity in these eminent subjects was a critical factor in their uniqueness and success. Examples are abundant but the three most prominent were Thurgood Marshall, Colin Powell, and Paul Robeson. Marshall was known as the "Mulatto Lawyer" due to his mixed racial heritage. Powell was of African, English, Irish, Scottish, and Arawak Indian descent. Robeson was of African, Indian, and English ancestry. The very diversity of these three wunderkinds contributed to their uniqueness and imbued them wtih an inner resolve to become individuals, not stereotypes of a given race. As our society intermarries it will gravitate toward a variegated mix of white, black, and brown, and the twenty-first century will close on a society that is colorless; classifying a person by color will have gone the way of the horse and buggy. When this occurs, the words *black, yellow,* and *brown* will be relegated to the trashcan of bigoted history.

20

Key Secrets of Black Success

Life is a comedy for those who think and a tragedy for those who feel.
Horace Walpole

Are there any discernable differences between the races in achieving super-stardom? None! Can anyone with normal intelligence and health get to the very top? You bet! Is there a pathway that is best suited for achieving eminence in life? Yes, and for these thirteen black wunderkinds it was the performing arts (Cosby, Jackson, Robeson, Winfrey), business (Gordy, Johnson, Lewis), politics/government (Chisholm, Mandela, Marshall, Powell), and sports (Jordan). The sample is far too small to draw any substantive conclusions but one thing is certain: Success is colorless as are the key traits necessary for achieving greatness in life. Attitude, not color, is the operative word in all great success stories.

Stereotypes

Based on my research successful people fall into specific stereotypes. The word *stereotype* is a dangerous one to use since it has grown to have a negative connotation, especially for any group that has been victimized or carries the scars of discrimination. However, the word can carry a very positive message, especially in the sense that "drive" and "aggressiveness" are stereotypical terms used to define success regardless of race. Words like *drive, passion,* and *aggressiveness* describe the dominant traits found in all eminent people whether they are of Asian, European, or African ancestry. These words are highly correlated to great achievement in business, the arts, sports, and most other disciplines. Few Jewish power brokers become incensed over being referred to as stereotypically driven, passionate, or aggressive. The reason is that they see the truth in the names and therefore do not

369

become defensive over such comments. Name-calling never bothered these thirteen since they knew the truth and they always considered the source as less than credible. Those who use degrading epithets to label a person are not defining the person, only themselves.

I was told by a number of people not to use the words *passionate, aggressive,* or *driven* to describe black males since the words are stereotypes and not appropriate for this book. The word *passion* just happens to be the most accurate description of Bill Gates just as it was for Sammy Davis, Jr. *Passion* described Golda Meir the same as it does Maya Angelou. It is precisely what made Pablo Picasso a master painter, Maria Callas a great diva, Martin Luther King, Jr., a civil rights activist, and Paul Robeson a great Shakespearean actor. It is also the driving force behind the eminence of Michael Jackson and Michael Jordan. Anyone desirous of getting to the top had better be passionate to a fault no matter their race, religion, or ethnicity. The very negativity conjured up by decrying the use of the truth or an accurate description of greatness is antithetic to the process of discovery.

The use of stereotypes in the negative are by the bigots and also-rans who see the negativity in everything. They key on the impossibilities and have hang-ups about words when they should be more concerned about actions. Fear is their god and defensiveness their sword. Instead of looking for the possibilities and opportunities in life they look for the problems and use those to make themselves feel better. The black subjects in this book never allowed stereotypes or degrading epithets to interfere with the pursuit of their goals and that is what made them so great.

Success Imprints the Key

Colin Powell discovered as a teenager that working hard as a janitor led to a promotion and ultimate success. He decided to be the best mopper in Pepsi history and said of the experience, "I had learned a valuable lesson. All work is honorable. Always do your best, because someone is watching." Maya Angelou experienced a similar imprint as a teenager. Her survival imprint occurred when she was stranded alone in the depths of Mexico with a drunken father. She survived the experience saying, "No matter what happened after that I had won." John Johnson's success imprint came from reading Horatio Alger stories after a despicable childhood in Mississippi, Cosby's came from Mark Twain, Gordy's from Joe Louis defeating the master race model Max Schmeling, and Michael Jordan's from the devastation of being cut from his high school basketball team. It isn't what happened to these people that made them great, it is how they dealt with the adversity that makes them great. All of them were able to use adversity to their advantage and the resulting "success imprint" launched them on their way to the top of their professions. They refused to allow any of the myriad of "failure imprints" to take hold of them. Our prisons are filled with those who bought into the "failure imprints." The creative geniuses of the world refused to accept anything but "success imprints." Wally Amos wrote, "Everyone on this earth has the power to tap into their own greatness." These thirteen had a handle on that power. Their "success imprints" were a valuable support system for their long treks to the top. These "success imprints" helped mold their internal self-images and armed them with the power to overcome all adversity.

Psychology of Greatness

These thirteen visionaries had a unique ability to take the right road to success. They were able to differentiate between the "success roads" and the "failure roads" and successfully avoided the many detours along the way. Confirmation of this comes from Stanford psychologist Albert Bandura. He concluded that "self-efficacy" was a key factor in one's ability to succeed in life. He wrote: "People's beliefs about their abilities have a profound effect on those abilities. . . . People who have a sense of self-efficacy bounce back from failures; they approach things in terms of how to handle them rather than worrying about what can go wrong." In his best-selling book *Emotional Intelligence* (1995), Daniel Goleman argues for an "EQ or Emotional Intelligence" as the critical factor in "predicting people's success." He said: "We are not necessarily limited to a specific emotional menu by our inherited traits," which is essentially in agreement with this book's argument that our key traits are learned not inherited.

Different Intelligences

Harvard psychologist Howard Gardner concluded that there are seven different intelligences that all humans can attain. This is contrary to the dogma that one's IQ is the critical factor in greatness. Gardner's intelligences were delineated in his book *Frames of Mind: The Theory of Multiple Intelligences* (1983). He used one supersuccessful individual to define each intelligence: interpersonal (Freud), visual/spatial (Picasso), musical (Stravinsky), linguistic (T. S. Eliot), bodily/kinesthetic (Martha Graham), logical-mathematical (Einstein), and intrapersonal (Gandhi). These thirteen all fit into one of Gardner's categories but none quite so well as the bodily-kinesthetic intelligence.

Gardner's work gives authenticity to many of the different types of intelligences found in these subjects. No person has just one of Gardner's intelligences. We all share some elements of introversion and extroversion as well as the other personality factors that make us what we are. We are all located somewhere on a continuum where degrees of myopic or visionary, introversion or extroversion, mania or lethargy, type A or type B, dependence or independence, and feeling or thinking become two faces within us.

Bodily/Kinesthetic Example

It appears from this research that blacks have more "kinesthetic" intelligence than other groups. Success in sports and the performing arts demands a kinesthetic intelligence just as winning a gold medal in the Olympic sprints, dunking a basketball in the NBA, or doing the moonwalk where rhythmic movement is critical to superstardom. This appears to be an intelligence where blacks have an advantage over nonblacks and they should take advantage of that advantage. We all have far too few areas in which we excel and those of us who are so blessed should see the blessing as an advantage, not something to be ashamed of.

The rhythm, style, and grace of Michael Jordan and Carl Lewis are testimony to their kinesthetic intelligence. Bill Cosby, Berry Gordy, Michael Jackson, Michael Jordan, and Paul Robeson all had more than their fair share of this "kinesthetic/bodily intelligence." The media has labeled this physical genius in the music world as "soul" and more recently the genre has come to be known as "rap." This was the genius demonstrated by Gordy's "Motown Sound," Jordan's "Hang Time," Michael Jackson's "moonwalk," and the artistry of Cosby and Robeson. Even Winfrey has some unique sense of timing that defies logic. The argument for this special intelligence is further substantiated by Wynton Marsalis in an article, "Why We Must Preserve Jazz" (*Ebony,* February 1986): "Jazz is the most modern expression of the way black people look at the world. It's not like what black people did in sports. . . . Jazz is something Negroes *invented* and it said the most profound things about what modern democratic life is really about. It is the nobility of the race put into sound; it is the sensuousness of romance in our dialect; it is the picture of the people in all their glory, which is what swinging is all about."

This appears to be consistent with the research findings of scientists who find that blacks dominate professional sports. Black athletes represent over 50 percent of NFL rosters and 80 percent of NBA rosters despite representing only 12 percent of the general population. Boxing and track and field sprints would be a joke without blacks competing since they have dominated every category for over thirty years. During the 1993 World Track & Field Championships in Germany, blacks won every single sprint and long-distance event. Blacks have dominated jazz, rhythm and blues, and pop music for half a century. Jazz composers like Duke Ellington and stage performers like Sammy Davis, Jr., had few equals.

Why are blacks so proficient in the above areas? According to James Comer and Alvin Poussaint of Harvard, "There may be some physical reasons why blacks are better dancers and singers than whites." Scientists have found that a black's "motor development takes place faster during the first year among many African-American babies than among European babies." Even if the scientists are correct, it remains fundamental that success does beget success. As long as blacks are supersuccessful in any area of expertise they will continue to pursue those areas in which they can experience positive financial rewards and emotional reinforcement from their peers.

Musical Intelligence

Jazz is just one dimension of Gardner's "musical intelligence." Ralph Wiley wrote in *Why Black People Tend to Shout* (1991), "Creativity is at the root of all forms of music, which is why black people are so adept at it. Creativity is black people's middle name." This premise adds credence to the magnificence of Paul Robeson singing "Ol' Man River," Maya Angelou doing *Calypso Heat Wave,* or Michael Jackson's phenomenal success in the rock video *Thriller.* It also contributed to the monumental success of jazz composer Duke Ellington, the most prolific composer in history with twelve hundred compositions, and instrumental in the great success of Quincy Jones and Berry Gordy. Jazz was Gordy's first love and a jazz record shop his first enterprise prior to starting Motown.

Other Intelligences

John Johnson, Nelson Mandela, and Reginald Lewis could be said to have possessed Gardner's "intrapersonal" genius based on their special talents in the area of entrepreneurship, speaking and writing, and interpersonal skills. Martin Luther King, Jr., Maya Angelou, Shirley Chisholm, Bill Cosby, and Oprah Winfrey were especially adept at Gardner's "linguistic" and "intrapersonal" intelligences. George Washington Carver defines "logical-mathematical" genius and Bill Cosby, Colin Powell, and Thurgood Marshall are excellent examples of his "interpersonal genius." All of the subjects had some traces of other intelligences but the most prevalent was "kinesthetic" and the least were the "visual-spatial" (no artists of note) and "logical-mathematical."

Characteristics of Black Creative Genius

Figure 20 summarizes some of the key personality characteristics found in these superstars. As can be seen, eleven of the thirteen subjects were externally energized and therefore classified as *extroverts.* They represented a surprising 69 percent of the subjects. A like number had a macrovision of the world and were classified *intuitives* for a total of 85 percent of the subjects. Twelve of the thirteen, 92 percent, had a propensity for what David Kirton called an "innovator" style of behavior. These types prefer "being different" in contrast to their opposites, "adaptors," who prefer "being excellent" as a professional operating style. Only Colin Powell, of all these subjects, operated with an adaptor style.

The preponderance of the subjects (twelve of the thirteen) were live-on-the-edge risk-takers in terms of Frank Farley's Big T thrill-seeking and high testosterone personality types. The only subject who met Farley's definition of a "little t" or security-conscious and caretaking mentality was Colin Powell. All but one

FIGURE 20
BEHAVIORAL CHARACTERISTICS OF CREATIVE GENIUS

1. Jung's Archetypes   Extroverts (Externally energized) vs. Introverts (Internally energized)
Intuitiveness (Macrovision) vs. Sensors (Microvision)

2. Kiersey's Temperaments   Lifestyle choices:

Promethean: (Intuitive-thinking)	Visionaries
Apollonian: (Intuitive-feeling)	Catalysts
Dionysian: (Sensing-perceiving)	Trouble-shooters
Epithemean: (Sensing-judging)	Traditionalists

3. Kirton's Behavioral Styles

Adaptors:	Prefer "being excellent" to taking risk
Innovators:	Prefer "being different" to safety

4. Farley's Thrill-Seekers   Big Ts (high testosterone) vs. little ts (low testosterone)

5. Type A Personalities

Type A:	Impatient and competitive
Type B:	Patient and passive

6. Charismatics   Mesmerizing influence; attracts disciples in droves +++ cultlike attraction

Subjects	1 Jung's Introvert/ Extrovert	2 Jung's Intuitive/ Sensor	3 Kiersey's Tempera- ment Type	4 Kirton's Creative Type	5 Risk (Big T vs. little t)	6 Drive Type	Charisma
Maya Angelou	Extrovert	Intuitive	Apollonian	Innovator	T+	A	C++
Shirley Chisholm	Extrovert	Intuitive	Promethean	Innovator	T	A++	C
Bill Cosby	Extrovert	Intuitive	Promethean	Innovator	T	A	C+
Berry Gordy	Extrovert	Intuitive	Promethean	Innovator	T+++	A+++	C+
Michael Jackson	Introvert	Intuitive	Apollonian	Innovator	T+	A+	C++
John Johnson	Introvert	Intuitive	Promethean	Innovator	T++	A	C
Michael Jordan	Introvert	Intuitive	Promethean	Innovator	T+++	A+++	C+
Reginald Lewis	Introvert	Intuitive	Promethean	Innovator	T++	A+++	C+
Nelson Mandela	Extrovert	Intuitive	Promethean	Innovator	T+++	A	C+++
Thurgood Marshall	Extrovert	Sensor	Dionysian	Innovator	T++	A	C
Colin Powell	Extrovert	Sensor	Epithemean	Adaptor	T+	B	C
Paul Robeson	Extrovert	Intuitive	Promethean	Innovator	T+++	A++	C+++
Oprah Winfrey	Extrovert	Intuitive	Apollonian	Innovator	T++	A+	C+++
Summaries	9 = Extrovert	11 = Intuitive	8 = Promethean	12 = Innovator	4 = T+++	12 = A	3 = C+++
	4 = Introvert	2 = Sensors	3 = Apollonian	1 = Adaptor	4 = T++	1 = B	4 = C+
					3 = T+		4 = C
	69%	85%	62%	92%	100%	92%	100%

(92 percent) had the classic Type A personality characteristics and nine of the thirteen were highly charismatic. Only Chisholm, Johnson, Marshall, and Powell were not strongly charismatic but Mandela, Robeson, and Winfrey made up for them with their captivating personae.

Nine of the thirteen (69 percent) were classified as Promethean temperaments based on David Kiersey's definition of people who prefer to seek the opportunities and possibilities in life in contrast to the guardian and traditionalist behaviors. The Prometheans dominated this group, but no matter the personality preference, all used the ten key success traits for climbing the ladder of success: charisma, competitiveness, confidence, drive, independence, passion, perfectionism, temerity, tenacity, and vision.

Bred, Not Born

The data indicate these thirteen acquired those behaviors that led to their great success. Such findings are confirmed by the September 1995 *Science Digest*: "Research now indicates that creative people are made, not born." Harvard psychologist Jerome Kagan agrees, saying, "No human quality is beyond change." Novelist/philosopher Ayn Rand found the same to be true. She wrote in her book *We the Living* (1936): "No one is born with any kind of talent and therefore, every skill has to be acquired. Writers are made, not born. To be exact, writers are self-made." Maya Angelou confirms that more than any other in this book. Nelson Mandela also believes this to be the case: "I maintain that nurture, rather than nature, is the primary molder of personality."

Formation of Success-Oriented Personality

These wunderkinds acquired their key traits the old-fashioned way from positive role models, superlative parenting, early success imprints, and a "psychological unease" acquired as a survival mechanism from the basic insecurities of childhood and traumatic experiences. The most critical of these appear to be the "success imprints," mythical hero/mentors, and traumatic experiences of life.

These individuals appear to have stumbled onto success during their formative years and grabbed hold of that positive experience both consciously and unconsciously. Their imprints and positive experiences were indelibly imprinted on their psyche to such an extent it altered their inner values to one that had "greatness" written on it. Would Martin Luther King, Jr., have become a great civil rights leader and reformer had he not been named for the father of the Protestant Reformation? Maybe, but the impact of his having a label of religious revolutionary certainly affected his approach to life and established a model for him to follow to his destiny. Would Frederick Douglass have become as great had he not learned to read and write? I think not! Or what of George Washington Carver's life without the need to build a barrier—education—between himself and slavery? He would have been an also-ran had he not been driven to bring science to mankind.

Even the dastardly and horrific acts we experience can become motivators to us in later life. Winfrey is a greater success professionally because of her childhood molestations since she has lived her life to overcome that devastating experience. Finding oneself on the bottom often conditions one to what is necessary to reach the top. Maya Angelou is an example. She was transformed into a lover of poetry and books due to the childhood molestation that resulted in her becoming mute. It was poetry and books that became her solace and road back to normalcy. We grow due to a need to survive both emotionally and intellectually. That is the great secret of success. It is our armament against evil that proves to be our fuel to greatness. Money can't do it, or name, status, or formal education. Drive and motivation are learned through life experiences, both positive and negative. They come from within and the inner self is molded as a direct result of all of life's interfaces both good or bad.

As a freshman at the University of North Carolina, Michael Jordan was magically transformed into "Air Jordan." The moment he made that last-second shot to win the NCAA championship against Georgetown, Michael became a different person. This "success imprint" has become so fixated in Michael's psyche he insists on taking the last shot in every crucial Bulls game—and has been successful more times than Cleveland or the Lakers would like to remember.

When Reginald Lewis came home from camp and learned that his mother would keep his paper route money because she had delivered his papers, he was destroyed. But it taught him a valuable lesson he would never forget, causing him to write about it forty years later. He never again forgot to make his deals up front and was motivated to become a lawyer in order that he would be expert at contractual negotiations.

Fear and Success

Fear is a key motivator in successful people. Too much fear is debilitating. Too little and achievement goes wanting. Fear and ambition must be balanced. Insecurity does breed greatness but only if positive passion exists to overcome the crippling aspects of fear. High anxiety sharpens the wit, energizes the brain, and arms one with enough moxie to overcome complacency. Such is the nature of overcoming rejection and fueling one's drive to go for the gold. Most blacks intuitively "know" they have to be better to be successful in most any profession, especially those professions dominated by white males. The fear of failure gives minorities a special incentive to excel and this was found in all of these subjects.

Crisis—The Mother of Creativity

It appears from the psychohistories of these subjects that one cannot reach the top without having first visited the bottom (see chapter 3). It is at the bottom where all the important learning takes place and survival imprints are instilled. Little is learned from success other than self-confidence. We always learn more from adversity than success. To some people adversity is shattering and they never fully recover while others are renewed by the experience. Losers see traumatic experiences as a crutch and winners view it as a catalyst. These thirteen overcame many traumas which made them stronger for having the experience, and emerged from the chaos with a stronger character, more self-sufficiency, and an indomitable resilience.

Overprotective Parents—The Bane of Creativity

Parents who never allow their children to experience life, and learn from those experiences, are setting them up to fail later in life. Such parents shield the child from any harm and by doing so never allow the child to experience problems or learn the nuances of problem resolution. The child never learns to cope in a real-world environment. Confirmation of this thesis comes from Harvard psychologist Jerome Kagan who found: "It appears that mothers who protect their highly reactive infants from frustration and anxiety in hopes of effecting a beneficent outcome seem to exacerbate the infants' uncertainty and produce the opposite effect." Locking one's child in a room ensures he or she will never bruise a knee or psyche, or experience a bloody nose, but the child never learns to deal with the normal adversities of life. Needless to say, none of these subjects was raised by overprotective parents. Most were raised in permissive households, which allowed them to hone their coping skills at a very young age and to learn early to risk and fail without suffering a devastating experience emotionally.

Passion and Drive

Freud was convinced success was a zero-sum game with sex and professional achievement at opposite ends of a continuum. He said that any individual who successfully fulfilled all his sexual appetites for pleasure would be totally incapable of productive achievement in other pursuits. In his words: "For what motive would induce man to put his sexual energy to other uses if by any disposal of it he could obtain fully satisfying pleasure? He would never let go of this pleasure and would make no further progress." He cited Leonardo da Vinci as an example of an asexual man who was energy incarnate when it came to creative innovation but lacking in personal sexual gratification. Since other research shows successful people with very high sex drives, it was decided to list the sex drives, marriage and

FIGURE 21
MARITAL AND SEX DRIVE INFORMATION

Subject	# Marriages	# Children	# Children Born Out of Wedlock	Libidinal Energy Sex Drive
Maya Angelou	3	1	1	Highly sensual
Shirley Chisholm	2	0	0	Restrained
Bill Cosby	1	5	0	High
Berry Gordy	3	8	6	Highly promiscuous
Michael Jackson	2	1	0	Asexual
John Johnson	1	2	0	Restrained
Michael Jordan	1	3	1	High
Reginald Lewis	1	2	0	High
Nelson Mandela	2	4	0	High
Thurgood Marshall	2	2	0	Very high
Colin Powell	1	2	0	High
Paul Robeson	1	1	0	Highly promiscuous
Oprah Winfrey	0	1	1	Sensuous

divorce data, number of children, and other available data on the sexual proclivi-
ties of these subjects (see figure 21). They were married an average of 1.5 times
and had an average of 2.8 children (of the total thirty-two children, nine were illegitimate).

Napoleon Hill was convinced that "sex energy is the creative energy of all geniuses" and that "there never has been, and never will be a great leader, builder,
or artist lacking in this driving force of sex." These individuals did not meet that
expectation. Only Berry Gordy showed signs of extreme licentiousness, with Paul
Robeson a close second. Gordy had the most children, eight, and only two of these
born by women he married, with six born out of wedlock. Cosby had five children
and Mandela four, but the number of children and the number of marriages were
not out of the ordinary.

Most of these thirteen subjects were highly sensual but did not allow those
feelings to dominate their life. No alternative lifestyles such as homosexuality appeared in the research. Michael Jackson appears to be the only subject with any
deviant sexual orientation but he is more asexual than anything due to his preference for the company of teenage boys. Oprah Winfrey is the only subject who
never married. Shirley Chisholm and Winfrey are the only ones without children
although Winfrey had a child who died when she was fourteen. Gordy took the
most trips to the altar. The only unusual statistic is the nine illegitimate children,
but six of those were by one subject, Berry Gordy.

Age of Success for Creative Geniuses

Six of the thirteen visionaries (46 percent) found success prior to age thirty-five (see figure 22). Four of them were between ages thirty-five and fifty before they found success, and three were over fifty. The subject who demonstrated the most patience was Nelson Mandela. Mandela was awarded the Nobel Peace Prize at age seventy-four and was not elected to the presidency of South Africa until age seventy-five. Mandela began his career fighting for his nation's freedom during his twenties and worked diligently for fifty years to see his dreams come to fruition.

Maya Angelou reached the peak of her power and success at age sixty-four when she was asked to read a poem at Bill Clinton's inauguration. She was first published at age forty but did not become a successful author until age fifty. Thurgood Marshall first gained national recognition in his mid-twenties when he became the legal counsel for the NAACP, but he did not realize national acclaim until age fifty-nine when he was appointed to the Supreme Court in 1967. He had worked tirelessly for thirty years prior to achieving real success. Colin Powell is the other subject who was in his fifties prior to national recognition as a superstar. He was age fifty-two when President Bush appointed him to the chairmanship of the Joint Chiefs of Staff on October 1, 1989. He had been on a fast track in many prestigious positions during the interim but was unknown out of the military until he became head of America's military operations.

In stark contrast to these later successes were Michael Jackson, Michael Jordan, Bill Cosby, and Oprah Winfrey, all of whom made it to the very top before age thirty. Michael Jackson began performing in concerts at age five and was a national celebrity by age ten. He reached the pinnacle of success with release of the *Thriller* album in 1984, when he was still only twenty-five. This success made him enormously wealthy and guaranteed his status as one of the all-time great entertainers after *Thriller* became the highest-selling album in history and won him eight Grammys. Michael Jordan reached national acclaim as a basketball star at age nineteen when he was named college basketball's player of the year in his sophomore season at North Carolina University. But he didn't became a national superstar until two years later in 1984 when he was named the National Basketball Association's Rookie of the Year. He was still just twenty-one years old. By age twenty-five Michael had become all-universe and a multimillionaire. By age thirty he was the world's highest paid athlete at $35 million a year. Bill Cosby made it to the top as a national TV celebrity by age twenty-eight when he played a starring role in "I Spy." "The Oprah Winfrey Show" was launched when she was just thirty. John Johnson, Paul Robeson, and Berry Gordy all started their careers in their twenties but never reached the top until their mid-thirties.

FIGURE 22
AGE WHEN BROKE THROUGH BLACK CEILING

Subject	Success and Year	Age
Maya Angelou	Published author (1968)	40
	Read poem at inauguration (1992)	40
Shirley Chisholm	New York State legislature (1964)	40
	United States congresswoman (1968)	44
Bill Cosby	Premiere of "I Spy" television series (1965)	28
Berry Gordy	Supremes hit #1 at Copa/Ed Sullivan (1965)	37
Michael Jackson	*Thriller* #1 of all time—8 Grammys (1984)	25
John Johnson	*Ebony* and *Jet* solvent (1952)	34
Michael Jordan	Bulls Rookie of Year (1984)	21
Reginald Lewis	LBO of McCall Pattern $90M (1984–87)	45
Nelson Mandela	Nobel Peace Prize and president of South Africa	74/75
Thurgood Marshall	U.S.Supreme Court Justice(1967)	59
Colin Powell	Chairman, Joint Chiefs of Staff (1989)	52
Paul Robeson	London stage success and recording artist (1928)	30
Oprah Winfrey	"Oprah Winfrey Show" syndication/*Color Purple* (1985)	31

Physical Characteristics

Various researchers have shown that successful people tend to be taller than the norm, at least in United States politics. Dean Keith Simonton said in *Greatness* (1994), "In democratic systems . . . the taller of two candidates is more likely to win the election." He illustrated this with data on John Kennedy who was much taller than Richard Nixon; Ronald Reagan, who was taller than Walter Mondale and Jimmy Carter; George Bush, who hovered over Michael Dukakis and Walter Mondale; Bill Clinton, who at six feet, three inches was taller than the six-foot George Bush. History also gives credence to size as an important criteria for leadership. Abraham Lincoln was six feet, four inches; George Washington, Thomas Jefferson, and Franklin Roosevelt were six feet, two inches; and Andrew Jackson was six feet, one inch. Anthropologically speaking, "Alpha Males" are more dominant, virile, taller, and more aggressive than the other primates in the pack. They win the battles of the heart and the food.

Strikingly Powerful People

Were these subjects taller than the average? These thirteen subjects were all physically striking and impressive people. Most towered over their associates and adversaries and projected powerful personae. Maya Angelou is a female with a giant intellect and physical presence. She stands an imposing six feet tall and commands the respect of all those who come in contact with her. Oprah Winfrey is a stately five feet, eight inches. Berry Gordy, John Johnson, and Reginald Lewis were all males of average height, but were specimens who could be physically intimidating. Gordy fought as a professional boxer and Lewis was a four-letter athlete in high school who earned an athletic scholarship to Virginia State as quarterback.

Only Michael Jackson and Shirley Chisholm were what could be called average physically. All the others were well above average with most of the men well over six feet tall with a commanding presence. When they walked into a room, they were intimidating and soon became the center of attention. Most adversaries were frightened by their physical presence. Paul Robeson was six foot three and 230 pounds of solid muscle. Michael Jordan is an athletic six feet, six inches. Nelson Mandela is a huge presence at six feet, two inches. Thurgood Marshall and Colin Powell are massive six feet, one inch, and Bill Cosby an even six feet.

Catalysts for Equality

These subjects not only became rich and famous in their own right, they were the catalysts of change for their people. Berry Gordy legitimatized gospel music and took it mainstream, He took rhythm and blues out of Harlem and Watts and deposited it in mid-America as a respectable sound that Madison Avenue and Rodeo Drive accepted as their own. Motown pioneered in making the "Black Sound" synonymous with American musical culture and transformed the musical listening and dancing habits of a nation. If Elvis was the King then Berry is Prime Minister for his pervasive influence on American music.

In a similar manner Maya Angelou absorbed her Southern heritage—riddled with hatred and fear—and communicated it to a desensitized world. Colin Powell resorted to diplomacy and individual pride (esprit de corps) to meld a diverse group of people into one body with a common goal and spirit. Reginald Lewis also took the tack of gaining equality by beating the opposition on their own turf. He conquered Harvard Law School, Wall Street, and the world of finance, making hundreds of millions in the process but more importantly proving to the nonbelievers that color has nothing to do with achievement. Cosby elected to use the medium of the TV sitcom to effect change. He insisted on depicting blacks as normal people by placing them in ordinary, nonstereotypical environments. Michael Jackson recently followed Cosby's lead although he resorted to mental imagery and emotional shock in his recording albums aimed at effecting change. In Michael's defense it must be understood that the "outlandish" and "weird" are often the necessary vehicles to get the masses to see the obvious with candor. John Johnson launched *Ebony* and *Jet* magazines to portray black people as beautiful subjects and not as subjects of ridicule, which had been so common in white magazines. Michael "Air" Jordan has done more to tear down the lines of prejudice than most. As a sports icon he has maintained a "spartan" image that has done wonders for the sport.

Discrimination and Success

These visionaries took prejudice and discrimination and used them as catalysts to motivate them to be better. Rather than allow others to be obstacles in their paths, they used the issues as an incentive to drive themselves. Those people in life who allow other people to interfere with their success are allowing a bully to win. These thirteen never allowed any form of rejection and intolerance to get in their way. Sammy Davis, Jr., gives us some insight into how the superstars are able to deal with the race issue. He told the *Ann Arbor News* just prior to his death: "Racism had a profound effect on me. In one respect it was good for me because I used it as a motivating force. But it was also negative, because it made me get too deeply involved in trying to play a game that's impossible to play . . . pretending that if you get fame or if you become well known, it will eradicate the prejudice. Because there's no such eradication" (May 20, 1990).

Malcolm X went through a similar metamorphosis while in prison. On his release he was reborn into a freedom fighter without parallel. Others have experienced a similar plight as blacks in their drive to be great. The Jews have been discriminated against for two thousand years and have fought back by working in self-employed industries as merchants. They have become inordinately successful in many professions just as the blacks have. The reason is that their mothers raise them to believe they are special, great, and powerful in order to prepare them for the overt discrimination they are sure to face as adults. Consequently the Jewish people tend to grow up with extra-strong self-esteems and a special resilience. Often Jewish children grow up with stronger self-esteems than the bigots who would attack them for their religious beliefs. I found their career-pathing to be quite similar to the black subjects in this book and found a parallel that had to be noted. Jews and blacks take similar paths to the top. Both are typically loners, entrepreneurs, or entertainers who are self-sufficient. These professions are not dependent on others as they are evaluated on their personal performance, not on the whims of others. Like these blacks, the Jewish superstars pursue careers in the performing arts, business, and the humanities, since success in these professions is a function of personal performance not adhering to a bureaucratic class structure.

Gays and lesbians often face a similar problem. Gays have always taken a divergent path to the top. Fear of recrimination from an ignorant and bigoted world force them to stay in the closet instead of duking it out in the establishment which is typically intolerant of those who are different. Most minorities have consciously taken their destiny out of the hands of traditionalists by refusing to work in any discipline controlled by others. They have sought employment in the creative disciplines which tend to rate their efforts for their intrinsic value and not for their color, lifestyle, or gender. These people are found working on Broadway or in Hollywood, painting, writing, or in professions outside the mainstream. In many respects, women have had the same problem but not to the same degree as blacks and Jews.

Prescription for the Future—Dare to Be Great!

These thirteen individuals were risk-takers not care-takers, always willing to sacrifice the present for a better future. All were prepared to bet the farm in pursuit of their dreams. Gordy was by far the greatest risk-taker among this group but most of the others were not far behind. Maya Angelou gives testimony to the importance of taking risk to become great. She is quoted in the book *Genius: The Artist and the Process* (1990): "It is the desperate traveler who teaches us the most profound lesson and affords us the most exquisite thrills. She touches us with her boldness and vulnerability, for her sole preparation is the fierce determination to leave where she is, and her only certain destination is somewhere other than where she has been."

John Johnson wrote in his autobiography, *Succeeding Against the Odds* (1987), "living on the edge is the summit of life." Michael Jordan once told a sports reporter, "I was always the type of guy who went for the home run." Colin Powell told an Arts and Entertainment audience, "Teach children survival techniques and then send them out to experience survival." The other subjects, like all eminent people, learned to live right on the edge of the precipice, but had the prescience not to fall over that edge. They preferred the challenge of uncertainty with its high rewards to the tediousness of the more secure life. All were comfortable with ambiguity. Reflecting on the success of these consummate black innovative visionaries their behavioral characteristics can be summarized as follows: A driven person who is well steeped in charisma, competitiveness, confidence, and a strong work ethic. They are tenacious renegades and passionate perfectionists willing to risk everything in pursuit of their dreams. All were intuitive visionaries who used adversity and prejudice as a motivating force to success.

The book *The Bell Curve* has done the greatest disservice to blacks in the last decade. It espouses high IQ as the path to the top when all it does is test for cultural knowledge. The path to the top is steeped in the above personal characteristics, not in the size of the house where one is raised, scores on SAT or IQ tests, or a pedigree from an Ivy League college. Something else is at work in creative genius and it can be found in the success stories of these thirteen superstars. According to renowned University of Minnesota psychologist Paul Torrance, "no fallacy has done more harm to children or robbed society of more creative talent than the IQ test." Torrance discovered in his research that "IQ tests do not measure creativity." His work validates the findings in this book. Creative and innovative achievement has a lot more to do with internal drives and vision than it has to do with potential for intellectual processing. It has something to do with life's experiences and the attitudes and motivations derived from them.

FIGURE 23
TWELVE PRINCIPLES OF INSTILLING CREATIVITY

"Children grow up to fulfill their internal self-images"

It appears from the research on highly creative and entrepreneurial people that "success imprints," in contrast to "failure imprints," are critical to the process. The gifted child is intolerant of useless conformity and demands a stimulating and challenging environment. Research has shown that depositing children in impoverished or nonstimulating environments will make them less capable and placing dull children in enhanced or embellished environments will cause them to become more capable. Maria Montessori's success in this was dramatic and recent brain research at Berkeley and UCLA has cast light on the importance of environment in molding a person's ability to cope and maximize their potential. Overprotective mothers and authoritarian fathers are the bane of creativity, while doting and permissive parents appear to mold creative offspring.

Indulgent and Doting Parents. Treating a child as unique and special instills a strong self-esteem and builds personal confidence. The flip-side danger is creating an arrogant and/or egoistic adult. Such is the price of molding an indomitable will and optimistic persona.

Demonstrate Independent Action. Entrepreneurial or venturesome activities by parents mold the child with like behavioral styles. Independence is born of experience, not genetics, and children of self-employed parents learn independence and self-sufficiency, since they emulate positive role models. Example is far more important than words.

Extensive Travel or Transience. Moving and facing new cultures and relationships are positive influences for building self-sufficiency, coping skills, and comfort with risk taking. Learning to cope with the new and unknown is critical to molding an entrepreneurial personality. An around-the-world trip is far more valuable to a child than a year in school, especially for the gifted.

Freedom of Movement and Action. Encourage living on the edge without courting disaster. The child must be allowed to push the envelope to the edge without going over, with parental guidance and direction critical to survival. Indulgent parents are preferable to overprotective ones.

Ban "No" from the Vocabulary—Reinforce All Actions Positively. Magnify strengths and ignore weaknesses. Optimism should be paramount in all things personal or professional. Never allow negativity or rationalization to rule. "Success imprints" result from difficult but positive actions.

Preach "Different" Is Okay. Leaders are different. Mimicking the pack grooms only followers, not leaders. Leaders break new ground and by definition are renegades. Children should be encouraged to risk and fail and to experiment. They need to know it is okay to be unique; independence is the result.

Games of Abstract Problem Solving. Lego sets, erector sets, jigsaw puzzles, video games, and ham radios are the tools of genius. Heuristic problem solving builds holistic and intuitive skills.

Books, Movies, and Fantasy Heroes. Fictional and mythical heroes are excellent fantasy mentors. They tend to remove limits to achievement and channel energy toward positives.

Knowledge and Inquisitiveness Should Be Revered. Knowledge builds enthusiasm. It should be pursued relative to the arts, sciences, journal writing, poetry, philosophy, and the like.

Surround with Stimulating Challenges. The unconscious is absorbent and children become a product of their environment. Avoid impoverished environments; seek enhanced ones.

Hyperactivity and Mania. An extremely beneficial trait. High energy excels; speed wins. They should not be inhibited by drugs or punishment. Such behavior should be directed, managed, and focused on meaningful targets; it should not be changed. Most charismatics are hyperactive.

Imagination Should Be Encouraged. All adult creative endeavors are born of childlike fantasy, that is the by-product of right-brain, holistic vision. Intuition and imagination are golden.

These thirteen subjects are classic examples of individuals being molded early and thereby adopting those key personality traits necessary for greatness. All were nurtured or transformed into greatness at some critical period during their formative years. Figure 23 summarizes twelve recurring experiential factors found in these subjects. It appears these twelve factors were most responsible for the formation of their key behavior characteristics. To be successful in a dynamic world it is important to be dynamic and these twelve principles demonstrate how such personalities are formed.

Bibliography

Subject Selection and Success Data

Barntemps, Arna. *Famous Negro Athletes*. New York: Dodd, Mead, 1964.

Black Enterprise. "The B.E. 100's—Largest Black Businesses." June 1994, 1995.

Boyd, Herb, and Robert Allen. *Brotherman: The Odyssey of Black Men in America*. New York: Ballantine Books, 1995.

Ebony. "The One Hundred Most Influential Black Americans." May 1992, 62–68.

———. "American Black Achievement Awards," May 1994, 37–50, 118–20.

Franco, Robert. "Top 40," *Forbes*, September 25, 1995, 136.

Hart, Michael. *The One Hundred: A Ranking of the Most Influential Persons in History*. New York: Citadel Publishing, 1978.

Ludwig, Arnold. *The Price of Greatness*. New York: Guilford Press, 1995.

Pamplin, Robert. *American Heroes*. New York: Mastermedia, 1995.

Robinson, Wilhelma. *Negro Life and History*. New York: Publishers Co., 1967.

Salley, Columbus. *The Black One Hundred: A Ranking of the Most Influential African-Americans Past and Present*. New York: Citadel Press, 1993.

Smith, Jessie Carney. *Notable Black American Women*. Detroit, Mich.: Gale Research, 1992.

———. *Black Firsts: Two Thousand Years of Extraordinary Achievement*. Detroit, Mich.: Visible Ink Press, 1994.

Smith, Sande. *Who's Who in African-American History*. New York: Smithmark Publishers, 1994.

General References

Adler, Alfred. *Superiority and Social Interest*. New York: Norton and Co., 1979.

Amabile, Teresa. *Growing Up Creative: Nurturing a Lifetime of Creativity*. New York: Crown Publishing, 1989.

Aptheker, Herbert. *A Documentary History of the Negro People in the United States*. New York: The Citadel Press, 1966.

Baker, John. *Race*. New York: Oxford University Press, 1974.

Barzun, Jaques. "The Paradoxes of Creativity." *American Scholar,* Summer 1989, 337.

Blackbook—International Business and Entertainment Reference Guide. New York: National Publications, 1994.

Boden, Margaret. *The Creative Mind.* New York: HarperCollins, 1990.

Boorstin, Daniel. *The Creators.* (Dostoevsky section in particular). New York: Random House, 1992.

Branden, Nathaniel. *Six Pillars of Self-Esteem.* New York: Bantam Books, 1994.

Brigham, Deidre. *Imagery for Getting Well.* New York: Norton and Sons, 1994.

Broderick, Francis, and August Meier. *Negro Protest Thought in the Twentieth Century.* New York: Bobbs-Merrill, 1965.

Campbell, Joseph. *The Inner Reaches of Outer Space.* New York: Harper and Row, 1986.

———. *Transformations of Myth Through Time.* New York: Harper and Row, 1990.

Cantor, Dorothy, and Toni Bernay. *Women in Power: The Secrets of Leadership.* Boston: Houghton-Mifflin, 1992.

Cappon, Daniel. "The Anatomy of Intuition." *Psychology Today,* May/June 1993, 41.

Clark, Barbara. *Growing Up Gifted.* Columbus, Ohio: Merrill Publishing, 1988.

Colton, Elizabeth. *The Jackson Phenomenon: The Man, the Power, the Message.* New York: Doubleday, 1989.

Douglass, Frederick. *Narrative of the Life of Frederick Douglass: An American Slave.* Garden City, N.Y.: Dolphin Books, 1963.

D'Souza, Dinesh. *The End of Racism.* New York: The Free Press, 1995.

Estes, Clarissa. *Women Who Run with the Wolves.* 1993.

Farrell, Warren. *Why Men Are the Way They Are.* New York: McGraw-Hill, 1986.

Ferguson, Marilyn. *The Aquarian Conspiracy.* Los Angeles: J. P. Tarcher, 1976.

Fish, Jefferson. "Mixed Blood." *Psychology Today,* November/December 1995, 55.

Frankl, Victor. *In Search of Meaning.* New York: Pocket Books, 1959.

Freud, Sigmund. *On Creativity and the Unconscious.* New York: Harper, 1925.

Fucini, Joseph, and Suzy Fucini. *Entrepreneurs: The Men and Women behind Famous Brand Names and How They Made It.* Boston: G. K. Hall, 1985.

Gardner, Howard. *Framing Minds: The Theory of Multiple Intelligences.* New York: Basic Books, 1983.

———. *Creating Minds.* New York: Basic Books, 1993.

Garfield, Charles. *Peak Performers: The New Heroes of American Business.* New York: Avon, 1986.

Ghislin, Brewster. *The Creative Process.* Berkeley, Calif.: Berkeley Press, 1952.

Gilligan, Carol. *In a Different Voice: Psychological Theory and Women's Development.* Boston: Harvard University Press, 1982.

Goleman, Daniel, Paul Kaufman, and Ray Michael. *The Creative Spirit.* New York: Dutton, 1992.

Gomeman, Daniel. *Emotional Intelligence: Why It Can Matter More than IQ.* New York: Bantam, 1995.

Gornick, Vivian, and Barbara Moran. *Women in Sexist Society: Studies in Power and Powerlessness.* New York: New American Library, 1971.

Gray, John. *Men, Women and Relationships.* Hillsboro, Oreg.: Beyond Words Publishing, 1993.

Guiles, Fred L. *Norma Jean.* New York: Bantam, 1969.

Hallmandras, The Brothers. *Caring Quotes: A Compendium of Caring Thought.* Washington, D.C.: Caring Publishing, 1994.

Haygood, Wil. *King of the Cats: The Life and Times of Adam Clayton Powell, Jr.* Boston: Houghton-Mifflin, 1993.

Heatherton and Weinberger. *Can Personality Change?* Washington, D.C.: American Psychological Association, 1993.

Hershman D., and J. Lieb. *The Key to Genius: Manic Depression and the Creative Life.* Amherst, N.Y.: Prometheus Books, 1988.

———. *A Brotherhood of Tyrants: Manic Depression and Absolute Power* (analysis of Hitler, Napoleon, and Stalin). Amherst, N.Y.: Prometheus Books, 1994.

Hirsh, Sandra, and Jean Kummerow. *Life Types.* New York: Warner, 1989.

Hutchison, Michael. *The Anatomy of Sex and Power.* New York: Morrow, 1990.

Jamison, Kay. *Touched with Fire: Manic Depressive Illness.* New York: Free Press, 1994.

———. *An Unquiet Mind: A Memoir of Moods and Madness.* New York: Alfred Knopf, 1995.

Johnson, Robert. *Inner Work: Using Dreams and Active Imagination for Personal Growth.* San Francisco: Harper, 1986.

Jordan, B., and S. Hearon. *Barbara Jordan: A Self-Portrait.* New York: Doubleday and Co., 1979.

Jung, Carl. *The Portable Jung* (see "The Stages of Life"). New York: Penguin, 1976.

Keirsey, David. *Portraits of Temperament: Personality Types.* Del Mar, Calif.: Prometheus Nemesis Book Co., 1987.

Keirsey, D., and M. Bates. *Please Understand Me.* Del Mar, Calif.: Prometheus Nemesis Book Co., 1984.

Korda, Michael. *Power: How to Get It, How to Keep It.* New York: Random House, 1975.

Kroeger, Otto, and Janet Thuesen. *Type Talk at Work.* New York: Delacorte Press, 1992.

Landrum, Gene. *Profiles of Genius.* Amherst, N.Y.: Prometheus Books, 1993.

———. *Profiles of Female Genius.* Amherst, N.Y.: Prometheus Books, 1994.

———. *Profiles of Power and Success.* Amherst, N.Y.: Prometheus Books, 1996.

Leman, Kenneth. *The Birth Order Book.* New York: Dell Publishing, 1985.

Lemann, Nicholas. "Is There a Science of Success?" (on David McClelland's work on motivation). *Atlantic*, February 1994, 82.

Lommel, Cookie. *Madam C. J. Walker: Entrepreneur.* Los Angeles: Melrose Square Publishing, 1993.

McClelland, David. *Power: The Inner Science.* New York: John Wiley and Sons, 1978.

MacKinnon, David. "Personality and the Realization of Creative Potential," *American Psychologist*, 1965, 273–81.

Maslow, Abraham. *The Farther Reaches of Human Nature.* New York: Viking Press, 1971.

May, Rollo. *Love and Will.* New York: Norton and Co., 1969.

Moyers, Bill. "The Power of Myth" (PBS interviews with Joseph Campbell). Public Broadcasting System, October 1995, 1987.

Neyland, James. *Booker T. Washington—Educator.* Los Angeles: Melrose Square Publishing, 1992.

Ornstein, Robert. *The Psychology of Consciousness.* New York: Penguin, 1972.

Pacheco, Ferdie. *Muhammad Ali.* Secaucus, N.J.: Carol Publishing Group, 1992.

Pearsall, Paul. *Making Miracles.* New York: Avon Books, 1993.

Plomin, Robert, and Gerald E. McClearn. *Nature, Nurture and Psychology.* Washington, D.C.: American Psychological Association, 1993.

Prigogine, Ilya. *From Being to Becoming.* San Francisco: Freeman and Co., 1980.

Prigogine, Ilya, and Isabelle Stengers. *Order Out of Chaos.* New York: Bantam Books, 1984.

Quarles, Benjamin. *Frederick Douglass.* Washington, D.C.: Associated Publishers, 1948.

Rand, Ayn. *We the Living.* New York: New American Library, 1936.

Roucek, Joseph. *The Negro Impact on Western Civilization.* New York: Philosophical Library, 1970.

Science Digest. "Industry Tries to Teach Creativity." September 1995.

Scott, Randall. "Creative Employees: A Challenge to Managers." *Journal of Creative Behavior*, Second Quarter, 1995.

Segal, Robert. *Joseph Campbell: An Introduction.* New York: Mentor Books, 1987.

Silver, David. *Entrepreneurial Megabucks: The One Hundred Greatest Entrepreneurs of the Last Twenty-Five Years.* New York: John Wiley and Sons, 1985.

Storr, Anthony. *The Dynamics of Creation.* New York: Ballantine Books, 1993.

Taylor, I., and J. Gretzels. *Perspectives in Creativity.* Chicago, 1975.

Taylor-Guthrie, Danille. *Conversations with Toni Morrison.* Jackson: University Press of Mississippi, 1994.

Toffler, Alvin. *Power Shift.* Bantam Books, New York: 1990.

Walker, Marie, Richard Koestner, and Andrew Hum. "Personality Correlates of Depressive Style in Autobiographies of Creative Achievers." *Journal of Creative Behavior*, Second Quarter, 1995.

Walsh, Anthony, and Grace. *Vive la Difference: A Celebration of the Sexes.* Amherst, N.Y.: Prometheus Books, 1993.

Weatherby, W.J. *James Baldwin: Artist on Fire.* New York: Bantam Doubleday, 1989.

Wolf, Naomi. *The Beauty Myth.* New York: Anchor Books, Doubleday, 1991.

Maya Angelou

Angelou, Maya. *I Know Why the Caged Bird Sings*. New York: Bantam Books, 1969.

————. *Gather Together in My Name*. New York: Bantam Books, 1974.

————. *Singin and Swingin and Gettin Merry Like Christmas*. New York: Bantam Books, 1976.

————. *The Heart of a Woman*. New York: Bantam Books, 1981.

————. *Poems*. New York: Bantam Books, 1981.

————. *All God's Children Need Traveling Shoes*. New York: Random House, 1986.

————. "Phenomenal Woman." *Ladies Home Journal*, October 1993, 128.

————. "A Celebration of Spirit." *Good Housekeeping,* December 1993, 98.

Black Writers. "Maya Angelou." 1990, p. 13.

Bloom, Lynn Z. *Afro-American Writers After 1955*. 1985.

Collier, Eugenia. "Maya Angelou." *New Directions,* October 1986, 22–27.

Current Biography. "Maya Angelou." 1994, p. 25.

Gillespie, Marcie. "Profile of Maya Angelou." *Essence,* December 1992, 48–53.

Haynes, Karina. "Maya Angelou—Prime Time Poe." *Ebony,* April 1993, 71.

Mangold, Catherine. "Maya Angelou: Her Life and Her Career." *New York Times*, January 20, 1993, p. C1.

Shuker, Nancy. *Maya Angelou—Genius! The Artist and the Process*. Englewood Cliffs, N.J.: Silver Burdett Press, 1990.

Shirley Chisholm

Black Writers. "Shirley Chisholm." 1990, 103.

Brownmiller, Susan. *Shirley Chisholm*. New York: Pocket Books, 1972.

Chisholm, Shirley. *Shirley Chisolm: Unbought and Unbossed*. Boston: Houghton-Mifflin, 1970.

————. *The Good Fight: Shirley Chisolm*. Boston: Houghton-Mifflin, 1973.

Schraeder, Catherine. *Shirley Chisholm: Teacher and Congresswoman*. Hillside, N.J.: Enslow Publishers, 1990.

Smith, Jessie Carney. *Notable Black Women*. Detroit, Mich.: Gale Research, 1992.

Bill Cosby

Adler, Bill. *The Cosby Wit: His Life and Humor*. New York: Lorevan Publishing, 1986.

Black Writers. "Bill Cosby." 1992, p. 119.

Cosby, Bill. *Fatherhood*. New York: Doubleday, 1986.

————. *Time Flies*. New York: Bantam Books, 1987.

————. *Love and Marriage*. New York: Bantam, 1989.

Current Biography. "Bill Cosby." 1967, p. 82.

Ebony. "Why Cosby Attempted to Buy NBC in 1993." May 1994, 100.

Forbes. "Top 40 Earning Entertainers 1993." September 9, 1993, 97.

Jet. "Bill Cosby on Blacks and Jews." May 30, 1994, 33.

Pamplin, Robert. *American Heroes*. New York: Mastermedia, 1995.

Ruuth, Marianne. *Bill Cosby: Entertainer*. Los Angeles, Melrose Square Publications, 1992.

Smith, Ronald. *The Cosby Book*. New York: S.P.I. Books, 1986.

Frederick Douglass

Douglass, Frederick. *Narrative of the Life of Frederick Douglass: An American Slave*. Boston, Anti-Slavery Office, 1845.
Quarles, Benjamin. *Frederick Douglass*. Washington, D.C.: The Associated Publishers, 1948.

Berry Gordy

Bagwell, L. S. "Berry Gordy and Carol Publishing Suit." *Publishers Weekly,* June 29, 1995, 13.
Benjamison, Peter. *The Story of Motown*. New York: Grove Press, 1979.
Current Biography. "Berry Gordy." 1975, p. 168.
Gordy, Berry. *To Be Loved*. New York: Warner Books, 1994.
Jet. "Berry Gordy Files $250 Million Libel Suit against *New York Daily News*." May 9, 1994, 53.
Rolling Stone. "Berry Gordy." August 23, 1990.
Singleton, Raynoma. *Berry, Me and Motown*. 1991.
Taraborrelli, J. Randy. *Call Her Miss Ross*. New York: Ballantine Books, 1989.
———. *Michael Jackson: The Magic and the Madness*. New York: Carol Publishing Group, 1991.
Waller, Don. *The Motown Story*. New York: Charles Scribner's Sons, 1985.

Michael Jackson

Anderson, Christopher. *Michael Jackson Unauthorized*. 1995.
Current Biography. "Michael Jackson." 1983, p. 197.
Gunderson, Edna. "HIStory at Stake" *USA Today,* April 20, 1995, p. D-1.
Jackson, Michael. *Moonwalk*. New York: Doubleday, 1988.
Orth, Maureen. "The Jackson Jive," *Vanity Fair*. September 1995, p. 114.
Sawyer, Diane. "Prime Time Live" interview with Michael and Lisa Marie Jackson. June 7, 1995.
Taraborrelli, Randy. *Michael Jackson: The Magic and the Madness*. New York: Carol Publishing Company, 1991.

John Johnson

Boyd, Herb, and Robert Allen. *Brotherman: The Odyssey of Black Men in America*. New York, Ballantine Books, 1995.
Current Biography. "John Johnson," 1968, p. 201.
Johnson, John. *Succeeding Against the Odds*. New York, Warner Books, 1989.
Salley, Columbus. *The Black One Hundred*. New York: Carol Publishing Group, 1993.

Michael Jordan

Current Biography. "Michael Jordan." 1987, p. 87.
Ebony. "The Michael Jordan Nobody Knows." December 1993, 128.
———. "The Greatest Returns." June 1995, 25.
Greene, Bob. *Hang Time*. New York: St. Martin's Paperbacks, 1992.
Jet. "Michael Jordan Retires." October 25, 1993, 17.
Jordan, Michael. *I'm Back!: More Rare Air*. San Francisco: Collins Publishers, 1995.

Krugel, Mitchell. *Jordan: The Man, His Words, His Life*. New York: St. Martin's Press, 1994.
Levin, Bob. "Master of Midair." *Maclean's*, October 19, 1993, 62.
McCallum, Jack. "The Desire Isn't There." *Sports Illustrated*, October 18, 1993, 28.
Newsweek. "Air and Hare." July 3, 1995, 39.
Reilly, Rick. "Smells Like Another Rose." *Sports Illustrated*, June 21, 1993, p. 74.
Sports Illustrated. "Michael!: The Story of Michael Jordan, From his Childhood to His Comeback."
     Spring 1995.
Starr, Mark. "The Gambling Man," *Newsweek*, June 14, 1993, 72.

Martin Luther King, Jr.

Clayton, Ed. *Martin Luther King: The Peaceful Warrior*. New York: Simon and Schuster, 1964.
Cone, James. *Martin and Malcolm and America*. Maryknoll, N.Y.: Orbis Books, 1991.
Current Biography. "Martin Luther King." 1965, p. 220.
Garrow, David. *Bearing the Cross*. New York: Random House, 1986.
King, Coretta Scott. *My Life With Martin Luther King*. New York: Priffin Books, 1993.
Lischer, Richard. *The Preacher King*. New York: The Oxford Press, 1995.

Reginald Lewis

Berman, Phyllis. "Black Business Loses a Star." *Black Enterprise*, March 1993, 17.
———. "Payoff Time," *Forbes*, November 22, 1993, 100.
Jet. "Late Business Maganate Leaves $84.2M Estate." April, 26, 1993, 9.
Lewis, Reginald, and Blair Walker. *Why Should White Guys Have All the Fun?* New York: John Wiley
     and Sons, 1995.
U.S. News and World Report. "Reginald Lewis." February 1, 1993, 16.

Malcolm X

Asanti, Molefi. *Malcolm X as Cultural Hero*. Trenton, N.J.: Africa World Press, 1993.
Cone, James. *Martin and Malcolm and America*. Maryknoll, N.Y.: Orbis Books, 1991.
Gallen, David. *Malcolm A to X: The Man and His Ideas*. New York: Carroll and Graf Publishers, 1992.
Haley, Alex. *The Autobiography of Malcolm X*. New York: Ballantine Books, 1964.

Nelson Mandela

Benson, Mary. *Nelson Mandela: The Man and the Movement*. New York: Norton and Co., 1986.
Black Writers. "Nelson Mandela." 1992, p. 378.
Clark, Steve. *Nelson Mandela Speaks*. New York: Pathfinder Press, 1993.
Mandela, Nelson. *Long Walk to Freedom*. Boston: Little, Brown, 1994.
Mandela, Winnie. *Winnie Mandela: Part of My Soul Went With Him*. New York: Norton, 1984.
Time. "Nelson Mandela: Birth of a Nation." May 9, 1994, 24.

Thurgood Marshall

Davis, Michael, and Hunter Clark. *Marshall: The Rebel on the Bench*. New York: Birch Lane Press, 1993.

Goldman, Roger, and David Gallen. *Thurgood Marshall: Justice for All*. Caroll and Graf Publishers, New York: 1992.

Kennedy, Randall. "Fanfare for an Uncommon Man." *Time*, February 8, 1993, 32.

Lemann, Nicholas. "The Lawyer as Hero." *The New Republic*, September 13, 1993.

Lord, Lewis. "A Farewell to Mr. Civil Rights." *U.S. News and World Report*, February 8, 1993, 10.

People. "The Power of One." February 8, 1993, 40.

Rowan, Carl. *Dream Makers, Dream Breakers*. Boston: Back Bay Books, 1993.

Colin Powell

ABA Book Show speech. McCormick Center, Chicago, Ill., June 3, 1995.

Barrett, Laurence, Jeffrey Birnbaum, J. McAllister, and Mark Thompson. "The Powell Factor." *Time,* July 10, 1995, 22.

Gaiter, Dorothy, and Gerald Seib. "Many Voters Believe Powell Could Bridge Nations Racial Divide." *Wall Street Journal*, November 7, 1995, p. 1.

Keen, Judy. "Powell Won't Run in 96." *USA Today*, November 9, 1995, p. 1.

Means, Howard. *Colin Powell*. New York: Ballantine Books, 1992.

Pamplin, Robert. *American Heroes*. New York: Mastermedia, 1995.

Parker, Suzy. "Draft Colin Powell for President." *USA Today,* April 12, 1995, p. 11A.

Powell, Colin. *My American Journey*. New York: Random House, 1995.

Paul Robeson

Current Biography. "Paul Robeson." 1976, p. 345.

Gilliam, Dorothy. *Paul Robeson: All American*. Washington, D.C.: New Republic Book Company, 1976.

Robeson, Eslanda Goode. *Paul Robeson, Negro*. New York: Harper Bros., 1930.

Robeson, Paul. *Paul Robeson Speaks*, edited by Philip Foner. New York: Citadel Press, 1978.

———. *Here I Stand*. Boston: Beacon Press, 1958.

Salley, Columbus. *The Black One Hundred*. Secaucus, N.J.: Carol Publishing Company, 1993.

Oprah Winfrey

Current Biography. "Oprah Winfrey." 1987, p. 610.

Essence. "Oprah Opens Body and Soul." June 1991, 46.

Goodman, Fred. "Madonna and Oprah and the Companies They Keep." *Working Woman*, December 1991, 52.

King, Larry. CNN interview with Oprah Winfrey. Spring 1995.

King, Norman. *Everybody Loves Oprah*. New York: William Morrow, 1987.

Pamplin, Robert. *American Heroes*. New York: Mastermedia, 1995.

Rogers, Jackie. "Understanding Oprah." *Redbook,* September 1993, 91.

Waldron, Robert. *Oprah*. New York: St. Martin's, 1987.

Winfrey, Oprah. "What We All Can Do to Change TV." *TV Guide,* November 11, 1995, 12.

About the Author

Gene Landrum is a high-tech start-up executive turned teacher and writer. He originated the Chuck E. Cheese concept of family entertainment among other entrepreneurial ventures. After years of interacting with creative and overachieving personalities he decided to research the subject of What Makes the Great Tick? The result has been a doctorate on the innovator personality plus a number of books on innovation, creativity, and the entrepreneurial process. Gene is president of the Naples Entrepreneurial Network and teaches leadership, organizational behavior, marketing, entrepreneurship, and management at International College in Naples, Florida.

Dr. Landrum is considered a marketing visionary whose success has been a direct result of his unique ability to envision potential opportunities and act on them in a rational manner. He is a Promethean temperament who tests as a right-brain visionary with an intuitive-thinking personality on the Myers-Briggs Type Indicator. His communication and motivational speaking skills have led to hundreds of television and radio appearances in addition to a busy lecturing schedule on: genius and gender, visionary leadership, entrepreneurship at the millennium, and the psychology of risk taking.

Landrum's abiding interest in the behavioral characteristics of eminent people contributed to his following nonfiction books:

Profiles of Black Success: Thirteen Creative Geniuses Who Changed the World (1997)

Profiles of Power and Success: Fourteen Geniuses Who Broke the Rules (1996)

Profiles of Female Genius: Thirteen Creative Women Who Changed the World (1994)

Profiles of Male Genius: Thirteen Male Entrepreneurs Who Changed the World (1993)

The Innovator Personality (Published Dissertation, 1991)

Index